FUSION
Integrating IE, CASE, and JAD
A Handbook for Reengineering
the Systems Organization

Selected titles from the YOURDON PRESS COMPUTING SERIES
Ed Yourdon, *Advisor*

FUSION
Integrating IE, CASE, and JAD
A Handbook for Reengineering
the Systems Organization

Dorine C. Andrews
Value Systems, Inc.
Potomac, Maryland

Naomi S. Leventhal

PTR Prentice Hall, Englewood Cliffs, New Jersey 07632

Library of Congress Cataloging-in-Publication Data

ANDREWS, DORINE C.
    FUSION : integrating IE, CASE, and JAD : a handbook for
reengineering the systems organization / Dorine C. Andrews, Naomi S.
Leventhal.
        p.   cm.
    Includes bibliographical references and index.
    ISBN 0-13-325333-3
    1. Information resources management.   2. System design.
I. Leventhal, Naomi S.   II. Title.
T58.64.A437   1993
658.4'038—dc20

                                                          92-376
                                                          CIP

Editorial/production supervision & interior design: *Jean Lapidus*
Cover design: *Wanda Lubelska Design*
Copy editor: *Maria Caruso*
Pre-press buyer: *Mary Elizabeth McCartney*
Manufacturing buyer: *Susan Brunke*
Acquisition editor: *Paul Becker*
Editorial assistant: *Noreen Regina*

 © 1993 by PTR Prentice Hall
A Simon & Schuster Company
Englewood Cliffs, New Jersey 07632

The publisher offers discounts on this book when ordered in
bulk quantities. For more information, write: Special
Sales/Professional Marketing, Prentice Hall, Professional &
Technical Reference Division, Englewood Cliffs, NJ 07632.

Printed in the United States of America

10 9 8 7 6 5 4 3 2 1

ISBN   0-13-325333-3

PRENTICE-HALL INTERNATIONAL (UK) LIMITED, *London*
PRENTICE-HALL OF AUSTRALIA PTY. LIMITED, *Sydney*
PRENTICE-HALL CANADA INC., *Toronto*
PRENTICE-HALL HISPANOAMERICANA, S.A., *Mexico*
PRENTICE-HALL OF INDIA PRIVATE LIMITED, *New Delhi*
PRENTICE-HALL OF JAPAN, INC., *Tokyo*
SIMON & SCHUSTER ASIA PTE. LTD., *Singapore*
EDITORA PRENTICE-HALL DO BRASIL, LTDA., *Rio de Janeiro*

Contents

Preface

This book is designed to provide its readers with a practical guide for harnessing the energy of the three most powerful forces available to the systems organization today: information engineering, joint application development (JAD), and computer aided software engineering (CASE). Many organizations have experimented with one or more of these forces; some have even mastered the use of one or two. However, very few organizations have realized the productivity gains that are possible when these three forces are fully integrated and applied in a consistent manner to the solution of information management problems. It is the authors' hope that through this book the FUSION concept will reach a wide range of individuals within today's organizations. Information systems can no longer be said to belong only to the "systems people," and neither do information management problems. It is our belief that the solution to these problems is also the province of all of those involved in the management of organizations, from the lowest line manager to the chief executive officer. FUSION is for all of them.

FUSION is an approach that integrates methodology, technique, and tools in the service of enhancing the organization's management of information. It is embodied in the FUSION equation:

$$FUSION = IE + CASE + JAD$$

Simply put, the FUSION equation maintains that the whole is greater than the sum of its parts, that information engineering can only be fully implemented with the use of the JAD technique and the application of CASE technology, that JAD relies on a consistent methodology and automated support for its value to be fully realized, and that CASE tools are empty vessels without a sound set of analytical principles and a technique for gathering and evaluating information.

It should also be said that this book emphasizes a practical approach to solving information management problems. It assumes that the world in which most managers operate is less than ideal, that there are and always will be constraints on their actions. Time is always too short, qualified personnel are in short supply, and funding is limited. These factors might make some managers hesitant to try something new, but, in fact, these constraints all help to make the case for FUSION implementation. FUSION is the perfect approach for a world with limits.

The book is organized into eight chapters. Chapter one presents the basic assumptions that underlie the development and implementation of the FUSION concept. It describes the need for a unifying or integrated approach to the implementation of methodology, tools, and techniques, and defines the interrelationship of the three FUSION elements. It discusses the reasons why today's systems organizations are not more productive, and provides an approach for changing some of the basic assumptions with which these organizations operate.

Chapter two focuses on the joint application development technique. It defines the role of JAD in systems work and describes the dual nature of JAD, emphasizing both the technical and behavioral aspects of systems design and development. The role of the facilitator is defined, as well as the roles and responsibilities of the other individuals involved in the JAD process. The structure of the JAD project is presented in terms of preworkshop, workshop, and postworkshop objectives, tasks, and responsibilities. Deliverables are defined as well, and the relationship between the objectives of the project and the deliverables produced is delineated.

Chapter three follows with a practical guide for the use of JAD facilitation techniques. It presents facilitation techniques that are specifically designed for building commitment, structuring the JAD process, analyzing ideas, managing participant interaction, and for other purposes. Each technique is defined in terms of its purpose, advantages, timing, and preparation requirements, and each includes a set of step-by-step instructions for technique implementation.

Chapter four looks at CASE tools, the technical dimension of the FUSION approach. It identifies the critical success factors in tool selection and addresses the key issues in tool implementation. Among these are the prolonged learning curve associated with CASE, the problem of user resistance, and the need for specialized data collection techniques. Prerequisites for effective tool use are discussed, as well as impacts that the organization must anticipate if CASE is to be a success. These impacts include job restructuring requirements and change management challenges as well as the more obvious impacts in the financial and training arenas.

In chapter five, we address the element of methodology through a look at information engineering (IE) concepts. While FUSION can operate effectively within a number of different methodological constructs (including both structured analysis and object-oriented approaches), we think that IE concepts are particularly well suited to the approach. This chapter defines those characteristics of information engineering that contribute to the FUSION approach. It shows how the methodological principles of IE frame the FUSION project and lead to a high level of consistency and quality in project deliverables. We have chosen to utilize an IE life cycle with four basic components, and have presented these in a manner that should enable any organization to easily relate its own life cycle standards and vocabulary to our "generic" IE life cycle. For each component we identify basic objectives and related diagrammatic tools, and identify some ways in which JAD and CASE can be used to support these.

Chapter six brings together the three FUSION elements and defines how FUSION is created. We present seven steps for achieving FUSION and explain how each of the three elements contributes to its creation. In describing how FUSION is created, we draw upon real examples for our experience. These examples are designed to demonstrate that FUSION can be implemented under difficult conditions and on imperfectly designed projects. Chapter six also contains our plan for a "Breakthrough Project." This special project guide can satisfy several valuable objectives: to test the waters for FUSION within the organization; to demonstrate the value of FUSION principles, tools, and techniques; and to develop a specific strategy and plan for FUSION implementation.

Chapter seven addresses fully the issue of implementing FUSION within the organization. It presents a detailed approach to FUSION implementation, including start-up, proliferation, and support activities. It also discusses such critical success factors as the development of high-level commitment, the creation of coordination strategies, and the design of a FUSION marketing plan. Key mistakes are reviewed too, in order to enable the reader to avoid these. As an illustration, a real world example of FUSION implementation within a complex organization is presented. The discussion of the difficulties encountered here—and their solutions—can help other organizations both large and small.

Finally, in chapter eight we present concepts in the management of change. In implementing FUSION, it is vital that the organization make a commitment to change. FUSION cannot be successful if it is viewed as a superficial change. Properly implemented, it is a profound change, touching all aspects of the organization's future aspirations, self-image, and methods and procedures. This chapter describes how this change can threaten the individuals involved, how it can attack their need for consistency in their work environment, their desire for status, and their sense of self-actualization. Building on the ideas of Elizabeth Kubler-Ross, it portrays the stages to the acceptance of change, demonstrating how the individual caught up in the implementation of FUSION can be led from denial of the approaching change to an enthusiastic acceptance of it. Once again, we use examples of individuals addressing this problem, indicating some of the many strategies that can be used to manage the movement of individuals through the different stages of dealing with the threat of change.

Just as the FUSION approach seeks to be a comprehensive response to the need of the organization for a better approach to the solution of information management problems, this FUSION book seeks to provide a comprehensive guide to the implementation of new principles, tools, and techniques within the organization. We believe that this comprehensive approach will benefit those readers currently involved in the implementation of these new concepts, as well as those who are on the verge of making a commitment to change.

Dorine C. Andrews

Naomi S. Leventhal

1

FUSION = IE + CASE + JAD

THE FUSION EQUATION

The FUSION approach represents a new way of designing automated solutions for information management problems. It is composed of three dimensions: methodology, tool, and technique. The first dimension, the methodology that provides the guiding discipline and structural foundation for the FUSION approach, is information engineering (IE). While there are a number of methodologies that might have been chosen to support FUSION, we have selected this one because of two important contributions it makes to the analysis of information management needs and solutions. First, IE, as it is often abbreviated, emphasizes the connection between high-level business strategy and the details of application design. Second, IE provides us with a set of graphic tools that allow us to view data and process separately and at multiple levels within the organization.

The second dimension of the FUSION equation, tool, represents the principal means of automating the information engineering methodology available today, computer-aided software engineering (CASE) products. As in methodologies, there are a range of choices available in tools. However, no specific CASE tool is advocated here as the ''best'' answer. Rather the analysis and documentation capabilities generally shared by the major CASE tools are presented in support of the tool dimension of FUSION.

The third dimension of the equation, the technique that is recommended for implementing IE and supporting CASE, is joint application development (JAD), a team-based approach to analysis and decision making. This technique provides the practical "how to" for achieving the benefits of information engineering and CASE tools. JAD offers a structure that enables systems professionals and users to work together productively on information management projects. In fact, we believe it is the key to making the implementation of IE and CASE successful. Without a technique such as JAD, IE would remain largely in the hands of a small group of specialists. With JAD, IE can be effectively utilized by any skilled analyst. Without JAD, CASE would too often be used to provide technically correct solutions to the wrong information management problems. With JAD, the CASE user can be assured that the information he is analyzing and documenting represents the best information available.

The authors chose the term "FUSION" to refer to this multiacronym formula because the value of each dimension is greatly increased when all are combined together. In other words, when you add up IE + CASE + JAD, the result is significantly greater than the sum of the individual parts. The result is a rapid application development (RAD) approach (Fig. 1.1), where quality and speed provide complementary benefits. The FUSION approach can be summarized in the simple equation:

$$\text{IE} + \text{CASE} + \text{JAD} = \text{QUALITY} + \text{SPEED} + \text{COMMITMENT}$$

It is true, of course, that the many books and articles written about CASE technology can provide you with tips on how to improve your systems through the use of CASE tools. The same is true of single focus books that discuss the information engineering methodology or the JAD technique. But we maintain that none of these dimensions provides a sufficient return on investment when implemented alone. Each dimension requires the others in order to be successful. If their implementation is not "fused" into an integrated solution, the investment may fail to meet expectations and may result in wasted resources.

The approach presented here is a distinctly practical one. Far from being intended for mathematicians, physicists, or other practitioners of esoteric arts, the FUSION equation was created for people who are involved in the management, design, and use of computer systems on a daily basis. This book is written for managers charged with selecting new methodologies, tools, and techniques, managers responsible for directing the use of these methodologies, tools, and techniques on specific projects, and the many systems analysts and users who form the project teams that are on the front lines of the information management crisis.

WHY THE FUSION EQUATION?

Today's competitive business environment and volatile economy have greatly increased the difficulty of the systems professional's job. He is pressured to do more work than ever before, to do this work more quickly than ever before, to

AN IE LIFE CYCLE

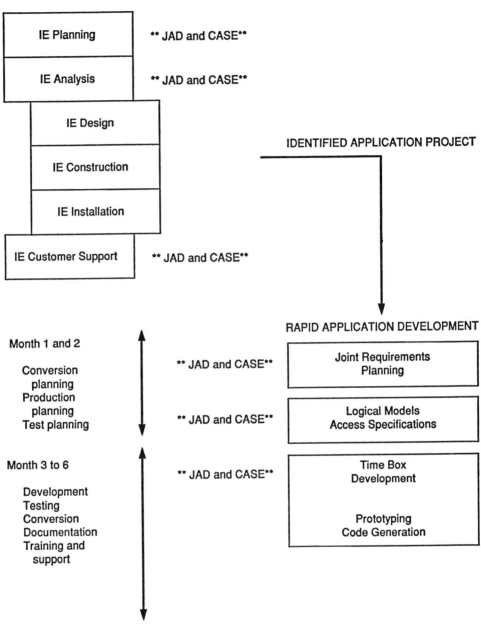

Figure 1.1 Rapid application development.

deliver a higher quality result than ever before, and to accomplish this magic with fewer resources than ever before. Systems professionals at all levels in the organization must work within a greatly constrained environment to deliver a greatly improved result in a dramatically reduced timeframe. The result? One retail manufacturing and distribution organization recently identified the following problems with their systems work:

- Late delivery of systems averaging twenty to fifty percent over schedule.
- User dissatisfaction with delivered applications as measured by the high number of change requests within the first six to twelve months of system operation.
- Unwillingness of systems managers to commit resources to projects for fear of failure.
- Conflicting objectives for systems managers (e.g., improve delivery time to users and hold the line on expenditures for personnel and tools).
- Rejection of new corporate roles such as that of data base administrator by individual project managers.
- Assignment of responsibility for complex projects to managers without providing them with authority for decision making or sufficient resources.
- Narrow short-term strategies that focus on "the quick fix."
- Rejection of Project Managers (viewed as "bulldogs" or "renegades") who are effective in accomplishing tasks but not in winning support within the organization.
- Desperation dictates from managers (e.g., "From now on everyone must produce every document specified in the standard methodology.") rather than commitment building behavior.
- Compensation for systems managers based on span-of-control head counts rather than delivered units of user accepted functionality.
- Nonteam playing within a project team as members attempt to protect their limited territory and authority.
- Failure to market new concepts and ideas to the user customer base.
- Snail-paced funding, multiple approval structures, and other bureaucratic mechanisms that lengthen project downtime.

Not only do systems professionals face the challenge of finding a new way to work, but they also face the challenge of implementing change within an environment that seldom welcomes change. Any organization that spends up to eighty percent of its time on fixing old systems is likely to be wedded to its old way of doing business. Too often the attempt to implement a new tool, technique, or methodology fails because no one has considered the impact the change will have on the individuals or the organization. The solution oriented, short-term mentality makes it easy to say: "This new tool (technique, methodology) is the answer to all our problems." But, as recent research in CASE implementation clearly shows, it is far more difficult to achieve this, especially if the organization is not prepared for change or if it views change with suspicion. Even those charged with selecting new tools, techniques, or methodologies often find themselves the victim of this antichange psychology. Instead of implementing change, they focus on gathering data and preparing endless studies.

But if "change" is a word not to be spoken out loud within the halls of systems organizations, there is no such ban against "productivity." It must be easily one of the most abused words in our language today. Unable to consider the concept of change directly, we instead talk about the importance of improving our productivity. To show that we are serious, we buy "productivity solutions," preferably the kind that can be implemented without actually changing the way we work. What we say is: "Here's something new. But don't worry. It won't really change things. You'll hardly notice it's here." But if we were honest, what we would say is: "It's time to change the rules of the game. Let's look at the way we work, how we do business as a systems organization, and figure out why it takes so long to get new systems built and why we have so many unhappy users. Let's improve our systems design and development approach with the objective of supporting the organization's business strategy, not just automating its manual processes."

The authors believe that the successful implementation of the FUSION approach must be supported by a detailed change management strategy. The development of that strategy must involve all of the individuals who will be affected and address political and cultural issues as well as technical concerns. Therefore, it is important not only to define the three dimensions of FUSION, but to define the behavioral aspects of successfully implementing this approach. In today's systems environment, the technical and the behavioral are inextricably joined.

Consider the example of one major manufacturing company that took on the challenge of implementing FUSION and creating a rapid application development (RAD) environment. In addition to purchasing new technology, redefining the life cycle, and adding new techniques, top executives recognized that they had to:

- Clarify and define roles and responsibilities for middle managers.
- Restructure the physical work facilities to create a FUSION Center and improve project team communication.
- Redefine current roles and division of authority among project team members and add new roles where necessary.
- Develop FUSION skills in project team members.
- Create and sustain new working relationships between systems creators and systems users throughout the development life cycle.

By facing all of these issues at the beginning of a conversion to a RAD environment, the organization greatly increased the chances for success.

HOW ARE IE, CASE, AND JAD RELATED?

Of the three dimensions of FUSION, you are probably most familiar with CASE tools, not least of all because the CASE tool vendors have very large advertising budgets and a vested interest in ensuring that you are aware of their products. You may have seen demonstrations of these tools at special meetings or at the trade shows. Rapidly gaining popularity since 1987, they are now considered a necessity for any systems organization that considers itself "on the leading edge." The effectiveness with which they are utilized, however, is another matter. A 1989 study revealed that although eighty percent of all U.S. companies have purchased CASE tools, only twenty-five percent had used a tool at least once and only five percent were using the tool in a production environment.

Most of the organizations that have tried to install CASE tools recognize that if CASE is clearly part of the answer, it is just as clearly not the whole answer. CASE doesn't address organization sociology or individual psychology. It is estimated that the hardware and software costs of CASE are only thirty-five percent of the total cost needed for successful implementation. It is wrong, however, to focus on the failure of CASE to provide a quick and easy solution. In a roundabout way, CASE tools may have actually delivered more than they promised. The difficulty of effectively integrating CASE tools into the systems organization has forced systems managers to examine the way they design and develop systems. CASE does not often fit neatly into the existing project team structure. In addition, CASE has forced us to confront the need for reviewing and updating staff selection and training procedures, life cycle activities and standards, strategic planning for systems, and the relationships between the customer (user) communities and the systems organization that serves them. It has forced a recognition at all levels within the systems organization that change is a necessity.

Most systems organizations today claim that they have a life cycle methodology. The typical systems manager may, in fact, be able to point to a fine multivolume set of standards and defined activities. But try applying the white glove test here, and you will quickly discover that these standards are dusty from lack of use. Not only are these standards seldom consulted, it is likely that they have not been reviewed for years. People talk openly about the way in which standards are by-passed and life cycle requirements are ignored. "Let the quality assurance guys worry about that stuff. We've got a job to do," is the common refrain.

Why then, should we care that systems are being built in less than an engineered manner? While the artistic approach to systems development may provide great job satisfaction for employees, it provides very uneven results. Not every analyst is a Leonardo da Vinci, and not every system is a Mona Lisa. Too many systems are undocumented masses of fixes knitted into antiquated, complex networks of code. Any documentation that exists probably hasn't been updated for years. These systems are accidents waiting to happen.

If we want to avoid these accidents and decrease the probability of their occurring in the future, our only choice is to build a common set of methods and activities based on the best options that technology has to offer. This must be done for several reasons. First, without standards, we cannot develop integrated data bases or implement them on compatible platforms. Second, without standards, we cannot automate the systems analysis, design, and construction process. No civil engineer would settle for the undisciplined methods we use in building systems to build bridges and road networks. And if he did something so foolish, none of us would want to drive over them. No systems engineer should settle for less in the construction of his "bridges and roads" in the world of information.

Today's systems provide strategic, critical support to business. If the systems fail, products do not get manufactured and distributed, and customers are not serviced. From the sophisticated markets of the financial services industry to our basic manufacturing businesses, systems make a significant difference to the bottom line.

CASE fails without standards and a life-cycle methodology to define how the tool is to be utilized. Successful implementation of CASE tools requires, therefore, that we redefine and reassert standards and methodology. But that is not the end of the task. The CASE crisis has also taught us that if we ignore the importance of thoughtful, detailed input into systems design, we will only produce unacceptable systems faster.

This is where the JAD technique comes in. For decades, it was assumed that the most important part of building a software application was the programming. In our rush to code, we ignored the sometimes difficult and time consuming task of design. This is akin to hiring a contractor and telling him to add a garage onto your house. He knows what a garage looks like—four walls, a roof and a door—and he'll build you something that will shelter your car next winter. But when he's done, will you have room for your lawn mower and power tools? Will the walls be insulated? Will the door open on the front or side? And will the addition fit in with the appearance of the rest of the house or stand out like a sore thumb?

The distinction between design and construction is equally valuable whether you are building a structure or an automated system. Design cannot be slighted or skipped. If this is done, experts agree, the average defect removal time of fifty percent of the construction time may actually approach one hundred percent of construction (Fig. 1.2). If CASE cannot be successful without a set of standard business practices behind it, then neither can it be successful without a set of procedures for obtaining high quality design information.

JAD is a technique that enables us to build the blueprints we need before coding begins. It is a technique for involving users in the decision making as well as the data gathering of their information and processing needs. JAD involves users in translating their needs into a solution that fits within the possibilities offered by the technological, financial, and human resources available to a project. JAD ensures as well that all political, cultural, and organizational factors that may impact the successful implementation of a project are addressed early in the

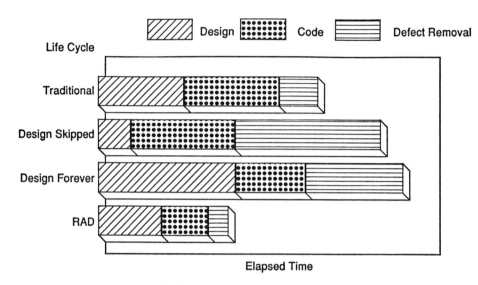

Figure 1.2 Traditional versus RAD life cycle timing patterns.

life cycle of the project. JAD creates a partnership among the systems professionals (analysts, programmers, database administrators) and the prospective system
customers who may reside in many different organizations and at different levels. JAD does this through team building, diffusing the hostility and confusion
that has arisen over the years as a result of that all too common slip between
customer expectations and the reality of the delivered system. Some analysts
claim that "users don't know what they want." Whether this is true or not (the
authors believe it is not) is beside the point. The systems organization should
provide appropriate mechanisms to uncover needs, assist people in clarifying
and defining them, and ensure that they are articulated in terms developers can
understand.

    When the traditional series of individual iterative interviews is used to gather
and refine user requirements, it is easy to defer decision making and point responsibility in many different directions. In addition, the traditional interview process
can easily miss important functionality and information requirements. A 1989
study of over sixty projects by Capers Jones showed that those projects that did
not use JAD missed up to thirty-five percent of required functionality resulting in
the need for up to fifty percent more program code. Those projects that used JAD
with prototyping missed only five to ten percent of the required functionality and
code was minimally impacted (Fig. 1.3). JAD, on the other hand, ensures that all
required functionality and information needs are addressed. As partners in JAD,
users and systems professionals reach consensus and make decisions under the
direction of a trained JAD facilitator, an individual with experience and skills
in systems analysis, group dynamics, behavioral psychology and commitment
building. The JAD facilitator is trained in techniques to structure the decision

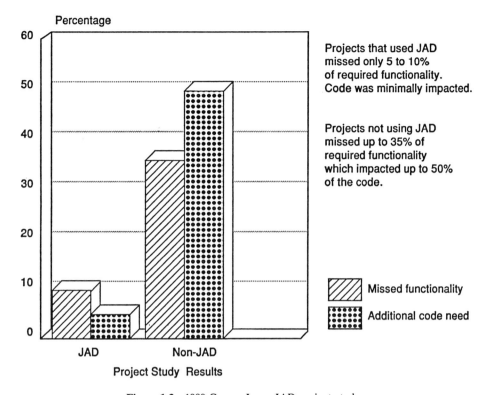

Figure 1.3 1989 Capers Jones JAD project study.

making experience, to reduce conflict and to focus the group's activity. In a JAD session, the assembled participant group is specifically tasked to make decisions and is under the pressure of time to do so quickly and efficiently. The result is a common set of design requirements, a common set of expectations for application functionality and performance, the early identification of potentially damaging issues, and a joint enthusiasm for the end result that overcomes any disappointment about limitations or constraints that cannot be avoided.

The methodology dimension of FUSION, information engineering, provides the common foundation for both CASE and JAD. This methodology ensures that our system solutions to information management problems will reflect the complexity of today's competitive business environment. IE helps us meet this challenge in two ways: first, by emphasizing the link between business strategy and application design; and second, by providing us with a set of graphic devices that analyze data separately from process and permit us to view these data and process models at multiple levels within the organization. By emphasizing the corporate (or "global") view of information management problems, and by linking high-level information resource planning to the design and construction of specific applications, IE places the design and development of individual applications within a set of overall architectures for data, application, and technology. In this way, it provides us with a view of both the "parts" (individual applications) and the "whole" (the total corporate information management resource). From a practical view, it changes the nature of application priority setting from a "shouting and bidding" auction to a strategically oriented selection process.

IE diagramming techniques (which include many of those commonly used by practitioners of the structured analysis approach) provide the most systematic and consistent approach available to systems professionals today. These techniques offer a variety of approaches to the documenting of data and process models at different levels of specificity and complexity. IE is still an evolving methodology, however. The various advocates of the approach do not all agree on a single set of diagrams or on the appropriate way to sequence them. Nor is there unanimity concerning all of the principles and practices that comprise IE. Nevertheless, the commonality among the different versions of information engineering is more than adequate to provide a sound basis for the FUSION approach and to provide strong support for the other dimensions of FUSION—JAD and CASE. By setting CASE and JAD on the foundation of IE, we can create an unequalled force for productivity and quality in the systems business (Fig. 1.4).

Is IE + CASE + JAD the ultimate solution? No, there will surely be advances that will take us another step on the evolutionary path. But for now, this equation represents the best available approach for improving the management of our most vital business resource, information.

DOES YOUR ORGANIZATION FACE A COMPUTING CRISIS?

Is it time for your organization to consider FUSION? Look behind the doors of many systems organizations today, and you will find people struggling to maintain a viable, credible organization, respected by the customers they serve. On the surface, it may appear that everything is under control. Programmers are programming, and analysts are meeting with users to gather requirements for new systems or discuss changes to existing systems. But just below the surface, fundamental problems of poor quality, late delivery, overwhelming maintenance, and limited resources are festering, dramatically limiting the ability of those programmers and analysts to serve their customers.

The optimists see this situation as an opportunity for innovation and change. The pessimists ignore the situation and hope it will go away. To the outsider it looks like a John Wayne movie, where the last defenders of the fort are getting ready for the final assault by the Indians.

This situation has created enormous stress on the systems organization and has had a negative impact on the ability of its people to perform. As the stress

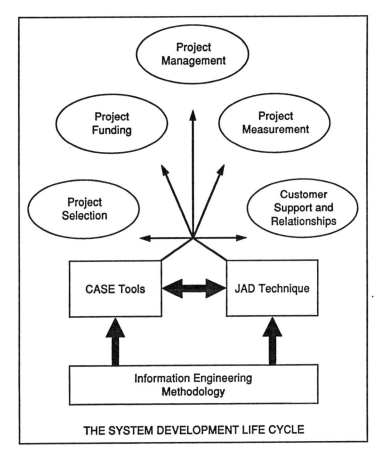

Figure 1.4   IE—The foundation for JAD and CASE.

grows, the organization may try various tactics for reducing the strain. Some of the stress is absorbed. It may even have a positive effect, waking the systems group out of a sense of complacency, reminding the group that its function is to serve its customers, not dole out the occasional favor of a program enhancement. However, as the stresses compound, they can become unmanageable. Members of the group may begin to exhibit certain telltale behavior in an attempt to reduce the stress and survive the pressure.

The forces operating on systems organizations today can provide us with important clues in understanding where we are, how we got there, and where we need to go in the future. Let's look then, at the manifestations of unhealthy stress that were exhibited on a very large cross-functional project as problems were encountered. The first sign of trouble came as due dates for interim deliverables began to be missed.

Stage One

Key project and systems managers stay in their offices during the day, not talking with their customers or their subordinates. They claim to be busy working on budgets and other administrative matters. In essence, the organization leaders abandon their leadership role as they become more and more overwhelmed by the project. In the absence of any leadership, individuals and groups within the systems community begin to act randomly, not coordinating their activities with other individuals and groups. With a leadership vacuum in place, new individuals appoint themselves leaders, rising to save the situation. Several renegade leaders also appear, ready to instigate a rebellion to kill off the floundering project.

Stage Two

As the leadership crisis deepens, some first line project managers begin to fight with each other, each believing that he has the answer to their difficulties. Others begin to form factions, spending their time on the petty politics of transitory alliances. Deadlines slip by, and the project is now three months behind schedule. The pressure to deliver increases and shortcuts start to replace standard quality assurance practices. Overall project plans begin to fall apart as individuals make the protection of their posteriors their first priority. Those managers who attempt to work together have difficulty making decisions. They are afraid of making mistakes. No decision, they feel, is better than a wrong decision.

Stage Three

Systems analysts and programmers struggle to complete their individual tasks. As the stress percolates down into all levels of the organization, the early mistakes committed during design activities generate more mistakes in development. Three separate programming teams attempt to build screens and databases without an integrated data model or a set of screen design standards (Fig. 1.5). Overtime increases to compensate for the earlier mistakes. All quality assurance practices are abandoned. Change control procedures are thrown out the window as design changes are repeatedly pushed through at the last minute at heated meetings. In desperation, the managers hire a consultant to shield them from the complaints of customer groups. The consultant recommends a series of team building seminars.

Stage Four

The user community becomes more and more hostile as the stress of mistakes and missed deadlines increases. Sometimes the attack is direct: "Let's throw out the systems group and bring someone in from the outside to finish the system." Sometimes the attack is indirect. They refuse to make decisions, reject requests

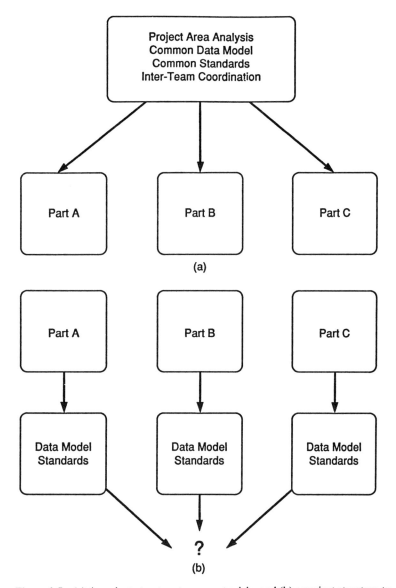

Figure 1.5 (a) A project structure to prevent crisis, and (b) a project structure to invite crisis.

for user participation, and continue to add functionality to designs on which they had previously signed off. As the hostility increases, the attacks become personal. Rumors about imminent firings and threats of resignation fill the air.

An organization whose members exhibit this type of behavior is ill-equipped to work proactively on even simple maintenance projects; complex new designs for multiuser applications are out of the question. In this example, the systems group has been effectively reduced to a state of leaderless confusion. It does not have the focus, structure or skill base necessary to build systems that integrate common business processes across multiple business units, in this case, manufacturing plants. As we look to the future, however, these are just the type of systems that will be most critical to our success. These systems will link manufacturing operations, integrate information access, and introduce common business practices across diverse business units. We are no longer concerned with building stand-alone payroll systems. We are building integrated systems that support financial decision making, resource allocation, process management, and strategic planning. Yesterday's systems development methods and management and communication practices are inadequate to meet these challenges, as the company in our example discovered.

The crisis we face in computing involves four major areas of concern:

- Quality of functionality
- Time required to deliver
- Maintenance of existing applications
- Limited resources

An understanding of each of these areas is important if we are to devise a comprehensive FUSION-based solution to our problems and not just apply another "productivity band-aid."

CRISIS: QUALITY OF FUNCTIONALITY

Functionality is represented in four different ways within the traditional systems development life cycle (Fig. 1.6). In the user requirements phase, functionality is defined from the perspective of the users. In the logical design phase, functionality is defined from the perspective of the systems analyst who translates the broad requirements identified by the users into specific system functionality and business rules expressed as data and process models. In the physical design phase, functionality is seen from the viewpoint of the database designer who is concerned about response time, volume performance, and capacity handling. In the construction phase, functionality is viewed from the viewpoint of the programmer who focuses on effective screen processing and efficient handling of data. Clearly, if there is not agreement among all viewpoints, there will be a surprise in store for the users when the application is implemented. As in the children's game of "telephone," where each player independently passes on a message to another, in the multiphased life cycle there is a strikingly high chance that the message received by the last player will bear only a passing resemblance to the message communicated by the first player. Research indicates that seventy-five percent of

THE QUALITY VIEWPOINT

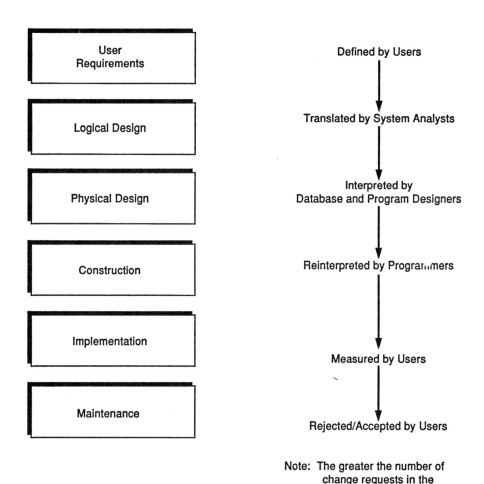

Figure 1.6   Quality in the traditional systems life cycle.

our postdevelopment maintenance work is generated by errors made in the definition of the original functional requirements through mistakes, omissions, ambigu-
ities, and poor communication (Fig. 1.7). Some might say that the systems development business is just a grown-up version of "telephone."

The children's game plays off of an absence of precise, legible documentation
of the message. Once written down, the message cannot become garbled. In the
systems life cycle, the problem of the garbled message can be solved in the same

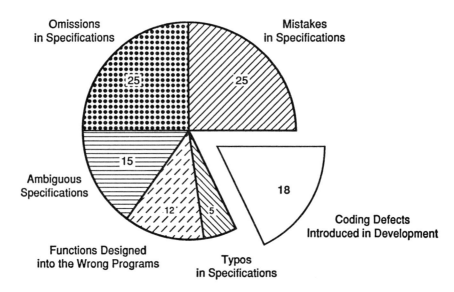

Figure 1.7 Origin of maintenance requests.

way. However, we can only write down a precise and legible message if we all—users and systems professionals—agree on what the message is. This is becoming more difficult as our systems are built to service many users who legitimately have different needs and priorities.

In the traditional iterative interview approach to functional requirements definition, a systems analyst, who may have a limited understanding of the business area he is defining, sets up a series of interviews with different individuals or small user groups. This process can be both painful and unproductive. The pain starts when interviews are repeatedly canceled and rescheduled due to crises in the business area. It intensifies when, after getting one user to fully define his needs, the analyst discovers other users define their needs very differently, and the analyst is forced to integrate unrelated, even conflicting requirements. Productivity decreases as the analyst must constantly revisit users he has already interviewed to clarify points that were not fully explained the first time. If the analyst is not consistent or thorough in his questioning, each return visit can reveal new functional requirements. The problem is exacerbated when the analyst discovers that the users do not understand how the technology can assist them and merely want to automate the manual environment.

What is the analyst to do? He has two choices, neither of them good. The analyst can take responsibility for resolving discrepancies and decide, for example, whether or not the system will provide access to historical data on noncurrent customers. Not a very good choice if the analyst has no experience or education in retail sales. Or, he can avoid the responsibility, opting to continue the series of interviews and discussions until everyone is exhausted. At this point, the analyst

YESTERDAY'S SYSTEMS	TODAY'S SYSTEMS
Single Function	Multiple Functions
Single User	Multiple Users
Process Oriented	Data Oriented
Back Office Transactions	Front Office Decisions
Hardware and Software Limited and Expensive	Hardware and Software Increased Capabilities
Technology Driven	Business Decision Driven
Operational and Tactical	Strategic and Competitive Edge

Figure 1.8   Differences between yesterday's and today's systems.

can go with the answer provided by the last user left standing or the one with the loudest voice. Sometimes, in a situation almost too horrific to contemplate, an analyst will, in a rush to get to code, actually toss the unresolved issue into the hands of the programmer, figuring that he can always make a change postimplementation if the users complain enough.

While the iterative interview technique has sometimes worked well in the past (when the functionality was limited, transaction-based, and noncontroversial), it is not a technique that is viable for the systems we are building today. These systems are substantially different from those we are accustomed to building (Fig. 1.8). We can identify these new systems by looking at several key factors.

Multiple Priorities/Multiple Perspectives

Today's systems must serve multiple cross-functional user groups that have differing priorities and perspectives. Example: A large international bank with many different lines of business recently made its third attempt in five years to build a customer information system. This system was to serve four organizations within a single business unit, sales management, product management, market research, and customer account management. The executives of the four functional organizations were asked to write summary descriptions of their requirements. When all of the executives submitted their descriptions, it appeared that all were describing different systems. The suggestion was made that four separate system development efforts be funded. This was vetoed because of the expense involved, leaving the participants no choice but to devise a common set of functional and data requirements. It was a clear case of fiscal responsibility driving functional integrity, and a clear indication of things to come.

Common Information Needs/Different Process Needs

Today's systems must support organizations where multiple decentralized business units share common data requirements, but they must also continue to support certain unique business practices and procedures. For example, one midwest manufacturer has eighteen separate divisions, each with its own location, organizational structure, and existing automated systems. The divisions represent different functional areas for the manufacturer. Some manufacture parts; others assemble products. At one time eighteen different payroll systems and eighteen different accounts payable systems supported these divisions. However, a strategic directive from top management, citing inefficiency, high cost and information confusion mandated that a set of common systems be created to serve the divisions. For this goal to be achieved, a common set of functional requirements had to be derived. But, in addition, certain requirements for flexibility had to be respected in order to allow each division to maintain certain unique business practices where these were required.

Strategic, Tactical, and Operational Information Needs

Today's systems face another challenge. They must provide information to support strategic decision making at the highest levels of the organization as well as tactical and operational decision making at the working level. For example, a national retailer wanted its corporate financial managers, warehouse managers, and store managers to have access to the same information on product purchasing, inventory levels and transportation. However, information on these areas was resident in over two thousand data items stored on seven different and sometimes overlapping databases. Clearly, a unified central data repository was needed. But how should the data be stored? The corporate managers needed information that would assist them in long range planning. They wanted to answer such questions as: "How is profit on product X impacted by the inventory costs associated with it?" "Should we contract out our transportation requirements or continue to maintain a full in-house shipping operation?" and "What is the purchase trend for processed as opposed to fresh foods?" The warehouse and store managers needed information that would assist them in their day-to-day operational activities. They wanted to be able to answer such questions as: "Will we be able to deliver sufficient quantities of product X to all of our stores in the tri-state region to support a Labor Day television sales campaign?" and "If we are forced to issue rain checks for out-of-stock items, how long will it take to replace our inventory?" A full review of the relationship of data requirements to decision making had to be undertaken.

CRISIS: TIME TO DELIVER

The backlog of development projects for most systems organizations ranges from two to three years. Yet, the time allowed for delivery of new business functionality, whether in the form of new systems or enhancements to existing systems has decreased dramatically, and the time squeeze is increasing. In the financial sector in particular, the rush is on to create new products and services. Marketing is leading the way, announcing new investment vehicles on a regular basis. Not only are these new products pushed out the door more quickly than ever before, but the products themselves require more sophisticated information processing and automated management support than ever before. With rates of return tied to variables in the financial marketplace, accuracy and flexibility in processing are of paramount importance. For a company to remain competitive, it must act fast and act right.

Some organizations have addressed the time constraint issue by purchasing packaged software. For smaller applications, this can be successful. However, on larger projects where customization of packages is required, disasters have occurred. When the package is seen as a shortcut, little or no time is devoted to customization needs. But no large package can be implemented successfully without customization. In one insurance company, a policy processing package was purchased at a cost of over one million dollars. The purchasers of the package believed they were saving time by bypassing the user requirements and logical design life cycle phases. Consequently, they were unequipped to recognize the need for package customization, and when an unending (not to mention unreviewed and uncoordinated) stream of requests for system modifications began to arrive, the systems group was unprepared. Instead of spending the six months that would have been required to develop a complete set of user requirements and logical design before package installation, they spent three years implementing their "time-saving" package and spent three times their original investment in recoding the system.

Similarly, when organizations choose to develop their own systems, time constraints and the desire to rush into coding too often prevent the preparation of a complete logical design. The result is uncontrollable "scope creep," a major source of pain for the systems organization. As programmers and analysts ask questions to clarify functional and data requirements for the system, they find that users keep developing new needs. This leaves the systems organization with more instead of less work to do in the same amount of time.

As the customer base for a system expands, the multiplicity of potential input from users and conflicting requirements also expand. The time needed to gather requirements and construct designs using traditional data collection and review techniques lengthens, often placing considerable stress on the organization. Other types of stress caused by the pressure to work fast include the following.

Time Lost

One of the great project time wasters is the bureaucracy of the approval process. In the worst cases, project "downtime" can exceed project "up-time." Politics and organization change are two additional causes of downtime. Politics can take a simple decision and turn it into a major battle between competing executives or organization units. These battles occur frequently in situations where common systems are being built to support multiple work groups and a leadership vacuum exists. Whose business practices will be supported? Whose will have to change? Who will pay for the system work? Who owns the system? Who will authorize access to "my" data? Then there are the situations where we all wait for the strike to end, or for the new chairman of the board to be appointed, or for Congress to pass the budget, or for the agency to write the new regulations. In these situations, individuals may be very productive, but the culture, or environment, is exceedingly nonproductive.

Time Denied

Because of the pressure to act fast, strategic information systems planning projects lose out to "must have it now" application development projects. In the end, mixed priorities are a terrible time waster, resulting in applications that use data inefficiently and perpetuate outmoded processing standards. New database management products that may have been purchased are used ineffectively, thereby reducing their return on investment, and corporate competitive position can be severely impacted. It is not possible, of course, to stop all application modification and development work while high-level strategic information needs are addressed. However, it is necessary that these needs be addressed as quickly as possible if we are to avoid introducing more inefficiency into our systems even as we rush to complete them.

Time Unavailable

In some organizations, it is never the right time to send people to training. There is always time to purchase a new productivity enhancing tool or technique, but there is no time to ensure that its users are prepared to exercise it properly. We have seen this happen with the acquisition of CASE products and other advanced software packages, but it also happens when organizations adopt a new life cycle methodology (such as IE) or a new technique (such as JAD). Without the time needed to learn the proper use of a new tool, technique, or methodology, and without the time to develop on-the-job skills in its application, these time savers can quickly become time wasters. The usual result is a round

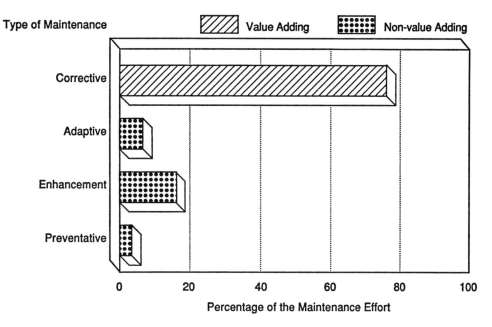

Figure 1.9 Maintenance resource allocation in the traditional systems environment.

of finger pointing, followed by the hunt for the next "real" answer to productivity problems.

CRISIS: MAINTENANCE OF EXISTING APPLICATIONS

From sixty to ninety percent of the work performed by most systems organizations can be classified as maintenance. The time available for the development of new applications is therefore limited, and the time available for strategic information systems planning is even more constrained. However, while the heavy load of maintenance is a problem, part of that problem is more perception than reality. Many organizations do not sufficiently analyze their maintenance requests in order to evaluate the nature of the changes they are asked to make. One company that did take a strategic look at its maintenance requests found that over forty percent of them were for a system that top management wanted to replace in two years. The result was a decision to stop maintenance activities on the old system and reallocate resources to the development of the new system.

To understand the maintenance issue better, it is useful to look at the different types of maintenance projects that occupy so much of our time (Fig. 1.9).

Corrective Maintenance

This type of maintenance project aims at fixing errors in the representation of business functionality within an existing system. Most corrective maintenance occurs within the first three to six months of system utilization, although, in some cases, errors are not found until exception functionality is utilized. The time required for this type of maintenance can be decreased by improving the definition of information and processing requirements and the quality of the logical design of applications in order to remove errors before physical design or coding begin. Improvements in application quality can then be measured through the decreased number of change requests for corrective maintenance. Corrective maintenance adds no value to the systems we create, and yet it consumes up to seventy-five percent of all maintenance work.

Adaptive Maintenance

This type of maintenance is performed in order to accommodate upgrades and changes in technology, generally with the goal of improving capacity, efficiency, and performance of existing applications. This type of maintenance is often the target of re-engineering tools. The time required for adaptive maintenance can most easily be reduced by improving the skills of the personnel performing the adaptive maintenance work. The introduction of new technology requires a commitment to education in that technology and the ability of its implementors to secure a sufficient amount of time for practice. Mistakes will be made. It is best that the mistakes are made in either a formal training program or in on-the-job practice sessions. Mistakes made under the pressure of real deadlines can be very costly.

Enhancement Maintenance

This type of maintenance should not be included under the category of "maintenance" at all. Enhancements represent additions to in-place system functionality that occur because a new requirement has been identified in the business environment. New reports and inquiries are often mistakenly classified as enhancement maintenance. Enhancement maintenance adds real value to an application and should more appropriately be termed "design modification" or "redevelopment." If it is only viewed as a series of quick and dirty fixes, enhancement maintenance is likely to create as many problems as it attempts to solve, thereby increasing the likelihood of premature system obsolescence. Instead of looking at a particular system enhancement requirement in isolation, we need to bundle our enhancement requests and address them as redevelopment issues at the business level. This is a case of the whole being greater than the sum of its parts.

Preventative Maintenance

This type of maintenance is only a problem when it is ignored. But like that annual visit to the dentist, the regular preventative maintenance check-up is as important as it is disliked. Periodic audits of systems for stress and failure points are essential if we are to reduce the number of midnight disasters that occur. While the average organization spends a great deal of time on other maintenance activities, this type of maintenance receives very little attention.

With many of our systems approaching retirement age, we need to understand maintenance better and to begin to reduce its consumption of our valuable resources. Strategic knowledge of where the business is headed is critical to making maintenance support decisions.

CRISIS: LIMITED RESOURCES

Systems organizations have two basic resources with which to operate, people and money. Historically, we have put the emphasis on the money needed to purchase new hardware, software, and facilities. In today's economy, the continuing downward pressure on budgets limits our resources even more. That, of course, is one of the reasons for the interest in productivity tools and techniques: we hope to do more with less.

We have not thought very hard, however, about our other major resource, people. Personnel issues, in general, are not at the top of the list for most systems managers. Some of these managers see people as interchangeable parts. "Let's replace the batch programmers with on-line experts," they say. But the time is long past for this attitude. For one thing, good people are getting harder to find. Pick up any newspaper want ad section. You will find that we solicit people with specific technical skills (e.g., ". . . minimum three years COBOL and CICS experience plus two years of DB2"). We should be looking instead for the ability to learn new languages and technologies, to think and follow through. The move to open architecture simply confirms the need for people who have the ability to learn rapidly and transfer skills from one technology to another. In the postbaby boom era, the number of people available for systems positions will continue to drop. But the call for these people is increasing. In the coming years, it will be more difficult to attract and keep high quality systems professionals. It will take more than just high salaries.

But what about the staff we currently have? There are a number of people around with ten to twenty years of systems experience. Won't that help? No, not without a substantial investment in retraining, and even then we may still be in trouble. The individual who chose a systems career twenty or even ten years ago generally was looking for a highly technical environment with a minimum of personal interaction. Many researchers have noted the existence of this systems personality type. This individual wants a job that has clearly defined parameters, and he wants to be left alone (preferably in a quiet corner) to do it. Ambiguity is not his style.

Organizational politics is a nuisance. The "customer" for his systems is someone who lives outside the world of computer technology. Communication is best carried on through written correspondence. His motto is: "Memos, not meetings."

Today's systems environment requires professionals who have the skills to manage organizational politics, who enjoy personal interaction, and who are not afraid of working in a world of shifting priorities and changing agendas. Some of yesterday's systems professionals may be able to make this leap in attitude and skills. Others will not. Efforts are underway today in a number of systems organizations to provide skills training in communication, marketing, and facilitation techniques. These courses are extremely important for the organization that wants to build and maintain a positive relationship with its customers.

One early indication of the change taking place in the nature of the work performed by today's systems professionals can be seen in changes to job titles. Where once the key job title in the systems business was "programmer," today it is "analyst." We are about due for another change, this time to a title that will increase the emphasis on the front-end of the life cycle, "information architect" or "information designer," perhaps? Many are considering this issue of nomenclature. James Martin, for example, talks about the "information engineer" as the successor to the "systems engineer" and suggests that the new role of "knowledge coordinator" be created.

HOW DOES INFORMATION ENGINEERING ADDRESS THE CRISIS?

A good methodology contains both theory (how things should be done in a perfect world) and practice (how things really are done in an imperfect one). It provides its users with a coherent and compelling presentation of ideas and an orderly systematic process for applying those ideas to the real world. The result of the implementation of such a methodology should be a high level of quality in the performance of the work it supports. We believe that the methodology known as information engineering provides this, and therefore should be included in any approach to addressing the crises in computing that we have outlined (Fig. 1.10). IE can assist us in addressing the components of the crisis in the following ways:

Solution: Quality of Functionality

Information engineering forces a formal, disciplined, and rigorous analysis of business strategy and needs at a level above that of the individual application. It asks corporate executives to define their business plans and to participate in the design of architectures to support the strategic implementation of these

Solution / Crisis	IE Methodology	Case Tools	JAD Technique
Function Quality	Forces business focus Provides discipline and rigor Demands new user involvement Provides seamless trail	Reduces analysis and design errors Links logical and physical designs Automates complex and routine analysis	Reduces analysis and design errors Reduces effort Increases completeness Makes systems and users partners
Time to Deliver	Redistributes where time is spent Requires more front end time	Shortens life cycle elapsed time Requires more front end time Reduces programming time	Reduces life cycle elapsed time Reduces front end time
Maintenance	Reduces effort Reduces costs Design drives changes	Enables change Changes at design level, not source code level Reduces analysis effort	Improves priority setting Improves decision making Forces full analysis of change needs
Limited Resources	Increases system role in business planning Redistributes system staff Requires new skills	Provides standards Requires new skills	Requires new skills Redistributes resources Ensures user decision making

Figure 1.10   FUSION: Addressing the quality crisis.

plans. Further, IE emphasizes the development of top-down, integrated views of information and process support needs, while at the same time maintaining a separation between the process support needs of a specific application and the corporate databases that serve it. As James Martin has repeatedly advocated, IE separates the analysis of the (relatively) stable information that an organization requires from its more volatile business processes, procedures, and practices. Because of this, IE changes the way projects are structured, planned for, and ultimately managed.

Because of its emphasis on business strategy, IE calls for a new involvement by users in the definition and clarification of their information and processing needs. It requires that they examine their business strategies and tactical implementation needs and link these to specific requirements for databases and applications. In an IE environment, applications are not prioritized by reference to the political weight of their supporters. They are prioritized in accordance with reference to their satisfaction of strategic, tactical and operational business needs.

In the IE driven environment, the systems organization becomes the supplier to the business unit, and the performance of the systems group is measured by the effectiveness of the business unit in supporting business goals and strategies. IE asks that programmers and analysts become information engineers, specialists in linking business unit and area information and processing needs to the delivery of applications and databases. The technical aspects of systems solutions (physical database structures, communication networks, operating platforms, etc.) are important. They are important, though, not because of abstract performance values, but because they enable us to better implement business strategies. IE asks us to judge the success of the systems organization by the extent to which it delivers comprehensive and flexible business information in support of the organization's goals and strategies.

Solution: Time Required to Deliver

Information engineering addresses time constraints by redistributing resources throughout the life cycle (Fig. 1.11). This is true both on the "micro" level for the application development life cycle, and on the "macro" level for the corporate information management life cycle of which the former is a part. IE puts more time into application planning and design activities for the specific purpose of obtaining substantial time reductions in construction, testing and implementation activities. In this way, the overall time required on any project is reduced.

Similarly, information engineering increases the time required for strategic information planning and architecture activities, with the objective of reducing the duplication and inefficiency produced when applications and databases are developed without reference to an overall plan. Again, this should reduce overall life cycle requirements. The truth, of course, is that many (perhaps most) organi-

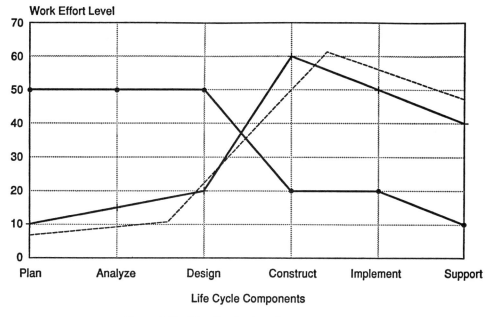

Figure 1.11 IE redistribution of systems resources.

zations today spend minimal time on strategic information planning and architecture development efforts, pursuing tactical and operational application development projects with little or no regard to corporate and business unit goals and strategies. This saves time in the short run, but can cost heavily in the long run.

Solution: Maintenance of Existing Applications

It may seem at first glance that the implementation of an information engineering methodology has no direct impact on maintenance. The indirect impacts are significant, however. With the improvement in planning that IE brings, systems are designed to match strategic business needs. Applications and databases are designed independently to support business needs that cross organization boundaries and to provide a balance of standardization and flexibility. As a result, maintenance requests are reduced. IE is not the only force driving us in this direction. Ultimately, the introduction of such new technologies as re-engineering will change the way we look at all of our maintenance activities. But IE is a part of this movement.

Solution: Limited Resources

Implementing an information engineering methodology can impact system development costs. The most obvious way it does this is to cut the time required to develop and maintain systems. In effect, it uses personnel time more efficiently. But we must acknowledge that these personnel resources will be more expensive on a per capita basis than those we have used in the past. The new information engineer will be more difficult to hire and retain than the COBOL programmer, thus increasing the cost per person of the typical system staff. When we add in the costs incurred in the purchase of expensive productivity enhancement tools, it seems likely that our future resources will remain as limited as our present resources. This does not negate the many advantages of the new approach, however. In addition to the better systems we will build, there may be a further corporate advantage to be gained. Today's CEOs generally come from either financial or marketing organizations. The increase in status and expertise of the typical systems executive may mean that a time will come when the CEO is a former information engineer. This could prove important both for the systems organization and the corporation as a whole. While the introduction of an IE methodology will not significantly reduce resource costs, then, it will surely increase resource quality and ultimately the impact of those resources on corporate goals and strategy.

HOW DOES CASE ADDRESS THE CRISIS?

CASE tools support the automation of our systems development life cycle. Some do this better than others, and as of today, no one tool has proven to have the total answer. But the benefits of CASE are clear. While the full implementation of a CASE tool can have a profound effect on the systems organization, even limited use of CASE can assist the organization in addressing the crises found in today's systems environment.

Solution: Quality of Functionality

First, CASE can assist us in reducing the number of errors built into information plans, models, and application designs by providing us with automated analysis. Through this analysis, we can uncover inconsistencies and omissions in our designs and repair these at an early point in a project. On a large project, where it can be impossible to make all of these checks by hand and eye, this is no small benefit. Second, CASE can assist us by generating code based on a logical design entered into the tool. This increases the accuracy and quality of the delivered application and databases. Changes in design can then drive new code generation. Design changes are easier to understand and maintain than source code changes.

In addition, most CASE tools enforce a set of standards. In some tools, these standards are tied to a specific methodology. In others, they represent a simple requirement for consistency. Many tools require that tool functions be performed in a predefined sequence and prohibit exceptions to this sequence. For example, a tool may require that all entities be identified before their attributes are identified. This constrains those users who favor a "bottom-up" approach to logical data design. While occasionally these rules may seem confining, however, they almost always prove useful in increasing the quality of the delivered product. For the organization that has only the most basic life cycle standards in place, they can prove invaluable.

Solution: Time Required to Deliver

Using CASE tools may slow down a project initially. Traditionally, the front end of the life cycle has been shortcut. As a result, when adequate time is devoted to these activities, the result is the appearance of a lengthened life cycle. Appearance is not reality, however. Lengthening the front end of the life cycle shortens the back end of the cycle, and, in fact, the overall time required for a project. In addition, when code generators are added to the picture, cutting the time required for the construction phase, time savings increase still more. Does CASE alone cut system development time in half? No, not on the typical project. Match CASE with IE and JAD, however, and the probability of dramatic savings increases greatly.

Solution: Maintenance of Existing Applications

CASE tools provide an important part of the solution to today's maintenance backlog. CASE tools reduce the amount of time needed to identify and design changes for applications. When the specifications for logical and physical designs are well documented, it becomes much easier to make changes and manage the impacts of those changes. As more sophisticated tools evolve, the process of transforming logical design changes into physical design changes and then into generated code will become totally automated. New code will be integrated automatically into the existing code without generating errors.

Solution: Limited Resources

CASE tools cost money, some thousands of dollars generally for just one workstation. Yet for CASE to be successfully implemented, all analysts must have ready access to these tools. Whether or not this represents a major expenditure will depend on the health of your budget. For most organizations, this purchase is cause for careful financial consideration. The first concern many prospective buyers will have is how soon they can recoup their investment. CASE does not provide an instant payback, however. In addition to the initial purchase price,

CASE will cost money in project downtime while analysts develop their CASE knowledge and skills. However, given a CASE-knowledgeable staff, sufficient access to the tools, and a reasonable implementation and transition plan, CASE can start saving the organization money in less than one year. Over time, the return on investment that will be gained through enhanced system quality and performance will ensure that savings continue to increase.

CASE tools can also have an important impact on the resource of people. CASE tools improve the communication among systems professionals and between these individuals and the customers they serve by providing standards for communication and automated graphics capabilities. Correctly used, CASE tools ensure that decisions are accurately represented and that all parties understand and agree to these decisions. This places a burden on the user community. It may need to become familiar with certain graphic representation standards it does not currently understand. If systems analysts can accept the burden of learning the CASE tool, however, it would not seem inappropriate to ask the user community to learn a few new communication concepts as well.

Because we are still in the infancy of the CASE revolution, we sometimes find ourselves more concerned with the frustrations than the opportunities these tools provide. It is clear, however, that the automation of systems planning, design, and development activities is both required and inevitable. The "retooling" of our systems professionals represents a special challenge for the future if we are to ensure that the increasing sophistication of our personnel resources keeps pace with the increasing sophistication of our tools.

HOW DOES JAD ADDRESS THE CRISIS?

JAD techniques are the data gathering and consensus building mechanism for systems life cycle activities. JAD forces user commitment and involvement and relieves the systems organization of what should be the user's responsibility for strategic business planning, information systems planning, and logical application design. Further, it makes a unique contribution by addressing the political component of projects as well as the technological one. By providing a structured process for the exchange of ideas and the resolution of conflicting opinions and priorities, JAD leads us to the development of systems that promote business goals and strategies. JAD techniques provide a structured approach for addressing the crisis currently facing the systems organization.

Solution: Quality of Functionality

JAD is an extremely effective technique for gathering and refining information on strategic goals, high-level information and processing needs, and detailed application designs from a diverse set of participants. It provides a structured forum in which business and systems professionals can together construct flexible solutions that accurately reflect the goals and strategy of the business without violating the constraints of available technology and resources. JAD also resolves the problem of system ownership, or rather, the lack thereof. Too often in the past users have disowned an application once it was implemented. Whether the cause was faulty functionality or organizational politics, this was a difficult problem. Through JAD, users develop ownership as they build consensus. It is easy to reject someone else's design, but not so easy or desirable to reject your own.

When integrated with information engineering concepts and supported with CASE tools, JAD can provide a coherent, disciplined structure for defining information and processing requirements at all levels of detail (Fig. 1.12). JAD is used at the business enterprise level to define strategic information plans and implementation architectures. It is used at the business area level to construct data and process models and re-engineer operations. At the application level, JAD is used for the creation and testing of logical designs. And JAD can do this in the real world of politics and competing (and sometimes rapidly changing) priorities. In this way, JAD significantly improves the quality of functionality delivered.

Solution: Time Required to Deliver

Properly implemented, JAD techniques can decrease the time needed to complete a project. This decrease, depending on the project type, can range from twenty to fifty percent of elapsed time (Fig. 1.13). JAD achieves these gains by bringing people together and eliminating the iterative interview and redundant approval process that characterizes most design efforts today. In addition, JAD, like CASE, provides important time savings downstream in the life cycle. When a design is improved, the system that results is improved, and change requests decrease.

Solution: Maintenance of Existing Applications

JAD is often thought of as a technique to be used only for the design of new applications. This is too narrow a view of the potential of this powerful process, however. JAD can be used effectively as well for high-level corporate information planning, data and process architecture design, and a variety of special project types (e.g., data model integration, process improvement). Even in the area of application design, the projects that can benefit from JAD are varied. They include new application development, major redevelopment, prototype evaluation, software package selection, and maintenance. In maintenance in particular (an area where JAD is currently under utilized), JAD can be quite effective when used to gather modification requests, prioritize those requests, and ensure that the impacts of those modifications are carefully analyzed and controlled.

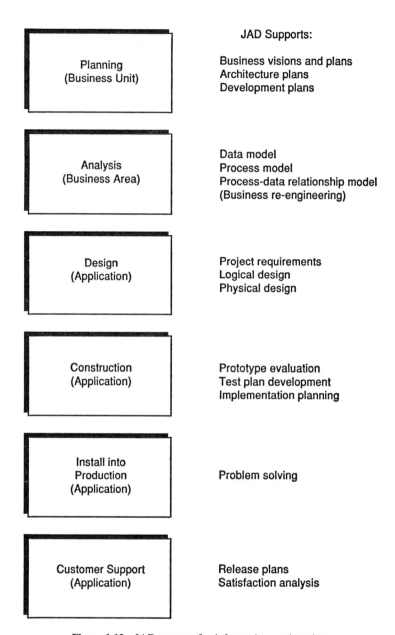

Figure 1.12 JAD support for information engineering.

1985 Insurance company study
Effort required to complete user specifications
for application projects

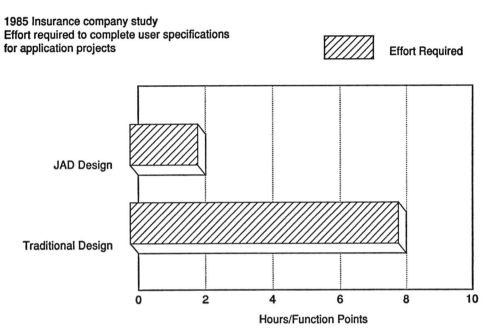

Figure 1.13   JAD time savings over traditional techniques.

Solution: Limited Resources

JAD is a cost-effective technique. Relatively few analysts need to be trained as JAD facilitators because each facilitator can support two to three projects at a time. The involvement of systems and business professionals is limited as well. The biggest commitment of time for all involved comes during the JAD workshop. This may require from three to five days from each workshop partici- pant. In large projects with multiple workshops, this requirement may increase, with each participant asked for a total commitment of about twenty days. To some, this commitment may seem too great, but this concentrated effort generally saves far more time than it consumes. By rounding up all of the key players at one time in one place, JAD eliminates the need for the repeated telephone calls, interviews, and review meetings that nibble away at productivity. While the per- sonnel resource costs with JAD are more obvious because they are concentrated, they are actually less than the hidden resource costs of the traditional approach.

A well-engineered JAD technique may also provide a valuable redistribution of time for the project manager. Instead of supervising a series of interviews and a prolonged review and approval process, he can devote more time to managing his team and ensuring that political and organization hurdles are cleared for the project. This leadership is critical to project success, especially for large, complex projects that cross organizational boundaries.

Finally, JAD helps define the new role of the systems analyst. The effective JAD facilitator is an individual who has one foot in the business world and one foot in the systems world. This individual understands the importance of the information resource as a competitive instrument in the marketplace, as well as the political realities of managing information in complex organizations. He knows how to ensure that all views are given a fair hearing, how to mediate among diverse perspectives, how to get commitment, and how to handle the variety of personality types that any project will contain. Individuals with the credentials to make good JAD facilitators are not to be found everywhere, but they are becoming more available all the time.

In summary, JAD techniques are a new and extremely effective way of enhancing communication and promoting sound decision making. JAD provides a structured and disciplined behavioral platform for work at multiple levels of systems design and development, from the broadest strategy and systems planning to the most detailed screen design. It provides strong support for the project manager, directly involves users in defining their information management needs, and relieves the systems group of the responsibility for making business decisions. As part of the FUSION equation, JAD supports an IE methodology and provides high-quality input to CASE tools. More structured than the typical business meeting, more focused than the typical walk through, and more productive than a series of iterative interviews, JAD workshops are a key to implementing rapid application development and a strategic approach to systems planning and information management.

IMPLEMENTING THE FUSION APPROACH

Information engineering is a discipline, a set of methodological principles that can be taught in a classroom, but this discipline only proves its value when implemented in the real world. And it can only be fully implemented when it is matched with practical tools and techniques. The tools and techniques discussed here, CASE and JAD, provide the practical foundation for the implementation of IE. The purpose of this book is to provide practical, not theoretical, guidance on how, when, and where to integrate these three dimensions of "FUSION."

No two organizations will choose to implement the FUSION concept in the same way. An organization's culture, technical environment, history, and strategic priorities will all play a part in determining the most effective implementation approach. Some will want to plunge right in, opting for a one-time revolution; others will want to stage their implementation, preferring a phased approach. There is no answer that will fit all organizations. Change is a difficult thing. If it is not carefully thought out and prepared for, it can cause more problems than it solves.

In considering the most effective implementation of FUSION, think about where you are today and where you want to be tomorrow. This will give you a framework for implementation and help you to identify areas that may need special attention. Before going any further consider the following questions:

The Present Environment

1. Does your organization currently have a systems development life cycle methodology in place? If not, consider your organization's "common practice and procedures" to be your de facto methodology. What is its theoretical basis? What diagramming conventions does it support?
2. Was the methodology purchased from a vendor or created in-house? If purchased, was it modified for in-house use? How much variation in use exists within different divisions and groups of the organization?
3. How widely is this methodology used? Where is it successful? Where unsuccessful? Are people rewarded for using it or punished for not using it? Is it perceived as a hinderance or enhancer to productive work?
4. Does this methodology incorporate new tools and techniques such as CASE and JAD? If so, how widely are these used? With what level of expertise?
5. What training is currently provided to systems professionals? Does this training cover methodology? CASE tools? JAD techniques? Project management techniques? Facilitation skills? Marketing and selling skills? Communication skills? How does the organization value development of its people? Is there a directed, planned effort to upgrade staff capabilities?
6. Who are the key political players and influencers at each level of the systems organization? What are their positions in the present environment? What are the hostilities and "camps" within the organization? What are the biggest problems and opportunities within the organization?
7. What is the nature of the relationship between the user community and the systems organization today? Do users set the agenda or does the systems organization create its own priorities for action?

The Future Environment

1. Does your organization have a strategic vision of what role systems will play in the future? Is that vision defined?
2. If there is a vision, what information and technical architectures will be required to support it? If there is no stated vision, what is likely to be the organization's approach to satisfying user needs and managing maintenance requirements over the next five to ten years?
3. Does this vision require that your organization adopt a highly structured approach to the life cycle? To what extent is flexibility important to the organization? How important is consistency?
4. How will the systems organization transition from the existing environment

to one that meets future needs? How will the role of the systems professional change?

5. How is change generally implemented and received within your organization? Are there tactics that can assist in the implementation of change that were successful in the past? What energizes people in your organization? What frightens them? What causes them to resist change?

6. How is the new environment generally regarded by leaders within the organization? Will these views enhance or inhibit the successful implementation of change?

7. To what extent may the user community be expected to support the systems organization in the implementation of change? What can be done to maximize their commitment and support for FUSION?

The answers to these questions should help you to define your major areas of concern. It may be that your organization has recently adopted an IE methodology, but you are not certain how to match the methodology to the CASE tool you just purchased. It may be that your organization has been operating without any formal methodology, but while you know this does not work, you do not want to give up all of the flexibility this situation affords. Perhaps it is the role of the systems analyst that is causing concern. Without a clear view of the future systems organization, it is difficult to define the role of this individual or hire new recruits.

You do not need to resolve all of these issues before you implement FUSION. But you do need to be aware of them. These issues will help you to identify the unique benefits and special challenges that await you in changing the way you do business. One thing is clear: our information management needs are changing, and the business of planning, constructing, and implementing systems to meet these needs must change along with them. Our only choice is whether we will define and direct that change, or whether we will let it overwhelm us. The FUSION equation provides us with a formula for mastering change. It is up to us to use it successfully.

2

The Technique Dimension: Joint Application Development

THE ROLE OF JAD IN SYSTEMS WORK

The most pressing issue in application development today is obtaining positive user involvement in the systems planning and development life cycle. There has long been a communication gap between systems professionals and the user community. Systems professionals have trouble talking to and working with users, finding it difficult to explain ideas to individuals who are unfamiliar with the terminology and concepts of the systems business. Users, on their side, find it difficult to work with systems people who are unfamiliar with the terminology and concepts involved in their business. Neither group has fully understood the constraints under which the other one operates, even though each group works in a world of budgets and deadlines. This flawed relationship has inevitably resulted in a sense of alienation, if not direct hostility, on both sides.

One cause of this problem is that, as a general rule, systems professionals have not been trained in how to work with people. It is not part of university computer science curricula, nor is it part of most corporate systems training programs. As a result, they know little about the concepts of group and individual behavior or the structure of effective communication. Neither do they generally have the skills for promoting user involvement and assisting people in constructing decisions and building consensus. Their focus has been on the engineering side of systems technology rather than its business application.

The project manager (sometimes called the *project team leader*) is a key component in the systems-users relationship. Traditionally, this person has shouldered the burden of communicating with users. His team is primarily composed of analysts and programmers, with the addition of a few "real" system users. Unfortunately the latter may be those who are most easily spared by their business units, rather than those who are most knowledgeable or who have the most influence. As a result, the project manager may have inadequate information on which to base his conclusions about user requirements. He may also anticipate serious problems in gaining final acceptance when the larger user community is finally introduced to the system.

Some project managers rise to the occasion. They insist on adequate user representation right from the start, as a nonnegotiable component of the systems life cycle. Others may see this initial lack of commitment and interest on the part of the users as a challenge or an insult. Some project managers view their role as protecting their "troops" from the unreasonable requests and ever changing needs of the user community. This type of project manager is willing to go into battle to get necessary input from users, but his approach is that of the general, not the mediator. If he fails to get a response that meets with his expectations, or if he gets no definitive response at all, he will take responsibility for making the decisions necessary to keep the project moving forward. In a choice between progress at any price and an endless series of delays and evasions, he chooses progress.

In the past, the techniques available to a project manager and his team for involving users have been limited. These included user interviews, design walk throughs, and prototype reviews led by the project manager or team members. There are several problems with these approaches, however, not the least of which is that they are basically iterative in nature. They begin with the assumption that it is impossible to fix on a set of requirements as the result of a single information gathering/decision making event. Therefore, they emphasize repetition and modification. The theory seems to be something of a variation on "practice makes perfect." Add to this the communication gap between the systems and user communities previously mentioned, and it is no wonder that the more "practice" that goes on here, the more opportunity confusion and error has to creep in. These traditional techniques too often fail, a situation that results when the project team takes on the responsibility to:

- Identify and define information management needs for users while obtaining only limited participation of the users in this process.
- Translate generalized statements and incomplete information into logical application models and designs.
- Resolve conflicts among different user groups with legitimately different needs and priorities.

A further problem with these techniques is that they provide little help for handling the very real political and organizational issues that surround most important projects. The result is that some projects stay in the planning, analysis, or design phases of the life cycle for years, never proceeding to construction. Some die from lack of commitment by users, and others result in systems that, when installed, are severely criticized or rejected by users as inadequate.

Joint application development (JAD) is different from the traditional techniques previously described. JAD is a team-oriented approach to the development of information management solutions that emphasizes a consensus-based problem solving model. It provides a structured approach for increasing user involvement and commitment, managing project politics, and promoting objective and unbiased project leadership. JAD builds a positive, nonhostile, team-oriented partnership among the systems and user communities and creates an atmosphere of mutual respect and a willingness to compromise among all of the parties to the process. Best of all, it results in systems that are enthusiastically accepted by their users and accomplishes this in a greatly reduced timeframe.

JAD's most important role in systems work comes at the front end of the systems development life cycle (Fig. 2.1), where JAD focuses on improving front end planning, analysis, and design life cycle deliverables. Because JAD so dramatically improves the quality of application designs and reduces the number and extent of design modifications, its impact on defect removal can be quite significant, with defect removal time reduced to as little as one fourth the time required in a non-JAD project. Recent studies indicate that in a project where JAD is not used to define requirements, the initial design can fail to capture up to thirty-five percent of user required functionality. This can result in the need to add up to fifty percent more code to bring the application in line with requirements. In contrast, in a project where JAD is used to define requirements, the design fails to capture only ten percent of required functionality. This number is reduced to only five percent if JAD is combined with prototyping, thus reducing the need for additional code substantially.

JAD AND RAPID APPLICATION DEVELOPMENT

JAD is a key to implementing a rapid application development approach to the life cycle. Both JAD and RAD share the same goals: high-quality output, a greatly reduced project timeframe, and a clear connection among all phases of systems activities, from high-level planning to information architecture development to application design. Both favor a team-based orientation to problem solving and the use of prototyping techniques and CASE tools, and both emphasize the importance of breaking down large projects into manageable smaller ones, each with its own set of specific objectives and a clearly defined connection to the larger project goal. JAD and RAD are clearly complementary (Fig. 2.2).

Systems Work	JAD Role	User Involvement
Plan for systems	Primary	Decision making
Analyze business area data/process needs	Primary	Decision making
Define application requirements	Primary	Decision making
Create application logical design	Primary	Decision making
Database administration in business unit/area	Optional	Advisory
Prototype application	Primary	Validation/ confirmation
Complete physical design of databases/applications	N/A	N/A
Construct databases/ applications	N/A	N/A
Test applications	Optional	Test plan development
Maintain/correct/ enhance applications	Primary	Decision making

Figure 2.1 The role of JAD in systems work.

JAD DISTINGUISHING CHARACTERISTICS

The term "JAD" originally meant Joint Application Design. It was coined by an IBM sales executive in the late 1970s. When faced with systems managers who could not reach a decision to purchase hardware, the sales executive invited some users to join the systems managers in a discussion of their needs. The result was a better understanding of user requirements by the systems managers and a big sale for the sales executive. We might say that JAD was first used as a closing technique to expedite a buying decision. It has come a long way since then. Today many large corporations are using proprietary versions of JAD developed by the vendors that specialize in providing training and consulting services in the technique. Other organizations have built their own customized versions of

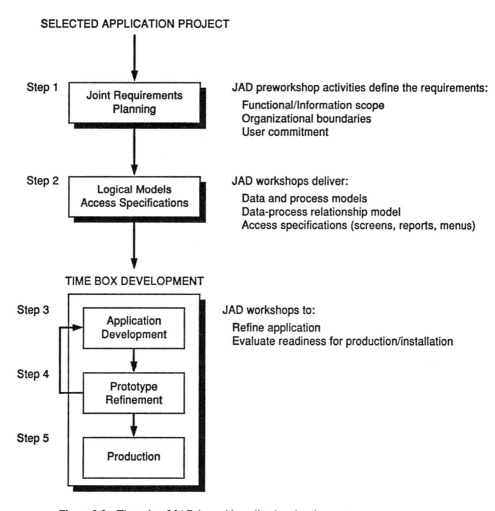

Figure 2.2 The role of JAD in rapid application development.

JAD. In fact, the popularity of JAD is such that some people use the term to refer to any well run meeting where more than two users and systems people get together. But while approaches to JAD may differ, there are some distinguishing characteristics that all true JAD approaches share. A description of these characteristics follows.

Unbiased Facilitation

The application of the JAD technique to a particular project must be directed by an unbiased specially trained facilitator. This individual is neither a member of the project team nor the project manager. The JAD facilitator himself has no stake in the project; rather his role is to facilitate the decision making process for the team. He does not need to have extensive expertise in the business area under consideration, but he must be an expert in many other areas, including: systems analysis, life cycle methodology, group dynamics, individual behavior, conflict management, and commitment building.

Deliverable Accountability

JAD always produces specific outputs, including both workshop deliverables and other project support deliverables. The content and format of the workshop deliverable, which we refer to as the "JAD workshop deliverable" for the sake of simplicity, varies from project to project and from one organization to another. It is detailed, carefully structured, and appropriate to the needs of the project and the standards of the organization. One or more workshops and postworkshop activities may be required to create and finalize the JAD workshop deliverable. Other project support deliverables may include a project evaluation document designed to review applicability of the JAD process to the project, a project definition document designed to define project scope, and an educational document designed to assist workshop participants in understanding the JAD process. The responsibility for preparation of all the deliverables belongs to a JAD/CASE specialist, who works with the JAD facilitator during the JAD process.

Participant Roles and Responsibilities

JAD requires that certain roles be filled in order to ensure project commitment and JAD success. These predefined roles include: JAD facilitator, JAD/CASE specialist, executive sponsor, project manager, business user experts, and systems experts. Optional roles include technical experts and observers. For each role there is a specific, defined set of responsibilities.

Process Structure

Although the focal point of the JAD technique is a workshop or series of workshop sessions, JAD is not a meeting or series of meetings. JAD is a rigorous process consisting of three distinct phases—preworkshop activities, workshop activities, and postworkshop activities, each formally structured to ensure a high quality of accomplishment and a clear connection to the other phases. Each phase has its own objectives, participant profile, and delivery strategies.

Forum Structure

JAD uses three different types of group sessions to promote participant involvement in a project: the target meeting, the focus group interview and the workshop. Each type of session has its own objectives, preparation requirements, operating rules, facilitation style, and participant responsibilities.

Exercise Structure

JAD facilitators are not just discussion leaders who happen to produce technical system models and designs. JAD facilitators design and direct exercises that integrate behavioral and technical principles with specific project objectives. While each exercise has a specific contribution to make to the final JAD workshop deliverable, each is also structured to stimulate and motivate the group, keep participants from becoming overtired, and ensure that final decisions represent a consensus of the entire group.

CRITICAL SUCCESS FACTORS

Four critical success factors are recognized and addressed by most JAD practitioners. One is the necessity of preventing "scope creep" through the clear definition of project objectives and domain. Another is the need to identify and address "killer" political and organizational issues early in the JAD process. A third is the need to ensure commitment to the JAD technique both by all project participants and by key executive management. The fourth is the need to modularize large projects into manageable units to allow for a module linked delivery approach, with each module delivered to the client within a four to six-month timeframe. This last strategy is adhered to with particular strictness by those committed to a joint JAD/RAD approach.

For the most part, the different proprietary approaches to JAD subscribe to the earlier identified principles. Each of these approaches, however, is structured somewhat differently. The proprietary approach offered by M.G. Rush & Associates, for example, stresses methodology independence and provides a series of predefined agendas to the new JAD facilitator to define the structure of JAD projects. Rush's agendas for what he terms the "FAST" technique include a Planning JAD agenda, a Requirements JAD agenda, a Design JAD agenda, and others. Other vendors drive the process based on a specific methodology. The JAD technique promoted by IBM and discussed in a recent book by Jane Wood and Denise Silver supports structured analysis theory and principles. ATLIS Performance Resources, Inc. (ATLIS/PRI) offers a JAD technique called *The METHOD*. This technique incorporates elements of structured analysis, but is generally oriented toward an information engineering methodology.

A great deal can be learned about the way JAD is thought of and used today from the differences among these proprietary approaches. Each utilizes its own terminology for JAD process structure and deliverables. Each also defines the objectives and content of each phase in the JAD process somewhat differently. This is particularly apparent in looking at preworkshop activities. *The METHOD*, for example, is heavily "front end loaded." It requires two to three weeks of preworkshop activities using small target meetings and focus group interviews before moving to the workshop phase. Other JAD approaches move more rapidly, requiring only three to five days of workshop preparation. Some approaches recommend that each workshop session last from three to five days, with the option of one or several sessions depending on project requirements. Others endorse short sessions of one half to one day in length, a structure that may result in a series of ten to twenty-five short workshop sessions. Some approaches favor the "single group" technique, where all exercises are completed by all participants together in the same room under the strong direction of the JAD facilitator. Others use a variety of large group and subteam exercises, where single group exercises are alternated with small group exercises that divide responsibilities among three to five subteams that work on their own for a time in separate locations. Some approaches are tied very closely to specific CASE tools, devoting much time in postworkshop activities to CASE tool utilization. Others emphasize fast turnaround time for workshop deliverables, and use word processing tools (sometimes requiring twenty-four hour word processing availability) to achieve this.

THE JAD FACILITATOR

The JAD facilitator is a consultant to the project manager, with responsibility for managing the JAD process and ensuring that the project proceeds through all JAD activities to a successful and appropriate conclusion. The technical job of the JAD facilitator is to deliver a high quality result quickly. The political job of the JAD facilitator is to make the project manager a "hero," to assist him in making the right decisions for the project and for the business as a whole. The behavioral job of the JAD facilitator is to create a project team that will work productively throughout the project and will carry a new attitude and commitment into other project work as well.

The JAD facilitator sets the rules for the JAD process, guides project decision making within those rules, and assists the project manager in selecting participants and arranging other aspects of the JAD activities. The JAD facilitator is responsible for creating the JAD workshop structure and for designing and managing all workshop exercises and activities. Ultimately, JAD success is judged by the planning and facilitation skills of this individual.

By definition the JAD facilitator is not a member of the project team or the business organizations involved in the project, and as such, is unbiased and objective. Beyond this, the facilitator must be well trained and experienced in both technical and behavioral areas. It clearly helps if the facilitator is part of a larger group of facilitation professionals to whom he can turn for support and guidance. Some organizations hire JAD consultants either as a temporary or a permanent answer to the question of how to find these exemplary individuals. Other organizations develop their own facilitator teams, generally locating them in the systems group. In either case, selection and training of facilitators is an important key to JAD success. A poor facilitator can quickly undermine organization confidence in the technique. It is not a good idea, however, for an organization to depend on the special skills of one or two expert JAD facilitators. While the skill of the facilitator is an important key to JAD project success, the focus of attention should always be on the JAD process itself, not the individual facilitator. This is the best way to ensure that the process will be proliferated throughout the organization.

WHAT IS A FACILITATOR?

A facilitator is someone who is an expert in leading a group of individuals in the achievement of objectives defined by the group itself. This person will fulfill many different roles. One of those roles is that of the timekeeper. The facilitator must ensure that each target meeting, focus group interview, and workshop session moves along properly, accomplishes its agenda and keeps on track. Another role is that of summarizer, with the responsibility to listen carefully to all discussion, feed back key points succinctly to the group and moderate the analysis, evaluation, and decision making that follows. A third role is that of clarifier. In this role, the facilitator must untie the verbal knots that participants can create in trying to address complex issues. The facilitator must always keep in mind the core elements of the discussion and be able to direct participants back onto the proper path when they wander off. Fourth, the facilitator is an analyzer, both of what is said and what is conveyed through other means. The facilitator must look for similarities, differences, agreements, disagreements, discontinuities, paradoxes, and contradictions in the discussion, and be prepared to deal with all of these. At the same time, he must be aware of nonverbal behavior that indicates agreement, disagreement, and confusion as well. The role of mediator is another one filled by the facilitator. He must be able to help individuals to resolve disputes without himself taking sides in the controversy, even if he believes that one position is superior to another. In other words, he must never forget that his role is to assist the group in creating a solution that meets its common needs, not to advance a solution of his own. A facilitator may suggest alternatives, ask questions, or assist the group to evaluate proposed ideas, but he is not a decision maker. The success of any facilitated approach, and the JAD technique is no exception, depends heavily on preworkshop planning and preparation activities. These present the facilitator with additional responsibilities. In addition to the roles identified earlier, the facilitator must be prepared to fill the role of researcher, even to the extent of ferreting out information and perspectives on the project that others may wish to conceal. If the facilitator is to be successful in the workshop, he needs to understand all aspects of the issue that will be addressed, complete with hidden agendas and political perspectives. He must be able to walk into the workshop convinced that he will meet with no surprises there.

In addition, the facilitator must be skilled in workshop agenda design. He must be able to create an agenda that meets the technical needs of the project while acknowledging the constraints of the time and facilities available and the strengths and weaknesses of the participant group. Finally, a facilitator must be a coordinator, able to manage the timing and execution of all JAD activities to ensure that the desired result is produced.

Because the facilitator is a consultant to the project manager, he cannot order the project manager to do as he wishes. Therefore, the facilitator also must be a diplomat, someone willing to let the "other guy" take the credit for an idea, even if this is not the case. A facilitator must be a counselor as well, willing to listen to the project manager's concerns and problems, but he nevertheless must impose a sense of discipline on the process. The facilitator cannot be backed into a corner or allow JAD critical success factors to be violated by the project manager. If necessary, the facilitator must be a salesman. He must sell the project manager on following these critical success factors, even when it might be easier not to do so. He must be willing to delay or stop the JAD process if executive commitment is not adequate, if user participation is uncertain, or if political issues override the potential for technical success.

WHAT MAKES A GOOD JAD FACILITATOR?

JAD facilitators are made, not born, but there is a typical experience and personality profile that strong candidate facilitators bring to a training program. The prospective JAD facilitator needs training and experience in systems analysis principles and techniques, methodology concepts, and life cycle approaches. A programming background is not required, nor is extensive, detailed experience in such technical areas as physical database design, hardware platform selection, or network design. What is helpful, on the other hand, is any experience in conducting analysis activities for large complex projects, or in teaching, training, or leading groups. The ideal JAD candidate is a person who has a "foot in both worlds," who has a broad based understanding of technical issues but who also enjoys the people part of the systems business.

In identifying prospective JAD facilitators who have the "people-oriented" characteristics required, it is necessary to look for the following type of individuals:

- They enjoy working with people.
- They like being on "center stage."
- They think analytically and are quick on their feet.
- They tend not to offer solutions quickly and are patient when others need time to explain a thought or reach a decision.
- They trust the abilities of other people, and are able to view the opinions of others as legitimate and interesting, even if they do not share them.
- They are good listeners, able to sort out complex arguments in "real time."

- They are organized, like to plan, and can anticipate potential problems rather than relying on a "seat of the pants" approach.

JAD facilitators do not have to be performers. Quiet, nondemonstrative people can be good facilitators as well as boisterous and charismatic people. Extreme personalities of any type do not fare well as facilitators, however. People who are too dictatorial or too laid back often fail to become good facilitators. Their personalities are too prominent; they become the focus of group discussion. This, of course, is the opposite of the concept of "facilitation," because the facilitator, if he is to be successful, must disappear behind his role, using his skills to put the spotlight on others. Facilitation requires a balance between directive and supportive skills and the ability to provide the proper leadership given a particular situation.

WHAT IS JAD LEADERSHIP?

While the JAD facilitator does not make decisions for participants within the workshop, there are many points in the JAD process at which he must move the group to a specific conclusion. Well qualified JAD facilitators are able to apply four different leadership styles in such situations and know when to use each style appropriately. Each of the four styles is selected based upon the amount of direction the facilitator must provide to the group and the amount of trust the facilitator has in the individuals that make up the group. A more directive style is needed when participants are inexperienced with or unwilling to commit to the JAD process. As people become more experienced and committed, the facilitator's style may become less directive and more supportive (Fig. 2.3).

The four basic leadership styles important to the JAD technique are telling, selling, consulting, and joining. These styles are defined as follows.

Telling

This style is most appropriate in emergency or crisis situations, or where the JAD process itself is threatened. The "telling" leadership style is appropriate when the JAD facilitator has been unable to convince a project manager that a particular JAD critical success factor must be followed. In such a situation, the facilitator must rely on his authority as the technique expert and present the project manager with two choices: he acts to support the critical success factor, or he gives up the opportunity to use the JAD technique on the project. The "telling" style may also be particularly useful at the beginning of a workshop where participants may not fully understand the process or their responsibilities. The "telling" style should be used in a gentle way, however. The JAD facilitator does not and should not act like a general going to war.

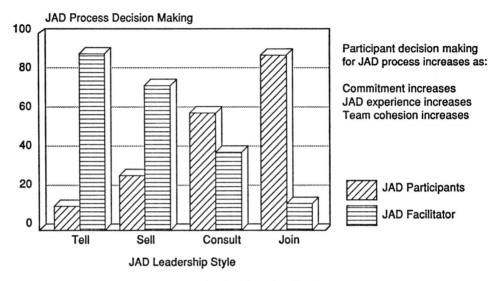

Figure 2.3 JAD leadership style utilization.

Selling

The "selling" style is appropriate when the leader wants to convince the group of something. This something may be the rules of the JAD process or the necessity of acknowledging the built-in constraints of the project or the importance of accepting responsibility for decision making. Commitment building, too, fits within the category of "selling." This style is used often in JAD preworkshop activities to build executive sponsor and project manager commitment. While the facilitator must be an unbiased nondecision maker within a workshop, there are times (most often outside the workshop) when he must focus on gaining agreement to a decision that has already been made. This type of skill is required, for example, when the JAD facilitator wants to convince the project manager to allow him five days for the workshop when the project manager thinks he can only spare three. Here the facilitator's selling skills can come in very handy.

Consulting

The facilitator's use of the "consulting" style is in evidence when he asks the group for ideas from which he can choose. The risk with this style is that if the leader does not proceed with one of the ideas offered, then he loses the credibility of the group. In JAD, the consulting style is slightly modified to make it more effective for the facilitator. The JAD facilitator offers the group alternatives or options which the facilitator already knows will work. This might occur if it becomes apparent that not enough time is left to complete all workshop exercises on the agenda. At this point, the facilitator might ask for suggestions from the group as to how to proceed. The group might offer several suggestions. They might offer to add an extra day onto the workshop, to meet until midnight for the next two days, to reconvene for a day the following week, or to assign specific exercises to a subteam as an off-line activity. The facilitator might evaluate these alternatives, eliminate some (e.g., the offer to remain until midnight), and then pass on the choice among the remaining alternatives to the group itself. This style is utilized most effectively in the later days of a workshop or after the first workshop in a series. At that point, the group and project manager will have established a commitment to the JAD technique and will be unlikely to jeopardize it.

Joining

In this last leadership style, the facilitator declines to make any final decisions and becomes just one voting member of the group. Trust, commitment, knowledge, and teamwork must be very high for this style to be effective. In the JAD technique, the facilitator generally uses this style at the end of a workshop as he leads the group in developing next step activities and in the postworkshop activities as the group reviews and edits the JAD workshop deliverable.

Most of us have been educated and trained to be consultative leaders in our supervision of people. As a result we find this style particularly comfortable and often think that it is better than the others. However, that is not always true. Styles are different, with one not necessarily better than another. Each style has advantages and disadvantages. JAD facilitators must be aware of their natural style bias so that they can learn to change styles when necessary, and when they change to select the most appropriate style.

JAD FACILITATOR TRAINING

A key to the successful implementation of JAD in an organization is the ability to develop facilitators who consistently and reliably produce high-quality JAD workshop deliverables. Just like programmers and analysts, facilitators should be trained to conduct their work to a high-quality standard and to produce a consistent outcome. If one facilitator gets sick in the middle of a JAD process, another facilitator should be able to pick up where the first facilitator left off. Therefore, excellent training must follow careful facilitator candidate selection.

Training for JAD facilitators should build the five knowledge and skill sets of: (1) JAD structure and activities; (2) methodology and CASE tool concepts; (3) group dynamics and behavioral psychology, (4) basic facilitation, and (5) selling. Each knowledge and skill set contributes to the development of fully qualified JAD facilitators.

JAD Structure and Activity Skills

The foundation of a high-quality JAD technique (i.e., one that can be reproduced consistently) is the JAD facilitator handbook that contains the rule set for the JAD process. Just as a FUSION expert needs a methodology handbook and a CASE tool users guide, he also needs a rule book for JAD. This guidebook, which should be the foundation as well for a JAD facilitator training program, is a manual defining the rules, critical success factors, and standard operating procedures for the JAD technique and all of its component activities. It should contain techniques for obtaining preliminary project information, strategies for defining the type, scope and size of projects, and standards for designing and facilitating target meetings, focus group interviews, workshops, and the creation of JAD deliverables. The guidebook should also contain instructions for customizing the JAD process to meet the needs of particular project situations. Workshop exercises should be defined in specific detail, and the guidebook should show the facilitator how to use nontechnical language to achieve high-quality technical results. Without a handbook, there can be no real structure and consistency to the process. Then it is up to the individual facilitator to make things work. This does not result in a consistent, reliable, and predictable process. It results instead in reliance on the unique performance of a charismatic facilitator, sometimes succeeding exceptionally well, and sometimes failing just as badly. A JAD technique within an organization should live beyond the tenure of a particular individual facilitator.

Methodology and CASE Tool Concepts/Skills

While different methodologies may form the basis for the JAD approach, the information engineering (IE) methodology lends itself particularly well to JAD because of its emphasis on the initial definition of high-level business objectives, its use of a progressive, integrated set of diagrams, its separation of data and process, and the integration it provides from highest level business planning down through the most detailed physical implementation of a screen. While full methodology training may take place outside of formal JAD facilitator training, JAD training must nevertheless refer to the principles of the methodology. At a high level, it must specify how the principles of the methodology are implemented through the JAD process and how its goals are achieved. At a more detailed level, it must specify when, where, why, and how to use the diagrams supported by the methodology to create the JAD workshop deliverable. It must specify, for example, the specific data and process information that is required for defining an information architecture, for creating a corporate data model, for building an application prototype, for writing a request for proposal, or for selecting a software package. It must answer the questions: Which diagrams are essential? Which are optional? How are the diagrams to be integrated into a total design? In addition, the use of an appropriate CASE tool in supporting the diagramming techniques must be defined. The JAD facilitator must be trained in the use of this tool for supporting the methodology. While he need not be an expert user, he must have a solid working knowledge of the tool and should be fully aware of the constraints it presents as well as the diagrams it supports.

Group Dynamics and Behavioral Psychology Skills

JAD facilitators must understand the forces that hold groups together, the forces that drive them apart, and most of all, how to guide groups toward the achievement of a specific goal. This involves being able to handle different personality types, being able to manage problem behavior that can inhibit a group, being able to motivate the individuals within a group, and being able to utilize the four basic leadership styles discussed earlier. JAD facilitators must have sufficient knowledge about human behavior in order to control the group's behavior for the benefit of the project. This type of training must involve both principles and strategies for action, theory, and practice, in other words. It must arm the facilitator with the techniques he needs to ensure that he is in control of all individual behavior within the group at all times. The JAD facilitator is a strong facilitator, a director, not a reactor, and he needs a strong set of behavioral skills to accomplish this.

Basic Facilitation Skills

JAD facilitators must know the basic rules for group operation and be able to execute a variety of different exercises to assist groups in analyzing problems, creating possible solutions, evaluating alternatives, and reaching consensus. One useful source of information on facilitation skills is a short film from the British company, Video Arts, called "More Bloody Meetings." It explains and demonstrates three principles of group facilitation. These are: (1) unite the group, (2) focus the group, (3) mobilize the group. The JAD facilitator must know how to redirect a group if they get off the point by helping people to stay alert, restating objectives, testing for comprehension, and paraphrasing their ideas. In addition, he must know how to motivate the group to construct a common solution and prevent rejection of good ideas by protecting the weak, checking with each person in the group, recording suggestions, and building on the ideas presented.

The facilitator's specialized skills also come into play when implementing the JAD structure discussed earlier. This can best be seen in the workshop. In preparation for the workshop, JAD facilitators must review the alternative structures that workshops can take and be able to design a structure to meet the needs of the particular project in which they are involved. This means identifying appropriate exercises and deciding the sequence those exercises will take. Typical exercise sequences include:

- Serial exercises where one exercise builds on the results of another.
- Parallel exercises where subteams do the same exercise or different exercises concurrently.
- High-intensity exercises where the facilitator leads the total group to focus decision making and move quickly.
- Low-intensity exercises where subteams detail an idea and allow shy participants the opportunity to participate more effectively.

Selling Skills

The ability to create a positive attitude and commitment among people who are sometimes reluctant to take on a new challenge and its inherent risks is a critical JAD facilitator skill. As our JAD experience shows, the first thing a strong project manager wants to do is change the JAD process structure and rule set to suit his own agenda. Such actions may doom the JAD technique right from the start. Therefore, JAD facilitators must have the skills to convince project managers to follow the critical success factors of the JAD process structure. This requires skills in specific questioning techniques to build commitment and overcome objections. Tom Hopkins, in his book, *How to Master the Art of Selling*, refers to these questioning techniques as: "tie downs, alternative advances, porcupine questions, involvement questions, discovery questions, and leading questions." Some of the popular sales and marketing books make useful guides for developing these skills.

Listening is another important aspect of the selling skills used throughout the JAD technique. Facilitators need to be able to recognize both the facts and the emotions of a situation, validate what people are thinking and feeling, answer their objections and questions, solicit feedback for confirmation and move the discussion forward. The development of these skills may be difficult for some JAD facilitators since many people have a negative image of salespeople in general and are reluctant to take the time required to convince. For many people, "telling" comes easier than "selling," even though this is not always the most appropriate strategy in a given situation.

JAD Training Programs

An excellent training program for JAD facilitators should provide a combination of experiences involving basic skill development, protected practice, and supervised "live" practice. Such a training program might involve these steps (Fig. 2.4):

1. Observation of an experienced JAD facilitator.
2. Five to ten days formal basic skills training.
3. Apprentice work with an experienced JAD facilitator.

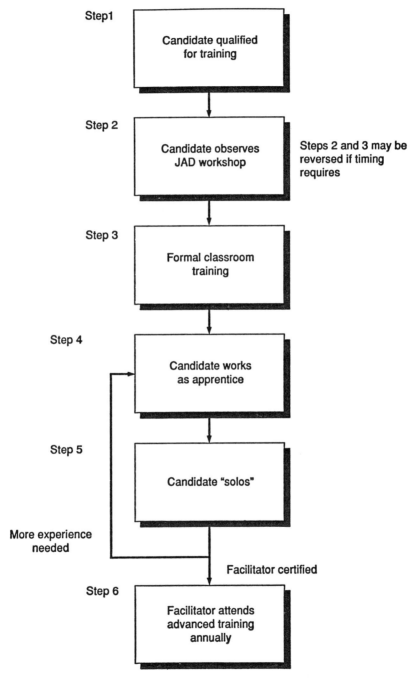

Figure 2.4 JAD training program example.

4. Observed "solo" work with feedback for skill refinement and certification.

5. Advanced skills training.

The training program (steps one through four) should take approximately two to three months depending on the skill set of the individual candidate. The number of days of formal training will vary, depending on the technical skills that the candidate brings to the training program. Candidates, for example, who need some additional training in methodology principles or CASE utilization will require more classroom time than candidates who bring strong skills in these areas with them.

There tends to be an impression among many JAD facilitator candidates before their training that the facilitator's job is not a particularly difficult one. This is balanced, interestingly, by a perception voiced after training that the job is close to impossible. Both conclusions are wrong, of course. The best correction for these perceptions is involvement in actual JAD workshops, both as an observer and as a participant. For this reason, whenever possible it is wise to have a prospective JAD facilitator serve in the role of the JAD/CASE specialist, responsible for documentation production and for assisting the JAD facilitator to manage workshop subteams. In addition, the selection of less complex, less political projects for initial solo work is often helpful for new facilitators.

Advanced skills training is another important area to consider. This type of in-service training should be an annual or semiannual requirement. In fact, it is generally valued quite highly by JAD facilitators. Once on the job, they quickly come to understand their own strengths and weaknesses and are eager to continue to build their skills in advanced training programs that offer specialized skills training. Also, as part of their on-the-job support, JAD facilitators benefit greatly from having a network of other facilitators to whom they can turn for a second opinion when a difficult problem presents itself. They also benefit from the opportunity to share their experiences with other JAD facilitators.

JAD PARTICIPANT ROLES AND RESPONSIBILITIES

JAD delivers as promised only if the right people are involved and committed to their roles in the process. These critical players include:

- Executive sponsor
- Project manager
- JAD/CASE specialist
- Business user experts
- Systems experts
- Outside technical experts (optional)
- Observers (optional)

Executive Sponsor

The executive sponsor is the individual within the business organization who charters the project to use JAD. His organization will benefit directly from the project effort, and often it is his budget that will be tapped to carry any special costs associated with the use of the JAD technique. In a large, cross-functional project, this role may be taken on by a small group of executives. Whether the role is filled by one individual or several, the executive sponsor's role is to ensure that the project team has access to and the commitment of the right business user experts, that the business users attend all appropriate JAD activities as requested by the JAD facilitator, and that the results of the JAD process are honored. This last point requires that the executive sponsor understand that the decision making that goes on in a JAD workshop is not just an exercise or a rehearsal, that it is, indeed, the real thing, not to be second guessed later by others in the organization. The executive sponsor must be willing to live with the results of the JAD project, even if the decisions or recommendations are not precisely those he would have made himself.

The executive sponsor must be positioned high enough within the organization authority structure to clear the calendars of the individuals selected to participate in all required preworkshop, workshop, and postworkshop activities. He must also be willing to demonstrate his own commitment to the JAD process, preferably by making a personal statement to the group, or if necessary, by other means. He may, for example, choose to use an intermediary to speak for him if scheduling makes his own participation difficult. He should also be willing to provide the JAD facilitator and project manager with any information they might need to give them strategic direction and help them to define the scope of the project. Finally, he should be willing to make policy decisions when necessary and to do so in a timely manner in order to avoid a breakdown in the momentum of the JAD process.

Project Manager

The project manager leads the project team and is operationally responsible for the delivery of project results. Depending on the organization, the project manager may be located in the systems group or in a business area. In some cases, the project manager will be part of a team, where one individual represents the systems organization and the other represents the business users. The project manager is the client of the JAD facilitator. His role is to ensure deliverable quality and project effectiveness. He is responsible for coordinating the project effort and ensuring that strong communication exists between the systems and user communities. This includes staying personally involved with and communicating with all other JAD participants (including the executive sponsor). He must keep the JAD facilitator informed of organizational issues that may impact the project, make logistical arrangements for the JAD workshop, and arrange a manageable schedule for all JAD activities.

The JAD facilitator should have as one of his goals making the project manager a "hero." The project manager should be seen as the individual in charge, the one who brought the project to an appropriate and timely completion. The project manager is a full JAD participant in all workshop decision making and participates in all JAD activities.

JAD/CASE Specialist

The JAD/CASE specialist, sometimes referred to as a design analyst or scribe, is responsible for ensuring that the results of the JAD are documented and delivered as planned. This person is a partner to the JAD facilitator and is involved in all JAD activities before, during, and after the workshops. Depending on the project team structure utilized, the JAD/CASE specialist may be a member of the project team or from the JAD facilitator group. This person should be an expert CASE tool user and a qualified systems analyst. On complex projects, there may even be more than one JAD/CASE specialist supporting a JAD facilitator. Without this role, the JAD technique can fail to produce the required deliverables for the project. In the workshop sessions, the JAD/CASE specialist is not a participant in decision making, but works with the JAD facilitator to ensure that all knowledge, issues, and decisions are recorded and documented properly. As the facilitator's second set of eyes and ears, he monitors all JAD activities and may even assist in facilitating during the workshop sessions.

Business User Experts

Business users make up the largest subgroup of JAD participants, about sixty-five to seventy-five percent of the total group. All business users who will be impacted by the project should play a part in the JAD process, although some will play a more direct role than others. Those business users who are workshop participants have a primary and vital role in reaching decisions during the sessions. Obviously, not all users can be present in the workshop, except in very rare cases. Many other users, though, can be brought into the process during pre-workshop activities when they are contacted for information on their perspectives on the functional and information needs to be met by the system, as well as the issues and politics surrounding the project. Each user who participates in the process should be made aware that he represents many others.

There are two types of users. Some users represent the strategic, tactical, or operational direction of the business. Their participation ensures that the JAD workshop deliverable will support the long term future of the business. Other users are true end users, those people who must live with the results of the project on a daily basis. Their participation provides the insurance that the JAD workshop deliverable will be accepted by field personnel. True end users can often be found at multiple levels within the organization. Individuals from all levels affected by the project should participate in the workshop sessions to build commitment at all levels and establish better interlevel understanding. An effort should be made also to ensure that the participants represent all major user groups or factions affected by the project. The greater the number of users who participate in preworkshop activities and the actual workshop sessions, the greater will be the buy-in and commitment across the business organization.

In some cases, true end users reside outside the organization. The most common example of this occurs when an organization designs software for sale to another organization or to an industry. In this case, business users from the software purchasing organization may be requested to join in the process. If this is not possible, then individuals from the organization designing and selling the software must represent their interests. Generally, these individuals will be systems support professionals, well aware of the functionality of the proposed system and the needs of those who will use it. This presents a more difficult problem, but not an insurmountable one. A number of software sellers have found this approach particularly successful in cases where major upgrades of their packages are being designed.

Systems Experts

JAD workshops are not about users getting together to discuss "blue sky" ideas. Rather, JAD is about building a strong working partnership among users and systems professionals, who together create a realistic solution to information management problems. Systems experts have a direct role to play in workshops in ensuring that all technological constraints (and their monetary consequences) are represented. They assist the process by ensuring that the project will result in a solution that is realistic for the users' budget, can be delivered when the users require it, and takes advantage of the available technology most effectively. The level of participation by systems professionals will differ, however, depending on the nature of the project to be addressed. For projects that focus on business planning and business analysis, systems experts will tend to play more of an advisory role. They themselves will benefit by developing a better understanding of user business goals, priorities, and strategies. For projects that focus on architecture planning, application design, and prototype evaluation, systems experts will play a stronger decision making role. For most of these projects, systems professionals will make up from twenty-five to thirty-five percent of the workshop participant group.

Several different job functions within the systems organization may be represented at the workshops, including such functions as data administration, systems/business analysis, programming, prototyping, and production/operations management. In some cases, some of these individuals may be invited to act as workshop observers rather than participants. This will depend on the nature of the project and its objectives.

Outside Technical Experts

In some projects, the business expertise present within the user community must be supplemented from outside the organization. For example, in a project where an organization wants to create a database to support targeted mailings to customers, a direct mail marketing consultant may be asked to join the business users as a full participant in a workshop. This outside technical expert plays an advisory role in the workshop. He does not participate in making final decisions because he does not have to live with the results of his decisions. Sometimes an outside technical advisor is asked to wear a badge saying "advisor" to reinforce this role. Generally, no more than five to ten percent of the workshop participant group would consist of outside technical experts, and many workshops will not have this role represented at all.

Observers

Many people are curious to see what a JAD workshop looks like. The observer role has been created to allow for observation of the JAD technique. In addition to satisfying the curiosity of some individuals, this benefits the project by enabling a wide variety of individuals to play a small part in the process. In addition, observation can be an effective selling tool for the JAD technique. Prospective users of JAD are allowed to observe for this purpose. There is no better way to convince a prospective JAD participant or project executive sponsor of the value of the process than by letting him see it in action. The role of observer can also be educational. Sometimes junior members of the project team (often assigned as programmers on the project), will play the part of workshop observers. This helps them to increase their understanding of user needs and workshop decisions, and will help them when the time comes to start programming or preparing a prototype.

The responsibility of all observers is to watch and listen. No matter what the provocation, they must refrain from participating in workshop discussions and decision making. They may interact with participants and the JAD facilitator only during breaks, meals, or before and after sessions. Some observers will find these rules easy to follow. Others will not. But it is up to the JAD facilitator to enforce them. If these rules are not enforced, workshop direction, scope, and control will be lost. Isn't it then possible that some valuable idea may be missed? No, this is not likely. It should not happen if the JAD facilitator has done his job well. The JAD facilitator will have taken all steps necessary to ensure that the ideas and opinions of all parties to the process are well researched and represented as fully as possible both before and during the workshop.

Business, systems and outside technical experts all have the responsibility of participating in preworkshop, workshop and postworkshop activities as directed by the JAD facilitator. This may include reading materials and researching issues prior to the workshop, actively participating in the workshop sessions and carrying out assigned postworkshop activities.

WHO SHOULD BE A WORKSHOP PARTICIPANT?

Generally, it is not feasible for everyone involved in or affected by a project to participate in a JAD workshop. Consequently, the participants in the JAD process will be required to represent the interest of a much larger group of people. In an ideal world, workshop sessions would have ten to twelve participants. Studies of group behavior indicate that this size is good for promoting group synergy, team building, and effective decision making. But in the real world, this number is often too small for full representation. In practice, most JAD teams are larger, and experience indicates that a JAD workshop group of sixteen to twenty is acceptable.

There is a natural limit to size, however. In projects where groups are larger than this, both the quality and speed of decision making start to suffer. In a large group, there is a likelihood that someone who has a good idea may not speak up. As the size of the group increases, the number of quiet people tends to increase. That is one important reason why it is very useful to break up the total workshop group into subteams. This provides more opportunity for active participation, creativity, problem solving, and decision making.

Having more than twenty participants in a workshop session seriously slows the decision-making process and makes team building almost impossible. In addition, "crowd control" becomes an issue in total group discussions. The JAD facilitator may be forced to spend so much time controlling participant behavior that he will have too little time to spend monitoring the quality of the discussion and the decisions produced. Size can represent a critical success factor for JAD workshops, and the facilitator must be prepared to enforce reasonable standards in regard to this aspect of the process.

Considering that we have a limited number of slots, then, getting the right people assigned to the workshop becomes a serious preworkshop activity. The project manager, JAD facilitator, joined in some cases by the executive sponsor, should create a list of candidate participants who are:

- Competent performers in their jobs and are valued by other organization members.
- Available or can make themselves available for the workshop sessions.
- Experienced in more than one relevant functional area within the organization.

- Willing to make decisions.
- Open to the JAD technique and who have a positive attitude about the project.
- Are good communicators.

Workshops run more effectively, accomplish more, and produce higher quality results when the JAD facilitator carefully chooses to assign certain exercises to the large group and others to smaller subteams. These subteams must be structured before the workshop. The facilitator will divide the workshop participants into three or four subteams of four to six people each. These subteams will meet periodically during the workshop sessions as directed by the JAD facilitator. Expertise and perspectives should be spread across the teams. In creating teams, the facilitator will want to consider first whether heterogeneous or homogeneous business function teams are most appropriate. In some cases, a workshop will have different types of teams, depending on the exercise to be addressed. Most often, however, the facilitator will create heterogeneous teams, mixing business and systems expertise. In addition, he must make sure that teams do not have conflicting personalities who will slow down the work, and that individuals from different levels within the organization are fairly represented on each team.

JAD DELIVERABLE ACCOUNTABILITY

The authors know of few systems professionals who actually enjoy creating and managing project documentation with or without the automated support of CASE tools. The discipline that JAD brings to the documentation process, however, makes it a considerably less painful experience. The principal responsibility for documentation in the JAD process belongs to the JAD facilitator and the JAD/CASE specialist. They are responsible for designing, creating, and finalizing the JAD deliverables, with the advice and assistance of the project manager.

There are two types of deliverables produced by the JAD technique. The first type can be referred to as ''preparation'' deliverables. These may consist of one or more documents prepared prior to the first workshop. While CASE tools may be used to provide graphic support in the preparation of deliverables, these deliverables are more often produced using word processing tools. The second type of deliverable we will call the JAD workshop deliverable. This deliverable, produced in one or more JAD workshops, generally is designed to satisfy a documentation requirement associated with the systems development life cycle. CASE tools are often used to produce the JAD workshop deliverable. This is, in fact, highly recommended. Both types of deliverables are important to the JAD process.

Preparation Deliverables

JAD preparation deliverables are created during preworkshop activities. Some JAD vendors recommend the creation of one document; others recommend two documents. These documents are given names such as Familiarization Guide, Project Scope Definition Document, Management Definition Guide, Briefing Package, and Preview Package. Whatever they are called, these preparation documents are important. They help to ensure that the early phases of the JAD process proceed successfully and set the stage for the JAD workshop(s). It is important, therefore, that these documents be relatively short and clearly written, and that they provide those participating in the workshop with a consistent knowledge base concerning the project. They may be written by the JAD facilitator and/or the JAD/CASE specialist, and should always be reviewed and approved by the project manager prior to distribution. Although they are descriptive prose, they may be supported with graphic aids such as decomposition diagrams, matrices, entity relationship diagrams, and any other diagrams the JAD facilitator believes will be helpful in promoting understanding. The information gathered for the project knowledge base should include, but is not limited to the following:

- The history and context of the project, highlighting relevant political and organizational factors that placed it on the agenda.
- High-level strategic, tactical and/or operational business goals that will be supported by the project. Project objectives and measures of accomplishment may be defined based on these business goals, as well as project limits. Project limits may be defined in terms of business organizations, areas, functions, and/or existing systems and subject data areas supported by the project.
- Activities in the business environment that may affect the success of the project, as well as potential impacts of the project on the business environment.
- The hidden issues and built-in constraints that must be understood in order to keep the project from going out of control. Staffing resources, existing hardware and software, budgets, regulations, laws, and so forth, may all be included. In addition, important open issues should be identified in order that they may be resolved early in the JAD process.
- Benefits to the organization that will result from the project should be identified as an aid in building commitment. Commitment can also be strengthened by documenting the risks of noncompletion of the project.

In addition, information that will be helpful to the prospective JAD participant may concern the JAD technique and how it is structured, the workshop agenda and exercises, and the roles and responsibilities of each participant before, during, and after the workshop. Individual JAD participants may also have special responsibilities for gathering information (user perspectives, data dictionary, corporate strategy statement, etc.) prior to the workshop. These workshop preparation tasks should be written down so that everyone can reference his given assignment.

JAD Workshop Deliverable

A detailed design for the JAD workshop deliverable must be approved by the project manager prior to the first JAD workshop. The word "detailed" is significant. The JAD facilitator cannot proceed on the basis of a vague statement from the project manager that: "I need a user requirements document"; or "We need to build a data model." This leaves open the possibility that a great deal of work will go into the creation of a deliverable that will be rejected or found barely acceptable. It is important that the JAD facilitator be able to evaluate the effectiveness of the workshop, and the best evaluation criteria is the JAD deliverable design. If this is a detailed document, and if the JAD facilitator can show that the final deliverable closely follows the design, then it is easy to demonstrate that the workshop has been a success.

In addition to providing a success measurement, the design for the JAD workshop deliverable provides the framework on which the workshop agenda, supporting materials, and exercises are built. Without a detailed definition of this deliverable, JAD workshop sessions may drift from topic to topic and fail to result in decision making or consensus building. The JAD process is an interrelated set of activities customized to ensure that this deliverable is built. An agenda is structured based on the deliverable design; exercises are created to support the agenda; and CASE input is built from the results of the exercises. In order for this set of activities to proceed without loss of quality or consistency along the way, a detailed design is vital. It is the road map to a successful JAD experience.

The design for the JAD workshop deliverable will generally require that a physical document be created, but it may also require that this information be stored in a CASE tool repository, and/or that an application prototype be built. The JAD workshop deliverable design should define:

- Content
- Media
- Format
- Level of detail

"Content" defines the information to be included in the deliverable. Whenever possible, content is defined by the relevant components in an existing life cycle methodology. "Media" identifies the means of storing and displaying the content of the deliverable. Examples of media would be paper, a CASE encyclopedia, or a prototype. "Format" defines how the content will be displayed within a given media. It must first provide a "table of contents" for the document, if, as is generally the case, a physical document is produced. This may include an executive summary, or other material in addition to the technical information that the document will contain. In addition, it must include a definition of the graphic techniques to be utilized to display information in the technical sections of the document or within a CASE tool. If entity information is to be displayed, for example, it may be formatted in entity relationship diagrams, entity tables, and/or dictionary/encyclopedia definitions. Business transactions may be formatted and displayed through the use of dependency diagrams, data flow diagrams, state transaction diagrams, or other formats. With content, media and format defined, it is then possible to define the level of detail needed for each diagram, narrative, summary or prototype screen. It will be necessary for the JAD facilitator to determine, for example, if full normalization is required for entity relationship diagrams and entity tables; if prototype screens will accept sample data; or if certain data characteristics are required for attribute definitions.

As we know, JAD was first used to develop user requirement definitions and logical designs for databases and applications. However, when JAD is integrated with the information engineering methodology, the JAD workshop deliverable may be used to support any of the IE components of planning, analysis, and design. These include:

- Component I: Planning—business unit or enterprise business plans, architecture plans, and development plans.
- Component II: Analysis—business area process model, data model and process-data relationship model.
- Component III: Design—logical application design.

JAD workshops can also deliver physical designs, information for package purchase or make or buy decisions, test plans, and prototypes evaluations. By defining what is needed in terms of content, media, format and level of detail, an appropriate JAD workshop deliverable can be designed.

The definition of the JAD workshop deliverable will vary based on an organization's particular methodology standards and the unique needs of the project at hand. Since the FUSION approach advocates an information engineering methodology, this book offers a set of diagram standards for each IE component deliverable. It also presents a set of JAD exercises that may be used to create these diagrams and identifies how CASE tools may be used to document and validate them.

There are situations where a more customized JAD workshop deliverable is required. In such cases, the JAD facilitator designs the deliverable by working with the project manager and his team. He first documents the decisions or actions the team wishes to take after the JAD workshop and then defines the information they need to make the decisions and take actions (Fig. 2.5). For example, a JAD project may have as its goal process improvement for a business unit. In this case,

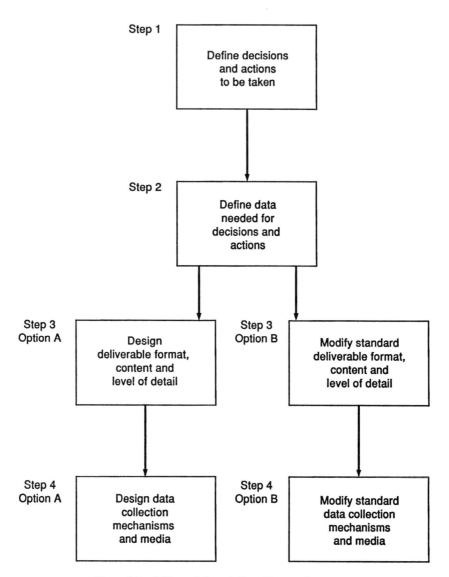

Figure 2.5   JAD workshop deliverable creation steps.

the JAD facilitator will define what the business unit hopes to achieve through the process improvement project and what critical decisions it wants to make. It may also be important to define a plan for implementing improved processes, including tasks, responsibilities, critical success factors, measurement standards, schedules, and other key items. In this case, the JAD workshop deliverable will contain a plan of action in addition to a full process analysis.

JAD PROCESS STRUCTURE

The JAD process structure consists of three general phases: preworkshop activities, workshop activities, and postworkshop activities. Vendors have taken different approaches to detailing this structure. For example, the IBM JAD approach, as defined by Wood and Silver, includes five steps: project definition, research, preparation, the JAD session itself, and production of the final document. ATLIS/PRI's proprietary METHOD technique defines seven steps: scoping, planning, work analysis, briefing, preparation, workshop, and transition and validation. Each approach includes all three phases and all of them generally agree as to the major objectives of the phases. Figure 2.6 illustrates approaches to each phase.

JAD PREWORKSHOP ACTIVITIES

The principal objective of preworkshop JAD activities is to make certain that the critical success factors for the JAD process are in place and that the workshop will be a success. Specifically, preworkshop activities must be designed to ensure that:

- Commitment to the project and the JAD process is strong.
- All participants understand what part they play in the JAD process.
- The JAD workshop structure, exercises and deliverable(s) are designed to meet project needs.

Generally, preworkshop activities should not require more than three weeks, and the work can be accomplished in one to two weeks if participant schedules are sufficiently flexible. These activities can also be expanded to four or five weeks if extended research in the user organization is required. However, because a JAD project should exhibit strong momentum and seek to deliver a high-quality result in a short period of time, delays should be kept to a minimum.

The key activities required to meet the preworkshop objectives are:

- Defining the scope of the JAD project.
- Researching the background of the JAD project.
- Defining the structure of the JAD project.
- Defining the JAD deliverable(s).
- Preparing required materials.
- Selecting and educating participants.

All of these activities are performed under the direction of the JAD facilitator, although they involve others as well, including the JAD/CASE specialist, the

JAD Process Structure	ATLIS/PRI	MG Rush Systems, Inc.	IBM Silver & Wood
Preworkshop	Scoping Planning Work Analysis Briefing Preparation	Preparation	Project Definition Research Preparation
Workshop	Workshop(s)	Workshop(s)	JAD Sessions(s)
Postworkshop	Transition and Validation	Review and Resolution	Final Document

Figure 2.6   Sample JAD phases.

project manager, and the JAD participants. They can be accomplished using target meetings, focus group interviews and workshops.

Defining the Scope of the JAD Project

This activity is particularly critical to the success of the JAD process. In fact, this activity may be seen as a qualification step for the project. If a clear definition of project scope cannot be obtained because of confusion on the part of the client organization(s), missing information, or a lack of decision making, the JAD facilitator may recommend that the project is not ready for the JAD process to proceed further. Working with key individuals from the project team, including both systems and user personnel, the JAD facilitator should identify the:

- User executive or group of executives who will sponsor the project and assume the role of JAD executive sponsor.
- Project objectives in specific measurable terms.
- Business unit(s), area(s), and/or specific business functions/information areas to be included within the scope of the project.
- Critical success factors for the project.
- Project concerns, including any known resource limitations, political/organizational issues and critical areas where key decisions are required but have not been made.

If the project scope cannot be clearly defined and some reason exists to doubt the level of commitment within the organization, the JAD facilitator must work closely with the project manager to decide on the best course of action. Sometimes the situation can be corrected with a small amount of effort. A direct meeting with the project's executive sponsor in which the difficulties are spelled out (as well as the consequences of not overcoming them) may be all that is necessary. More attention to education of key managers or prospective participants may remove any serious anxiety that is getting in the way of success. Resolution of organizational issues outside of the project itself (e.g., appointment of a new CEO or confirmation of a rumored acquisition) may solve the problem without any action on the part of the JAD team at all. If the problems in the project are more intransigent than this, the JAD facilitator and project manager may decide to hold a project initiation workshop with the objectives of: building project commitment, resolving key open issues, and defining a clear project scope. Such a workshop should emphasize participation by higher level managers who can make decisions and plan a strategy for building commitment. This can be very effective in getting a stalled project off to a good start. A project initiation workshop can rely on the JAD process for pointers as to creation of a strong agenda, creation of workshop exercises, and facilitation approach. In this way, it may also serve as a demonstration of some of the important characteristics of a JAD workshop. This will be valuable in reducing anxiety about the JAD process and getting the project moving.

If a project initiation workshop is not viable and a lack of commitment or other types of problems prevent further JAD activities, the JAD facilitator and project manager may agree to delay or defer the project until there is sufficient support to proceed. This may be disappointing to those who are committed and eager to move forward, but it may save the organization from a great deal of wasted effort.

Researching the Background of the JAD Project

While it is not necessary for the JAD facilitator to be an expert in the business functionality that will be the focus of the workshop, it is important for the facilitator to be as familiar as possible with the different political and cultural perspectives of all key players regarding the project and its impact on the organization. The JAD facilitator should lead this research effort, in some cases choosing to involve the JAD/CASE specialist and project manager. The purpose of the research effort is not requirements gathering. JAD workshops should not merely confirm or modify a previously defined "strawman" model or design. The purpose of the research rather is to ensure that there are no hidden issues or major disagreements as to project scope. Neither should research time be spent examining existing systems at a great level of detail. JAD always focuses on the future, on what is needed to meet the business challenges of tomorrow.

Research for a project that will result in a four to five-day JAD workshop usually takes two to five days, unless there are special circumstances involved. This frequently occurs in a project with strong political overtones, as in the case where it is important to meet with a great many more people than is strictly necessary in order to ensure that no one feels left out. It also occurs, reasonably enough, in cases where the number of organizations involved in the project or the extent of the functionality is such that more research time is required.

In understanding the background of the project, it is always necessary to conduct an interview with the executive sponsor to confirm his commitment and to ensure that his sense of the strategic objectives of the project accord with those of the project manager and other key players. The identification of others who should be interviewed should be a task jointly performed by the JAD facilitator and the project manager. The executive may also have some recommendations on this, and frequently new names come up as initial meetings or focus groups are held. It is also necessary to read and review any written materials that exist pertaining to the project. These may include high-level business plans, a statement by a second vice president on the future of the organization, or a set of project objectives prepared by the project manager.

Most JAD approaches recommend that the findings of all background research conducted in the preworkshop phase of the process be documented. In some cases, this documentation will be distributed to the JAD team as a whole after review and approval by the project manager and/or the executive sponsor.

In some cases, a project manager will pressure the JAD facilitator to skip this activity. Generally, this is because he believes that research represents wasted time and that he and one or two others can tell the JAD facilitator everything he needs to know in order to structure the workshops. Experience tells us, however, that this is a bad idea. When research is skipped, the JAD facilitator will almost certainly experience one or more surprises during the workshop which may have a negative effect on its outcome. Consider an example. The objective of one JAD project was to build an investment portfolio analysis application. Only one of the three key business economists could participate in the background research activities, but the JAD facilitator was assured by the project manager that all three economists were in complete agreement on the structure of a typical portfolio. There was even a prototype application in operation. However, on the second day of the workshop, the three economists discovered that each had a unique view of the portfolio data structure. Therefore, the rest of the workshop dealt with defining those differences and constructing a portfolio data model that the economists could agree to and that administrators could understand. An additional three day session was required to complete the work originally planned.

Defining the Structure of the JAD Project

No two JAD projects are exactly alike. In each case, the JAD facilitator must match the scope and objectives of a project to a unique workshop structure. He does this by using his training and past experience as a guide. The ability to design an appropriate structure, particularly in support of a complex project, is one of the distinguishing marks of an excellent JAD facilitator (Figs. 2.7 and 2.8).

The JAD project structure must include the number, sequence, and schedule of workshops. It is difficult to define hard and fast rules for determining the number of JAD workshops required for any particular project type. Judgment plays a major role in determining how many workshops are required to produce the required workshop deliverables. However, three parameters are important in determining how many workshops are needed. These are: (1) organization size and politics, (2) number and complexity of business functions to be supported, and (3) level and type of detail required in the JAD workshop deliverable. As a guideline, it is wise to consider the use of multiple workshops if:

- More than three to five organization units are involved in or directly impacted by the project.
- More than four to seven well defined but related business functions (or a single complex business function with four to seven subfunctions) are included within the scope of the project.
- Multiple job levels and/or large numbers of people are impacted in a profound way by the project.
- Longstanding hostility exists among the participating organization units.
- The participating organization units will be interacting with each other in the future, although they have not had close contact in the past.
- Business functions and/or roles and responsibilities are poorly defined and tend to overlap, indicating a lack of clear direction and focus in the project or organization.
- The business functions within the scope of the project are widely diverse (e.g., sales support, account reconciliation, and inventory warehousing), indicating a pervasive impact on the organization.
- Multiple, detailed life cycle deliverables must be produced by the project.
- Very extensive detail is required in the JAD workshop deliverable. It is clear that extra time will be needed to generate and validate that detail.

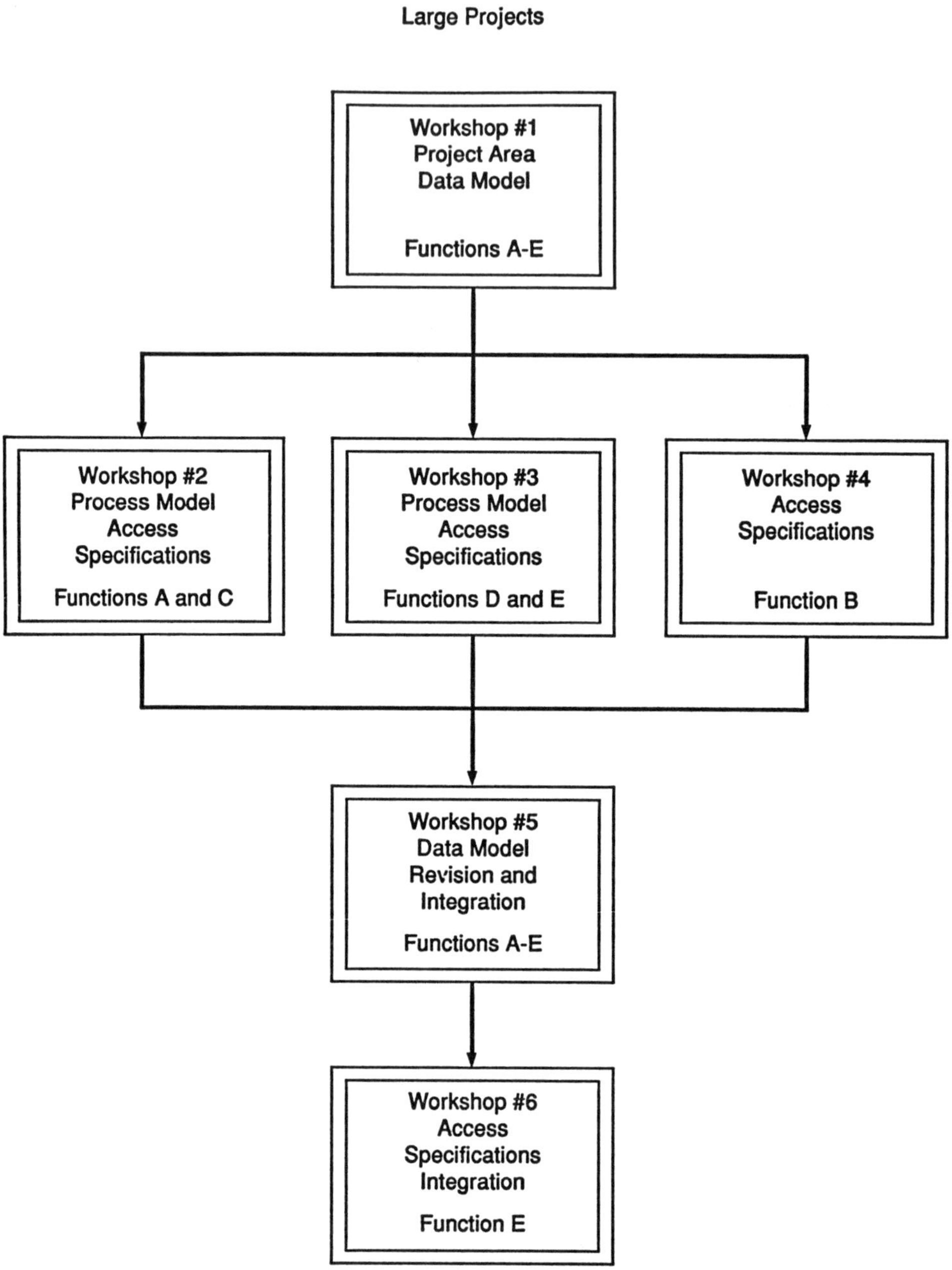

Large Projects

```
                        ┌───────────────────────┐
                        │  ┌─────────────────┐  │
                        │  │   Workshop #1   │  │
                        │  │   Project Area  │  │
                        │  │   Data Model    │  │
                        │  │                 │  │
                        │  │   Functions A-E │  │
                        │  └─────────────────┘  │
                        └───────────────────────┘
```

┌─────────────────────┐   ┌─────────────────────┐   ┌─────────────────────┐
│ Workshop #2   │   │ Workshop #3   │   │ Workshop #4   │
│ Process Model   │   │ Process Model   │   │ Access   │
│ Access   │   │ Access   │   │ Specifications   │
│ Specifications   │   │ Specifications   │   │   │
│   │   │   │   │   │
│ Functions A and C │   │ Functions D and E │   │ Function B   │
└─────────────────────┘   └─────────────────────┘   └─────────────────────┘

┌─────────────────────┐
│ Workshop #5   │
│ Data Model   │
│ Revision and   │
│ Integration   │
│   │
│ Functions A-E   │
└─────────────────────┘

┌─────────────────────┐
│ Workshop #6   │
│ Access   │
│ Specifications   │
│ Integration   │
│   │
│ Function E   │
└─────────────────────┘

Figure 2.7   Sample multiple workshops—data first.

Large Projects

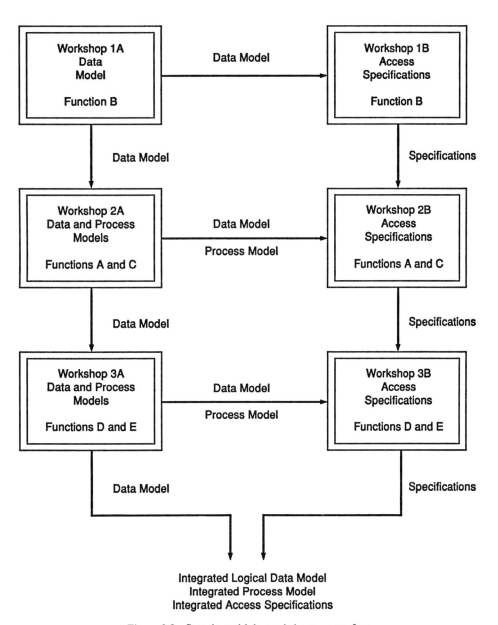

Figure 2.8 Sample multiple workshops—core first.

To demonstrate the importance of correctly defining the structure of the JAD project and to indicate the number of different approaches that are possible, it is helpful to look at some examples. Let's take the case of an organization where nine key managers were responsible for inventory management in an environment that included multiple warehouse locations. In this project, one five-day workshop was determined to be sufficient to define the logical design for a materials management system. This one workshop provided sufficient deliverable detail to allow the systems team to transition to physical design.

In another example, a retail company with over 200 stores identified eighteen participants to define the logical design for a point of sale inventory and accounting application. It was determined that two four-day workshops would be required here, one to define logical process and data models, and one to complete data and process integration and screen design. A two-day workshop was also tentatively planned to allow users to evaluate a prototype of the application.

A transportation company where five regional organizations supported the nationwide scheduling and routing of trains identified eighteen people to construct a logical design for automation of those business functions. This project contained limited but extremely complex functionality. It was also very important that the solution to this information management problem be highly integrated and efficient. It was determined that three five-day workshops attended by all the participants would be required. In addition, three two-day project team integration and refinement workshops were required.

In another example, a national retail organization with 250 stores wanted to define information management requirements for strategic, tactical and operational decision making both at the store level and the corporate level. The outcome of the project was to include both an analysis of the specific decision making that was required and the design of a detailed data model to support it. Because of the many organizational units involved, the participation of multiple levels of management within the organization, and the complexity of decision making within the organization, it was determined that the project required six three-day sessions. Spreading out the workshop schedule in this way enabled the JAD facilitator to obtain greater commitment and participation by key individuals and allow the organization some thinking time to ensure that no areas of importance were overlooked.

A final example looks at a project where an organization wanted to integrate two different payroll systems. The need for the integration of the systems came about because of a business merger. The organization, a telecommunications company, identified five key people from each company who were authorized to define new payroll editing and processing rules. Two three-day workshops were held, one in each location, where these rules were defined and action diagrams were created to support the processing required. In addition to the technical information gathered and decisions made, however, there was another important project outcome. A strong, positive relationship developed between the two payroll organizations. In many ways this was as important to the success of the merger as the new system that was designed.

Once the scope of the project is identified and the background of the project is known, schedules for multiple workshops are not difficult to construct (Figs. 2.9 and 2.10). These guidelines may be used effectively to determine which workshops should be scheduled first:

- Identify those core business function(s) and/or information areas which, if defined, will provide fifty percent or more of the deliverable. Address these core functions and information needs first.
- Identify what in the project is critical to the success of the organization and address this first. If a project focuses on problems/opportunities and business functionality, identify the business functions most in need of modification, enhancement and/or support. Involve those people and organizations that have the most to gain from the success of the project.
- When analyzing organizations, business functions, and information areas, identify those with the most intense organization involvement. Involve these primary users first. Secondary, or downstream users of information, can be involved in subsequent validation sessions.

Simple projects will, quite naturally, lend themselves to simple structures. Complex projects can present a few extra challenges, however. Consider one example. A bank initiated a project to support the business functions of customer platform sales, account executive management, product analysis, and market research planning. Analysis of the relevant organizations, functions, and problems/opportunities revealed that the core function was customer platform sales. It was determined that this function provided eighty percent of the information required for the data and process models, involved a great many people (six line divisions that supported 230 branches), and was extremely critical to the business's ability to compete in the marketplace. An initial workshop of five days addressed that function alone, resulting in a first draft logical application design. Subsequently, two one-day sessions supplemented this design by examining, respectively, the account executive management and product analysis functions. Information obtained from these later workshops was used to enhance and modify the initial design wherever necessary.

That left the function of market research planning, but at this point an interesting thing happened. The workshop structure approach used here made it possible to identify a mistake made early on in the definition of project scope. When the first draft data model was defined, it became clear that this function could not fairly be considered "within scope." A look at the initial data model clearly demonstrated that data requirements for this function were substantially different from those defined in support of the primary function. A carefully performed high-level analysis of business information needs, had one been conducted, would have told the organization this ahead of time. But living

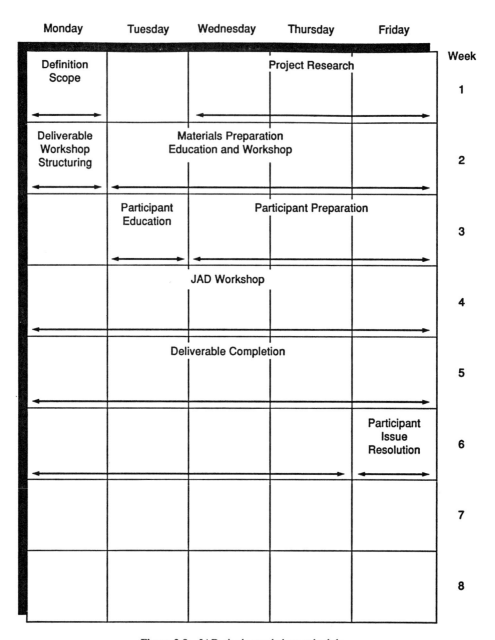

Figure 2.9   JAD single workshop schedule.

To Support Rapid Application Development

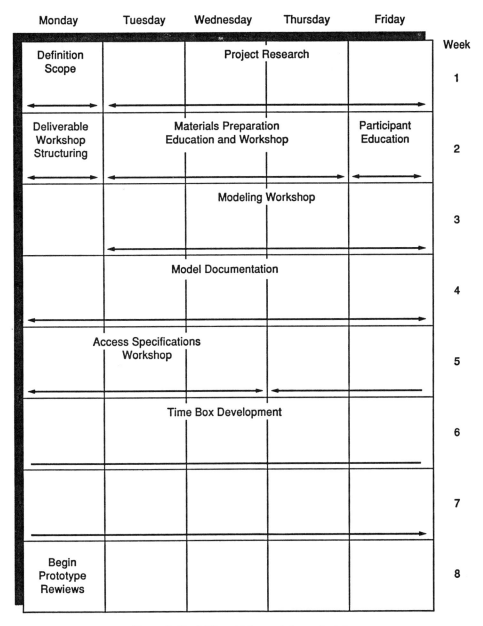

	Monday	Tuesday	Wednesday	Thursday	Friday	Week
	Definition Scope		Project Research			1
	Deliverable Workshop Structuring	Materials Preparation Education and Workshop			Participant Education	2
			Modeling Workshop			3
			Model Documentation			4
		Access Specifications Workshop				5
			Time Box Development			6
						7
	Begin Prototype Rewiews					8

Figure 2.10   JAD multiple workshop schedule.

in the real world, we know that the preferred progression from high-level strategy to specific application is not always realized, and it is good to have an opportunity to correct such mistakes when they occur. A clearly thought out structure for a JAD project can make this possible.

The definition of an appropriate project team is dependent on the project structure. Full representation of all organization units is required. However, when a project involves multiple workshops, it is also necessary to determine what type and level of participation will be required throughout the workshop process. Will all business users from all participating organizations be required to attend all workshops? Will some participants attend some workshops and not others?

There are several factors to consider in answering these questions. Given that the goal of any JAD project must be to develop a single solution to an information management problem (e.g., one integrated data model and one integrated process model), it is necessary that there be some continuity of participants across the workshop schedule. This can be accomplished by retaining the same set of participants for all workshops or by creating a core group of participants who will attend every workshop and appointing other special focus participants who will attend only the workshop(s) where their expertise is specifically required. In a smaller project, the first alternative is often used successfully; for larger projects, the second is almost always the preferred choice. When a single group of participants is used, it is important to create a project schedule that will not overtax their time or span of attention. When a core group is used, it is important to balance their contribution toward project continuity with the contribution of the special focus participants in their areas of expertise. Whatever approach is used, it is critical that the models (or other information) developed in any one workshop be carried into all succeeding workshops in the form of written documentation.

Defining the JAD Workshop Deliverable

As a rule of thumb, the JAD facilitator should anticipate that every one day of workshop time will result in from one to one and one-half days of documentation preparation time. The amount of time required will depend on the complexity of the tools utilized for document preparation, the familiarity of the CASE/JAD specialist with those tools, and the level of detail produced by the workshop. If a CASE tool is utilized within the workshop itself, this can save time, but it will not substantially reduce the estimate given earlier. CASE speeds up some operations, but it delays final production of the deliverable by providing analysis and validation capabilities. This is not a criticism of those capabilities; rather it is a warning to set aside adequate time to fully utilize the benefits of the tools. It may be beneficial to assign more than one JAD/CASE specialist to a project, particularly if it is a multiworkshop project. One of these individuals may be primarily responsible for data entry and the other may be assigned the specific task of ensuring that all workshop information is fully integrated, and that the final document is consistent, accurate, and complete.

Because the exercises selected for use in the workshop are largely dictated by the needs of the deliverable, the format and the content of the deliverable must be clearly defined in advance of the workshop. In some cases, this will be easy. If an organization has a set of standards for documentation, if those standards are well supported by the CASE tools in use, and if the project itself is fairly straightforward, then it should not be difficult to define what is needed. The weaker the standards, the less experienced the organization with CASE and the more complex the project, the more difficult it will be to define the format and content of the deliverable. This, however, does not release the JAD facilitator from his responsibility of doing so. In fact, it makes his role in this activity all the more important. JAD facilitators have even found themselves thrust into the role of standards creators. If no clear standards exist within the organization, and if a JAD project successfully demonstrates the value of a clear up-front definition of deliverable form and content, then JAD can become the force behind the implementation of a de facto set of standards. This is even more likely to occur if CASE tools are used successfully in connection with the project.

In defining the content of the deliverable, the JAD facilitator must make an educated guess as to the amount of information that can be collected during the workshop (or series of workshops). The more experienced the JAD facilitator, the more accurate the projection will be. If at any time during the workshop, he begins to suspect that he has over promised, it is his responsibility to inform the project manager of this. The two should then consider alternatives for action. A reduced deliverable may be acceptable. If it is not, the project manager may want to schedule additional workshop days, or possibly to allow some work to proceed in another format (e.g., mini-workshop, special teams) after the workshop is completed. The reason for this situation, however, is generally an inexperienced facilitator who has missed something important in researching the project. Whether that "something" is a result of a poorly defined scope or a lack of knowledge of key political issues, the facilitator should consider this part of his education and do his best to scout out these problems in the future.

Preparing Required Materials

At this point, the JAD facilitator must define the materials required for the workshop. He should ensure first that the physical site and all logistical requirements will be met, so that all workshop equipment will be present. Generally, JAD approaches agree that a number of easel boards are required. Many approaches use overhead projectors and screens. Some use special magnetics on white boards, and many use CASE tools on PC's, some with and some without screen projection capabilities. If CASE tools are to be used, it is particularly important that these tools be loaded and checked out well before the session begins. Printer capabilities available at the workshop site are also highly recommended.

The facilitator must then select or design any data collection forms that will be used in the workshop. While it may be technically possible for the CASE/JAD specialist to enter information directly into the PC as the discussion proceeds, this is not a good idea. It does not provide an adequate amount of time for thinking and, more important, rethinking by participants. In addition, it will make life rather difficult for the JAD/CASE specialist, who will spend a lot of time re-entering information that has already been entered. CASE tools were not designed to support this type of "court reporting."

It is much more valuable, rather, to create an intermediary set of paper forms to be used to collect, edit, and refine workshop discussion results. The structure that these forms can impart to the discussion and decision-making process can be a valuable asset in helping participants to stay on topic and focus on the issue at hand. These forms should be carefully designed to reflect the documentation objectives of the workshop and should use a vocabulary and format that is as "friendly" as possible. In fact, there is a certain similarity between the design of good quality screens in a computer application and the design of good quality forms in a JAD workshop. They should simplify the user's task, guiding him through his job with a minimum of confusion.

These forms can be working forms or consensus forms. Working forms are designed to provide workshop participants with a paper and pencil structure for decision making. A working form, for example, might be designed to allow partici-pants to prepare a preliminary functional decomposition or data dictionary. The information on the working form would not be final, but would be subject to later rethinking and modification. These forms may be used during the course of the workshop and then thrown away.

A consensus form, on the other hand, would represent the final agreement of all participants on any issue discussed in the workshop. This, again, might involve a functional decomposition or data dictionary, but here the information would represent the final agreement of all participants in the workshop. Consensus forms, therefore, can serve as CASE input forms or as the basis for constructing the final documentation through the use of other tools. These forms may be completed by the workshop participants or by the CASE/JAD specialist. The JAD facilitator should choose an approach that best meets the needs of the work-shop. Again, as with working forms, consensus forms benefit greatly from careful attention to design. If they are to be used as CASE input forms, the CASE/JAD specialist should play a role in their design. This will ensure that a minimum of time is wasted in translating paper information into CASE input.

Selecting and Educating Participants

When selecting participants, the most important step the JAD facilitator can take is to identify those individuals who can least be spared by their organiza-tions. These are the people who always have the most to contribute to a proj-ect. The individual who has experience and expertise meets the first criterion for a workshop participant candidate. That is, the individual should have served in the organization for more than a minimal length of time and should have in-depth knowledge of an area pertinent to the project. The length of experience required may vary from project to project, as may the degree of expertise. The JAD facilitator will have to rely on the project manager to assist him in determining how much of each is required for a given project. It is never necessary, though, for any one individual to have all the answers. The nature of the JAD process is such that it takes the best that everyone can bring to the process and emerges with a stronger result than any one individual could provide on his own.

The second criterion is an open attitude. If possible, participants should be chosen who are interested in the JAD process, enjoy working with others, and want to be a part of a consensus based approach to decision making. A corollary of this criterion is commitment. The strong candidate for participation in the workshop will exhibit a commitment to the organization, to the project, to the JAD process, and to the other members of the project team. This person is the opposite of the jaded, seen-it-all individual who thinks there is nothing new under the sun, that every new idea has been tried before and found wanting. While the JAD facilitator cannot create an individual with experience and expertise, he can have some effect in building and supporting a positive attitude toward the project and the JAD process within the organization.

The third criterion is availability. Here, too, the JAD facilitator can have some impact. Along with the project manager and, if necessary, the executive sponsor, the JAD facilitator should do his best to ensure that those individuals best qualified are made available for the workshop. Since the facilitator is already looking for the people least available, this will undoubtedly make it difficult to schedule workshop dates. Work on scheduling workshop dates should begin as soon as possible in the JAD process. When possible, dates should accommodate the work demands of participants, avoiding peak load times for participant involvement in JAD activities. When not possible, the organization should find ways to accommodate the requirements of the JAD process.

Once participants are selected, they should be educated. If they are unaware of the full nature of the project, they should be educated about its scope and objectives, and if they have had no contact with the JAD process, they should be educated about its activities and strategies. This can be done in a formal education session, and/or through written materials distributed to participants, and/or by providing participants with the opportunity to observe an actual JAD workshop if one is being held at an appropriate time. If it is difficult to bring all participants together for an education session, teleconferencing should be considered. In addition, each participant needs to be educated about his own role and responsibilities in the JAD process and about the roles played by other participants as well. Most of the JAD approaches emphasize the importance of education, and most suggest that participants receive some type of written document reinforcing education both on project background and the JAD process as a part of that process.

There is one area in which JAD approaches differ in respect to participant education, however. Some JAD approaches favor educating participants in a specialized vocabulary and in the technical details of such concepts as data modeling or screen design. Other JAD approaches favor a "common language/common concepts" type of JAD process and, therefore, do not require this special type of training. Instead, these approaches rely on the skill of the facilitator to translate technical vocabulary into a more common set of terms and to present technical concepts in an accessible format. Either approach can work. The first requires more emphasis on the education of participants before the workshop, while the second requires good translation skills on the part of the JAD facilitator. In either case, education of participants is an important part of the JAD process. The more participants understand about the project and the process, the more useful their contributions will be.

JAD WORKSHOP ACTIVITIES

The JAD workshop or workshops are the heart of the JAD process. They make it what it is, a team-oriented, consensus-based decision-making process. While the JAD facilitator works closely with the project manager throughout the JAD process, once the workshop begins, the facilitator becomes the general and the project manager is just one of the privates. The project manager may be consulted about special issues during workshop breaks, but he is an equal partner with all other participants while the workshop is in session. While the JAD facilitator is not a decision maker in the workshop, he is in charge of all activities and is ultimately responsible for the satisfaction of all workshop objectives.

Each workshop will have its own specific technical objectives. In addition to these, each JAD workshop must meet the following objectives:

- Identify and resolve critical project issues.
- Achieve consensus through structured exercises.
- Construct a solution documented in a deliverable.

The tight structure and facilitated style of the workshop make it different from other types of user group meetings led by users or systems professionals. A workshop provides an intense, carefully orchestrated environment in which people can resolve information management problems as well as build team relationships. This works because the JAD environment provides the opportunity for people from different areas of expertise to learn from each other, to develop a common view of a project, and to resolve conflicts in a nonhostile atmosphere where each person is assured of being heard. This can work in two ways. Often, it is as important for individuals from different user organizations to learn from each other as it is for the user group as a whole and the systems professionals to learn from each other.

A related value in the workshop environment is that it protects the "weak," those who are less demonstrative in their manner of expression or simply lower on the organization totem pole. It ensures that all participants will have an equal ability to influence decision making, not just the most vocal or the highest in authority. One of the many responsibilities of the facilitator is to ensure that all voices are heard and are represented in the final product of the workshop.

Too many meetings meander from one topic to another with no clear sense of purpose. This cannot happen in a JAD workshop. The structured agenda, reflective of specific objectives, is an inseparable part of the JAD concept. The "great chain of being" for the JAD process is: objectives—agenda—exercises—deliverable. All the links in the chain are tightly connected. JAD makes this promise to the project manager: If you and your team can clearly specify the objectives of the project, then JAD can produce the product (i.e., deliverable) you want. In an information management project, this means that both business functionality and data will be clearly defined, the scope of the project will be respected, and the level of detail required will be produced.

JAD approaches vary in their recommendations for workshop length. While the "classic" JAD workshop lasts for three to five days, some approaches advocate workshops as short as a day in length. Others require a minimum of five days. The authors' experience in hundreds of workshops indicates that the most successful workshops are three to five days in length. While shorter workshops can produce good results, a three to five-day workshop will by far produce the best return for the time invested. An important reason for this has to do with the principles of group dynamics. It takes approximately three days for a group to develop into an effective team. While effective decision making goes on throughout the workshop, the first day is often spent by the participants in staking out territory. During the second day, the participants begin to realize the need for a common language and understanding of each other's perspectives. On the third day, group synergy takes over and creates a team that will not only effectively build consensus on a solution but will continue to support that solution well after the workshop is concluded. For this reason, it can be very valuable to push participants to a fourth or fifth day. Their productivity is likely to be high, as is their enthusiasm.

Workshops running more than five days in length are probably a mistake. If a weekend intervenes between day five and six, momentum will be lost. If participants are pushed to work through a weekend (and there are many project managers who have suggested this), their momentum and enthusiasm will diminish significantly, as will their productivity. This may be because of the burden of giving up weekend time or because of the strain of going into a sixth day. In either case, the JAD facilitator must help the project manager and sometimes the overenthusiastic participants themselves understand that peak productivity cannot be sustained over a long period of time.

Not all JAD projects are limited to a single workshop, however, and if it becomes clear during preworkshop activities that more than one workshop will be required, these multiple workshops must be scheduled as carefully as a single one. Generally, the first workshop in a series will last at least two days and may well last up to four or five. This workshop may be used to refine the scope of a project or create a high-level view of process and/or data or produce a detailed view of core functionality and/or data. After the first workshop, subsequent sessions can last anywhere from one to five days. As mentioned earlier, no one workshop session should last for more than five days; neither should a session last less than one day. The productivity level, even of a subsequent session where team integrity has been established, does not justify a workshop of less than a day. After a break between workshop days, time will be required to re-establish group interaction norms and to bring the technical concerns of the project back into focus.

There are occasions, however, where unusual workshop schedules should be considered. The difficulty in securing the participation of key individuals or other organization priorities may sometimes lead the facilitator to look for a creative alternative to more traditional JAD scheduling approaches. JAD facilitators have experimented with using a week of five half-day sessions and with a long series (ten to twenty) of two-day sessions. However, experience teaches that the best results are obtained through less creative approaches. Correct scheduling is a critical success factor for the JAD process, and compromise on this issue can result in a breakdown in the integrity of group interaction, a reduction in the quality of workshop output, and, perhaps most dangerous of all, the call for further compromises and ultimately the reduction of the JAD workshop into just another meeting. No "creative" approach to scheduling should ever be considered without an extreme justification. Above all, this should not be done to appease a stubborn project manager or project participant who simply "can't spare the time." If a key individual says that he cannot meet the schedule required by the project, the JAD facilitator has the options of replacing him, convincing him (either through education or the heavy hand of the executive sponsor), or, if necessary, recommending that the project be deferred to a time when he will be available.

One other note here. Some of those involved in implementing the rapid application development (RAD) approach within their systems development life cycle have advocated a two workshop JAD approach to the development of a logical application design, with the result being a prototype that can be brought into active production within a two to four-month timeframe. In this scenario, the first workshop defines required process and data models. The second workshop defines access requirements, action diagrams, screens, and application navigation. This particular approach to scheduling can work very effectively. The only special concern for the JAD facilitator is that the scope of the application be carefully limited to what can be defined within the space of two five-day workshops. When this approach is applied to a large project, each application developed within the two workshops may represent a separate application module. In such a case, it is critical that the order in which modules are developed be carefully considered beforehand, and that the need to integrate related modules be addressed early in the process as well.

JAD POSTWORKSHOP ACTIVITIES

The JAD process is deliverable oriented. That is to say that while the team spirit built and communication barriers destroyed during the process are important, the process cannot be said to have succeeded if the required deliverable is not produced. Therefore, the objectives for postworkshop activities are very important. They are to:

- Validate workshop information.
- Produce the JAD deliverable.
- If appropriate, integrate this JAD workshop deliverable with other JAD workshop deliverables.
- Transition to post-JAD activities.

The second and third items identified are fairly straightforward technical activities for which the JAD/CASE specialist assumes responsibility. The first activity may be very simple or somewhat complex depending on the project. Validation may consist of no more than a review of the final document and/or prototype by the workshop participant group, with individuals requested to identify any errors that they find. On the other hand, validation may take the form of a more complex group activity where additional analytical tools are introduced to ensure accuracy and completeness. It should be noted first, however, that the need for the validation of workshop information does not imply that any decisions made during the workshop will be second guessed after it is over. Neither does it imply that the JAD facilitator should be prepared to find major inconsistencies or inaccuracies in that information. The need for validation is simply an acknowledgment that many JAD projects produce highly complex design information and that this information must be checked for accuracy and completeness if the little problems that can cause big problems are to be identified in a timely fashion. This is one of the benefits brought to the process by CASE technology. Many CASE tools are capable of providing analytical reports that can assist the JAD/CASE specialist in validating design information.

In addition, there are other techniques that can be used by the JAD facilitator to ensure accuracy and completeness in the design. These may include the use of analytical tools such as data navigation diagrams, state transition diagrams, and data flow diagrams. While these graphic techniques are not typically seen as ''validation'' tools, they can be very useful for this purpose. To the extent that these diagrams allow us to review the same information from different perspectives, they can provide valuable validation assistance.

CASE tools can greatly assist us in validation by enabling us to:

- Validate the data model by constructing a data navigation diagram.
- Identify differences among multiple models, resolve those differences and integrate them into a single model.
- Validate the models using state transition diagrams, data flow diagrams, or data navigation diagrams.
- Identify omissions in and complete draft diagrams created in the workshop.
- Automate screen and application navigation specifications in a prototype.
- Validate or build test data for an application by analyzing all potential processing situations.

The minimum activity required for completing the JAD workshop deliverable includes the presentation of all validated workshop information in an appropriate physical format. Usually this means producing a well-edited document including both text and graphics. In some situations, it also means constructing a prototype. The content of the document will, of course, vary from project-to-project, but for most projects, it will include a data and/or process model at some level of detail. If a prototype is produced, it may be a minimally functional prototype, a fully functional one, or something in between. The type of prototype created would reflect the needs of the project, the time available, the tools available, and the decision of the project manager and executive sponsor. This should have been determined in preworkshop activities.

The definition of a JAD workshop deliverable need not be so limited, however. For example, if CASE tools are used to create the deliverable, an interim deliverable document may also be created. This would consist of the analytical reports produced by the CASE tools used to validate design information. These reports are not generally presented as part of the final deliverable, but they may be included if the project manager wishes, or they may be shared with those members of the project team who represent the systems group as part of the process of validating and refining workshop information.

While the emphasis in this discussion has been on the development of a logical design, it is also possible to include within the deliverable information that will assist the systems organization in making the transition to the physical design stage. This may include information that was developed within the workshop or it may represent additional work performed by an appointed subteam subsequent to the workshop. Logical to physical transition information may include:

- The use of action diagrams to define programming requirements.
- The identification of single or multiple sources for each data attribute, and strategies and structures for creating the physical database.
- A review of existing production applications and databases and a recommen-

dation on which may be utilized to support the solution, which may be salvaged and incorporated into the solution, and which must be replaced when the solution is implemented.

- The identification of volume, frequency, sequence access, and capacity information using the logical data model to guide the development of physical database design.
- The development of action plans with assignments, tasks, and activities to ensure project completion and success.

JAD FORUM STRUCTURE

The central concept behind the JAD process is that more can be accomplished in a group environment than in isolated interview or analysis situations. But JAD offers more than one type of group environment for action, each with its own benefits. There are three types of forums for involving participants in JAD activities. They are the target meeting, the focus group interview, and the workshop. In order to make the best use of each approach, JAD facilitators should understand the purpose of each type of forum, the techniques for conducting it, and the critical success factors associated with it.

TARGET MEETINGS

The target meeting is a meeting with a very carefully defined purpose. Both data collection and decision making can occur in a target meeting. But unlike the typical project team status meeting held every Monday morning, a target meeting is a unique event designed by the JAD facilitator to obtain specific results. Figure 2.11 suggests some typical target meetings held before and after workshops. A target meeting is one day or less in length, has specific objectives, an agenda, is led by the JAD facilitator, and is documented by the JAD/CASE specialist. Meeting minutes are not issued. Instead, the information collected at preworkshop target meetings may be incorporated into the JAD preparation deliverable. The information collected in postworkshop target meetings is used to complete the JAD workshop deliverable and develop project plans.

A target meeting is similar to a workshop in that it is led by a JAD facilitator and adheres to a clearly defined agenda. Its purpose is different from that of a workshop, however, in that it does not focus on consensus building or attempt to create a comprehensive information design of some type. The purpose of a target meeting is to gather high quality information quickly from a number of sources at one time. The structure and techniques used in a target meeting also are different from those we find in a workshop. In a workshop, the JAD facilitator conducts both technical and team building exercises, uses data collection materials, and

Meeting Purpose	Length In Hours	Attendees	Results
Sales	2	Project Team Business Users	Commitment to use JAD process
Project Definition and Scope	4 - 8	Project Team Key Users Executive Sponsor	Set project boundaries
Deliverable Definition	2	Project Team	Detailed deliverable table of contents
Workshop Structuring	2 - 4	Project Team	JAD workshop structure, agenda and logistics
Participant Education	2 - 4	Workshop Participants	Prepared participants
Deliverable Review	2 - 8	Workshop Participants	Finalized deliverable
Postworkshop Issue Resolution	2 - 8	Workshop Participants	Updated issues
Postworkshop Executive Briefing	1 - 2	Project Team	Decisions to move forward

Figure 2.11   Typical target meetings for JAD.

focuses on building the JAD workshop deliverable. In a target meeting, the JAD facilitator does not execute formal exercises. Instead, he leads discussions that are structured around a predetermined format. Often this format includes a set of questions or a blank matrix or series of matrices. If the facilitator chooses, he may use the meeting to construct a graphic of particular relevance such as a hierarchy chart or a context-level data flow diagram.

Just as the JAD facilitator must be aware of the importance of the physical environment to the success of a workshop, the facilitator must be aware of the environment in which a target meeting is held. It should be held in a quiet, spacious conference room free from interruptions. The room should provide any visual aids required, particularly the easel boards that are used by so many facilitators. The room should be located in "neutral" territory, especially if the meeting participants come from different organizations and see themselves as being involved in a competitive situation of some type. In addition, the agenda for the meeting should be prepared ahead of time and circulated among the prospective participants. Finally, the participants should be well chosen. They should be selected for their knowledge and willingness to share information.

FOCUS GROUP INTERVIEWS

Focus group interviews have been used in market and product research for decades. The benefits of using this technique for obtaining lots of information about consumer preferences quickly are clear. But researchers recognized that there was a further benefit to be obtained from focus group interviews that went beyond speed and quantity. The quality of the information obtained increased as well. This was a result of two things: the interaction of the participants and the guidance of the focus group leader, or "facilitator."

It was not difficult for JAD facilitators to recognize the link between this technique and the objectives and strategies of the JAD process, and to apply it to the process of systems development. For JAD facilitators, the focus group interview is the primary forum for project research activities. The purpose of focus group interviews is data collection, not decision making. Focus group interviews are better than individual one-on-one interviews because the four to eight people who participate in the focus group share and build on each other's views thus providing the JAD facilitator with a much richer information resource. Generally, a series of such interviews are held, with the same questions and facilitation techniques used in each.

Focus group interviews are specially planned for and conducted. Questions are developed ahead of time, and the JAD facilitator should be aware of the pertinent political background of the project to the extent that this is possible. This will enable him to more effectively evaluate and control the discussion. The "no surprises" objective of the workshop is useful here too. Each focus group interview should last approximately two hours, and as a reasonable guideline the number of questions asked should be from eight to twelve. It is useful to have another individual appointed to take notes and to be responsible for documenting the results of the session. It is just not possible for the JAD facilitator to do a good job of facilitating a focus group interview if the facilitator also has to think about note taking. The JAD/CASE specialist may serve in this capacity.

It is also useful for the project manager to be present. His role would be that of a listener, similar to the observer role in the workshop. He is there to learn, not to intervene to correct the comments of the participants or to steer the discussion in a particular direction. If it is feared that his presence may inhibit participants, this problem may be dealt with by placing him in a physically inconspicuous position or by asking him to forego participation altogether. The need to ban the project manager from a focus group session should be viewed very seriously, however. It can indicate a project with major political problems. In such a case, a more acceptable representative of the project manager may be substituted during the session, but all results of the session should be discussed with the project manager to evaluate the potential for project success.

In evaluating the results of the focus group interview, the JAD facilitator should determine if a pattern of information exists. This might be a consistency in the type of technical or political issues that are cited, a similarity in the way current problems or project objectives are defined, or a repetition of critical assumptions about the project. In order for these patterns to be revealed, it is important that the same questions be asked in each interview and that all focus groups be facilitated in the same way.

Just as with all group activities, it is important that focus group interviews be conducted away from participant desks and telephones. A good location would be within the territory of the participant group in a quiet and comfortable conference room free from interruptions. Again, too, it is critical that the right people, those who are well informed and prepared to communicate their information, be present. While the structure of the session may be governed by no more than a list of questions, it is important that the discussion not be permitted to drift into unrelated areas. Finally, it is also critical that the participant group know why they are being asked questions and how the information may be used. The JAD facilitator should introduce himself and any other nonparticipants present before the session and explain how the results of the session will contribute to the project as a whole.

WORKSHOPS

In contrast to the other types of forum previously discussed, JAD workshops have the distinct purpose of promoting decision making and building consensus in the service of creating the JAD workshop deliverable. They are led by the JAD facilitator, documented by the JAD/CASE specialist, and are attended by a mix of business and systems experts and outside technical advisors. The physical facility in which the workshop is held should contribute to this purpose by creating an atmosphere conducive to conversation and decision making (Fig. 2.12). The "U" shaped table in the main workshop room allows participants to have eye contact with each other at all times. The "U" also provides direct access to each participant for the JAD facilitator. In addition to the main JAD room, there should be several "break away" rooms available for the many subteam activities that can occur during a workshop. These rooms should provide a more informal opportunity for discussion and a change in environment for the participants during the workshop.

The workshop agenda for a JAD project reflects the objectives of the project and is dictated by the agreed upon content of the JAD workshop deliverable. In addition, the structure of the workshop (or multiple workshops if these are required) is constrained by the amount of time available, the number and character of the participants, and the complexity of the information needs being analyzed.

OPENING AND CLOSING THE WORKSHOP

Many JAD facilitators begin and end each workshop with a behavioral exercise to reinforce the team building experience. Start-up exercises should not consume more than an hour of the time available and may have several uses. They may be used to establish group norms and interaction rules for the workshop environment, bring participants to a common level of understanding to ensure good communication, and set the tone for the workshop environment. In a large project where a series of workshops will be held, the first workshop is critical to the creation of a positive team spirit. In such a case, these exercises can be invaluable in removing participant doubt about the JAD experience, overcoming longstanding animosity among different groups, and in establishing an atmosphere of cooperation. If the JAD facilitator is concerned that participants will come to a workshop uneasy about their individual roles and anxious about what will happen throughout the workshop sessions, an opening behavioral exercise can address these issues up front. In subsequent workshops conducted with the same group of people, opening exercises can be abbreviated to include only the necessary review of rules for operation, a review of the status of the project to date, and an overview of the workshop and project agenda.

Just as start-up exercises help participants to transition into the workshop environment, closing exercises help the participants to transition out of the workshop environment. This is particularly critical for the project manager and his technical team since they will have to carry on the project after the JAD workshop is completed. Workshop closure activities generally take about one to two hours. One purpose that may be served by closure activities is to have participants consider what steps must be taken to carry the activity of the workshop further. Assignments may be made and dates assigned for task completion. Another purpose that may be served by closure activities is the review of any issues

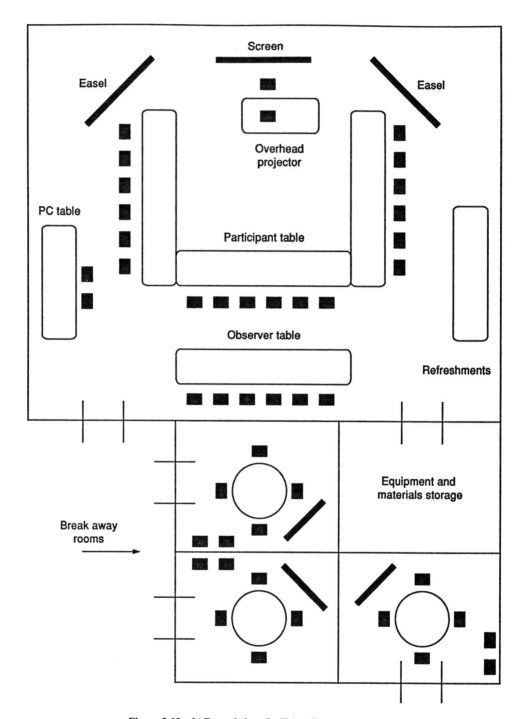

Figure 2.12 JAD workshop facilities diagram.

Sample JAD Workshops

Sample JAD Deliverable — Logical Design

Data Model

    Entity relationship diagrams
    Entity tables

Process Model

    Decomposition diagrams
    Dependency diagrams

Process-Data Relationship Model

    Navigation diagrams
    Data flow diagrams

Access Specifications
    Query statements
    Screens and reports
    Action diagrams
    Application dialogues

Workshop #1
    Entity relationships
    Entity tables
    Decompostion diagrams
    Dependency diagrams

Workshop #2

    Navigation diagrams
    Data flow diagrams

Workshop #3

    Query statements
    Screens and reports
    Action diagrams
    Application dialogues

Figure 2.13 JAD deliverable and workshop agendas.

that remain unresolved by the workshop. These issues may also be assigned to individuals with dates for completion.

At the end of a workshop almost all JAD facilitators use some type of evaluation tool. This feedback may be either verbal or written, but most facilitators prefer to use a written form in order to obtain a more detailed view of participant attitudes. Generally, the evaluation will focus on both the JAD process in general and its application to the project at hand in particular. The information presented can provide the JAD facilitator with valuable ideas for enhancing the technique and improving his own skills.

WORKSHOP TECHNICAL CONTENT

The core of every workshop or workshop series is a series of technical exercises designed to produce the content of the JAD workshop deliverable (Fig. 2.13). If a project focuses on a logical application design, for example, the technical agenda for a given workshop will consist of exercises designed to accomplish one or more of the following:

- Definition of the project framework
- Analysis of data requirements
- Analysis of process requirements
- Integration of data and process requirements
- Specification of access requirements

The definition of the timing, pacing, and structure of workshop exercises is a key responsibility of the JAD facilitator. The facilitator may choose to present some exercises sequentially so that one builds on the results of another. Other exercises may be presented in parallel through the use of subteams to speed the progress of the group as a whole and to provide a more intimate environment in which people can wrestle with difficult issues. Parallel exercises, however, require a second step in which the subteam presents its conclusions to the larger group for modification, integration and final decision making.

Exercises can have different objectives. Exercises may be used to:

- Establish group norms and rules.
- Bring people to the same level of understanding.
- Change the mood or tone of the workshop environment.
- Generate ideas without judgment.
- Analyze and evaluate ideas.
- Make decisions.

Definition of the Project Framework

It has already been noted that no project should begin without a clear definition of scope. However, prior to the workshop, this definition will necessarily be somewhat brief. It is the purpose of this workshop activity to provide a much more detailed view of the project, its content and its boundaries, than has been available before. This is particularly important for large, complex projects where multiple workshops will be required. The results of this work may be documented using any of the following:

- Strategic, tactical, or operational statement narratives
- Analytical matrices
- Entity relationship diagram(s)
- Business function decomposition diagram(s)

Analysis of Data Requirements

The definition of a data model may precede or follow some level of process analysis. It requires participants to define the information needs of the business and to identify how that data is used. The level of detail provided will vary from project to project. In some cases, a JAD facilitator will introduce the concept of data normalization and work with the group to refine the data model into first, second, or even, in some cases, third normal form. The normalization process, when employed in a workshop, can provide up to ninety percent of the business rules governing the organization. The only caveat is that the use of the normalization exercise in a workshop requires great skill on the part of the JAD facilitator. It is one of the most demanding exercises he can lead, and many facilitators do not attempt it until they are confident that both their technical and behavioral skills are quite strong. The data model produced through the exercises conducted under this heading can be documented through the use of:

- Entity relationship diagrams
- Entity tables
- Definitions for all entities and attributes

Analysis of Process Requirements

The definition of a process model should be easy, but often this is not true. The definition of process is not the same as the definition of procedure. Participants are generally quite comfortable with the definition of the procedures that they employ on a daily basis to, for example, manage inventory or calculate commissions. They are not so comfortable, however, when asked to rise to a higher level of abstraction and define the processes that make up a business operation. It is the job of the JAD facilitator to make sure that the participants understand the nature of the process model. The facilitator must also clarify the status of the model being developed. Some workshops will focus on a future view of the business as seen through a proposed process model. Other workshops that focus on the re-engineering of business operations may look at a current process model and at problem areas within that model. The process model produced through the exercises conducted under this heading can be documented through the use of:

- Functional decomposition diagrams
- Dependency diagrams
- Action diagrams

Integration of Data and Process Requirements

In a logical application design project, participants are asked to define how data is manipulated by different processes. In addition, integration also assists in validating the process and data model relationships and beginning the work of transitioning from logical to physical design. The integrated model(s) produced through the exercises conducted under this heading can be documented through the use of:

- Data flow diagrams
- Data navigation diagrams
- State transition diagrams
- Decision table diagrams

Specification of Access Requirements

The first concern for many users involves requirements for ad hoc inquiry and "on demand" reporting. In many cases, their inquiries are unique. But for most businesses, eighty to ninety percent of all reporting and inquiry requirements can easily be defined once the proper data models have been completed. This may be even more true for expert systems that are based on the predictability of certain judgments and diagnostic decision making. Therefore, for a logical application design, participants will be involved in defining how the user will access and interact with the application and/or database.

This work begins the transitioning from logical to physical design. The specifications resulting from this work may be directly handed off to programming staff for prototype development. The access requirements produced through the exercises conducted under this heading can be documented through the use of:

- Display/dialogue standards
- Data entry/report screen layouts
- Sample printed reports
- Interface requirements
- Application access and navigation requirements

WORKSHOP DOCUMENTATION

Early versions of the JAD process required that the JAD/CASE specialist act like a court clerk recording every point in the discussion that took place during a workshop. For this reason the person in charge of documentation was generally referred to as the "scribe." This approach was not very successful, however. It tended to emphasize the discussions that supported group decision making rather than the decisions that were made. Most JAD approaches today focus on the end result, not the many false starts and disagreements that can lead up to consensus. This approach was also very tedious for the note taker, who contributed little to the deliverable on his own. No JAD approach that includes CASE can afford to view the documentation expert in this light.

The JAD workshop deliverable is defined in very specific detail prior to a workshop. From this definition, the JAD facilitator and the JAD/CASE specialist know exactly what information they need to gather in the workshop. Several types of information collection media are available to record that information as it is generated within the workshop. The three most commonly used are the worksheet, the room display, and the PC. The JAD facilitator will select from these alternatives as appropriate for a given project. Generally, though, once a facilitator develops a sense of his own personal leadership style, he will tend to rely on the tools with which he feels most comfortable.

Workshop Data Collection Forms

One medium is the workshop data collection form, or "worksheet" (Figs. 2.14 and 2.15). Most JAD approaches rely on the use of worksheets to guide participants in their efforts. The worksheet is the JAD facilitator's best defense against the wandering conversation. It enforces a sense of structure on the workshop. JAD forms can be standardized based on the specific deliverable requirements of an organization, and some proprietary approaches to JAD offer those trained in the approach a standard set of worksheets. Generally, however, even if standard forms are used, the JAD facilitator will find that he must either modify certain forms or design one or more unique forms to meet specific deliverable needs. This is done when the JAD facilitator designs the JAD agenda and exercises. During the workshop, forms may be completed by the participants, by the JAD/CASE specialist or by both as appropriate for a given activity. Ultimately the content of the forms will appear, although perhaps altered in format, in the JAD workshop deliverable.

Room Displays

Another type of media is the room display, a useful type of tool because a JAD facilitator often needs to display and document information in front of the group. Such displays keep conversations on track and provide a single, easy-to-see reference for all to use throughout the workshop. This type of information collection tool comes in many forms, from the sophistication of predefined magnetic symbols to the simplicity of blank easel pads. Blackboards or white boards can be used as well, and many facilitators find that overhead projectors and transparencies are useful. However, many facilitators find that the least expensive and most flexible type of room display is the easel board and Post-It® combination. Easel sheets can be taped on the walls of a room and moved as needed. Post-Its® of various sizes and colors can be used to capture information, analyze the information and modify it as conclusions are reached. Not all facilitators favor the "low tech" approach, of course, and some use electronic white boards. These work somewhat better than a standard

```
Process Name _____
Process Reference Number _____
Process Description


Performance volume per frequency (pick one)
  ___/sec.  ___/min.  ___/hr.  ___/day  ___/week

Process Performer(s)                          Number
_____                              _____
_____                              _____
_____                              _____
_____                              _____


Process Output(s) Data                        Process Input(s)/Data
_____                              _____
_____                              _____
_____                              _____
_____                              _____



Data Created, Changed or Deleted by process
_____                              _____
_____                              _____
_____                              _____


Process Status      (OK) Process should continue as is
                    (mod) Process is modified
                    (new) This is a new process

Process Automation Status
                    (man) Is and should remain manual
                    (OK) Is supported by _____
                    (auto) Should be supported by new systems
```

Figure 2.14 JAD process analysis form example.

set of magnetics on a white board in that they make it easier to modify information captured. However, electronic white boards are expensive and have less than one hundred percent reliability. The more high tech the workshop environment, the less flexible the workshop is and the more the facilitator must tie the exercises to the capabilities of the technology rather than the needs of the JAD workshop deliverable.

Again, the ultimate destination for information captured through the use of this media is the JAD workshop deliverable. Today, this generally means that the intermediate destination is a CASE tool. After the information defined through the use of worksheets and room displays is entered, the JAD/CASE specialist may supplement it by including such items as an executive summary, table of contents, and additional graphic representations.

```
┌─────────────────────────────────────────────────────────────┐
│                                                               │
│   Data Entity Name _____                        │
│   Data Entity Reference Number _____                       │
│                                                               │
│                                                               │
│   One-to-one relationships with entities                      │
│   _____          _____                │
│   _____          _____                │
│                                                               │
│                                                               │
│   One-to-many relationships with entities                     │
│   _____          _____                │
│   _____          _____                │
│                                                               │
│                                                               │
│   Entity definition                                           │
│                                                               │
│                                                               │
│                                                               │
│   Entity KEY Attributes                                       │
│        Primary _____   _____             │
│        Secondary _____   _____             │
│                                                               │
│                                                               │
│   Entity utilization estimates for data base/application      │
│        Initial Volume _____                │
│        Maximum Volume _____                │
│        Stored on-line for how long _____              │
│        Archived for how long _____              │
│                                                               │
│                                                               │
│   Current source data bases/applications for entity           │
│   _____          _____                │
│   _____          _____                │
│                                                               │
│      Entity           Entity              Entity              │
│      Occurance        Frequency           Volume/Frequency    │
│                                                               │
│      Created          _____            _____            │
│      Read             _____            _____            │
│      Updated          _____            _____            │
│      Deleted          _____            _____            │
│                                                               │
└─────────────────────────────────────────────────────────────┘
```

Figure 2.15   JAD data analysis form example.

CASE Tools

Most JAD facilitators today place the CASE tool in the background of the workshop, the better to get a head start on CASE input when other workshop responsibilities permit. But for some facilitators the urge to go "high tech" results in their placement of the CASE tool center stage. They choose to avoid the middleman, preferring direct input from the participant group into the CASE tool. Along with the CASE software, this approach requires a high quality PC and electronic screen projection unit. This approach has the obvious advantage of moving participants quickly along a highly structured path to a predictable re-sult. But it has certain drawbacks as well. The principal one is that the participants become an audience rather than a work group (Fig. 2.16). They are a resource from which the facilitator extracts information, with the result that communication is one way, or at best two way. What is missing is the free exchange of ideas among the participants themselves that leads to the team building benefits common to most JAD approaches. Rather than working together to solve a common prob-lem, the participants in a CASE centered JAD workshop become the servants of the tool.

This may change, however, if the new groupware products are customized to the needs of the JAD approach. In effect, groupware could automate both worksheets and room displays, without reducing group interaction. In a group-ware situation, each participant (or group) has a PC, resulting in a different work-shop automation model. Once again the participants are center stage, not the tool. As in a typical JAD workshop, participants in a groupware workshop sit at a "U" shaped table and work together to solve a common problem. Promoters of the groupware approach place less emphasis on satisfying the demands of specific tool input requirements than on building consensus from many different ideas. It is easy to imagine that the software supporting this approach could be adapted to the requirements of the JAD workshop, perhaps at least initially with JAD subteams each assigned a PC to analyze and document their work. Subsequent presentations to the whole participant group could be expedited electronically as well. Ideally, once the entire group had reached consensus, the information gathered through the use of the tool could then be directly loaded into the target CASE tool. This would place automation at the service of the participants, rather than the other way around.

WORKSHOP SITES

The ideal location for a JAD workshop is away from the participant work place where people can work in a casual and relaxed environment. For this reason, hotels and conference centers which provide support services are often used. However, in tight economic conditions, it may not be possible to provide such luxurious accommodations. The next best choice is the organization's own conference or training center. The last choice is a conference room in the same building as most of the participants' offices. The tendency to return to the desk is very great. Although this approach can be used successfully, all too often participants will be late in returning to the on-site location after lunch or a break and will have trouble concentrating on workshop activities. In addition, the average conference room tends to be too small to accommodate a JAD workshop, and separate subteam work rooms are difficult to find.

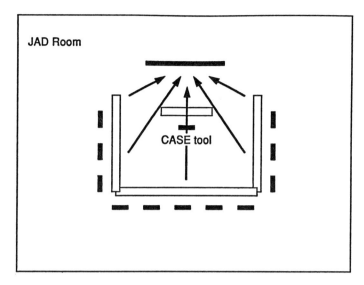

CASE as interference
in communication

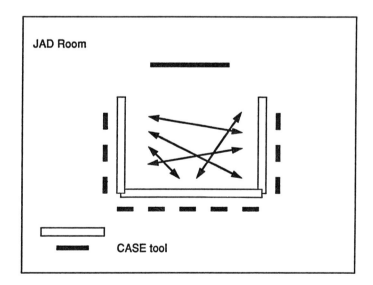

CASE as decision support
in communication

Figure 2.16   CASE tool communication interference.

HOW DO JAD TECHNIQUES VARY?

Some organizations introduce the JAD approach by hiring consultants to deliver JAD services. This provides a quick start, a safe opportunity for experimentation and a learning experience for everyone involved. However, this can also be expensive, and most organizations that have successfully experimented with JAD want to bring the process in-house eventually. By doing so, they not only save money, but they also achieve the benefit of making JAD a standard organization practice, integrated into the systems life cycle.

There are two options for bringing JAD into the organization. The first is for the organization to create a customized JAD process from scratch, and the second is to buy a proprietary JAD process from one of the vendors that specialize in this area. The first approach takes a great deal of time and JAD expertise. Because these resources are in short supply in many organizations, the second approach has generally proven to be the more popular one. In looking at the different proprietary JAD approaches, you will find that there are several key factors that distinguish one from another. Considering these factors can assist you in choosing the approach that is right for your organization. It can also give you a few insights into the questions you will face if you decide to develop your own approach. These key factors include:

- Methodology focus
- Life cycle focus
- JAD process structure
- Participant roles and responsibilities
- JAD–CASE relationship
- Vendor support

Methodology Focus

Some JAD techniques are aligned with a specific systems design methodology. ATLIS/PRI's METHOD, for example, has an information engineering orientation, while IBM's JAD maintains a perspective more compatible with the concepts of structured analysis. Other techniques, such as the FAST approach offered by M.G. Rush & Associates, attempt to stay methodology independent by emphasizing process flexibility and multiple exercise and agenda options. Each organization considering JAD must identify an appropriate balance of rigor and flexibility. Generally, the more rigorous the adherence to a particular methodology, the fewer the options presented to the JAD facilitator and the more standardized the JAD process. This approach particularly benefits two types of organizations, those where a specific methodology is already in place (or is strongly desired), and those where the typical JAD facilitator is moderately experienced and/or functions as a JAD facilitator on a limited or part time basis.

A more open and flexible approach to methodology may be better suited to the organization where multiple standards exist among different organizational subgroups. If one division favors a very strict adherence to structured analysis principles, while another is experimenting with information engineering concepts and is moving toward a RAD environment, then a methodology independent approach may be best. The difficulty inherent in this choice, however, is that the more open the JAD technique, the more that is required on the part of the JAD facilitator. The more choices available to the facilitator, the more training and expertise are required. In such an environment, the establishment of a core group of full time facilitators is almost mandatory.

The materials provided to new JAD facilitators by vendors of any of the proprietary approaches should clearly define the relationship between their approach and the most commonly practiced methodologies.

Life Cycle Focus

Some JAD techniques focus only on the development of logical application designs. Others offer support for such predesign activities as information systems planning projects and corporate data modeling, as well as such postdesign activities as prototyping and testing. The organization that wants to introduce JAD should consider where JAD will be active in their life cycle and determine what type of JAD approach will best support their needs. Just as the relationship between JAD and methodology comes down to a balance between rigor and flexibility, the relationship between JAD and the life cycle comes down to the same balancing act. A JAD process that can be implemented at many points in the life cycle can have great potential benefit, but it also requires a very high standard of performance on the part of the JAD facilitator and a high degree of support by the organization that adopts it.

The benefits of extending JAD into areas of the life cycle beyond logical application design are very real; the dangers are real as well. Trying for too much too soon can result in a rejection of JAD at all points. There are, in fact, a few organizations where too much ambition and too little experience have earned the approach a negative reputation. Rather than looking for a process that is either too limited or too all encompassing, it may be best to steer a middle course. This can be accomplished by seeking out a process that allows for initial implementation within the logical design phase and yet supports the extension of the process into other life cycle phases as a record of success is achieved.

JAD Process Structure

All JAD approaches can be divided into three general phases, preworkshop, workshop, and postworkshop. However, approaches can vary greatly in the way they balance these three phases, with some putting great emphasis on preworkshop activity and others moving quickly to the workshop with few preliminaries. Similarly, some approaches greatly emphasize postworkshop validation activities, while others see the production of a workshop document as a mechanical formality. But certainly the phase in which the greatest degree of diversity exists is the workshop phase.

If you could eavesdrop on a selection of JAD workshops conducted in accordance with a variety of JAD approaches, you would probably notice more differences than similarities. All would present you with a group of people in a room, and all would be presided over by a JAD facilitator assisted by a second individual. But the number of participants present might vary from four to forty, and the performance style of the facilitator might range from timid to terrifying. Even the room itself might be a sparsely furnished ex-storeroom or a high tech set from "Star Trek."

Most important of all, the work being conducted will vary greatly from approach to approach. The exercises which are orchestrated by the facilitator and performed by the participants are the heart of the workshop. They are the musical score, the instructions that when properly executed will produce the product of all this activity, the deliverable document. In looking at the various JAD approaches, one of the most important factors to consider is whether the nature and content of these exercises are appropriate to the needs of your organization. If the typical exercises in a workshop are designed to produced Brahms when you want Stravinsky, you need to look further. In reviewing the different JAD approaches, consider a typical exercise from each and ask what its objectives are and what techniques it uses to reach those objectives.

Finally, in addition to the exercises and their execution, you need to examine the techniques and strategies the JAD approach uses to create a team environment and build consensus. The development of a cohesive project team and the establishment of communication rapport should represent supporting objectives for any JAD technique. Some JAD approaches balance the need for technical productivity with behavioral control quite well. Others focus primarily on technical considerations, assuming that JAD facilitators will come equipped with a kit bag of strategies for group management or that they will acquire these skills from another source. If an organization has ready access to individuals already adept at facilitation principles and techniques, it need not be so concerned about the inclusion of behavioral concepts within the JAD approach. But for most organizations, the marriage of the technical and behavioral within one approach has proven to offer a greater degree of success.

Participant Roles and Responsibilities

The type and extent of involvement of the different individuals who participate in a JAD project vary from approach to approach. Some JAD approaches, particularly those following the early IBM standard, call for workshops composed primarily of business users with very limited participation by the systems organization. There are two problems with this approach. First, it misses the opportunity to build a partnership between the business and systems organizations and perpetuates the traditional separation between the groups. The users will be no closer to understanding the technical boundaries in which they must live, and the systems professionals will miss the opportunity to increase their understanding of why the users need what they need. Both will miss the opportunity to produce a creative solution within a real world environment. Second, it may (and in fact often does) generate a "blue sky" solution to the information management problem addressed. By not taking advantage of the valuable advisory role systems experts can play, it is likely that the requirements and design decisions documented in the workshop will fail to reflect real technical constraints or to propose the most efficient solution to an information management problem. Ultimately, this results in the systems organization rejecting all or part of the user proposed solution, which in turn results in disappointment on the part of the users and increased hostility between the two groups. In the most extreme cases, the result is a JAD solution that is worse than one that might have been created through more traditional means.

At the other end of the spectrum are the JAD approaches that elevate the role of the systems organization and discount the participation of the business users. In the "Rapid" JAD approach marketed by CEC, for example, users play a somewhat limited role in decision making. This approach favors a series of workshops, with initial workshops where the solution is defined including only six to eight business users. Subsequent workshops do include many more users (sometimes as many as thirty), but these are review meetings held to validate the JAD workshop deliverable. The advantage to this approach is that it reduces the amount of time spent on discussion and speeds the workshop process. It is, in terms of facilitation style as well, a heavily managed JAD process. But the drawback is that it reduces the emphasis on consensus, generally seen as a principal JAD objective, and ultimately risks reducing the commitment of the user community to the implemented solution. The greater the participation in workshop decision making, the greater the buy-in attained across the organization. Hostile users, asked to validate someone else's design, may react negatively by throwing it out and demanding to start over, regardless of the quality of the design. Participation in workshops is important to creating positive attitudes at all levels of the organization.

Another way in which JAD approaches vary is in regard to their expectations for participant knowledge. Some approaches require workshop participants to be trained in the principles and graphic representation techniques of a specific methodology prior to the workshop. Others require only briefings on the project and the workshop agenda. Clearly, there is great value in making participants aware of and comfortable with what will be expected of them in a prospective workshop. Whether it is necessary, however, to train them in the tenets of a methodology is another question. The education itself cannot be harmful, but it may be resented by participants who see it as a further burden on their time and as another attempt by the systems organization to force them to speak their language. A better solution may be for the JAD facilitator to take the responsibility for translating those concepts and terms that can be expressed in a more "user friendly" language. Then only those elements of the methodology that cannot otherwise be expressed can be introduced and illustrated when necessary. This does place a certain burden on the facilitator, but a JAD facilitator who cannot meet this challenge is probably not ready for "prime time" anyway.

JAD–CASE Relationship

Ideally, the results of a JAD workshop should be captured in a CASE tool. Some JAD approaches are tied to a specific CASE tool, while others are adapted to multiple tools. For an organization that has made a commitment to a specific tool, either approach will work. For an organization that has not committed to a single tool, the second approach would be preferable. The benefit of the first approach is that less work will have to be done to integrate CASE tool and JAD technique. The benefit of the second is that adopting JAD will not require the organization to make a premature commitment to a specific tool and will allow those organizations where multiple tools are in use to continue to follow this policy.

In examining different JAD approaches, it is also useful to consider how the CASE tool is used before, during and after the workshop. An approach may make little or extensive use of a tool in any of these three phases. Probably, though, the most critical phase to examine is the workshop phase. In some JAD approaches, the tool takes a central role, quite literally. It is placed in the center of the room, and the participant group becomes an extension of it, feeding it information and reviewing the results of that input on a projection screen. In others, the tool plays a background role, supporting the activities of the group, but not dictating them. At this point in time, it is difficult to imagine JAD without CASE. Any organization considering the implementation of a JAD approach must consider its relationship to one or more CASE tools as well.

Vendor Support

Some organizations have developed their own JAD approaches. Typically, organizations that have done this find that it takes two people approximately one year to write the JAD facilitator handbook, test the JAD technique, develop a facilitator training program, and train the first JAD facilitators. These organizations are relatively few in number, however. Most organizations utilize the services of JAD vendors. JAD vendors vary in the type of services that they provide. Some limit their services to supplying JAD facilitators and JAD/CASE specialists to organizations for specific project work. Other vendors focus on JAD facilitator training. Some license their JAD technique to organizations so that it can be customized to the organization's culture and standards.

Those vendor companies most committed to the discipline offer a variety of proprietary JAD products and services. Those with the greatest depth offer a JAD technique that is updated and enhanced on a regular basis, offer customization support, provide training for both facilitators and CASE experts, and provide ongoing support in the form of advanced training programs, conferences, and newsletters.

Even in the mid 1980s, there were relatively few organizations specializing in JAD. Today, many organizations have added JAD to their list of service offerings. Many companies offering CASE or information engineering services also offer some type of JAD facilitation services. Their degree of expertise, however, can range from a serious commitment and training program for their consultants, to a couple of on call experts, to little more than a claim to knowledge of the process. For this reason, it is important for the organization that is interested in working with a JAD vendor to check JAD references, review JAD materials, and above all, ask lots of questions.

THE EMERGING ROLE OF JAD

When JAD first came into use in the early 1980s, the technique was an informal one that depended almost entirely on the knowledge of an individual facilitator for its structure and technique. JAD workshop deliverable format and content also varied widely. Automated analysis and documentation support was not widely utilized, aside from word processing, and CASE was considered optional. The JAD leader was generally a "Lone Ranger" working without the strong support and commitment of the systems organization. Today's emerging JAD technique takes an opposite approach. Often JAD is the driver behind the examination, development, and/or selection of life cycle standards, methodology principles and CASE tools (Fig. 2.17).

The JAD facilitator is no longer a Lone Ranger, but is a central point of contact for a new approach to project support. This is best exemplified in the development of the "FUSION Center," a physical space in which these new concepts, tools, and techniques can be joined. The term "FUSION Center" was coined by an innovative group working for the U.S. Army Corps of Engineers at Ft. Belvoir in Virginia. These early innovators specialized in the development of team approaches to problem solving. Today there are many groups, both in private industry and in the academic world, specializing in different aspects of the group approach to problem solving. It should be fascinating to watch where they lead in the years to come.

WHY JAD FAILS

Many companies have implemented JAD, some more successfully than others. Fortunately for us, we can learn a great deal from their mistakes. Any organi-

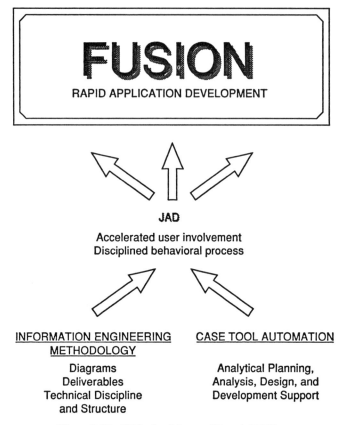

Figure 2.17   JAD: the driver to IE and CASE.

zation on the verge of implementing JAD should pay close attention. Early attempts often failed for one or more of these reasons.

Endless Session Syndrome

In some organizations, there are too few facilitators, but lots of interest in JAD. This good news versus bad news situation results in delayed projects and overworked facilitators who are forced to move continually from one workshop to the next. The result is facilitator burnout and organization frustration. This syndrome can be exacerbated by poor preworkshop analysis. Even the largest application projects seldom require more than five to seven workshops, each four or five days in length. Yet the authors have heard of workshop series lasting as long as twenty-five sessions. This happens when the true scope of a project was not determined before the first workshop was held or the JAD facilitator did not understand how to structure a workshop series to meet a specific set of objectives.

Musical Chairs Participation

Participants must make a clear commitment to the JAD process. If they do not do this, they will slow down the process at best, or invalidate it entirely at worst. It is not possible to facilitate a focus group interview or a workshop effectively if people are popping in and out of sessions as suits their convenience (or sense of self importance). This type of behavior on the part of some participants not only indicates a lack of support for the process, but also betrays a lack of respect for their colleagues.

Wandering Workshops

Some workshops never seem to develop a sense of purpose or direction. This can be caused by an early failure to clearly define the requirements for the JAD workshop deliverable or to construct a set of workshop exercises that support this deliverable. It can also be caused by a lack of experience on the part of a facilitator who fails to keep the group on track, who does not know when to bring discussion to closure or who does not know how to force a resolution of a critical issue. Too many of us have already had the experience of listening to aimless discussions in time wasting meetings. Put simply, JAD without structure is not JAD.

Charismatic Facilitators

A reliance on one or two charismatic facilitators who are in such demand that they burn out quickly is very dangerous to the JAD technique. If no facilitator training program exists, or if a process is not in place to identify potential trainees on a regular basis, then this is a real danger. While their personal skills may make these exceptional facilitators extremely popular, the JAD process should stand on its own merits and not be tied to the reputation of one or two individuals. If it cannot stand on its own, the process may be discarded when these facilitators get promoted or leave the job.

Poorly Trained Facilitators

Some people think that anyone can facilitate a workshop. Generally, these people have never seen a workshop. This attitude can sometimes be found in a project manager who wants to implement JAD, but who is disinclined to develop the resources needed to do so properly. Unfortunately, the idea that anyone can be a JAD facilitator results in very weak facilitation and poor project results. If this "anyone can do it" approach is pursued, the JAD technique will never develop the type of support it needs to be successful within the organization.

Unsatisfactory JAD Workshop Deliverable

No JAD project can be considered a success if the required deliverable is not produced as planned. When this occurs, the reason is often improper selection and training of individuals responsible for documentation production. These individuals are an intrinsic part of the team and cannot be asked, as if in an afterthought, to take on the responsibility for this most important task. It is the job of the JAD facilitator to see that deliverable objectives are clearly defined ahead of time, that these objectives are reasonable and attainable given the constraints of the project, and that the individual responsible for producing the deliverable understands what is required.

JAD IMPLEMENTATION CRITICAL SUCCESS FACTORS

The critical success factors required to introduce and maintain a JAD process within the organization fall into four categories:

- JAD project definition
- JAD engineering concepts
- JAD facilitator support
- Commitment to change

JAD Project Definition

No JAD project can be successful without a clear and early definition of the scope of the project and the format and content of the JAD workshop deliverable. This is the most difficult and ambiguous aspect of JAD work. The JAD technique must spell out the deliverable options and identify what is included at various levels of detail for each option. The technique should also distinguish which of the life cycle deliverables are not supported or are only partially supported by the JAD technique and indicate what must be addressed in postworkshop activities to ensure satisfaction of life cycle deliverable requirements. The more definitive the procedures for performing these activities, the more certainty that the JAD technique can be executed with consistency and high quality.

The JAD technique must also define the political climate of the project in order to ensure project success. It must reach beyond the project team for perspectives on the project and its impact on the various user organizations. If this is not done, commitment to the project may be overestimated and there will be surprises in the workshop which could derail the effort.

JAD Engineering Concepts

For JAD to be successful, it must be a fully engineered technique. This implies a high degree of structure, planning, and predictability. A fully engineered JAD process will provide: (1) A clear definition of the difference between preworkshop activities that focus on the data collection required for workshop preparation and planning and the decision making activities that take place inside the workshop environment. (2) A standard set of exercises, both technical and behavioral, from which to construct a workshop agenda to achieve specific workshop objectives. (3) A clear explanation of the options for adapting these exercises to meet different project objectives and to match different organization cultures. (4) Guidance on the use of different group management techniques, including the use of small and large teams, serial and parallel exercises, and distinctions among identification, generation, evaluation, and decision making exercises. (5) Specific directions for constructing each deliverable option using the approved CASE technology before, during and after the workshops, creating or modifying worksheets used by the participants during the workshop, and translating workshop results into the final deliverable. (6) A clear definition of the commitment expected from and responsibilities of the executive sponsor and other JAD participants. While this is not a fully comprehensive list, it should indicate the type of characteristics required in a fully engineered JAD approach.

JAD Facilitator Support

For consistent and high-quality JAD facilitation, JAD facilitators require proper training, an easy to use guidebook on the JAD technique, its rules and options, and the support of the systems organization in the execution of the JAD rules. For example, if a JAD facilitator tells a project manager that he cannot proceed until an executive sponsor from the user side is identified, the JAD facilitator's management should support that decision and not undermine the technique by saying, "Go ahead without a sponsor this time." If in-house JAD facilitators consistently suffer from one weakness over facilitators provided by outside vendors, it is a reluctance to enforce critical JAD rules when they run counter to organization culture or a project manager's prejudices or priorities. Vocal and action-oriented support for facilitators in the planning and preparation of JAD workshops is critical to successful implementation and long-term effectiveness of the technique.

Commitment to Change

Organizations committed to implementing JAD and improving the management of their information resources must take on the challenge of managing political and cultural change. The first commitment they must make is the development of a core of trained facilitators who can support each other and who are consistently supported by top management in their efforts to enforce the JAD technique rule set. The development of this group should not require an increase in the head count of the organization. It does, however, require a realignment of resources. Specially developed job titles and job descriptions are required for both JAD facilitators and JAD/CASE specialists. In addition, a JAD manager with a job title and definition of responsibilities must be appointed. Effort and patience must be given to helping people understand that a new approach to project work is being created and that the realignment does not mean there are fewer people for projects, but that project team member roles will be defined differently in the new systems environment.

The support for JAD should also be expressed through the recommendation of the technique in the organization's life cycle documentation and its adoption as the standard that all projects use unless an exception can be justified. While JAD can be adopted initially in an experimental mode, a full commitment to the JAD process requires more than the use of JAD as a sometime alternative. It requires that it become a part of the way business is done by the systems organization.

QUESTIONS FREQUENTLY ASKED ABOUT JAD

For the past five years, large organizations have been turning to JAD to assist in the definition of user requirements and logical application design. These early successful users are now expanding their JAD requirements definition services to business area data and process analysis and other high-level systems planning work. Their questions will provide insight into some of the implementation issues surrounding the JAD technique.

1. How do I know if my organization is ready for JAD?

    An organization is ready for JAD when its backlog of application enhancement requests is out of control. It is ready when users are starting to distrust each other as much as they distrust the systems organization. It is ready when the recognition surfaces that multiple overlapping and poorly maintained databases are not adequate to support the organization's competitive position in the marketplace.

2. Will users commit to the JAD approach? Will the systems organization?

    The main issue is not user buy-in, but rather systems buy-in. It is generally easy to convince users to give JAD a try. After all, JAD provides them with an opportunity to participate directly in a process from which many have been excluded in the past. Users consistently react positively to JAD, are willing to experiment with it, and are pleased with the results. The systems organization, on the other hand, may not be so enthusiastic. Trying to sell CASE tools to the systems organization is easy. With their split screens and blinking lights, these tools have the built-in advantage of resembling video games. JAD does not have this advantage. JAD is a business process, a way of working, and its benefits cannot be proven in an hour's demo by a flashy salesperson. Rather, the case for JAD must be built carefully, with reference to the unique needs and character of the organization. Special selling skills and innovative strategies are required here.

One useful strategy is the pilot project. A pilot project can demonstrate the power of JAD in a real world situation. If it is well chosen, the pilot project can also demonstrate JAD's impact on the life cycle practices and methodology principles adhered to by the organization. Clearly, the greater the span of influence of the project, the more substantial the reward. But choosing a pilot project involves a daring balancing act, balancing the risk of failure on one hand and the chance for a very public, high impact success on the other. This is a winning strategy, but one which must be implemented carefully.

3. Can JAD be used for all types of projects successfully?

While JAD can be applied successfully to a wide range of projects, not all projects are good candidates for the technique. An appropriate project will exhibit at least some of the following characteristics:

- The project will impact multiple groups of business users whose responsibilities cross traditional department or division boundaries.
- Users play different roles and are at different levels within their organizations.
- Project team members have differing business and/or project priorities.
- Users have different information needs.
- The project under consideration is a first for the organization.
- There are political or policy issues that will impact the success of the project effort.
- The project has time and budget constraints.
- The history of the project or the relationship between the systems organization and user organizations has been troubled.
- The project is critical to the future success of the organization.
- User acceptance and/or commitment may be a problem for the project.
- The reputation of the systems organization is at stake.
- There is a risk of failure if a traditional interview approach is used.
- The benefits of the project are unclear to some of the users.
- The business goals and objectives supporting the project are not clear to some users and/or systems professionals.

4. What is the best way to manage participant expectations?

Most pilot JAD workshops result in tremendous user enthusiasm and, sometimes, an unrealistic expectation for project completion. This can be particularly difficult if the project is a logical application design and the users expect to see an up and running system almost at once. Unreasonable expectations can be avoided, however, by insisting that workshop participants jointly prepare a careful, detailed definition of next step activities for the project. This definition should include a list of tasks, reasonable completion dates, and an identification of responsibilities. It should be presented in written form as part of the JAD workshop deliverable.

It is also important for JAD facilitators to be reasonable in the expectations they encourage in the course of selling the JAD process to the organization or project group. Too often new facilitators overestimate how much problem solving and decision making can be accomplished in one workshop. Most projects in today's complex business and systems environment require multiple workshops and a strict attention to integration with other information management activities being conducted by the organization. Within a workshop, even a single apparently simple point of conflict may require extensive discussion and negotiation before everyone present is prepared to live with the result. Controlling expectations is an important task for the JAD facilitator because even a successful workshop can look like a failure if too many unfulfilled promises are made.

5. How should the JAD facilitator interact with the project manager?

Sometimes a project manager sees the JAD facilitator as a threat to his authority. Ignoring the benefits of speed and quality produced by the JAD process and misinterpreting the supportive role played by the facilitator, the project manager sees his position being undermined. The resulting behavior exhibited by such an individual may range from aggressively trying to dictate the conduct of all JAD activities to passively resisting all requests to carry through on his JAD responsibilities. This type of situation can spell failure for a project. If it is to be avoided, the JAD facilitator must convince the project manager to support the process and to allow the facilitator his own area of authority and responsibility within it. The successful facilitator will need strong marketing strategies, questioning techniques, and negotiation skills in attempting to overcome the project manager's objections.

6. How do you know if your JAD project is in trouble?

Sometimes, especially if the JAD technique does not have the discipline and rigor of a fully implemented technique, warning signs appear that should tell the JAD facilitator to step back and take a second look before proceeding to a workshop. If too many of these warning signals appear, the JAD facilitator should stop the process or call a meeting with the project manager and executive sponsor to resolve the problems indicated. Such problems may include the following:

- Users can define detailed methods and procedures, but cannot talk about business functions or distinguish detailed tasks from concepts.
- Participants for workshops keep changing or are selected at the last minute so that they are not educated about the project or JAD process and have no time to prepare.
- Selected participants are at the wrong level within the organization and, as a result, do not have the knowledge or authority needed to make sound decisions.

- Dates for preworkshop activities are constantly reshuffled or are unrealistic. This indicates a lack of commitment on the part of either the project manager or executive sponsor or both.
- There is difficulty in defining or getting approval for project scope boundaries, objectives, users or business functions to be supported. This indicates the organization is not as yet politically committed to the project.
- A substantial number of individuals connected with the project have hidden agendas. This can undermine the entire JAD effort. For example, in one company a JAD leader was not told who the actual users of the proposed application were. The project manager selected the users secretly and refused JAD facilitator input. The workshop was canceled in mid-stream when the selected participants rebelled, denied their status as users, and identified an entirely different group of "real" users for the application.

7. How do I estimate the amount of effort required for a proposed JAD project?

Estimating the amount of effort required for a specific JAD project is important for all concerned. The first place to look in preparing an estimate is at the number of workshop days. Generally, the longer the workshop (or workshops), the more complex the project, and the more time that will be required for both pre- and postworkshop activities. As a general guideline, consider that a project that will result in one three to four-day workshop will require a total of about twelve days of effort from the JAD facilitator and approximately eighteen days of effort from the JAD/CASE specialist.

Each JAD approach will have its own rule of thumb for arriving at an estimate, and each will vary in the amount of time specified for different JAD activities. For this reason, predicting the level of effort is difficult without knowing the precise JAD process structure. However, these statements are true for most JAD approaches:

- Preworkshop activities do not need to be repeated for every workshop in a series.
- For every day spent in the workshop, one to one and one-half days of effort will be required following the workshop to complete the JAD workshop deliverable.
- In a multiple workshop series, for every two workshops of three to five days each, there will be a need for an additional two days of integration work.

THE IMPACT OF JAD ON THE SYSTEMS ORGANIZATION

The successful implementation of a JAD technique can provide an enormous boost in energy and vitality to the systems organization. The belief that things are changing for the better, the perception that the level of stress has been reduced, and the feeling that good products will result from the effort expended can energize an organization like nothing else. In addition to the establishment of a common language and a commitment to shared decision making, benefits already discussed in detail, the implementation of JAD can result in the following.

New Career Paths for Systems Analysts

Systems analysts gain a new path for professional growth. Experienced JAD leaders are highly valued for their facilitation skills, their ability to negotiate agreements and their knowledge of the business, the people and the organization's system life cycle and methodology. Because of their broad experience, JAD facilitators make excellent candidates for management positions. It is not unusual for experienced facilitators to find they have gained new opportunities for growth within the organization. This means losing some excellent facilitators, of course, but training will replace them, and facilitation's loss is the organization's gain.

Quick Productivity Gains

Because JAD depends on the skill and expertise of the facilitator and JAD/ CASE specialist and does not require all project participants to be JAD experts, it can be introduced into an organization very quickly. If participants are willing to commit to the process and follow the lead of the JAD facilitator, project teams can achieve the productivity benefits of JAD in a short period of time. If reasonable schedules can be set for workshops, the time required for a logical design effort that would have taken two months can be reduced by twenty percent and one that would have taken six months by forty percent. The larger the project, the greater the opportunity for productivity increases.

Consensus Model for Decision Making

The use of the consensus based decision making model offered by JAD can have an important impact on the organization. In its demonstration of the value of compromise and negotiation in working out conflicts between individuals and organization groups, it can suggest a model for problem resolution in other situations. JAD participants quickly become advocates of this problem solving model and apply it to situations where conflicts might otherwise seriously undermine the effectiveness of the organization.

Enhanced Project Management Skills

The rigor and discipline of the JAD technique greatly enhance the pace, decision making and momentum of projects. By employing the JAD process, the project manager finds objectives being met on time and without an atmosphere of crisis. Users are no longer combatants in a clash over differing priorities and petty politics. Project team members know their responsibilities and understand what is expected of them. In such an environment, the project manager can focus on the essentials of project success: providing the best solution possible within the constraints of the project and building commitment to support that solution. As a result of the project management model established by the JAD experience, the project manager should feel more comfortable and productive in working both with users and with the project team.

Enhanced Meeting Management Skills

As more systems professionals become exposed to the JAD technique either through workshop participation or training, project teams will start to adopt some of the basic JAD facilitation principles in their other group activities. Organizations that previously held frustrating, nonproductive meetings will be seen to emphasize the use of structured agendas, rules for operation, and open issues listing when even a few individuals gather together. A new professionalism about group responsibility will emerge, as will a willingness to compromise in order to achieve the benefits of consensus.

Enhanced Selling Skills

In addition to transferring project management and meeting management skills into the organization, JAD can provide an infusion of selling skills. Few technically trained individuals also receive education in the fine art of promoting ideas. This is unfortunate because good technical concepts and plans need a constituency just as surely as political proposals. Because it emphasizes the importance of convincing individuals to adopt a new way of doing business and a new set of assumptions about their business, JAD can effectively introduce the art of selling ideas to a community that may have few skills in this area.

Business Focus

JAD workshops quickly reveal that the most difficult issues to resolve in a systems project are business issues, not technical issues. Although these issues can sometimes be traced to the lack of understanding between the systems and user communities, they quite often arise from misunderstandings among different user groups. These issues may be serious enough to impact project success when they involve such concepts as:

- Business policies and practices.
- Organization structure and accountabilities.
- Long-range goals and strategies.
- Overlapping activities and redundancy of work groups.
- The quality of management and supervision.
- External forces over which people have little or no control.

- Discrepancies between strategies promoted by business executives and those advocated by middle management.

JAD provides an excellent model for addressing these issues. Through its team-based approach and emphasis on consensus building, JAD offers the organization a vehicle for both identifying and resolving the business issues that can undermine project success.

3

The Technique Dimension: Joint Application Development Facilitation Techniques

FACILITATING THE JAD PROCESS

The structure of the JAD process is defined by a series of steps that can be grouped together in three phases: preworkshop, workshop, and postworkshop. Each of these phases has specific technical and behavioral objectives. For the JAD facilitator to be successful, he has to take into account both the behavioral and technical aspects of the process. This can be seen most clearly in the workshop phase. The workshop agenda specifies the technical objectives of this phase through the identification of the specific exercises that the participants will complete. In order to select and order these exercises, the facilitator considers the methodology principles that the organization supports. In the FUSION approach, for example, we turn to the diagrams generally used to support information engineering concepts to provide guidance in the selection of exercises. Depending on the nature of the project, these exercises might support the development of matrices, dependency diagrams, an entity relationship diagram, or other information display format. Organizations more comfortable with a structured analysis approach might select other diagrams.

Also important in selecting a set of technical exercises is the purpose of the project. The agenda constructed to build a corporate-level data model will undoubtedly differ from that constructed to build a logical application design. Other factors that may influence the selection of exercises may be the amount of workshop time available and the level of sophistication of participants. Even the use or nonuse of a CASE tool can impact selection. The facilitator will have done a good job of satisfying the technical objectives of the workshop phase if the exercises chosen result in a comprehensive design that meets the deliverable requirements identified in preworkshop activities. The behavioral objectives of the workshop phase are generally not specifically represented in the agenda, however. The reason for this is that while technical objectives may vary greatly from workshop to workshop, behavioral objectives are quite consistent across all JAD workshops. All JAD workshops seek to create consensus, build commitment, and build communication bridges. These behavioral objectives are critical to the success of the JAD process.

What is typical of the workshop phase is also true of the pre and postworkshop phases. While the technical content of these phases may vary considerably because of methodology and project purpose, the behavioral objectives and content of these phases is remarkably consistent. For this reason, we have chosen to present in this chapter a set of JAD facilitation techniques that can be used to support the behavioral objectives of the JAD process no matter what the technical objectives of the project may be. These facilitation techniques are grouped in categories, with each category representing a specific behavioral objective. These categories are:

- Building commitment.
- Structuring the process.
- Creating a common understanding.
- Changing the tone of the workshop.
- Generating ideas without judgment.
- Analyzing and evaluating ideas.
- Supporting decision making.
- Managing participant interaction.

TECHNIQUE FORMAT

A standard format is used to define the key JAD facilitation techniques presented. First, a case study is presented to illustrate the need for a specific facilitation technique. Then a description of the technique is presented. That description includes:

> **Technique Name:** A short name that can be used to uniquely identify the technique.
>
> **Technique Purpose:** Objective(s) to be achieved through use of the technique.

Technique Advantages: Benefits to be gained through use of the technique.

Technique Timing: Information on when to use the technique.

Technique Preparation: Information on how to set the stage for use of the technique.

Technique Instructions: Step-by-step instructions for executing the technique.

Each of the techniques presented here has been tested and used many times and in many different circumstances. Many have uses outside of the JAD environment as well as within it, but the emphasis here is on their use in JAD facilitation. Both new and experienced JAD facilitators may benefit from adopting their use. While these techniques are presented for the facilitator, others involved in the JAD process, particularly the project manager, may find them useful as well.

BUILDING COMMITMENT

Without the commitment of the executive sponsor, the project manager and key participants in the JAD process, the JAD facilitator will find it difficult to manage the process and produce a successful result. Difficulties in building commitment can arise from many sources. The history of the project, the culture of the organization, the behavior of the project manager, and the relationship between the systems and user communities are all potential sources of commitment problems.

The key to creating a commitment building climate is to get the people who need to make the commitment excited about the potential of JAD. Always respond enthusiastically to their positive statements. Vary your style of presentation to keep people interested, but always try to speak the language of your audience. Try to avoid outright manipulation of the participant group. This can have quite the opposite effect of the one you are trying to achieve.

The Case of the Timid Project Manager

The project had quite a history. Over a period of five years, three attempts had been made to develop a design for a customer information system for a unit of a large bank. Each time, however, disagreements over requirements and the politics of the organization had prevented the systems organization from making any progress. In a fourth try, Sam, the JAD facilitator, was attempting to help Jim, the most recent project manager for the project. Jim had been a project manager for over fifteen years. A nervous person, he did not wish to make political waves, but he did want to succeed. When it was suggested that the JAD technique might help him, he welcomed Sam, hoping that the six different user groups could be brought to agreement.

Preworkshop activities went well. A clear scope was defined, key players identified, and workshop facilities obtained. Only one problem remained for Sam. He had been denied access to the executive sponsor by the project manager. Jim believed that the executive sponsor, an executive vice president, was too busy to be bothered. He told Sam he could give him all the information and assistance necessary. Sam was uneasy about the situation, but he agreed to go along with the plan. He did, however, secure a promise that the executive vice president would speak at a preworkshop participant education meeting. He wondered, with good cause, if the lack of commitment on the part of the executive vice president had been a major factor in the failure of the project in the past.

A combined project kick-off and JAD education meeting was to start at 9:00 AM on Friday, but only eight of the eighteen participants had shown up for the meeting by 9:20. The executive vice president was not there either. Sam turned to Jim and asked, "Where is everyone?" Jim replied, "I don't know. You better get started anyway." Sam knew they were headed for trouble. He knew he had made a mistake in not insisting on a meeting with the executive vice president and knew also that he had only one chance left to avoid failure in the workshop. He decided to act. When Jim turned the meeting over to Sam, he stood up and instead of the usual "nice to see everyone" speech said to the group, "This project is in serious trouble. Fewer than half of the participants invited are here this morning, and the executive vice president has not been able to join us. Neither has he been available for a meeting to prepare for the project. Therefore, I am recommending to Jim and the rest of you that we do not hold the workshop until the proper commitments are in place. I don't want to waste the time of those of you who have agreed to participate." The room was silent.

The group was clearly startled. Jim was shaking. After Sam made his statement, he kept quiet, waiting for someone to speak. Finally, one of the participants, George, said, "What do you need to hold this workshop? Those of us here today really need this system." Sam replied, "I need the people on this list to be committed to a five-day workshop. They need to show up for all scheduled activities and contribute their best efforts. I also need someone to act as executive sponsor, to take the responsibility for making that happen." George looked to the colleagues on his left and right, huddled with them for two minutes, and then turned to Sam and Jim. "We three will be your executive sponsor team," he said. "The executive vice president is our boss, and we will see that he agrees to allow us to represent him. Give me your participant list. We will be there on Monday and so will everyone else. We promise." Sam replied, "My job is to make sure that this project succeeds this time. It will if we have commitment. I accept your commitment. You, gentlemen, are the three musketeers who will make this project a success."

Seven months later, the first phase of the bank's customer information system was installed in 230 branches. Commitment made the difference.

Sam took quite a chance in letting the process go forward without the demonstrated support of the executive sponsor. If he had demonstrated better commitment building skills, he would not have found himself in the position of taking a last ditch stand. Without commitment, this project was just an accident waiting to happen. Use the following techniques to handle this and other commitment problems.

Technique Name:	**CREATING A BAND WAGON**
Technique Purpose:	**BUILDING COMMITMENT**
Technique Advantages:	Provides a foundation of commitment on which to build. Makes participants feel that they are a part of something important and exciting.
Technique Timing:	Sometime during preworkshop activities.
Technique Preparation:	Identify two or three key individuals who are willing to lend their credibility to the JAD process and the project. It is not vital that these individuals be directly involved in the project, but it is important that they be respected and liked throughout the organization.

Technique Instructions:

1. Ask these individuals to demonstrate their interest in the process and project by appearing at JAD education sessions or project orientation meetings, even if only in an observer status. Make sure that their presence is noted by prospective project participants.
2. Ask these individuals to lobby other key individuals who are important to the success of the project.
3. Publicly document the support of these key individuals and others as they sign on to the project. This can be done in writing through a memo or corporate newsletter or verbally through an announcement at an appropriate meeting.

Technique Name:	**TEAM COLORS**
Technique Purpose:	**BUILDING COMMITMENT**
Technique Advantages:	Rewards people for their participation and reinforces their sense of group identity.
Technique Timing:	Often used at the beginning of a workshop. Can also be used in connection with a preworkshop or postworkshop activity.
Technique Preparation:	With the consent of the project manager, select and order hats, t-shirts or other appropriate items with a customized logo. The same color can be ordered for the whole group, or to encourage subteam identification, a unique color

for each subteam may be ordered. The back of the shirt or hat may carry a project slogan or project name.

Arrange for someone to take pictures of the group with their team colors displayed.

Technique Instructions:

1. With the assistance of the project manager and/or executive sponsor, distribute the team colors to participants and discuss the importance of commitment to the success of the project.

2. Pictures of the team may be taken at the end of the workshop or at the conclusion of a significant postworkshop activity. Post them in work areas and send a copy to each participant with a thank you note from the executive sponsor and project manager.

Technique Name:	**ASKING QUESTIONS**
Technique Purpose:	**BUILDING COMMITMENT**
Technique Advantages:	To gain and maintain control of discussions. To get participants to make the small commitments that will eventually lead to larger ones. To give participants a sense of involvement in making decisions. To bring an issue to closure.
Technique Timing:	Often used during preworkshop activities. May be used whenever you want to get buy-in from a project participant.
Technique Preparation:	Make these questioning techniques a part of your communication pattern. Avoid relying on one questioning technique exclusively. This can make the conversation appear forced or pressured. For additional questioning techniques, consult Tom Hopkins's book, *How to Master the Art of Selling*.

Technique Instructions:

1. Tie Down Questions
   The purpose of this technique is to get a respondent to say "yes." A "tie down" is a set of words, which when added to a statement, turn it into a question. Tie down words are words such as "aren't they," "isn't it," "hasn't it," "wouldn't it," and "shouldn't it." The tie down helps to establish a common ground for discussion. Examples include:

- "Meeting that difficult deadline would really make the project team look good, wouldn't it?"
- "There has been a great deal of change here in the last year, hasn't there?"
- "After we understand the issues better, won't you have more ammunition to get additional resources?"

If someone responds with "no" instead of "yes," don't feel stumped. Ask a "what" question such as, "Well, then, what will enable you to get additional resources?"

2. **Alternate Advance Questions**

   The purpose of the "alternate advance" is to suggest two answers, both of which confirm a commitment. Examples include:
   - "We'll start off with a team meeting to define the scope of the project. Would you like to meet on Tuesday morning or Wednesday at noon?"
   - "Which would be better, a four-day or a five-day workshop session?"

   If, in the first example, the individual responds by saying that neither of those days is good, then offer two other alternatives or ask for a date within a set limit. Suggest selecting a date that falls within the next ten days. If, in the second example, the individual responds by saying that even four days is too much, then offer another alternative. Depending on what is appropriate in the situation, you may want to offer two sessions, perhaps one of three and one of two days. In this way, you can be responsive without compromising on a key issue and losing control.

3. **Porcupine Questions**

   The purpose of this type of question is to confirm the commitment implied by an individual's statement. Examples include:
   - A participant asks, "Will the workshop produce a complete logical design?" Respond, "Is a complete logical design important to you?" If the response is "no," then ask a "what" question to uncover the participant's real need. If the response is "yes," then proceed with the requirements for getting that logical design delivered. Say, "The workshop will deliver a complete logical design if we have two four-day sessions.
   - A participant asks, "Can we start next week?" Say, "If we start next week, will all of the assigned users be available?" If the response is "yes," then proceed with defining workshop logistics. If the response is "no," then ask a "what" question such as, "What is critical about starting next week?"

4. **Involvement Questions**

   This type of question helps the individual to focus on both the benefits of the JAD process and his own responsibility for contributing to its success. Examples include:
   - "Paul, after the JAD workshops, will the team developing the application be using a code generation tool or a fourth generation language?"
   - "Margaret, after the business area analysis is completed, will your staff

begin to restructure the operation immediately, or will you wait until after the first of the year?''

- "Mr. Johnson, after we get the agreements from the marketing and accounting people, what is your next step in the development process?''

5. Leading Questions

These questions move participants past immediate objections and get them to make a commitment. Examples include:

- "If the requirement for three days of workshop time were not an issue, whom would you invite to the workshop?''
- "Let's suppose we could find the budget. Then what would be your highest priorities for the workshop?''
- "If people from Accounts Receivable were made available, who would be good participants?''

Once an understanding with the participant group has been reached on a key issue, it is important to finalize or confirm that commitment. To confirm a commitment, follow these guidelines.

- When people appear ready to make a good decision, review their key needs and the way in which the JAD process meets these needs.
- Ask for the order as if you were a salesman. Use a statement such as, "Then, since JAD meets your requirements, would you like to start the project on Monday or Tuesday of next week?'' Use one or more of the questioning techniques previously listed. Once you have the order, make a closing statement. Don't manipulate or intimidate the group, but do be firm and specific. Don't be afraid to sound authoritative or to let your confidence in the process show.
- Don't talk. Use the pregnant pause. Wait until the someone in the group speaks first. If he says, "yes,'' then move ahead. If he rejects the idea or plan, bridge the situation with an apology and another leading question. For example, "I must have been caught up in the excitement of the project. Let's step back for a moment. What other information do you need to make a decision?'' or "What are the critical criteria needed to make a decision today?''

Technique Name:	**OVERCOMING OBJECTIONS**
Technique Purpose:	**BUILDING COMMITMENT**
Technique Advantages:	Diffuses hostility and defensiveness found in difficult participants.
	Dissipates aggression of participants who object to the process, project, or personalities involved.
Technique Timing:	Often used during preworkshop activities to win over participants and build commitment. Used during and after the workshop as necessary.

| Technique Preparation: | You must be familiar with the basic questioning techniques, history of the project, and politics of the environment. It can be helpful to understand the source of the participant's unhappiness. |
| Technique Instructions: | |

1. Even when directly challenged, never argue. Never attack the person who issues the challenge. Do not take a challenge as a personal affront. Ignore the style in which the objection is presented and consider it a request, however awkwardly stated, for more information.

2. Never get defensive, and don't be too quick to respond to the objection. Delay your response by taking a breath and asking for more information. Ask for examples or details to get the individual to let all of his dissatisfaction surface.

3. Restate an objection in a neutral way to make sure you understand it. You might respond, for example: "So what you're saying is that you are very concerned about having people away from the job for more than two days?"

4. After restating an objection, you can answer it in a number of ways: by defining the benefits delivered, by showing how any negative impacts can be minimized, by providing additional information, and by clarifying a previous statement.

5. If an objection focuses on a very small point, highlight one or two key benefits that dwarf the minor objection. You might respond, for example: "Remember that even though two of your key people will be out of the office for four days, the result will be a savings of twenty percent of direct project costs and the creation of a logical design for your application in four weeks."

6. Sometimes objections are more indirect. A project manager or executive sponsor might put you off by saying, "We'll get back to you," or "We'll think about it." This can stop a project as surely as a more directly stated objection. You can respond by mentioning again the benefits of the project and then asking directly why it is necessary to wait until further action is taken. You might say, for example, "If JAD meets your critical need for involving the key players in the organization and can deliver results before the end of the year, then what is your concern about moving ahead with the project?" Then work to overcome the objection.

7. When people object because they are reluctant to try something new, ask questions to help them focus on the results they will get and not the procedures to be used. Ask, for example: "If I can show you how we can make the situation comfortable for everyone, then would you be willing to proceed?"

8. Always confirm that you have answered an objection by asking, "Does that answer your question?" Then go on to the next topic. Do not dwell on the objection.

Technique Name: **OVERCOMING INTIMIDATING PERSONALITIES**

Technique Purpose: **BUILDING COMMITMENT**

Technique Advantages: Enables you to turn individuals who are detractors into supporters. Some people attempt to manipulate a situation by intimidating others. These individuals are often very vocal, but sometimes they offer a more subtle attack. It isn't wise to discount their support immediately. Sometimes they end up as JAD's biggest advocates.

Technique Timing: Often used during preworkshop activities. Can also be used at other times during and after workshops.

Technique Preparation: You must be familiar with the basic questioning techniques, history of the project, and politics of the environment. It can also be helpful to understand the source of the participant's need to dominate the situation.

Technique Instructions:

1. Look directly at the individual who is attempting to intimidate you or the group. Find out what motivates the person with questions like: "What really makes the difference to you?" or "What are your priorities?"

2. Use questioning techniques to create small agreements. Say, for example: "Then, what you're saying is that the JAD process must not take more than six weeks, and that your staff can contribute to the process, although not on a full time basis? Is that right?"

3. Focus on substance. Don't let yourself be distracted by ad hominem arguments.

4. Show a positive attitude through your body language and the expression on your face, but don't be afraid to be direct in what you say. Never play one-ups-man-ship, get defensive, or embarrass the intimidator.

Technique Name: **OVERCOMING UNSPOKEN OBJECTIONS**

Technique Purpose: **BUILDING COMMITMENT**

Technique Advantages: Enables you to handle the behind the scenes objections that can undermine participant commitment.

Technique Timing:	Often used during preworkshop activities. Can also be used at other times during and after workshops.
Technique Preparation:	You must be familiar with the basic questioning techniques, history of the project, and politics of the environment. It can also be helpful to understand the motivation of the individual(s) involved.
Technique Instructions:	

1. Directly contact the person who is making negative statements. Do not attack the individual. Begin the conversation by telling him what you have heard and asking for more information. Say, for example: "Joe, I hear that you are upset about what happened in last week's workshop. Please tell me what concerns you."

2. Hear the individual out, even if you have taken steps to correct the condition or situation that is mentioned. Then explain what you have done.

3. Ask if the person has any other ideas for action about this or another relevant issue. If he presents a legitimate concern that you have not yet addressed, ask: "If you were in my shoes, what would you do to correct the situation?" Listen and thank him for his ideas. Then reassure him that you will act to correct the situation and will let him know what you have done.

Technique Name:	**FOLLOW-UP**
Technique Purpose:	**BUILDING COMMITMENT**
Technique Advantages:	Assists in building strong relationships with the project manager and participants. Reinforces commitment to the project schedule and to the responsibilities assigned to all participants.
Technique Timing:	Should be used throughout the JAD process.
Technique Preparation:	None.
Technique Instructions:	

1. Contact all individuals involved in the JAD process on a regular basis. Do not wait for them to call you.

2. Find out what is happening within the organization that may impact the project. Volunteer help or moral support if either is appropriate.

3. Share information with others. Do not be just a question asker.

4. Show interest in the individuals involved in the project. Provide assistance in solving some problem if appropriate.

STRUCTURING THE PROCESS

While the JAD process is a highly interactive one, it can never be permitted to become a free-for-all. The JAD facilitator must maintain firm control at all times over the direction of the discussion in order to ensure that the specific objectives of the project are achieved. He does not, however, want to control the outcome of any particular point of dispute. This is an important distinction. While the facilitator must be the master of the process, the participants are the masters of the final product. This can require quite a balancing act on the part of the facilitator. In order to perform it effectively, he needs specific objective techniques for maintaining control.

The techniques described in this section are designed to enable the facilitator to assert authority over the process without diminishing the decision-making power of the participants or diluting their responsibility for the final outcome.

The Case of the Uncontrolled Observer

Janice Jones, a JAD facilitator, was in the morning of the third day of a four-day pilot JAD workshop for an insurance company. The eighteen participants included midlevel managers representing claims, marketing, underwriting, and finance. Each of these individuals had at least ten years of experience in the business. The previous days had gone very well, and the word was out in the organization that something special was happening on the JAD project. For the first time, several observers joined the group. One of these, Ed Jamison, the vice president of marketing, arrived twenty minutes after the session had started and insisted on greeting everyone by name when he entered the room. Janice stopped the discussion briefly, and then continued a data modeling exercise begun the previous day. A strong data model had been built, including identification of required data entities. Some of the most difficult definitions, however, had not yet been obtained. Janice started the day's work by asking for a definition of the key entity, "customer." One of the participants, Mary, who was an underwriter, volunteered. However, before she was halfway through with her explanation, she was interrupted by Ed. "Now the problem with that definition, Mary," he said, "is that it would put this company out of business. We've got to deal with people as individuals. You're making them statistics." Janice's suspicions were confirmed. Ed was not going to be a quiet observer.

Attempting to regain control, she said, "We appreciate your input, Ed, but please remember that observers are not participants, and I'll have to ask you to defer any comments until we take a break." "Well, if you want to waste a lot of time going off in the wrong direction, it's all right with me," Ed replied, and he got up and left the room. Janice turned back to Mary to ask her to continue, but she, like the others, was clearly very uncomfortable about saying anything.

This type of problem can quickly turn a positive workshop experience into a negative one. Use the following techniques to avoid these problems by establishing group rules and norms.

Technique Name:	**RULES FOR OPERATION FOR PARTICIPANTS**
Technique Purpose:	**STRUCTURING THE PROCESS**
Technique Advantages:	Allows the group to establish its own guidelines for operation. Gives the facilitator control of the group and ensures that proper gate keeping procedures are established and accepted.
Technique Timing:	May be used at the beginning of any group meeting. Particularly useful in workshops.
Technique Preparation:	First establish credibility at the beginning of the meeting or workshop. Progress made at a previous activity may be reviewed or the agenda for this activity previewed. Ensure that easel board paper and markers (or other documentation tools) are available.

Technique Instructions:

1. Ask participants to provide a few guidelines to control interaction and communication within the workshop. Ask them to focus on what makes some meetings succeed and others fail.

2. Offer suggestions if the group has trouble getting started. One suggestion might be a rule mandating that only one person speak at a time. Ask the group if this is a rule they can accept.

3. As each rule is identified and accepted by the participants, board the rule. The minimum rules which you will need to manage the group include:
   - Only one person may speak at a time.
   - Everyone has an equal voice in making decisions.
   - Stick to the facts. Be specific. Give examples.
   - Five minute limit to the discussion of any one point.

   You may also want to include rules about permissible times and places for smoking or about the importance of keeping to starting times, or the need for a sense of humor.

4. Post the list and keep it in a prominent place throughout the meeting or workshop.

Technique Name:	**RULES FOR OPERATION FOR OBSERVERS**
Technique Purpose:	**STRUCTURING THE PROCESS**

Technique Advantages:	Provides a standard for managing observers within a meeting or workshop environment. Ensures that observers understand what is expected of them.
Technique Timing:	May be used at the beginning of any group meeting. Particularly useful in workshops.
Technique Preparation:	Before the meeting or workshop, write a list of rules for observers. Provide these ahead of time to those who identify themselves as potential observers. Distribute copies of the list to observers or place copies where observers will see them when they enter the room. Participants should also be familiar with the role played by observers.
Technique Instructions:	

1. Ensure that each observer has a copy of the rules. If you are aware of individuals who will want to observe a session, provide them with a copy a day or two before the session. If necessary, discuss the rules with observers and/or participants. The minimum rules needed to control observer behavior include:
   - Observers may not talk with each other or to participants while the group is in session.
   - Observers may not enter or leave the room if this will disturb participants.
   - If an observer wishes to make a point, he must wait until a break and then speak first to the JAD facilitator.
   - Only the JAD facilitator may give an observer permission to violate one of these rules.

2. If a new observer enters the session, ensure that he also has a copy of the rules and understands them. Make certain that observers arrive at the beginning of the day or during a break so that you can discuss the rules with them.

Technique Name:	**TARGET MEETING AGENDA CONSTRUCTION**
Technique Purpose:	**STRUCTURING THE PROCESS**
Technique Advantages:	Ensures focus and objectives of meeting will be clear. Increases participant productivity.
Technique Timing:	Prior to any JAD target meeting.
Technique Preparation:	Identification of need for meeting and background research to educate the JAD facilita-

tor. Often the JAD facilitator will work with the project manager to design the meeting agenda.

Technique Instructions:

1. Define the purpose of the meeting. A target meeting may be designed to support:
   - Data collection: to gather facts, opinions, perspectives and ideas.
   - Presentation: to disseminate information, to educate and to share ideas.
   - Problem solving: to solve problems, resolve issues, make decisions, generate ideas, or develop plans.

2. Define the deliverable (if any) that will result from the target meeting. This may include:
   - Questions to be answered.
   - Decisions to be made.
   - Plans to be developed.

   If the deliverable is a formal document, the content, format, and level of detail expected in the document should be defined as well. An informal document (e.g., notes taken during the meeting) may be presented instead if this is clearly spelled out ahead of time.

3. Identify the most appropriate people to attend the meeting. Define participant roles for the meeting. Determine the most appropriate timing for the meeting and for inviting people. A mechanism for inviting them and ensuring their attendance should also be developed. Meeting size will vary with the purpose of the meeting, the facilities available and the nature of the issue addressed. Too large a number of participants can inhibit information gathering and problem solving meetings. Presentation meetings can easily be larger.

4. Identify the logical flow of the meeting needed to accomplish the objectives and produce the deliverables. Identify the activities and the sequence of those activities. Be sure to include activities for getting the meeting started, breaking every one and one-half to two hours, and closing the meeting.

5. For each activity, define the exercise(s) to be used. Vary exercises from activity to activity to ensure participant involvement and momentum. Define the timing for the meeting given activities and exercises. Adjust them as needed to fit within the target meeting start and end times.

6. Construct an agenda for distribution to participants. It is better not to include detailed comments on timing or techniques. It is important to include subject areas/topics to be covered.

7. Construct a detailed agenda for your own use so that you can effectively manage the timing of all activities. Construct or obtain the materials needed (e.g., handouts, room displays and forms).

8. Arrange for a pleasant and appropriate meeting room. Provide refreshments as appropriate. Allow adequate room for movement. Check seating, equipment needed, ventilation and temperature.

9. If a specific individual will be responsible for taking notes and/or collecting forms, prepare this person for his responsibilities.

10. Start the meeting on time and end it on time. Use facilitation and questioning skills to keep the meeting on track.

Technique Name:	**FOCUS GROUP INTERVIEW CONSTRUCTION**
Technique Purpose:	**STRUCTURING THE PROCESS**
Technique Advantages:	Ensures consistent and thorough data collection to support JAD preworkshop activities.
Technique Timing:	Prior to any JAD focus group meeting.
Technique Preparation:	Identification of questions to be asked. Often the JAD facilitator will work with the project manager to define questions and conduct the meeting.
Technique Instructions:	

1. Construct ten to twelve open ended questions (e.g., "What on-going activities in your organization may impact this project?") that will be asked in each focus group interview. Write these down for quick reference during the focus group interview.

2. Prepare an introduction for the project manager to use to open the interview. Prepare some opening remarks for yourself.

3. Identify the focus groups to be interviewed. The number of groups will depend on the size and complexity of the project. Identify four to six people for each group. A group should consist of people who do the same type of work and are at the same level within the organization. Generally, subordinates and supervisors should not be in the same group. Issue invitations mentioning the purpose of the meeting and confirm attendance. Do not provide questions ahead of time.

4. Arrange for interview facilities in the territory of the focus group participants. Find a room that is large, pleasant, and free from distractions.

5. Schedule the interviews to last one to two hours depending on the depth of responses required and the number of people attending each interview. Provide sufficient time (thirty to forty-five minutes) between interviews. Do not attempt more than three to four interviews per day.

6. Prepare the project manager before the interviews for his role as an observer. Assure him that he will have time before the end of the interview to ask questions if necessary.

7. Prepare the JAD/CASE specialist to take notes during the interviews. It is best to take separate notes for responses to each question. This allows you to combine the responses of all focus groups to each question to identify any response patterns. Note taking will be heaviest during the first few interviews. The information will begin to repeat by the third interview. Capture quotes whenever appropriate for emphasis. Attribution is not required.

8. When conducting an interview, control the discussion to see that it stays on target. Encourage all participants to contribute their ideas. Consensus is not necessary. The emphasis here is on differences of views and perspectives. Do not let one or two people dominate the discussion. Control time carefully. Gather examples of what people mean. Explore what appear to be new issues. Do not judge what people say. All contributions are welcome.

9. After each interview, take a few minutes to meet with the JAD/CASE specialist and project manager to confirm the key points made in the interview and to ensure the items were well documented for later reference.

10. In documenting the results of the focus group interviews, maintain anonymity. Identify patterns and key issues. Use examples to give definition to the more general statements.

11. Send thank you notes to participants. If appropriate, provide a written report on focus group results as well.

Technique Name:	**FORM CONSTRUCTION**
Technique Purpose:	**STRUCTURING THE PROCESS**
Technique Advantages:	Ensures accurate and complete collection of information and decisions in JAD workshops. Supports the maxim: "If it isn't written down, it doesn't exist." By completing forms, workshop participants confirm their commitment to the JAD process. By reviewing forms, the JAD/CASE specialist confirms that information has been collected.
Technique Timing:	Used during the workshop. May be used during preworkshop and postworkshop phases as well.
Technique Preparation:	Customize standard forms and design specialized forms with the assistance of the JAD/CASE specialist and, if appropriate, the project manager.
Technique Instructions:	

1. After the JAD workshop deliverable is defined, the workshop agenda is designed, and the exercises to support the agenda topics are selected. Then

the forms to be used to collect the information are prepared. Factors that go into the preparation of forms include:

- Workshop deliverable content and format requirements.
- Logical structure of information collected.
- Input requirements of a CASE tool if one is to be used.
- Need to reference information later in a workshop.

A single form may support more than one exercise and one exercise may use more than one form.

2. Forms should be clearly titled and numbered. Provide space to identify completers' names. Clearly identify the content of each field on the form. If narrative is required, provide adequate space.

3. Create a completed sample of each form to show participants. Create transparencies to be used for explanation during the workshop.

4. Make sufficient copies of each form prior to the workshop. Use different colors of paper to help distinguish each form, especially those used in combination during the same exercises.

Technique Name:	**REVIEWING PLANS AND PROGRESS**
Technique Purpose:	**STRUCTURING THE PROCESS**
Technique Advantages:	Ensures that participants know where they are and where they are going.
Technique Timing:	May be used at the beginning of any meeting or workshop and after any break in the session.
Technique Preparation:	Prepare a written copy of the objectives and/ or agenda for the session. Use transparencies and an overhead projector, easel board paper, or other display device.
Technique Instructions:	

1. Review items with the group to ensure that participants know where they are in the process and what they will be attempting to accomplish next.

2. Determine if activities are on schedule. Consider what actions should be taken if this is not the case. Comment positively on the progress made thus far.

BRINGING PEOPLE TO A COMMON LEVEL OF UNDERSTANDING

In a workshop situation, the absence of a common understanding among the participants can inhibit success. It is important to avoid such a situation by preparing participants to work together. This may be done in the preworkshop phase

or in an initial exercise in the workshop itself. The objective is to enable participants to develop a set of preliminary working assumptions and a common language for communicating with each other. If this is not done, there is a risk
that group decision making will be difficult and that the results will be unsatisfactory.

The Case of Too Many Points of View

Julie Goodman, the JAD facilitator, had just completed participant introduc-
tions and rules for operation on the opening morning of the workshop when
John Ackerman spoke up. "As you all know, my group has been involved in
the redesign of the parts management process for over a year now. Our studies
clearly show that the best way to streamline the operation is to eliminate the
Quality Control Unit, redistribute the supplier/vendor relations assignments
based on part type, not supplier, and install electronic ordering at customer
locations." Then looking at Julie directly, John stated, "I'll just come up to
the front, if you don't mind, to present the details. I think this will shorten our
work here by a couple of days." Julie hid her surprise, and turned to the
project manager to see his reaction. The project manager, Tim Jackson, just
shrugged his shoulders as if to say, "Julie, do whatever you like."

Julie decided she had to express her own reservations. "I'm not sure that
we all have the same understanding of the problem as yet," she said. "This means
that we don't have a common set of assumptions to guide our discussion of John's
proposal. What do the rest of you think?"

The first hand up was Sally Robinson's. "I want to discuss the Quality
Control Unit first," she said. "That's where all our problems are." Jerry added,
"Yeah, I agree and I don't want to be pushed into a decision before I'm ready."
"Why, who's pushing?" John replied. "I'm just trying to save us a little
time. We're all busy people aren't we?"

As the discussion continued, the group seemed to fracture still further, with
the more aggressive participants suggesting that only they understood what was
wrong with parts management. Finally, Julie tried to regain control by saying,
"You all seem to have different ideas on the problems associated with parts
management, but no one seems to be listening to anyone else." Julie knew that
something was wrong. She knew that JAD encouraged the presentation of different perspectives, and that it encouraged the presentation of all points of view. But
she also knew that a JAD workshop was not supposed to be a shouting match,
and she suspected that this workshop was rapidly heading in that direction. She
realized too that she should have been much better prepared to deal with the issue
of John's study and its results.

JAD benefits from a diversity of ideas among workshop participants. But
when the participants are more concerned with defending their positions than with
examining the issues, then diversity becomes a weakness rather than a
strength. For JAD to work, everyone must be united in their objective examination

of all points of view. The following techniques are designed to help encourage an appreciation for the multiple perspectives of all participants and to turn a potential problem into an opportunity.

Technique Name:	**UNDERSTANDING MULTIPLE PERSPECTIVES**
Technique Purpose:	**CREATING A COMMON UNDERSTANDING**
Technique Advantages:	Gives participants an opportunity to disagree about a neutral topic and to examine their differences without being concerned about the outcome.
	Demonstrates the value of different perspectives.
	Identifies the reasons for some of these differences.
Technique Timing:	May be used in the preworkshop stage at a meeting set up to educate participants in the JAD process, or as the opening exercise of a workshop.
Technique Preparation:	Find an item that can serve as the basis for discussion. This may be a picture from a magazine, a photograph, or an object with an unusual appearance and purpose. The item should be one that encourages multiple interpretations. A picture or photo should encourage multiple interpretations of what is happening. An unusual object should encourage multiple interpretations of usage.
Technique Instructions:	

1. Ask participants to work on their own for this exercise. Tell them to take out a pencil and paper and write down their interpretation of the item. Give them only one or two minutes to do this.
2. Ask for volunteers to read their interpretations. Encourage everyone to participate. A variety of perspectives should be brought out.
3. Reveal what is really happening in the picture or photo or the actual use of the object. Lead a short discussion on the reasons for multiple perspectives. Focus the group's attention on factors that filter our understanding and attitudes. Include such items as:

EXTERNAL FILTERS

Room environment
Work pressures
Outside interruptions
Time of day
Presentation style

INTERNAL FILTERS

Personal experiences
Job experiences
Values
Emotional state

Technique Name:	**UNDERSTANDING COMMUNICATION BARRIERS**
Technique Purpose:	**CREATING A COMMON UNDERSTANDING**
Technique Advantages:	Reinforces principles of effective communication.
	Demonstrates the problems of one way communication.
	Identifies the frustration people can experience when they do not receive feedback.
Technique Timing:	May be used in the preworkshop stage at a meeting set up to educate participants in the JAD process, or as the opening exercise of a workshop.
Technique Preparation:	Find or construct a somewhat complex geometric design that can be displayed to the group.
Technique Instructions:	

1. Ask for a volunteer from the group. Bring him to the front of the room and ask him to sit with his back to the group. Ask other participants to take out a pencil and paper. Tell them to work individually. Hand the geometric design to the volunteer and ask him to describe the design to the other participants so that they can draw it themselves based only on his description. Indicate that communication will be one way. No questions may be asked of the volunteer.

2. Allow the volunteer a set time (probably five minutes) for his description. Then ask participants to show their drawings and compare them to the original and to those of their colleagues.

3. Lead a discussion on the difficulties inherent in one way communication. Focus the group's attention on factors that inhibit and enhance communication. Include such items as:

ENHANCERS	INHIBITORS
Seeing speaker's face	Lack of physical proximity
Seeing gestures	Unspoken assumptions
Obtaining feedback	Unclear language
Common vocabulary	No feedback
Comfortable environment	Talking without listening
Listening closely	
Good use of examples	

4. Focus the discussion on the issue of active listening. Emphasize the difference between hearing and listening. Comment on those individuals who seem more concerned with formulating a response or defending a position than with listening. Help the group to develop a list of ideas for listening better. Include such items as:

- Accept the speaker's presentation style.
- Listen for the details, feelings, and emotions behind the facts.
- Acknowledge the importance of alternative points of view.
- Acknowledge the speaker physically and verbally.
- Ask questions for clarification or restatement, if necessary. Ask for examples.

Technique Name:	**UNDERSTANDING PROBLEM SOLVING**
Technique Purpose:	**CREATING A COMMON UNDERSTANDING**
Technique Advantages:	Examines the problem solving process. Demonstrates the power of team work. Demonstrates the importance of individual contributions to the group process.
Technique Timing:	May be used in the preworkshop stage at a meeting set up to educate participants in the JAD process, or as the opening exercise of a workshop.
Technique Preparation:	Obtain several Tinker Toys® sets. You will need one set for each of the subteams you organize for this exercise. Remove the instruction booklets from the sets. Review the booklet and select an item for the group to construct.
Technique Instructions:	

1. Ask for a volunteer from the group. Bring him to the front of the room and ask him to sit with his back to the group. Give him the instruction booklet.

2. Assign the participants to subteams. Tell them that they will have to work together to construct an object based on the instructions of the volunteer at the front of the room. Ask subteam members to rearrange their seats if necessary to enable them to work together, and give each team a set of Tinker Toys®.

3. Ask participants to follow the instructions of the volunteer in constructing the object that you have selected. Indicate that communication will be one way. No questions may be asked of the volunteer. The volunteer may not give an instruction that will reveal the nature of the object being constructed.

4. Tell the volunteer to begin. While the group is working, observe their problem solving style. Consider the following:
   - Which subteams organize their construction materials? Which ones do not?
   - Does a single individual in a subteam take control of the construction process? Is he appointed by the team or self appointed?
   - Are different roles assigned to or taken by individuals? What are these roles?
   - Does anyone withdraw from the problem solving process? What form does this withdrawal take?
   - How are disagreements about construction strategy handled?

5. When the subteams have each built an object, the construction process is stopped. Ask the subteams to compare their efforts with each other and to the picture of the object in the instruction book held by the volunteer.

6. Discuss their success or lack of success with all participants. Ask them to consider why they think they were or were not successful. Then focus the discussion on the observations you made while they were working. Place particular emphasis on which strategies work in a group problem solving situation and which ones do not. You may ask them to answer the previous questions listed above and/or comment on why those questions are important.

Technique Name:	**SOLICITING FEEDBACK**
Technique Purpose:	**CREATING A COMMON UNDERSTANDING**
Technique Advantages:	Ensures that everyone has an opportunity to provide the JAD facilitator with feedback. Provides the JAD facilitator with an opportunity to track the level of participant support and to uncover hidden concerns.
Technique Timing:	Most often used during (verbal feedback) and at the end (written feedback) of the workshop phase. Can also be used (in either verbal or

	written form) at other times in the JAD process.
Technique Preparation:	Create and copy the evaluation form if one is to be distributed.
Technique Instructions:	

1. It is always valuable to ask individuals informally how they feel about the JAD process. This is appropriate at any time. When soliciting verbal feedback from an assembled group (e.g., the workshop group), however, it is useful to use a more formal procedure, such as a round robin. Ask the participants to answer in turn two questions: "What was of greatest value to you today?" and, "What still concerns you?" Expect to get feedback indicating some level of participant confusion or uncertainty at the end of the first day of a workshop (or at any early point in the JAD process.) Reassure participants that their concerns will be addressed. Confer with the project manager and consider whether any adjustments to the workshop agenda (or JAD process) should be made based on this feedback.

2. Obtaining written feedback is particularly important at the end of the workshop. It can also be valuable at the end of the project, following the completion of all postworkshop activities. To obtain written feedback, distribute an evaluation form during the last day of the workshop (or at an end of project group meeting) and ask participants to complete it while they are present. In most cases, anonymity should be respected. It is helpful to provide both standardized and open ended questions. The standardized questions should have set answers that can later be quantified. Ample space should be provided for answers to open ended questions. Consider including the following topics in the evaluation form:

   • Whether objectives were reasonable; whether they were met.
   • Amount of progress made in the workshop.
   • Quality of results generated.
   • JAD facilitator performance.
   • Most/least useful exercises and activities.
   • Topics insufficiently covered.
   • Project next step concerns.
   • Recommendations for using JAD in the future.

CHANGING THE TONE OF THE WORKSHOP

When people work as intensely as they do in a workshop environment, they may get frustrated or burn out if they are not given a chance to re-energize themselves by having a little fun. A short break from the concentrated effort of completing technical exercises can help to alleviate stress and restore a positive attitude. The results of changing direction briefly by using one of these techniques can be restored creativity, renewed team spirit and enhanced commitment to the project after the workshop.

The Case of the Missing Team Spirit

The morale of the participant group for this project was at an all time low. The company, a frozen foods distributor, was in serious trouble. Budgets had been cut and people laid off as part of a total corporate cutback. Directors argued with each other, users were uncooperative and project managers had to fight for resources to get their work done. When a JAD workshop was planned to design a new systems development life cycle, skepticism was high. However, the vice president was committed, the project manager was an enthusiastic bulldog, and the best and brightest from all levels of the organization were represented. In the first three days of the four-day session, the participants accomplished a good deal, building most of the framework for an information engineering life cycle. On the fourth day, however, when the group assembled, participants were impatient and skeptical again. This return to their earlier attitude puzzled Kathryn, the JAD facilitator. When she asked the group directly why their attitude had changed, they told her that they had heard rumors about a corporate buy-out and a move to another city.

Kathryn realized that this new bout of uncertainty could undermine her ability to complete the workshop effectively. While she couldn't address the issue directly, however, she remembered a JAD technique for getting participants to refocus their attention. Thinking about an off hand remark made by Sally the previous day, she said, "Before we get back into the heart of the workshop, let's take a break and try to solve a related problem, one that will allow you to exercise some real creativity. Now that we have some idea of the outline of the new life cycle, it's time to come up with a new name for it."

"I'm holding a naming contest," she said. Each subteam will have half an hour to create a name. But that's not all. You also need to create a presentation of that name for the whole group that will convince them to adopt it." The exercise was a success. The challenge of choosing a name and the fun of creating a sales presentation to support it gave the participants something different and entertaining to focus on. The winning group not only came up with a name that could be expressed in a funny acronym, but a logo design and drawings for clothing and office decorations that included the logo.

The mood of the participants improved remarkably after the exercise. Following the break that concluded the exercise, participants were able to get back on track and finish their assignments without mentioning the many other distractions present in the work environment. The following techniques are designed to help you redirect and re-energize a group when they get off track for any reason.

Technique Name: **NEW PRODUCT IDEA**

Technique Purpose: **CHANGING THE TONE
                          OF THE WORKSHOP**

Technique Advantages: Re-energizes the group and emphasizes the importance of creativity.
                          Diffuses any negative feelings that may have developed.
                          Builds team spirit.

Technique Timing: Generally used during the second half of a workshop.

Technique Preparation: Prior to the workshop, select an unusual object (e.g., a rubber chicken).

Technique Instructions:

1. Before a lunch break, tell the group that it is time to recharge their batteries. Explain that a subteam competition will be held during lunch and that it will emphasize creativity. Tell them that the winning team will get a prize for their efforts.

2. Ask participants to assemble in their subteams. Then hold up the special object. Ask the participants to help out an old friend who invented this object but who does not know what to do with it. Their task is to prepare a five minute presentation on the object in the form of an advertisement for a new product. Tell them to use any of the workshop materials (paper, overheads, markers, etc.) they find useful. Encourage participants to use their imaginations to the fullest extent possible.

3. After lunch, ask each team to make its presentation. Ask the whole group to agree on a winning team. Then offer the object itself (or some other suitable item) as the prize to the winners. Encourage them to display the prize for the balance of the workshop.

Technique Name: **SCAVENGER HUNT**

Technique Purpose: **CHANGE THE TONE
                          OF THE WORKSHOP**

Technique Advantages: Re-energizes the group and emphasizes the importance of creativity.
                          Diffuses any negative feelings that may have developed.
                          Builds team spirit.

Technique Timing: Generally used during the second half of the workshop.

Technique Preparation: Prior to the workshop, create a list of objects for participants to find. Use a transparency or

easel sheet, or make copies of the list. Include both common and uncommon objects.
Prior to the workshop, get a prize for the winning team.

Technique Instructions:

1. Tell the group that it is time to recharge their batteries. Explain that a subteam competition will be held and that it will emphasize creativity. Tell them that the winning team will get a prize for their efforts.
2. Once participants are assembled in their subteams, give or show them the list of objects and ask them to set out on a hunt to locate as many as they can in fifteen minutes. Require them to be back in their seats at that time, and tell them that the team with the most items will win the prize. Encourage them to use their creativity and resourcefulness.
3. When time is called, ask each group to present its items and award the prize to the winning team. The prize for the winner should be a tangible reward which the team can display throughout the rest of the workshop. Encourage them to display the prize for the balance of the workshop.

GENERATING IDEAS WITHOUT JUDGMENT

One of the problems that facilitators have to face is how to get JAD participants to focus on the business issues at hand rather than issues of personality and politics. It is very easy for participants to mistake form for substance or to argue against a speaker rather than the idea spoken. The techniques included below are designed to structure a group discussion so that it focuses on ideas and information and not on extraneous issues. This improves the quality of the information that is generated and the decisions that are made. Most important of all, it ensures that the decisions made are supported by a consensus of the group. All participants will feel that they have an ownership interest in the outcome.

The Case of Too Many Right Answers

Lynn Smith was a systems project manager in charge of the sales reporting application for a large sports equipment manufacturing company. Over the past six months users had grown increasingly dissatisfied with the sales reports produced by the system and had submitted some twenty-five requests for enhancements. This situation was exacerbated by the corporate buy-out of a small but highly profitable ski equipment manufacturer in a neighboring state. The response of this new user group to the sales reporting system was highly negative. In an attempt to respond to all of the complaints, Lynn's team had developed a logical design for a new sales application, complete with enhanced reporting capability. She estimated that the redevelopment effort would require eighteen months of time, six programmers and about one million dollars to complete.

At this point, Lynn contacted Scott, a JAD facilitator with an excellent reputation for gaining commitment from users. She made it clear to him that she didn't need a JAD workshop to develop a set of requirements. She already had these. But she was interested in obtaining user buy-in before proceeding. She wanted the users to "sign on the dotted line," as she put it. Scott agreed that JAD could deliver user buy-in, but not to a finished idea. "You are forcing a solution on the users, and you will not get the commitment you want," he told her.

Scott suggested to Lynn that she present an overview of the key points in her design at an informal meeting of three or four key users to test them out. When she did this, she discovered that gaining commitment would not be as easy as she had hoped. One user balked at the cost of the proposed effort, another insisted that his change requests had not been considered in the new design, and a third, from the new ski equipment division, had rejected her ideas out of hand, complaining that they represented an outdated approach to sales and would seriously compromise future corporate profitability. The experience frightened Lynn. She did not want to take responsibility for a one million dollar effort that would be neither successful nor popular. As a result, she turned over the responsibility for developing a logical design for the redevelopment effort to Scott.

Scott proceeded to apply the JAD process to the project. In conducting focus groups in preparation for the workshop, he discovered that the participant group was even more divided than he had feared. Not only was the ski equipment division unhappy, but the other divisions had a long history of competing with each other for scarce resources and corporate recognition. Each group thought its requirements were unique, and that the systems organization was not equipped to understand them.

Scott knew that for the workshop to be a success he would have to provide a forum where these different ideas could be discussed without reference to ownership. He had to keep the focus on the development of one system for one company. To do this, he needed a set of techniques for transforming subjective ideas into objective ones. From his JAD facilitation skills training, he remembered the techniques for generating ideas without judgment that are described here. Using these concepts, he was able to build consensus on a single design. Not only was the design embraced by the total user community, it proved to be considerably less expensive to develop.

Technique Name:	**ROUND ROBIN DATA COLLECTION**
Technique Purpose:	**GENERATING IDEAS WITHOUT JUDGMENT**
Technique Advantages:	Keeps the whole group alert during the data collection process.
	Keeps one subteam or individual from dominating the data collection process.

Technique Timing:	Anytime after ideas have been generated individually or in small teams. Generally used in preworkshop and workshop phases to gather information.
Technique Preparation:	Prior to using the Round Robin technique, assign a data generation exercise. You might, for example, want the groups to generate a list of data elements or entities, or a list of processes contained within a functional area.

Technique Instructions:

1. After data generation is complete, reassemble everyone into a single group. Call on one team and ask the spokesperson to give you the first item on their list. Document the answer on an easel sheet, transparency, or other display device. Ask the other teams to cross this item off their lists. Call on the spokesperson for another team and follow the same format. Do not permit any discussion of the items generated until the combined list is complete.

   This exercise can be somewhat time consuming if the answers are lengthy or the number of items per team exceeds ten to fifteen. An alternative data collection method is to have each subteam display its answers by writing them on easel paper or Post-Its®.

2. When you have called on all teams, go back to the first team and repeat. Tell the teams to pass when they run out of items. When all teams pass, the exercise is completed. At this point, a discussion may take place. Note that the discussion can now focus on the jointly owned list and not on an item volunteered by one team.

Technique Name:	**DISPLAYED THINKING**
Technique Purpose:	**GENERATING IDEAS WITHOUT JUDGMENT**
Technique Advantages:	Provides a structured brainstorming experience to enable participants to generate ideas without judgment. Energizes the group. Generates a lot of information in a short period of time.
Technique Timing:	Anytime you need to generate a lot of information quickly. Generally used in preworkshop and workshop phases.
Technique Preparation:	Prior to using the displayed thinking technique, write each question you want the group to consider on an easel paper, transparency,

or other display device. Use questions that lend themselves to specific, briefly stated answers. You may, for example, want the group to respond to such questions as, "What type of improvements are needed in the processing of payments?" and "What information groups are associated with profitability analysis in the consumer products division?"

Technique Instructions:

1. Distribute markers and Post-It® note pads to each participant.
2. Display the first question to be considered, and ask the participants to generate as many answers as possible to this question. Ask the participants to shout out answers and then write them on Post-Its® as you acknowledge each one. Screen out the duplicates by pointing them out as they are offered. Continue to collect the answers that are offered until all ideas are exhausted.
3. When the group has generated all the answers it can, lead a discussion on the displayed items. You can choose here to have the group discuss each item as it is presented, or you can ask the individual who volunteered the item to discuss it. Focus on relationships among the items. You can identify, for example, similarities, differences, and dependencies.
4. For further analysis of the ideas generated, you may choose to organize the ideas in categories or in priority order. Using Post-Its® makes this easy. You can move the items around to suit the organization pattern that the participants provide. Establish a consensus on the placement of items in the pattern.
5. At this point, you may want to end the exercise or ask participants to meet in subteams to further refine the items discussed. You may also choose to address a second question.

Technique Name:	**NOMINAL GROUP TECHNIQUE**
Technique Purpose:	**GENERATING IDEAS WITHOUT JUDGMENT**
Technique Advantages:	Provides a structured brainstorming experience to generate information without prejudgment.
	Can be used as a quiet, thought provoking exercise for the group.
	Generates a lot of information quickly.

Technique Timing:	Anytime you want to generate a lot of information quickly. Generally used in preworkshop and workshop phases.
Technique Preparation:	Prior to using the nominal group technique, write each question you want the group to consider on an easel paper, transparency, or other display device. This is a good information generation technique to use with open ended questions, such as: "What strategic business decisions must the marketing group make in the next twelve months?" and, "What questions must the new productivity management system answer for us?" The difference between the use of this technique and the displayed thinking technique is that here the generation of information is less spontaneous. It is, therefore, more appropriate in a situation where creativity is less important than a thoughtful response.

Technique Instructions:

1. Distribute markers and Post-It® note pads to each participant, participant pair, or subteam. (Any of these formulations may be used, although subteams will be used most often in a workshop setting.)

2. Display the question to be considered, and ask the participants (working individually or in whatever type of group you have specified) to generate as many answers as possible to this question. Ask them to write each answer on a Post-It®.

3. Check with the participants as they work, and when they have generated all possible answers, ask each participant or a representative of each participant group to post all of their answers.

4. Lead a discussion on the displayed items. Ask the group to identify any duplications for removal. Then ask them to focus on relationships among the items. You can identify, for example, similarities, differences, and dependencies.

5. You may wish to have the participants classify each response as part of a larger category. You may want to ask for a volunteer from the participant group to physically place the items associated with a category together. As with all decisions, consensus of the whole group should be sought after a rough cut at categorization is made. You may also wish to have the participants assigned priorities to the items or categories.

6. At this point, you may want to end the exercise or to ask participants to meet in subteams to further refine the items discussed.

ANALYZING AND EVALUATING IDEAS

People have different ways of analyzing information and reaching conclusions. Each JAD participant group will do its thinking and deciding in its own way. It is possible, however, to help put them on the road to decision making through the use of certain analysis and evaluation techniques.

The Case of the Tower of Babel

A manufacturing company was composed of eight separate divisions. Historically, each division had operated on its own. Each had its own systems organization, its own human resources, accounting, and manufacturing MIS systems, and its own funding. Finally, corporate management, citing the need for increased efficiency and enhanced profitability, decreed that the time had come for common systems. This decision was not universally popular, but it was accepted. It was decided to begin by using the JAD technique to develop a common personnel/ payroll system. In the focus groups conducted to gather background information, the participants all were happy to offer their input. However, once in the workshop, Tony James, the JAD facilitator, could not seem to get the participants past a comparative analysis of "how my division does this" or "how we handle that." The tone of the discussion was pleasant, but it did not seem to be moving toward a consensus.

Tony had a problem he had not been trained to handle. In his JAD training, he had been told to keep the whole group together in one room for all decision making exercises. Unless this was done, he was told, a common agreement could not be obtained. But in this case, the advice did not seem appropriate. He clearly would have been better off in this situation if he could have divided the group into function based units. He might, for example, have created different subteams focused on time reporting, tax processing, insurance processing, and personnel profiles. This would have enabled the participants to focus on solving specific design problems.

Even the best JAD facilitator will find it almost impossible to turn eight different perspectives into one design. The use of functionally based subteams, on the other hand, provides a technique for analysis and evaluation that can enable the facilitator to turn this wealth of ideas into an opportunity rather than a disadvantage. The following techniques are designed to provide you with ideas on how to get the most out of group analysis and evaluation.

Technique Name:	**SUBTEAM PROBLEM SOLVING**
Technique Purpose:	**ANALYZING AND EVALUATING IDEAS**
Technique Advantages:	Participants can work more quickly within a small group where responsibilities for task completion can be assigned based on expertise.

	Some participants feel more comfortable communicating in a small group and will make a greater contribution in this type of setting.
	Certain work tasks are completed more easily in a small group. The small group technique is particularly appropriate for tasks requiring the specification of technical detail.
Technique Timing:	Generally used in the workshop phase for the development of detailed information.
Technique Preparation:	Identify technical exercises that will be completed during the workshop that may best be addressed by use of the subteam problem solving technique.
	Identify the data generation, collection, and display techniques that will be used by the subteams.
	Construct any information generation and collection forms that are required.
	Identify the membership of each subteam. Make sure each subteam has a place to meet where they will not disturb other subteams.
Technique Instructions:	

1. If the subteams are to meet in the same room, you can have them divide up before you give instructions. If they are to meet in separate rooms, you will need to give instructions before sending them off to their locations. In giving instructions, first describe the work assignment they will undertake. Each group may have the same assignment, or each may have a unique assignment.

2. Distribute any data collection forms, easel paper, markers, transparencies, or other materials needed to the subteams. Walk through an example of the assignment.

3. Make certain that all subteams have an identified subteam coordinator and that this individual knows that he is responsible for making sure that the assignment is completed. Remind the subteams to ask for help if it is needed.

4. After the subteams begin work, visit each team to see that they are off to a good start and understand the assignment.

5. About halfway through the time allotted for the exercise, check to see if progress is being made. Provide assistance where needed.

6. When time is almost up, check to see if the subteams will finish on time. Determine if additional time should be provided.

7. When time is up, review the results. Choose an appropriate method for information presentation. Consider the type and amount of information gen-

erated and the need for input from other members of the group on information
generated or decisions made. Options include:

- A round robin data collection exercise.
- A "read out presentation" by each team of their recommendations, asking
  for changes, additions, deletions and clarifications from the total group.
- A "summary only presentation" by each team.
- A "next team review," where one subteam member presents the results
  to another subteam, asking for changes, additions, deletions and clarifications.

Technique Name:	**STRAWMAN MODEL**
Technique Purpose:	**ANALYZING AND EVALUATING IDEAS**
Technique Advantages:	Provides a starting point for participant analysis. Some people find it easier to edit other people's ideas than to start from scratch.
	May provide a way to keep thinking focused on the primary issue.
	May provide a provocative solution to stimulate thinking.
	May demonstrate assumptions which must be included in the final solution.
Technique Timing:	Anytime during the workshop phase.
Technique Preparation:	Prior to the workshop, gather sufficient information to construct the strawman model. If needed, ask for assistance from other project participants. Be clear about the purpose you intend the model to serve. Do not violate one of the basic tenets of JAD by making it a "take it or leave it" answer to an information management problem. Select a method of displaying the model. Use transparencies, easel paper, or other devices as appropriate.
	Be ready to put the strawman model aside and build from scratch if the workshop participants demand to "start over."
Technique Instructions:	

1. Introduce the strawman model to the group and explain its purpose. Do not
   ask the project manager to present the model. This may result in it having
   too much or too little authority. In some cases, you may choose to have a
   participant present the model or assist in explaining it to the group.
2. Ask for questions. In this initial stage, ask participants to defer judgments.
3. Using an information generation and collection technique (e.g., subteam

proposal, nominal group, displayed thinking), have the group generate and discuss the positive and negative aspects of the model. Ask for examples.

4. Using an information generation and collection technique (e.g., subteam proposal, nominal group, displayed thinking), have the group generate and discuss a list of proposed changes, additions and deletions to the model.

5. Lead the group in reaching consensus on the amended model.

Technique Name:	**ISSUE MANAGEMENT**
Technique Purpose:	**ANALYZING AND EVALUATING IDEAS**
Technique Advantages:	Provides a systematic way of controlling discussions and keeping them on track.
	Prevents momentum from being lost when participants are stalled on an issue of minor importance to the outcome of the workshop.
Technique Timing:	Should be introduced at the beginning of a meeting or workshop, and then may be used at any time.
Technique Preparation:	Prepare easel board and markers or other means of display. It can be helpful to use two different color markers, alternating color with each issue documented.
	Be prepared to call an issue when one topic has held the group's attention for longer than five minutes with no resolution in sight.
Technique Instructions:	

1. Tell the group that it is time to call the issue. Offer a statement of the issue or ask one of the participants to offer one. Write it down where all can see it.

2. Ask the group to consider what type of issue it is. Offer suggestions for acting on the issue based on this information. Possible actions are identified as follows:

   • If resolution of the issue is not likely and is not vital to the session, place the issue on the issues list.
   • If resolution of the issue is possible and/or if resolution of the issue is vital to the workshop, then allow the group to pursue it for another five minutes or other set time.
   • If you suspect that the issue is a "workshop stopper," first confirm that the group cannot proceed until the issue is resolved. Help the group understand the implications of this situation. Then attempt to construct a resolution to the issue. Finally, it this is not possible, create a plan for resolving the issue. This might involve contacting someone outside the workshop for additional information or a decision.

3. You may in some cases choose to defer an issue raised by a participant to a later point in a session when it would be more appropriate. If this is done, the issue should be documented on the issues list so that it will not be forgotten. The participant should be asked to formulate the issue in a specific statement that can be added to the list.

SUPPORTING DECISION MAKING

Strange as it may seem, in some organizations, people are not rewarded for making decisions, but rather for avoiding them. They may even be punished if they make incorrect decisions. Participants who have been trained in decision avoidance do not make the most natural JAD participants. Neither, however, do participants who are too quick to rush to judgment. They can dominate a group, particularly a group of decision avoiders, to the detriment of the solution developed.

The JAD facilitator must be prepared with specific techniques to minimize both of these negative approaches to decision making. This is where it becomes obvious that the JAD facilitator is doing more than just mediating a discussion. He is applying a structured decision making process to the solution of technical problems.

The Case of the Foggy Workshop

An insurance company had several years of experience in using the JAD process to develop logical designs for systems applications. When a new division vice president wanted to develop a strategic plan for integrating all applications related to customer service, however, one JAD facilitator suggested using the process in a new way. In an advanced JAD facilitation training class, Donna Darcy had learned some techniques for applying JAD to the development of strategic information management plans and saw this as an excellent opportunity to try out her new skills.

Donna had no trouble convincing the vice president to use JAD to develop his strategic plan. He assigned one of his top aids, Bernard Wilson, to work with her. Anna Parker, an associate of Bernie's, was named project manager. Pre-workshop activities went well, and Donna was eager to begin the workshop.

The workshop itself was, in some respects, a difficult one to conduct. Donna found it more difficult to maintain a clear focus in a strategic planning workshop than in the application design workshops she was accustomed to leading. Participants always seemed to be one step away from taking off on a tangent about the future of the insurance industry or the changing role of the sales agent. Bernie was particularly prone to lead the group astray. Having been heavily influenced by his mentor, the vice president, he was primarily interested in issues related to management philosophy and the changing nature of the financial market-place. Anna was a help, though. Because she and Donna had worked out a specific design for the workshop deliverable during the preworkshop phase, she knew exactly where the participants had to focus their energies and did her best to assist Donna in keeping them on track.

The other participants were, like Donna, unaccustomed to dealing with strategic concerns and a bit uncomfortable with making decisions about high level issues that they had previously believed were the sole province of upper management. However, Donna pulled them through it. How? By refusing to allow the discussion to focus on the theoretical or conceptual. Instead, she brought specificity and focus to the discussion by using the new decision-making techniques she had learned in her advanced training class. These techniques kept the participants on track and helped them to recognize that the big issues could be managed easily if they were just broken down into small issues. These techniques are presented next. They may prove useful in a wide variety of project types, but they are particularly helpful for handling higher level strategic planning projects, such as the one addressed here.

Technique Name:	**FORCE FIELD ANALYSIS**
Technique Purpose:	**SUPPORTING DECISION MAKING**
Technique Advantages:	Looks at both positive and negative aspects of a problem.
	Identifies the most critical elements of a solution.
	Examines the relationships among different aspects of a particular problem.
Technique Timing:	May be used in preworkshop, workshop, and postworkshop phases.
Technique Preparation:	Prior to using the technique, prepare room displays as illustrated in Figs. 3.1 and 3.2.
Technique Instructions:	

1. Using an easel paper or other display device, write a problem statement to serve as the basis of the discussion.
2. Using a technique that will allow the group to generate ideas without judgment (e.g., displayed thinking, nominal group technique), have the group identify and list on Fig. 3.1 the forces that may influence the situation or be part of the proposed solution.
3. After the list is generated, lead the group in reaching consensus on each item with reference to its:

   • Status as an enhancer (a driver to possible success) or inhibiter (a restrainer to possible success),
   • Rank on a scale of zero (no force) to five (extreme force) to define the amount of force that item exerts.

Situation Forces	Force Direction	Force Strength

Force direction
- R = Restraining or inhibiting
- D = Driving or enhancing

Force strength
- 1 = Weak
- 2 = Somewhat weak
- 3 = Moderately strong
- 4 = Strong
- 5 = Very strong

Figure 3.1   Force field analysis form.

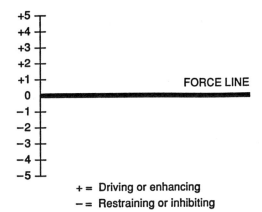

+ = Driving or enhancing
- = Restraining or inhibiting

Figure 3.2 Force field plot form.

4. Plot the results on the force field chart (Fig. 3.2) and draw a line from each factor to the baseline.

5. Lead a discussion on the results. Identify appropriate strategies to build on the greatest enhancers and overcome or convert the greatest restrainers.

6. If appropriate, prioritize these strategies. They can also be developed further using other techniques (e.g., subteam proposals).

Technique Name:	**PRO AND CON ANALYSIS**
Technique Purpose:	**SUPPORTING DECISION MAKING**
Technique Advantages:	Provides a way to summarize the advantages and disadvantages of a decision. Identifies specific objections to a decision and provides a way to develop strategies to overcome those objections.
Technique Timing:	May be used in preworkshop, workshop, and postworkshop phases.
Technique Preparation:	Identify a situation where the group is having trouble agreeing on a solution to a particular problem.
Technique Instructions:	

1. Using an easel paper or other display device, write a statement that offers a solution to a problem the group has been working on. Under the statement, set up two columns, one marked "pro" and one marked "con." Draw a vertical line between the two.

2. Ask the group to identify the advantages of the solution. Document these. Ask the group to identify the disadvantages of the solution. Document these as well.

3. Count the number of items in each column. If one list is longer than the other, ask the group if they are satisfied that a decision on the proposed solution has been made.

4. If the group feels that some items are more important than others, you can assign weights to the items and refigure the results. Or, if the group feels that while the pros are stronger, the cons must be addressed, you can work with them to develop a strategy to overcome these issues.

Technique Name:	**DECISION FACTOR ANALYSIS**
Technique Purpose:	**SUPPORTING DECISION MAKING**
Technique Advantages:	Provides participants with an opportunity to explore different actions that may be taken to address an information management problem. Ensures that a decision to select an option will be made with reference to its consequences.
Technique Timing:	May be used in preworkshop, workshop, and postworkshop phases. Particularly useful in specialized JAD workshops adapted to such needs as high level information management planning and system implementation planning.
Technique Preparation:	Identification of a specific information management problem and several different actions that can be taken to address it.
Technique Instructions:	

1. Display each proposed action as the header on an easel paper and post these in a prominent location.

2. Ask the group to identify a set of five impact categories to be used to evaluate all proposed actions. Divide each easel paper into five sections and label each section with one of the impact categories. Impact areas may include such items as: budget, personnel, schedules, facilities, and organization structure.

3. Divide the group into subteams and ask each subteam to address one or two of the proposed actions. They should evaluate the action in relation to all impact categories. The results of the evaluation of each impact category should be documented on a Post-It® and placed in the appropriate location on the easel paper. If, for example, the problem being addressed is an extensive backlog of change requests, one subteam might evaluate the proposed action of hiring an outside firm to assist with reducing the backlog. This action might affect the impact category of budget by eliminating dollars

previously planned for equipment purchase. If an impact category is not relevant to a proposed action, this should be documented as well.

4. Ask the subteams to present the results of their discussions to the whole group. You may wish to use one of the information presentation techniques previously identified. Participants should have the opportunity to comment on and modify the evaluation of all proposed actions.

5. At this point, there are several options. The group may be asked: to reject any actions that are inappropriate, to select for implementation any actions that are particularly appropriate, to prioritize all (or a subset) of the proposed actions, or to create another plan for addressing them further.

Technique Name:	**FORCED PAIR COMPARISONS**
Technique Purpose:	**SUPPORTING DECISION MAKING**
Technique Advantages:	Provides a quantitative method for evaluating a number of proposed actions.
	Adds objectivity to the decision making process and increases participant commitment to decisions.
Technique Timing:	May be used in preworkshop, workshop, and postworkshop phases. Particularly useful in specialized JAD workshops adapted to such needs as high-level information management planning and system implementation planning.
Technique Preparation:	Prepare a decision matrix (Fig. 3.3) on an easel paper, transparency, or other display device.
Technique Instructions:	

1. Using an easel paper or other display device, write down a key question that the group must address. You might ask, for example: "Which systems projects are most critical to the organization in the next twelve months?" Then enter the proposed answers to the question (e.g., names of key projects) on the horizontal and vertical axes of the decision matrix at the top of each column and at the beginning of each row.

2. Beginning with the first open cell, ask the group to answer the question: "Which of these two items is more critical?" If the group selects the item in the column heading, place a "1" in the right half of the cell and a "0" in the left half. If the group selects the item in the row heading, place a "0" in the right half of the cell and a "1" in the left half. Use this process to complete the matrix (Fig. 3.4).

3. To calculate the results, begin with the first row and add up the left hand cell numbers and write the results to the right of the row. The last row will have a "0" total. After this is done for all rows, add up each column and add the

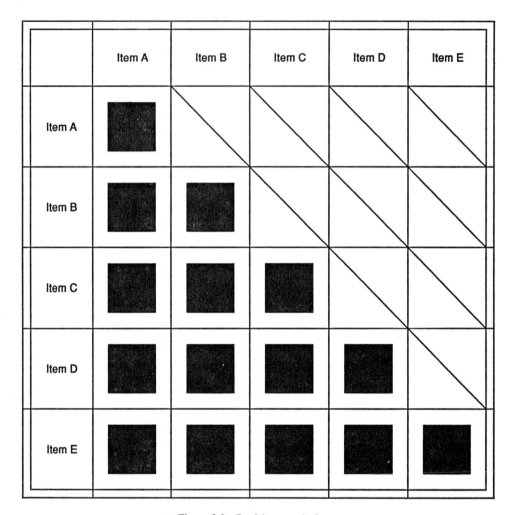

Figure 3.3 Decision matrix form.

column total to the previous row total for the item. The first column will have a "0" total. The combined row and column totals give the preference ranking or priority (Fig. 3.5). The item with the greatest total is that most preferred by the participants, and the one with the lowest total is the one least preferred.

Technique Name: **DECISION POINT ROUND ROBIN**
Technique Purpose: **SUPPORTING DECISION MAKING**
Technique Advantages: Provides a way to focus decision making.
                            Avoids voting. Prevents isolation when one

	Item A	Item B	Item C	Item D	Item E
Item A	■	1 / 0	0 / 1	1 / 0	1 / 0
Item B	■	■	1 / 0	0 / 1	0 / 1
Item C	■	■	■	0 / 1	1 / 0
Item D	■	■	■	■	0 / 1
Item E	■	■	■	■	■

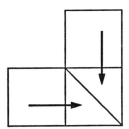

Record row preference in bottom of divided square.
Record column preference in top of divided square.

Figure 3.4 Decision matrix cell analysis.

	Item A	Item B	Item C	Item D	Item E
Item A		1 / 0	0 / 1	1 / 0	1 / 0
Item B			0 / 1	0 / 1	0 / 1
Item C				0 / 1	1 / 0
Item D					0 / 1
Item E					

	Add bottom of boxes across		Add top of boxes down		Add the two results	Priority
Item A	1	+	0	=	1	
Item B	3	+	1	=	4	*
Item C	1	+	0	=	1	
Item D	1	+	1	=	2	
Item E	0	+	2	=	2	

Figure 3.5 Decision matrix cell calculation.

or more of the participants cannot support a decision.

Provides a way to construct a decision which everyone can accept.

Technique Timing: Anytime during the workshop.

Technique Preparation: This is a final decision exercise. All analysis, discussions, and alternative development must have been completed previously.

Technique Instructions:

1. Based on the discussion leading up to this exercise, identify in specific terms the decision to be made and write it on an easel board.

2. Starting with one participant, point to the decision written on the board and ask: "Can you live with this decision?" If the person says "yes," then ask the next person the same question. Continue until someone answers "no." In this case, say: "Give me the specific change you want to make to this decision so you can live with it." Then rewrite the decision with the change incorporated and proceed to the next person.

3. Repeat step two until every participant accepts the decision. Permit short discussions for clarification, but do not allow extended discussion to interfere with the momentum of the exercise.

MANAGING PARTICIPANT INTERACTION

Managing the behavior of the participants in the JAD process is a critical challenge for the JAD facilitator. The facilitator must be aware of the behavior displayed by participants throughout the process and be prepared to take action if a disruptive behavior pattern arises. Such disruptive behavior can substantially reduce, and, in some cases, even destroy, the effectiveness of the JAD process in achieving the objectives of the project. For this reason it is important that participants know what is expected of them and that they be held to a high standard of cooperative interaction.

The Case of the Nervous Knitter

Bob Tasking, the JAD facilitator, noticed that Arlene, one of his key participants, had contributed very little to the discussion on the first day of the JAD workshop. Even when asked for her opinion directly, she had volunteered little. On the morning of the second day, she took out a pair of knitting needles and started in on what looked to be a very formidable sweater.

Bob was concerned that the group would find this behavior distracting, but when he asked them about it during a break, they all said that it was no problem. It was clear, however, that for Arlene this was only a symptom of a bigger problem. Arlene was not participating in the workshop more than absolutely necessary, and this frustrated Bob greatly because he knew she had important knowledge to contribute. He decided that the best course of action was to find a time to ask her privately why she was not contributing more. When he did so, she said that she was unaccustomed to working with so many other people. She said that knitting for her was like smoking for others. It helped to reduce the stress. When Bob asked if she thought she would be contributing more as the workshop went on, she said, "Well, I really don't know why I'm here. I don't know how this is going to get us to a good design. We haven't even talked about reports yet. Frankly, I'd really rather be back in my office getting something done."

Bob realized that there was a problem here and that he had caused it. He had not adequately prepared the participants before the workshop so that they would understand what was expected of them. He had believed that this was obvious. Providing only a cursory overview of JAD roles and responsibilities during his preworkshop education session, he had focused almost exclusively on the technical aspects of the project. Arlene's dysfunctional behavior, he knew, was due at least in part to his failure to prepare her adequately for the workshop.

Bob saved the situation by talking with Arlene during lunch that day about what he believed she could contribute to the process. But the next time he took on a JAD project, he worked much harder to address such issues as roles, responsibilities, and the nature of team problem solving at an early stage in the process.

Technique Name:	**CLARIFYING PARTICIPANT ROLES**
Technique Purpose:	**MANAGING PARTICIPANT INTERACTION**
Technique Advantages:	Helps participants understand what will be expected of them throughout the process.
	Provides an opportunity for participants to experience the subteam working group and the round robin data collection technique.
	Demonstrates to participants how the JAD facilitator will manage group work.
	Defines participant roles and positive/negative behavior.
Technique Timing:	May be used early in the JAD process in the preworkshop stage or specifically to prepare participants for their roles in the workshop. May be presented at a meeting specifically set up for this purpose, but often used at a meeting set up for participant education in the JAD process.

Technique Preparation: Create a transparency or use an easel board to list a short set of questions that participants will be asked to answer. The questions may include:

- How can I best play my role (e.g., during the workshop, during the project, etc.) in order to make the best contribution?
- What type of behavior might inhibit our success?
- What can I do to help others play their roles honestly and effectively?

Divide the participant group into homogeneous subteams that correspond to the roles that they will play (e.g., systems professionals in one subteam, users from the accounting department in another, etc.).

Technique Instructions:

1. Introduce the exercise by discussing the importance of each individual's contribution to the JAD process. Mention the different types of contributions that can be made. Explain that participants will be asked to work together in subteams to answer a few simple questions.

2. Display and read the questions, and present an example of an answer to each one. Then assign participants to subteams and ask them to appoint a subteam coordinator to take notes and present their results to the total group. Explain that they will be expected to work together to prepare one set of results. Give participants a time limit, probably about fifteen minutes.

3. Tell participants to rearrange their seating if necessary. Once the groups have formed and begun their discussion, visit each team to see that they have understood the instructions. Answer any questions they have.

4. Let the participants know when only five minutes are left. Tell them to begin documenting their answers, if they have not done so already.

5. After the time is up, reassemble the participants into a single group. Use a round robin data collection process, focusing on one question at a time. Begin with one team and ask it to present its answer to the first question. Display this answer on a transparency or easel board. Then ask the second team for its answer to the same question. Check items that have already been displayed and add new items to the list. Move to the next team until all have responded to the first question. Then use the same data collection technique to capture answers to the other questions. Ask participants to defer discussion until all answers have been collected.

6. After all answers have been collected, encourage discussion of these among the group as a whole. Then ask participants to discuss the use of subteams

and the round robin data collection process. Make sure that they see the benefits of this type of approach. Stress the importance of working in small groups for gathering and testing ideas and in a large group for final decision making.

Technique Name:	**GIVING AND RECEIVING FEEDBACK**
Technique Purpose:	**MANAGING PARTICIPANT INTERACTION**
Technique Advantages:	Assists in building positive relationships with all those involved in the JAD process. Improves the process by revealing hidden issues and concerns.
Technique Timing:	May be used in preworkshop, workshop, and postworkshop phases.
Technique Preparation:	No specific preparation required.
Technique Instructions:	

Feedback consists of two perspectives. Receiving feedback involves the ability to solicit information about your communication style and behavior from others. Providing feedback involves the ability to tell others about their communication style and behavior. A facilitator, to be effective, must be aware of how his communication style and behavior impact the project manager, the project team, and the workshop participants. To give and receive feedback effectively, follow these guidelines:

1. Never provide feedback unless you have permission to do so. Ask the individual if he would like to discuss some of your observations on the ideas he has presented or his style of behavior.

2. People are often reluctant to give feedback because they fear rejection or anger. As a professional JAD facilitator, you should always invite feedback from the project manager and workshop participants. Tell them that there are times when you may say or do something that causes concern. Ask them to let you know when this happens. Assure them that you look at this as an opportunity to improve your skills.

3. Use feedback to clarify a message. Ask the receivers of your message to rephrase it or to state what they think you said to confirm their understanding of the message.

4. Use feedback to describe to someone how his behavior or communication style has affected you. Emphasize your own confusion or need for clarification rather than his lack of clarity.

5. Feedback must be specific, not general, to be effective. If, for example, someone accuses you of forcing decisions on a participant group, ask for

specific examples. If you give feedback to someone else, be specific and descriptive. For example, don't say to your project manager, "You talked too much in that last session." Say, after getting permission, "You broke into the conversation three times in the last session when the group discussed the timing issue, scheduling priorities, and team selection. Is there some way I can help you make sure your concerns are addressed?"

Technique Name:	**MANAGING DISCUSSIONS**
Technique Purpose:	**MANAGING PARTICIPANT INTERACTION**
Technique Advantages:	Ensures effective control of workshop discussion.
Technique Timing:	May be used in preworkshop, workshop, and postworkshop phases.
Technique Preparation:	Familiarity with basic questioning techniques.
Technique Instructions:	

1. Keep people posted on their progress in relation to the objectives of the meeting or workshop. Review the agenda and objectives on a regular basis. For a workshop, this would be at the beginning and end of each day. Meet with the project manager regularly to review progress, discuss issues, and anticipate impacts on the workshop.

2. Manage interruptions in the workshop. Have a message board outside the room, so only real emergency calls are brought into the room. Do not let new participants join the discussion after it begins.

3. Help participants understand why they are being asked to perform certain activities. Explain how each activity or exercise relates to those that precede and follow it. Provide examples. If someone does not understand something, do not blame him. Be patient and take time with people.

4. Never embarrass participants. If someone breaks one of the rules for operation, tell him so politely but firmly. Follow through on actions you promise to take. In the ten years in which the authors have facilitated workshops, only twice has someone been asked to leave a session because of behavior problems. This should be the exception, not the rule.

5. Encourage participation, and do your best not to cut people off. However, you must also keep very verbal individuals from talking too long and dominating the discussion. Directly ask those who are reluctant to volunteer to offer their ideas. Make the dominant ones wait their turn to talk by telling them that you will get to them shortly. Recognize them and tell them that their turn will come after the next speaker.

6. Vary the pace and tone of the workshop to keep everyone alert and enthusiastic. Vary your use of facilitation techniques.

7. Ask open ended questions that cannot be answered ''yes'' or ''no.'' Consider using these questions:

- What demonstrates this point?
- Can you give us an example of what you mean?
- What do the rest of you think?
- What other perspectives are there?
- Who else has this concern?
- What can we do to remedy this situation?

8. Summarize and paraphrase often to keep participants on track and to increase the accuracy of information being collected. Write key points on a room display.

9. Do not permit side conversations. Do not permit observers to enter discussions or decision making. Keep people on track firmly, but politely. Tell them when it is time to move on.

10. Control timing of all activities. Start all sessions as planned. Readjust agenda topics if needed to slow or increase the pace. Look for signs of participant fatigue. Take breaks and/or stop early if the quality of participation declines. People need to be more fresh for some types of work than others.

Technique Name:	**HANDLING PROBLEM BEHAVIOR**
Technique Purpose:	**MANAGING PARTICIPANT INTERACTION**
Technique Advantages:	Enhances ability to reach objectives. Keeps problem behavior from interfering with the JAD process. Prevents other participants from suffering from the effects of inappropriate behavior of others.
Technique Timing:	May be used in preworkshop, workshop, and postworkshop phases.
Technique Preparation:	No specific preparation required.
Technique Instructions:	

1. Look for a pattern in problem behavior. If a person exhibits a problem behavior once, it may be appropriate to overlook it. When a pattern develops and begins to affect others, it is time to begin managing the behavior. This is particularly important in the workshop phase where it is important to recognize and address negative patterns quickly.

2. Find out the reason for the behavior. Do not assume you know the cause. One of the easiest ways to do this is to ask the person why he is exhibiting this behavior. You may want to ask the individual directly by saying, for example: ''You are very argumentative this afternoon. What is wrong?'' It is generally appropriate to do this outside of a workshop session, privately, on a one-to-one basis, but in some cases you may want to address the issue in front of the total workshop group. In making the decision, consider the specific behavior being exhibited, the reaction of the other participants, and your personal facilitation style. Be careful not to punish the rest of the group for one individual's behavior problem.

3. Based on the response of the individual, take appropriate action. Listed next are some types of behavior that may cause a problem in a session, along with some possible solutions. While you may observe these behavior problems in any type of meeting, they will be particularly critical in a JAD workshop.

BEHAVIOR	FACILITATOR ACTION
Talks too much	Do not stop the ideas. Do not embarrass the individual. Say: ''That's an interesting point. Now let's hear another perspective.''
Highly argumentative	Do not attack the individual or become defensive. Do not get angry. Do not let the group get frustrated with him. Pinpoint the issues of his argument, document them and then move on. Present the issues back to the group for their evaluation. Focus on the pros and cons, not the individual. Document the results and move on.
Apple polisher	Do not always go to this person first in a discussion. Let him summarize the discussion. Thank him for his enthusiasm, but remind him that everyone has to participate in JAD.
Rambler	Thank him for his contribution, then refocus his and the group's attention by restating the relevant points, and move on. Smile and say, ''I'm not sure that what you are saying is on target for the discussion.'' Then turn to the group and ask, ''Can someone help us here?'' Call an issue after five minutes.
Personality clash	(This clash may be between two participants or between the facilitator and a participant.) Sidestep the clash by bringing in a noncombatant participant and ask for another perspective. Tell the group: ''Everyone is entitled to his own perspec-

	tive. What are the facts here?'' Move from the subjective to the objective by referring to the objectives of the discussion and asking participants how a point is related to a specific objective. Document points of agreement.
Obstinate	Throw his view back to the group and ask: ''Who can help us here? What do you think?'' Call an open issue, document it, and move on.
Wrong subject	Take the blame saying: ''Something I said must have led you off the subject.'' Then restate the question or point. Call on a second individual to give the person a chance to rethink his position, and then get back to him.
Inarticulate	Attempt to clarify what he has just said, and ask for a confirmation. Ask for examples. Do not ignore this person. His ideas may be very important.
Wrong response	Do not embarrass this person. Respond by saying: ''That's one way of looking at it.'' Then move on.
Searching for your decision	Do not solve the problem or make the decision for the group. Remind the group that you are a facilitator, not a decision maker.'' Help them by asking for a restatement of the problem or decision point, or by asking them to restate the options and define key terms.
Complainer	Let the individual get it off his chest. Then call an open issue. Ask the group if anyone has a response to the issue. Then tell the group it is time to move on.
Side conversation	Call the people conversing by name, saying: ''Remember our rules for operation,'' or ''I'll get to your concerns in just a minute.'' Touch the two people on the shoulder if necessary.
Will not participate	Ask for the person's opinion directly during large group discussions. If he does not participate in the subteam exercises either, talk to him outside the workshop concerning the importance of his participation.

Technique Name:	**PROMOTING ACTIVE LISTENING**
Technique Purpose:	**MANAGING PARTICIPANT INTER-ACTION**
Technique Advantages:	Helps participants to stay alert. Helps participants increase their contribution to the JAD process.
Technique Timing:	May be used in preworkshop, workshop, and postworkshop phases.
Technique Preparation:	No specific preparation required.
Technique Instructions:	

1. Face participants when you are talking to them. Stop talking when you write on easel paper, transparency, or other display device. Speak clearly and at a speed appropriate for the group. Vary tone and pitch to sound animated and to keep people's attention.

2. Use eye contact as you speak. Stand up and move around without pacing. Do not plant yourself in the front of the room. Respond to the reactions of participants. When you see eyebrows go up, for example, you might say: "I see that some of you are skeptical about what I just said. What are your concerns?"

3. Do not use acronyms unless they have been defined first. Limit unnecessary technical language. Define any terms open to interpretation.

4. Do not lean on equipment or furniture. It makes you look tired and lazy. Do not look at your watch while someone is talking.

5. Write clearly on easel boards and transparencies. Use at least two different colors. Learn to write clearly. In some cases, it will be appropriate to ask someone else to board the results as you lead the discussion.

6. If you are using a pointer, do not wave it around.

7. Whenever it is possible that a participant has not been heard, restate the point made or question asked. Ask the participant to restate the point or question if it is not understood.

8. Ask questions for clarification and paraphrase to check for comprehension. Chances are you are not the only one who did not understand.

9. After giving instructions, walk through an example, and ask for clarification from the group.

10. Be aware of each person's personal space. Do not stand too close or too far away when talking.

11. Use body language to get your message across. Acknowledge your audience verbally and physically.

12. Dress in a way that indicates that your status is that of the leader.

13. Do not turn off the lights. If you use an overhead projector, make sure it projects with the lights on or with only the light in the front of the room off.

14. When listening to others, assume that people have something interesting and important to say. Accept their presentation style even if it is not easy to listen to. Listen for details, feelings, and emotions behind the facts, and when appropriate, acknowledge your own feelings and reactions before you speak.

15. Do not withdraw, fidget with markers, or daydream while someone is talking. Facilitation requires an exceptionally high degree of concentration on all of the issues at all times.

4

The Technology Dimension:
CASE Tools

THE IMPACT OF CASE TOOLS

Most systems managers spend a good deal of their time worrying about how to increase the productivity of their software development teams and how to increase the quality of the finished systems those teams produce. For this reason they have been quick to embrace new tools and techniques that are promoted with a view toward enhancing the life cycle. Sometimes the promises made for these tools and techniques are realized; sometimes they are not. Similar promises have been made for CASE (computer-aided software engineering) tools. They have been heavily promoted by their developers as the next major step toward enhanced productivity. The results so far, however, have been mixed. Some organizations have had great success with these tools, while others have been so disappointed that they have all but abandoned them, leaving expensive software sitting on a shelf and the hardware purchased to support that software underutilized or reassigned to other tasks.

The failure of some organizations to realize the value inherent in CASE technology is not generally a result of some inadequacy in the tool. Rather, it is most often caused by the unsuccessful implementation of that tool. To be more direct, it is not so much the fault of the tool vendor, but of the tool implementor. When tools are not carefully selected, introduced, and integrated into an organization, failure is not a surprise. It is almost a foregone conclusion. This would not be true if CASE tools were simple, easy to use, plug-it-in and watch it go machines. But they do not fit this description. They require a great deal of time, effort, and additional resources (e.g., people, training, money) to make them work. Take just one example of the introduction of a new technology into the work place. Consider what happened when robotics was introduced to the factory floor. An assembly line process that had taken years to create was turned upside down overnight. Not only did the mechanics of the assembly line change, but the jobs of the individuals who were responsible for production changed as well. Where once a worker performed such basic tasks as bolting and welding, he was suddenly in charge of machines that did those jobs. The level and type of expertise required for this new position required a new type of worker. The successful introduction of robotics, in other words, required more than just the purchase of new machines.

CASE tools, if they are to succeed as envisioned, require the same type of work place redesign effort. Too often this type of redesign effort does not take place. Instead, the tools are inserted into the existing systems development environment with little thought as to how they will impact that environment. Analysts and developers receive little or limited training, and existing systems development methods and procedures are not examined to reveal hidden inconsistencies between the tool and standard practices. Managers themselves may have little knowledge of the appropriate application of a tool to a given project. They probably have not considered how the tool will impact project management, interim deliverables, or resource requirements.

Neither have many considered what happens when these tools are integrated with other new concepts and techniques. Standard management tools such as critical path analysis and PERT charts are not designed for use in a rapid applications development environment where the typical project timeframe is four to six months rather than two to four years. Other questions confront the project manager as well. How does he motivate people to work closely in small, intense teams? How does he measure programmer productivity when a CASE tool (not a programming team) is generating lines of code?

Some of the early implementors of CASE, the "bleeding edge" experimenters, suffered through many false starts because they failed to pay adequate attention to the integration of these tools. One insurance company that purchased thirty five copies of a popular CASE tool tried unsuccessfully for two years to force people to use it. When no productivity improvements were realized, they decided the problem was with the tool and went back to the marketplace to look for a better tool, one that would really solve their problems. Other organizations, however, learned from their experience, stepped back to examine their systems design and development operation, and made fundamental changes in methodology, techniques, and management along with their tool implementation. These organizations have much to teach about the introduction of new technologies, and it is their experience we should emulate.

CRITICAL SUCCESS FACTORS FOR CASE
TOOL SELECTION

While not all CASE tools are created equal, there are many attractive options in the marketplace today for the organization that has not committed to a specific tool. It should be said at the outset that there is probably no one best tool choice for any organization. It is also true that what may be the best solution for the short term, may not be the best solution for the long term. Technology is evolving very rapidly, and any review of today's best selling tool solutions would provide old and, most likely, false information by the time this book was published. Quite recently, for example, it was possible to say that there were only two types of CASE tools in general use, back end code generators and front end planning and analysis tools. Nothing linked them together. The front end CASE tools were standalone workstations unable to share or transfer data with other workstations except through clumsy floppy disk file transfers. The back end CASE tools were centralized mainframe implementations. Cost was also a problem. It prohibited all but a few organizations from using CASE. Front end tools were priced from $5000 to $20,000 per workstation, and code generators required a minimum of $150,000 to $250,000 in direct investment.

Today the picture is entirely different. Today we have integrated CASE tools, where front end and back end capabilities are offered in a single tool set that provides data sharing and life cycle support all the way from systems planning through application code generation. Some tools offer mainframe implementations as well as networked solutions where code can be generated in multiple languages for multiple operating systems at a PC workstation. Prices have decreased dramatically, too, and code generation can be had for the price of a workstation. Some of the more limited front end CASE tools can be purchased for $495 to $2000 a workstation.

With all of this new technology available, however, it is still important to remember that the choice of a tool should be based on the needs of the organization, not the most capabilities per dollar. The factors identified next can greatly assist those who are in the process of making a buying decision, those who have purchased but not yet fully implemented their CASE tools, and those who wish to build on their current CASE investment. These factors include:

- Concepts driving CASE technology development.
- Essential functions, features, and variations of CASE products.
- Coherent strategies for purchasing CASE products.
- Typical problems with CASE implementation.
- Prerequisites for effective CASE use.
- Impacts of CASE on the systems development environment.

TYPES OF CASE TOOL PRODUCTS

Since "CASE" is a popular industry buzzword, all vendors attempt to classify their systems software products as CASE products. A utility to archive and backup databases may be called a CASE Database Support Manager by a clever vendor. Using this approach, the vendor may get his product listed in every computer magazine's CASE review, not just in the annual utility review issue. This is not very helpful to prospective CASE purchasers, however. They need a better sense of what CASE is.

Instead of relying on this generalized view of CASE, it is more useful to look at these tools as representing four primary types: front end, back end, seamless, and special function. Historically, front end and back end CASE products were developed independently. Later, an effort was undertaken to link them together into a single product. This is important because many organizations have already committed to a CASE tool for one phase of the life cycle, and they do not wish to give up a tool that has proven useful. They do, however, want to add other life cycle support capabilities, and they would prefer to have these presented in a compatible tool. Vendors are attempting to meet this need.

Front end CASE products support one or more of the business planning, business analysis, and application design methodology components (Fig. 4.1). Because their focus is on business needs and logical design, these products function independently of application and database development technology. Designed to bring order to the chaos of user requirements and specifications, most front end CASE products are methodology sensitive, supporting some or all aspects of one or more methodologies. The first versions of these products focused their support on application analysis and design, but today almost all front end CASE products support business planning, process and data analysis, as well as application analysis and logical design. Linkages to back end products are available. Some tools provide the ability to create files of "front end data" (logical design information) that can be exported to a separate back end tool. This tool compatibility may be offered by a single vendor or may be obtained when multiple vendors work out strategic alliances and commit to interproduct compatibility.

The best known front end CASE products are designed for IBM type environments, but tools have been developed as well for other environments, including DEC, UNIX, UNISYS, and Macintosh. Back end CASE products support application and database design and code generation methodology components. They focus on physical design, prototyping, and software development. Because of this, they are technology dependent, generating code for specific software languages (e.g., COBOL, PL/1, C) which run in specific operating and database management system environments (e.g., CICS, IMS, DB2, UNIX, ORACLE). Back end CASE products have been used by systems organizations longer than other CASE tools and have proven their effectiveness many times over. However, integration with front end CASE products is becoming a requirement, so some back end products now offer the ability to

Systems Work		Tool Type	Support Type
1. Planning for systems	T E C H	Front end Seamless	Documentation Decision support
2. Building data models and process models for business areas	I N	Front end Seamless	Documentation Analysis
3. Defining application requirements	D E P E	Front end Seamless	Documentation Logical design
4. Creating application design	N D E N	Front end Seamless	Documentation Analysis Logical design
5. Administering data for business area	T	Front end Seamless	Documentation Analysis

6. Application prototyping	T E C H	Front end Back end Seamless	Screens Simulation
7. Designing databases and programs	I	Back end Seamless	Documentation Physical design
8. Constructing programs	N D E	Back end Seamless	Generate code
9. Testing applications and databases	P E N	Special	Testing
10. Maintaining applications: adaptive enhancement corrective preventative	D E N T	Back end Seamless Special	Physical design Generate code

Figure 4.1 CASE tools and systems work.

import logical design information from different front end products as input to physical design.

Most of these products are mainframe products with workstation access. However, this is changing as new technology allows code generators to run on PC workstations. Most products run on IBM compatible equipment; a few support DEC, UNIX, or UNISYS.

The newest type of CASE product is the seamless CASE tool that integrates front end and back end product capabilities into a single solution. The advantage of the seamless product is that it eliminates the need for linking software to transfer logical design information from the front end tool to the back end tool. It provides an integrated resource (termed a "repository") for storing design and development information. The seamless tool set is constructed of a group of software modules that together support all methodology components—planning, analysis, design, and construction—although they may not equate one-for-one with the components named here. For example, Arthur Andersen's Foundation tool set contains CASE modules named Plan/1, Design/1, and Install/1 to support the four methodology components.

Generally, modules of these tool sets can be purchased one at a time or as a package. Some seamless tool sets have PC workstation modules and repositories for planning, analysis, and design, and a mainframe solution for the code generation module. Some support all four modules at the PC workstation with a central repository.

An important group of specialized software products is called "reverse engineering" tools. These tools are considered CASE tools because they support adaptive maintenance through automated design and construction methodology components. Their purpose is to structure, document, and convert existing applications and databases to new technology. Today reverse engineering products begin by accepting the business functionality supported by the current system. They do not support the redesign of business functionality to meet new or changed strategic business needs. However, this is an area that will see much useful enhancement in the future. Once reverse engineering tools can be used at the logical design level to address changes in business functionality, these tools will become invaluable for the organization with large in place systems that require modification.

Those CASE products used to structure and document previously implemented applications through the translation of object code and/or source code into structured source code and physical designs can provide important support to organizations that must maintain production systems after their creators either retire or are transferred to new work. The products that convert databases (e.g., IMS to DB2) propose a target logical or physical data model design and allow the user to "restructure" the model before generating the new database. These products are popular with organizations that must move massive historical databases to new technology.

REPOSITORY AND INFORMATION SHARING

When data is entered into a CASE tool, that data is stored in the form of diagrams, structures, supporting names, textual descriptions, and narrative. Early CASE products stored that data in a dictionary. Like a file cabinet, the dictionary accepted almost any type of data, because it had few or no rules regarding what could be put into the dictionary or how one item of data related to other data. Only if the user specified the relationships, would associations be established. Some analytical exception reporting could be performed to check for associations and find inconsistencies, but changes to the dictionary were not automatic. If data was changed in one diagram, the impact of that change on other diagrams could be traced through exception reporting, but corrections had to be made manually.

Newer CASE products have expanded the dictionary into what James Martin calls an "encyclopedia" and others have termed a "repository." The repository is more sophisticated than a dictionary because a repository:

- Stores data and the rules for relating each item of data to other items, in addition to policing the addition of new data. If the rules are violated, new data cannot be entered.
- Contains knowledge and rules for constructing and populating diagrams. If a rule is violated, some tools instruct the user on what is allowed. Others actually execute the correct rule. Extensive exception and comprehensive analytical reporting support the diagram rules.
- Contains knowledge and rules for selecting and bringing together the right diagrams and data for code generation.

In essence, a repository is a "smart dictionary." To maintain and control the knowledge base for the repository, CASE products tend to require data entry through the diagram function of the tool and to restrict direct access into the encyclopedia. Those that do not have this restriction in all cases (e.g., Foundation and Excelerator) provide sophisticated exception reporting for reconciling diagrams to repository content. The advantage of the restrictive approach is that it ensures repository integrity. The advantage of the nonrestrictive approach is that the repository is easier to use on projects where practical necessity often wins out over theoretical purity. Seamless CASE products require a repository strategy at the PC workstation level so that modules of the tool set can access and share the same data (Fig. 4.2).

The information engineering methodology promotes the creation of business process and data models that can be shared by a variety of different applications and databases. To implement this information sharing concept, a workstation repository must be able to access or retain parts of centrally stored models. In order to avoid massive model duplication, however, the CASE repository must be expanded beyond the individual workstation. Tool vendors have taken different approaches to achieving the shared repository. Some vendors have created a central repository which can be used by each designated PC workstation to download and upload data. Other vendors have created a multiple-level repository strategy. In this strategy, PC workstation repositories contain planning, analysis, and design data that can be shared with other PCs through a LAN network and file server. For code generation, a central repository is provided for physical

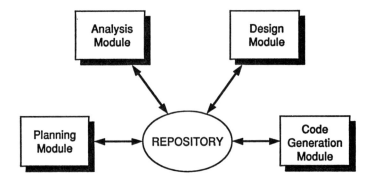

Note: Some data within the repository can be accessed through all modules.
Other data within the repository can be accessed only through certain modules.

Figure 4.2   CASE tool workstation level, respository strategy.

designs and generated applications and databases (Fig. 4.3). Again, the choice of strategy appears to be a case of the theoretical versus the practical. The central repository provides the most complete opportunity for information sharing, but communications channels and access to the mainframe may be strained with a full CASE implementation. A decentralized approach, where the central repository is used only for that information involved in the maintenance of the production databases and applications, reduces the need for access to the central repository. Logical models and designs remain locally maintained at the workstation or LAN level.

With the CASE repository centralized on a mainframe or accessible through LAN networks, knowledge and rules must be added to the repository so that information sharing and maintenance can be controlled. Management of the repository must include rules for:

• Tracking who is accessing what information.
• Assigning authority to manage the process of adding, changing, and deleting specific information in the repository.
• Ensuring consistency among existing repository information items and new information as added.
• Resolving access, consistency, and action conflicts on the same repository information.
• Down loading and up loading information from the central repository and the workstation repositories or among the workstations in a distributed, networked environment.

Repository and information sharing requires the creation of a new systems role—the knowledge coordinator. Just as concerns are raised when physical databases are shared by multiple applications, a number of important issues come up

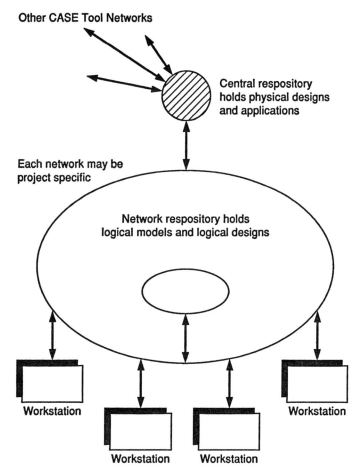

Figure 4.3 Multiple workstation respository configuration, example network structure.

when logical planning, analysis, and design information is used to support multiple application and databases. The most important of these are management issues that are unrelated to the technical capabilities of CASE repository technology. Systems professionals and users want to know, for example: "Who is responsible for knowledge coordination and access? Who is responsible for data administration? How many repositories are needed in the business unit? One? One for every business area? How is logical information synchronized with existing production physical databases?" The repository concept requires a degree of integration and coordination among systems professionals and business users that has not been tested in most systems organizations. These issues must be faced as the technology develops, particularly if we are to avoid creating the potential for great confusion and system failure.

OPEN VERSUS CLOSED ARCHITECTURE

The most volatile and controversial concept in CASE technology is the future direction of the hardware and software operating environment for CASE. Two competing approaches, or "architectures," are vying for prominence in the marketplace—open architecture and closed architecture. If we knew which architecture were most viable for the long term CASE solution, then today's purchase choices would be much easier. IBM, in announcing its AD/Cycle, wants to create an open architecture environment, but the reality is that open architecture does not exist as yet. Just getting the primary CASE product vendors to agree on logical and physical repository standards is a monumental task. Each has a commitment to and a large monetary investment in a specific approach to CASE implementation.

The open architecture concept is an exciting one, however. It promises to provide a CASE tool operating environment where different tools can exchange information through standard protocols for communication (gateways) and standard structures for repository creation, access, and management. Such an environment would enable multiple front end CASE tools to feed multiple code generators. All would share the same central repository without the need for special linkage software to make the tools compatible with each other. For the distributed, diverse, multivendor environments that some organizations support today, the open architecture would be a dream come true. It would allow those with an existing CASE tool investment to integrate currently incompatible CASE products. The organization would acquire only what is needed for complete life cycle support and could avoid the political and cultural conflicts surrounding the selection of a single solution.

The most appealing aspect of the open architecture concept is its flexibility. It promises a stable platform from which to expand, yet also offers opportunities for competitive creativity to flourish. However, we do not know with certainty when this promise will become a reality. A phased delivery of this architecture has been promised within the next five years, but everyone involved shares a healthy skepticism about the chances of meeting this goal.

Today's reality is the closed architecture approach. In this approach, automated and complete life cycle compatibility may be attained through one of two alternatives. The first alternative is the seamless CASE product consisting of modules and repository built to a single standard. The second alternative is the integration of separate front end and back end products through repository interface software. The first alternative is expensive; the second alternative cumbersome. In addition, the products that support this approach are constantly improving through the incorporation of increased standardization and enhanced capabilities. Many vendors offer standard linkages and are available to create unique linkages required by their customers. Some of the seamless CASE tool vendors also support linkages into and out of their front end modules. A typical strategy is to provide ASCII formatted files which the receiving CASE product can accept. Time, money, purchaser demands, and vendor staying power will provide a solution to the architecture dilemma. Although most organizations would prefer not to wait, they will have no choice but to accept advances as they are produced. To survive in the CASE business, vendors will have to have sufficient dollars for continual product improvement. To survive as CASE users, systems organizations will have to keep aware of new developments and determine how those developments impact their needs.

UNIQUE APPROACHES

In the long term, CASE tool technology will follow the hardware and software technology advances for application production. Each unique advance will be woven into CASE options. For example, the Foundation product has recently been expanded to offer options for building applications that run in a cooperative processing environment. New design and construction CASE modules utilize the latest OS2 presentation manager environment. Simply stated, the screen handling and editing of a cooperative processing application can be processed at the PC workstation level, and only the actual database affecting processing requires access and utilization of the mainframe processing power.

ESSENTIAL CASE TOOL FUNCTIONS AND CAPABILITIES

Each CASE product is packaged to make itself distinctive and attractive to buyers. Obviously, the more functions and features that are offered in a product and the more sophisticated their presentation, the greater is the potential impact of that product on the systems organization. But organizations seeking to purchase or upgrade CASE tools vary in their requirements, just as purchasers of new cars differ in their evaluation of the value of various automotive functions and features.

It is not possible to review in great detail here the capabilities of every tool on the marketplace today, but it is possible to review the standard functions and features and typical variations available. While there are six fundamental CASE tool functions, not all types of tools support every function. In addition, some vendors have integrated their CASE tool set with non-CASE capabilities such as project management and life cycle support functions. Andersen's Foundation product, for example, includes a METHOD/1 module to support the systems life cycle and a MANAGE/1 module to support project management in addition to the CASE modules of PLAN/1, DESIGN/1, and INSTALL/1. Other products will provide a different level of support for a given function or provide different strategies for function implementation. Tool functions and features are summarized in Fig. 4.4.

FUNCTIONS/ FEATURES	PURPOSE
Encyclopedia	Data storage and access
Graphics/ diagrams	Vehicles for data entry, analysis, documentation, and presentation
Analytical reports	Validation, consistency, accuracy checks (comprehensive and exception)
Prototyping	Application construction to see the effect of design decisions
Application and database generation	Automated code generation
Documentation	Project, diagram and application history
User materials	References for user "Help"
Data interfaces	Linkages for tools and data
Human interfaces	Features that make the tool user friendly
Vendor support	Customer service support
Configuration options	Hardware and software choices
Housekeeping support	Tool administration and management
Cost containment	Initial and support costs

Figure 4.4 CASE tool functions and features.

Function 1: Encyclopedia

The encyclopedia supports the storage and access of information for the CASE tool user. This information may be varied. Generally, it will include at least information about data entities and functional processes and their relationships. These encyclopedia items are sometimes referred to as "objects." When looking at the encyclopedia, ask these questions to clarify product features:

- How is the information stored in the encyclopedia? How does the storage technology affect access to the encyclopedia?
- Can the encyclopedia be accessed directly or must information be accessed through a diagram?
- How big is the encyclopedia? When must extra memory or hardware storage be added to accommodate large projects? How big can the diagrams become before the performance of the tool is affected?
- Is the encyclopedia centralized, and if so, how? Is it stored on a mainframe? What information is shared on the LAN network? What resides at the workstation level? How does that affect access speed and flexibility? What does the user need to know in order to access information in any of the encyclopedias?
- How is multiple user access to the encyclopedia managed or networked? How is encyclopedia information utilization monitored? How are access conflicts resolved? How many workstations can actually be supported by a single central repository?
- Can the repository learn? Can rules be added, or are they all predefined?

Function 2: Graphics/Diagrams

Information is captured in one of two ways in a CASE tool. It is entered through a diagram or through data fields on a screen. Diagrams, however, are the essential data entry, analysis, documentation, and presentation vehicle for most CASE tools. The diagrams supported are based on the methodology or methodologies underlying the CASE tool. The rules and symbols for diagram construction and the rules for connecting and relating diagrams are dependent on the vendor's approach to enforcing the underlying methodology. Different products may reference the same diagram by different names.

Questions to ask regarding the graphics and diagram features include:

- What methodology(s) are the diagrams based on? How rigorously is that methodology supported? Can users customize that methodology or insert their own methodology into the tool by creating new rules for constructing and relating diagrams?
- What symbologies are supported? Are symbol standards set by a single knowledge coordinator or are they defined by each user at his workstation? Once the standard is set, can the use of other symbols be blocked?
- What diagrams are supported (data, process and/or process-data integration)? Are standard "shells" provided for some diagrams like the matrix diagram or the decomposition diagram?
- What diagrams are required for code generation? Which are strictly optional?
- Must diagrams be drawn "manually" or is the product capable of generating a diagram automatically after the entry of essential data into the tool?

- Which combinations or sequences of diagrams are allowed? Which are required? Which are defaults?
- Does information in some diagrams automatically flow into related diagrams or does information have to be copied from one diagram to another? For example, can data from a decomposition diagram be copied into a matrix diagram, or is each diagram built separately? Must action diagrams developed at the logical level be re-entered at the physical level or can the same diagrams be called up and refined?
- How are diagrams constructed? How much of the diagram construction is tool driven? How much is manually defined by the tool user? For example, do diagrams automatically flow top to bottom or left to right or can a user create any diagram flow he wishes? Does the tool require a standard construction language for action diagrams or may the tool operator use any type of structured English? Can the standard constructs be accessed through PF keys and typing or must they be chosen from a list using the mouse?
- Must a diagram be used to add, change, or delete information in the encyclopedia? If not, are changes automatically recorded and potential impacts annotated on the diagrams?
- How many screens are required to complete a diagram? How much back and forth movement between screens is required to change a diagram?
- Can the tool learn new diagram rules or new diagram types?
- How is repository data updated and reconciled with screen data? For example, if an attribute used on multiple screens is deleted from an Entity Table, how is the attribute flagged or eliminated from the screens? Is the operator prevented from deleting the attribute from the model until all references on the screens have first been removed?

Function 3: Analytical Reporting

Analytical reporting is probably the most underutilized function of CASE tools, yet it is one of the most powerful functions provided. Analytical reporting validates the consistency and accuracy of diagrams developed in the CASE tool and other information entered into the encyclopedia. Exception analysis reporting uncovers inconsistencies and omissions in diagrams. As an example, a report might identify data fields used on screen layouts but not found in the entity relationship diagram. Comprehensive analyses provide summaries of diagram information and calculations for decision support. For example, a report might provide a narrative walk through of an entity relationship diagram, or it might cluster entities based on an analysis of the entities in the entity relationship diagram. Questions that may be used to evaluate features include:

- What types of analysis are available? What purpose does each analysis type serve?
- Which analysis types are required? Which are strictly user selected?
- Which analyses are conducted in real time as the diagrams are constructed or changed? What information is given to the user, what actions must he take, and what actions are taken automatically by the tool?
- Which analytical reports are created after a diagram has been completed? What information is given to the user, what actions must he take, and what actions are taken automatically by the tool?
- Can the user create his own analysis reports? How difficult is this to do?

Function 4: Prototyping

Prototyping is the construction of part or the whole of an application so that users can see the outcome of their design decisions. There are different levels of prototypes. Consider which of these levels is supported by the CASE tool and which you will require.

Screens only.   In this prototype level, specifications for screens and reports are painted on the screen for users to evaluate. In some cases, data may be entered, but no application functionality can be executed. Evaluate this feature with the following questions:

- How are screen specifications stored in the encyclopedia? What tool specific diagrams are required?
- Does the CASE tool automatically paint the screen, or must the user structure the screen initially?
- Can mandatory and optional data fields be displayed?
- How are the data fields on the screen validated against the data model? How are inconsistencies handled?
- What logical design work must be completed before a screens only prototype can be built?
- What standards support the screen design rule base? Can they be changed?
- How are data fields on screens added, moved, deleted, or changed?

Screen navigation.   This prototype level builds on the screens only prototype by linking the screens to menus so that screen sequencing and utilization patterns can be checked. Feature questions to ask regarding this prototype level include:

- How are screen linkages and sequencing defined in the CASE tool?
- How are the screens sequenced initially? How are they resequenced when necessary?

- What tool specific diagrams are required to define the navigation requirements? How are menus created and changed?
- What standards are used for the menu and navigation rule base? Can they be changed?

Fully and partially functional prototypes.   Building on the two previous prototype levels, some CASE tools offer a prototype level that processes transactions or accesses a database to respond to an inquiry. For a prototype to be fully functional, all processing and inquiries should be supported. The only difference between this prototype level and a production system is the size of the database it accesses and the number of users that can be supported by the application. In other words, it may be missing performance and capacity functionality, but otherwise the prototype runs just like the real thing. A partially functional prototype, as the name implies, implements only a slice of functionality of the total application. Feature questions to ask in examining this prototype level, in addition to those previously listed, include:

- What must be added to the prototype to make it a production application?
- Which components of the logical and physical designs are required for the functional prototype to be generated?

Function 5: Application and Database Generation

Code generation is at the heart of application and database generation. It is one of the principal goals of CASE technology. It may not warm the heart of the typical programmer, but the opportunity to generate code faster, at a consistent level of quality, and with automated documentation support fills the heart of many a manager with a warm glow. There appear to be at least two perspectives regarding code generation. Some vendors have chosen to generate code based on action diagrams written as a code generation language. Others have chosen to generate code based on action diagrams written in the programming language (e.g., COBOL2 and SQL). The former claim simplicity and understandability, and the latter point to the knowledge base within existing programmers as the advantage of their approach.

Feature questions to ask regarding code generation include:

- What are the minimum information requirements (diagrams and data) for transitioning from logical to physical design and then to code generation?
- What actions must the user take for each transition? Are there manual linkages to be made such as copying (translating) logical design action diagrams into physical design action diagrams or copying (translating) logical entity tables into data structure charts? What does the tool do automatically?

- What further work must be done to make the generated code run as an application?
- What type of assembly activities are required to tie together action diagrams into an application?
- What is required to generate a database structure, and populate it with data?
- What type of testing facilities are available?
- Once constructed, what diagrams are used to make changes to generated applications and databases? The physical design? The logical design? The source code? If code is not generated from the logical design, how is the logical design to be maintained in order to reflect the physical design of the application or database?
- What languages and operating environments are supported by the code generation function?
- What is required for code generation? A mainframe? A PC? Additional hardware and software?

Function 6: Documentation

CASE tools can provide systems professionals with documentation support. There are three possible types of support—project documentation, diagram documentation, and application and database documentation.

Project documentation.   This capability provides the ability to assemble information for presentation to reviewers and decision makers. Feature questions for project documentation include:

- What capabilities exist for storing, retrieving, and analyzing nondiagram project information such as project objectives, project schedules, interview notes, and so forth? Does the tool allow the creation of new information capture categories? (This is called repository extensibility by the vendors.)
- What are the text editing capabilities for diagrams, descriptive narrative, and reports? Are analysis reports and diagrams readable? Are there margins and cross references? Some tools, when preparing diagrams for printing, reduce and abbreviate diagrams to such an extent that they are not readable.
- What are the document assembly capabilities? Can progress toward completion be tracked? Can a table of contents be built? Can diagrams, reports and narrative be selected and ordered? Can a document be printed out of sequence with user defined page numbers?
- What are the document production capabilities? Can the output be exported to a desk top publisher?

Diagram documentation.   This capability provides the ability to print out diagrams of various sizes. Feature questions include:

• What is required to cut a large, complex diagram into segments that can be printed and then reassembled into one diagram? Is the work manual or automated by the tool?

• What is required to size a large diagram for a smaller scale? Are words cut up or abbreviated automatically? Are symbols elongated or squashed down? Is readability maintained?

Application and database documentation.   This capability provides the ability to analyze logic, correct errors, and maintain the application after installation. Feature questions include:

• Are printouts of the essential code generation diagrams such as action diagrams and data structure diagrams available?

• Does the tool allow access to source code files resulting from code generation? (Note: Access to source code may allow programmers to maintain applications at the source code level as is generally done today. In the future, changes will be made at the design level only.)

In addition, it is important to understand how these CASE tool functions are integrated. This can affect how the tool is used in an everyday work environment. The extent of integration can impact how long initial data entry takes and how the data is maintained once it has been input. Four key integration questions are as follows:

• How does the user access each function in the CASE tool?
    Some tools require the user to decide first what life cycle activity is going to be performed (e.g., planning, analysis, logical design, physical design, prototype, or code generation). The software then presents him with all the functions and subfunctions available for that life cycle activity. If data is entered into a diagram that is available only in one module, then the user may be unable to access that data from another module, even though both modules use the same repository.

• Can the encyclopedia be accessed directly by the user, or must the user access the encyclopedia through the graphics/diagram function?
    Some tools allow unrestricted access to the encyclopedia. Some tools allow direct access to the encyclopedia, but restrict this access to the knowledge coordinator. Other tools prohibit all direct access to the encyclopedia. If the user must access the encyclopedia through the graphics/diagram function, the integrity of the information entered will be enhanced, but the speed of entry will be slowed.

- Is the tool object oriented or task oriented?

  Many tools are task oriented requiring the tool user to switch tasks to accomplish a sequence of work. For example, to add an entity, the entity relationship diagram function is entered. To look at the relationships associated with that entity in the model, the user must exit the entity relationship diagram task, return to the selection menu, then select and enter the analysis or reporting function.

  An object-oriented user interface allows the tool user to select the object he wishes to work with, (e.g., an entity), and then perform any legal function on that object (e.g., add an entity, add attributes, build associations, examine associations, etc.).

- How are the diagrams connected? What diagrams and encyclopedia data are required to generate code?

  Some tools allow any diagram to be used with any other diagram. Other tools restrict diagram utilization to a given series or combination of series. When too many options are available, learning the tool can be difficult. When too few options are available, they may not support all project types required by the organization.

Although not functions in the true sense, other tool capabilities exist that should be explored in CASE tool evaluation and selection. These include:

Capability 1: User Materials

Reference documents and automated "Help" functions assist in operating the CASE tool, but the quality of the help provided by the tools varies greatly. This capability is important because none of the CASE tools is truly user friendly. Several of the vendors have compensated for this by providing skilled hot-line assistance, but for users who anticipate working at odd hours and on weekends, there is nothing as useful as a well-structured carefully written manual. Particularly useful are manuals with lots of problem solving examples and clear illustrations. Those manuals that demonstrate how to solve real business problems, with all of their inconsistencies and confusion, are among the best.

Capability 2: Data Interfaces

If the CASE tool is not a seamless tool, then compatibility among tool modules is critical. This includes the ability to import data from other tools as well (e.g., PRISM planning data into Excelerator, IE:Expert data into MAJEC, IEW files into SAGE/APS) and the ability to export data from the selected tool to other tools (e.g., Excelerator or IEW data into TELON or SAGE/APS). Some tools offer many compatibility interfaces. Others have few interfaces, supporting only one or two other vendors.

Capability 3: Human Interfaces

Color screens, drop down menus, windowing for multiple diagram viewing, a mouse, and function keys all assist the user in operating the CASE tool. But not all of these features are equally valuable for all users. Some apparently helpful features such as the ability to click on an item to select it from a list are excellent for the casual user, but may slow data entry for skilled users. The ability to type in commands or use PF keys quickens the pace of data entry for power users.

Machine response time, as it is related to moving from screen to screen, is another important human interface consideration. Slow screen response time can lead to frustration. Sometimes response time can be improved by installing the software on more powerful hardware with additional amounts of core and disk memory. Compromises on memory that result from budget constraints can have a big impact on user satisfaction and productivity.

Another human interface consideration is the number or depth of different screens needed to complete one diagram. One tool, for example, requires the use of four screens to fully populate entities and attributes within an entity relationship diagram. This up and down screen paging can be time consuming and tedious.

Capability 4: Vendor Support

Every manufacturer of CASE products, from such corporate giants as Texas Instruments, IBM, and DEC to the smallest data interface software company, promises customer service. Important customer service features to look for include:

Meeting product delivery dates for releases.   The ability to deliver as promised is an indicator of high-quality customer service and honesty. One company was over eighteen months behind on a promised release containing features already offered by its competition. This can cause significant problems for the organization that is counting on those new capabilities. Cost factors make it difficult to switch vendors to add on a new capability. For better or worse, once a major corporate commitment has been made, the organization is at the mercy of the vendor.

Multilevel training.   Training in hands-on tool use can generally be obtained either directly from the vendor or indirectly from an outside consulting organization. Training should include appropriate classes for systems managers, tool users, and project teams. Training in methodology principles should be considered as well. This will ensure a smooth transition between theory and practice.

Installation planning and consulting support.   A vendor should make available support assistance through first project use and the culture shock period. Not all organizations will require outside support for this transition, but for those that do, it may spell the difference between success and failure. Without this type of assistance, some CASE products will end up on the shelf gathering dust. This support can come from the vendor's own consulting group or an outside organization.

Hotline support.   Knowledgeable customer service representatives should be readily available to answer questions. Find out what the hours are for hotline support and ask about the qualifications of those who answer the phones. Vendors are generally aware of the importance of this service, and some are quite good at assisting users in problem solving. The only way to be certain, though, is to ask others who have had experience with the vendor's hotline service.

User groups.   Local meetings, regional and national conferences, newsletters, and other information sharing vehicles should be supported by the vendor. Local and regional meetings can be a good place to get information on tool usage and problem solving.

Capability 5: Configuration Options

Many tools can be installed on different types of PC or mainframe hardware. Important questions to ask regarding configuration options include:

- Can implementation begin with standalone workstations? Can workstations be linked together for information sharing? What functionality is offered at the workstation level or file server level versus the central mainframe level? In what situations are standalone workstations sufficient?
- Can implementation begin with mainframe functionality and then move to a distributed networked environment?
- How many workstations can access a central repository efficiently at the same time?
- How many workstations can be networked together to share repository information?
- What factors in the configuration will impact tool performance?

Capability 6: Housekeeping Support

Tool administration and management is an important aspect of long-term CASE tool utilization. Features should include such items as:

- File management
- Repository consistency and conflict management
- User ID assignment and management
- Performance and capacity management

Capability 7: Cost Containment

Both initial cost and maintenance costs should be closely scrutinized. Cost varies greatly from vendor to vendor. Where once the only CASE options available were expensive ones, today there are many lower priced alternatives available in the marketplace. The prospective purchaser should closely compare his needs to product capabilities. It is possible to save a great deal of money by refusing to buy more tool than you need. It is also possible, of course, to buy less than you need. Consider carefully any special deals that are offered. Many vendors provide multiple copy discounts and offer special packages just before new releases are issued. Buying into an "old" release may or may not suit your needs. While regret is a not uncommon result of the CASE procurement process, it is something you want to avoid. Also, do not forget that only thirty-five percent of the total cost for CASE can be attributed to software and hardware. Training, support, and many indirect costs raise the investment level. Forgetting this fact can lead to CASE failure.

THE QUESTION OF TOOL RIGOR

The successful selection of a CASE tool may depend less on the tool's functions and features than on the constraints imposed by that tool on the organization. The degree of rigor with which a CASE tool restricts or redefines existing work habits can be a significant element in determining the ultimate success of the tool. The more restrictions imposed by the tool and the fewer options it presents, the more rigorous it can be said to be. A CASE tool can be considered to be flexible if it presents a great many options and relies on the user to enforce methodological principles. The more flexible tool, for example, will not mandate that data flow diagrams be developed, or that they be carried out to a specified level of analysis, or that they be related to another specified diagram set. The option to do all or none of these tasks will be presented, but not required. The more rigorous tool, on the other hand, will have built-in constraints that will prevent the user from, for example, entering data elements (attributes) until their corresponding entities have been entered. These constraints or "rules" must be mastered for effective use of the tool.

No one tool is completely rigorous or completely flexible. Rather, rigor and flexibility should be viewed as end points along a continuum. Examining the place of a given tool along the continuum can prove helpful in determining which tool is right for your organization (Fig. 4.5). What are the advantages of rigor and why is it more important to some buyers more than to others? Rigor makes a tool:

- Easier to learn.
- Faster to use.

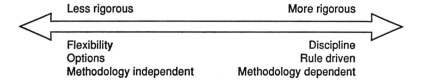

Figure 4.5 The CASE tool rigor continuum.

- Easier to support.
- Capable of delivering a higher degree of consistency across projects.

Rigor is important to those organizations that need assistance in bringing discipline and consistency to their systems life cycles. Rigorous tools encourage the development of transferable knowledge and skills. This gives flexibility to managers, enhancing their ability to manage projects, measure performance, and assign people to projects. If there is a common way of working, a common way of communicating and a common way of developing systems, then there is a higher likelihood of project success and user satisfaction. It is probably true that the more sophistication there is present in the organization, the less there is the need for this external imposition of standards, but it is safe to say that the organization that supports a strong set of standards is more likely to be successful in the long term than the one that relies on the creativity of its personnel.

While many organizations give lip service to the need for rigor, however, in practice the extent to which they impose standards varies greatly from project to project. Many programmers and analysts pride themselves on their creative, craftsman like approach to their jobs and enjoy the individual freedom and options of their work. They may measure success by the cleverness of their solutions and view any type of policing action as an intrusion. Therefore, the more rigorous the tool that is selected, the more likely the resistance to it. A high degree of tool flexibility makes these individuals more comfortable, but too great a degree of flexibility can make CASE long term success more difficult to achieve. Tools with many options and paths are more difficult to learn and rely much more on individual analyst knowledge and self-discipline for successful use. Their installation in the organization may be easier initially, but, in the long run, the potential benefits of CASE may be lost.

The rigor and flexibility of a particular CASE tool product can be examined from two perspectives:

- Methodology and common language
- Access and navigation strategies

METHODOLOGY AND COMMON LANGUAGE

The more closely a CASE tool supports a particular methodology, the more rigorous the tool is. A methodology defines a unified set of diagrams, symbols, and procedural instructions for planning, designing, and building systems. Although there can be multiple interpretations of a methodology, if the analyst understands a given methodology and a specific CASE tool closely follows that methodology, the analyst will begin his work with the tool already knowing a great deal about how the tool works. For example, information engineering separates data and process analysis. A tool that supports the information engineering methodology will present separate diagrams for data and process analysis, diagrams which will be readily understood by the analyst trained in this methodology. Tools with rigor will require the tool user to follow certain procedural instructions. The more automatic this enforcement, the more consistency there will be in tool use by the individual user and across the user base. For example, IEF and IEW, in adhering to the information engineering methodology and its top down approach to data analysis, will not allow an attribute to be entered into the encyclopedia unless it is defined through and related to an entity. Therefore, tool users will always enter entities first, then attributes. Dangling attributes can never exist as they would in a tool like Excelerator, which allows the analyst to define entities and attributes separately and relate them at a later time.

There is a down side, however, to this type of rigor. Using the tool may be cumbersome for individuals who may find that a given theory does not always fit the practices they engage in. This may happen for example, when constructing a data model and using the IEW or IEF CASE tool. The data modeler often starts with entity definitions. He moves on to identify and define attributes, but returns again to confirm, delete, and modify entity definitions through the normalization process. With IEW or IEF, the tool user cannot enter attribute information as it is defined. If attributes are identified that do not support a previously defined entity, he must create a dummy entity through which these attributes can be recorded in order not to lose them. After definition and normalization is complete, he must go back into the tool to move the attributes into the proper entities. This requires a tremendous amount of screen navigation. In other words, the tool does not perform well "interactively." Such tools require a utilization strategy which will avoid this cumbersome data entry. The only answer may be to delay entering the data model until it has been completed.

A tool is also rigorous when it provides only essential diagrams within the supported methodology and omits any optional diagrams. Such a tool takes the decision of, "Is this diagram needed?" out of the hands of the tool user. For example, IEF does not support the development of data flow diagrams or state transition diagrams because they are optional in the information engineering methodology. This should not be a problem unless these diagrams have been previously used as a standard by the organization.

Another consideration is whether or not a tool supports more than one methodology. Some vendors emphasize that their tools are "methodology independent." This may be particularly appealing to the organization that has no one accepted methodology or where several different competing methodologies exist. The result here is to expand diagram options and place the burden of selection on the shoulders of the tool users. They must be prepared to select options based on the nature of the project, the needs of the development team, and the knowledge base of the user communities. For example, the IEW strategy is to provide a single tool that can support both a structured analysis and an information engineering methodology. This flexibility allows people to transition from one methodology to the other using the same tool, but it increases the complexity of tool use, adds to education and support requirements, and transfers the burden of consistency for tool use to the CASE tool user.

Symbology, the grammar of diagrams, is another rigor issue. If multiple symbologies are allowed, systems professionals and business users will have difficulty reading diagrams. Many CASE tools offer more than one symbology. The issue, then, is whether or not the symbology can be defined at each workstation or whether it is centrally defined. For example, one tool allows entity relation diagram symbols to default to Backman, Chen, Martin, or user selected symbols with the touch of a function key. Clearly any organization would be better off with one standard here. Decisions on both methodology and symbology choice should really fall within the realm of management decision making. If the tool does not create a standard, management must.

A last aspect of rigor concerns the variations among CASE tools. Some organizations have purchased two or more CASE tools and want tool users to have access to multiple tools. Presumably, tool users would select a tool with the needs of a particular project in mind. Even if these tools follow the same methodologies and have the same symbologies defined as a standard, however, they may use language differently. Language consistency among CASE products (and sometimes even within the different modules of a single CASE product) may be lacking. A word may have two, three or four meanings. This may cause confusion and create learning difficulties. For example, one popular tool calls any item of data entered into the tool an "entity." But "entity" also has a specific technical meaning in the realm of data analysis. One tool calls the items of data entered into the tool "objects," but then refers to "entities" as "objects." Another tool defines "activity" as a function or process, defines a "function" as a group of processes and calls a "process" a repeatedly executed activity. It is not surprising that this lack of clarity causes a great deal of confusion.

ACCESS AND NAVIGATION STRATEGIES

Rigor is also a factor in the CASE tool user's ability to access and navigate among a tool's functions and features. The more direction given by the tool automatically, the more rigor is imposed. The more options offered, the more flexible the tool. The access and navigation features that should be examined include:

- Access control
- Diagram selection and navigation
- Analytical reporting requirements
- Prototyping and code generation access
- Project documentation access

Access Control

The more controlled the access into and out of the encyclopedia function, the greater the integrity and consistency of encyclopedia information. The greater the user's ability to access the encyclopedia directly, the more flexible the tool is considered. Direct access may allow for fast data collection, but there is a trade off. The less data entry discipline the tool imposes on the analyst, the greater the ability of the analyst to introduce error into the models and designs. By restricting access to the encyclopedia to diagram data entry, the tool can prevent the entry of errors. Diagram driven data entry requires anywhere from one to three screen interactions. For example, to define an attribute in one tool, the user must first define an entity in an entity relationship diagram (screen one); then after entering an entity name, key, and definition, the user adds the attribute (screen two) to an attribute list; and defines the attribute and its characteristics (screen three). The user then returns to screen one to access another entity or screen two to add another attribute. In another tool, which allows direct access to the encyclopedia, the attribute can be identified and detailed on a single screen. He may choose to wait until a later time (and use another screen) to relate the attribute to a particular defined entity.

The stronger the encyclopedia access control, the less exception analysis reporting is required to identify discrepancies. The more screen interaction required for data entry, the more difficult the tool is to use interactively.

Diagram Selection and Navigation

The more discretion the tool user has in selecting and sequencing diagrams, the more flexible the tool is. Selection and access will vary based on: (1) how the six tool functions are integrated (encyclopedia, diagrams, analytical reporting, prototyping, code generation, and project documentation); and (2) how strictly the tool follows a given methodology. The more automated the process of diagram selection and navigation, the less flexibility in diagram sequencing. If this sequencing does not mirror the analytical process, however, it can result in extra work. For example, in one tool the user can build matrices comparing any two items (e.g., organization groups and business processes) to identify patterns or groupings of data for decision making (e.g., Which groups appear to be duplicating work?).

However, in this tool, items on the horizontal and vertical axes cannot be transferred from the decomposition diagrams where the items might have been first defined. Therefore, duplicate data entry of business processes and organization groups is required to populate the matrix.

Some tools allow the user to construct a diagram indirectly. This may be helpful when a tool is missing a desired capability. For example, one tool has no defined diagram support for the decomposition diagram. However, this tool's data flow diagram capability can be used in a hierarchial format to "fake" a decomposition diagram.

To assess a tool's diagram connectivity rigor, each diagram's selection options must be examined. If the tool does not permit two diagrams to be connected, they cannot share information, as with the example of the decomposition diagram and the matrix mentioned. In many tools, there are few or no rules for building diagram sequences and relationships. Consider, for example, the possible sequences and relationships of the decomposition, dependency, data-flow diagram, action, and entity relationship diagrams. A process on a decomposition diagram could explode into an entity relationship diagram to define the data used by that process or a dependency diagram or an action diagram. A process on a dependency diagram could explode into a data-flow diagram which could display a process that explodes into an entity relationship diagram. Other tools might allow only the explosion sequence of decomposition to dependency to action diagram, but might allow entity relationship diagram explosions for any process within any level of decomposition or dependency. This can be very confusing to beginning tool users.

Analytical Reporting Requirements

Exception reporting, whether predefined by the tool or custom built by the tool user, is a critical function for tools which do not enforce methodology rigor. Inconsistencies, missing or freestanding items, illegal associations, and redundancies, can be reported and subsequently corrected using this capability. In some cases, certain reported inconsistencies are acceptable for the level of detail at which the diagram is presented. In other cases, the correction of inconsistency is vital to the integrity of the design.

Comprehensive reporting can be provided to users through tool defined or customization options, just as with exception reporting. In some cases, the predefined reports are sufficient, although in other cases, they may provide more or less information than is really needed for the intended audience and purpose.

Predefined reports take the guesswork out of analytical reporting for the tool user, are easier to teach, and more likely to be used consistently. Customized reports may take several days to perfect and introduce a new level of tool complexity. But, once defined, the user defined report may be best for a particular purpose. The greater the number of predefined reports that exist and the more often the tool requires such reports to be run, the more rigorous the CASE tool.

Prototyping and Code Generation Access

Rigor in prototyping is found in the amount of automated interactive checking the tool performs between the data fields on an application screen and the data model in the encyclopedia. The tools that do not provide this checking, either comprehensively or on an exception report basis, allow errors and omissions to creep into models and designs.

With linked front end and back end CASE tools, rigor can be lost as information is transferred from one tool to the other, before or after prototyping. For example, extra care must be taken to reflect changes in prototype screen data fields made in the back end tool in the front end tool data model. This may require manual editing of the data model entity relationship diagram and entity tables.

This concern extends to code generation as well. Some tools allow users to modify generated code without forcing changes in design diagrams. The more flexible these change control procedures are, the more errors and discrepancies may be introduced into the design diagrams. This lack of rigor can make later maintenance difficult.

Project Documentation Access

CASE tools are not documentation tools. The quality and consistency of their presentation of information on paper is not what most users would wish it to be. The production of large or reduced diagrams and charts can take days and produce awkward results. Often printed pages must be pasted together and photocopied. The degree of elegance in the presentation of diagrams and text is pretty much left to the individual skill and experience of the tool user. Only a few tools offer documentation management capabilities.

STRATEGIES FOR CASE TOOL SELECTION

Before examining the functions and features of one or more CASE products, a systems organization will need to define the overall strategy it wishes to pursue regarding CASE technology. Based on the strategy, the most appropriate types of tools can be nominated for selection and a direction can be set for implementation. There are four basic strategies for CASE implementation:

- Investment retention strategy
- State-of-the-art strategy
- Experimentation strategy
- Wait and see strategy

Investment Retention Strategy

The investment retention strategy is the right one for organizations that have previously made an investment in CASE products and that want to use those tools already acquired as a basis for expansion. It is likely that these organizations were early users of front end or back end CASE products. They may have used these tools experimentally as many groups have done with front end tools like Excelerator, or they may have used only the planning and analysis modules of a seamless tool like IEW. They may be at the point where they wish to add back end functionality and/or expand utilization beyond a standalone workstation. Other organizations may have begun CASE tool use with a code generator and may even have used the tool in production rather than experimental situations. These tool users are going to want to expand their front end CASE capabilities.

This investment retention strategy will dictate a linkage solution unless the early CASE tool consisted of modules of the now seamless tool. In the former situation, selection of any new CASE products begins with an examination of the installed CASE product to identify: (1) other CASE products that are compatible with it now, (2) linkages planned for the tool, and (3) product strategy for addressing the repository issue for information sharing between front end and back end linked products. In the latter situation, where other modules of the seamless tool are now available, the strategy may be simply to acquire those modules.

The challenge in this approach is to know when to give up, that is, to know when it is better to move away from a commitment to a particular tool and to adopt a new, more comprehensive solution. A multiple product solution can be productive, but an organization that wants to adopt such a solution must be realistic about the efficiency and effectiveness that can be achieved when considering the constraints its current tool inventory imposes.

State-of-the-Art Strategy

Organizations that want the best technical solution offered today will select a state-of-the-art strategy. These organizations may or may not have a previous investment in tools. If they do, they are willing to replace them with something better. Today this strategy will dictate the selection of a seamless CASE tool that operates with a central repository, offers a networked communication environment, and is capable of code generation at the PC workstation level as well as on the mainframe. The organization that wants a state-of-the-art solution had better pay close attention to the many conferences and journals available to educate them on the latest and the best, however, because this list is subject to change at any time.

This strategy is an expensive, all encompassing one, and an organization that embraces it must be prepared to accept these terms. The organization must also accept the fact that it will have to make a commitment eventually if it is to make progress with a strong implementation plan. It cannot forever be looking over the horizon to see what the next big advancement looks like. Therefore, it is best implemented in an organization that is not afraid to tackle difficult political and cultural issues head-on.

Experimentation Strategy

The experimentation strategy is for those organizations that wish to learn more about CASE. They do not want to stand still, but they are reluctant to take the "big plunge" for a variety of reasons. This reluctance might stem from:

- Insufficient funding for total immersion in CASE.
- Lack of knowledge about the true needs of the organization regarding CASE.
- A fairly stable development and enhancement environment and a high level of success with fourth generation languages and end user computing.

The experimentation strategy can accommodate all types of CASE tools. These tools may be purchased, or as with some mainframe tools, they can be leased. This strategy allows for the incremental adoption of CASE. It makes possible a quick acceptance of one or more tools while the organization is investing its energy in planning for and implementing other tools. It also makes it possible for individual groups or projects to act as pilots for various tools, enabling the organization to gain experience quickly on a variety of tools. However, experimentation must end and commitment must begin at some point. The price that may be paid for this approach is that different groups will become committed to different incompatible tools, and they will not want to sign on as eager users of a single CASE solution. It is also possible, with new tools coming on the market so often, that the experimentation stage can be prolonged indefinitely by the addition of another pilot to test yet another new tool. As with the other approaches, a strong sense of objectives and strategy on the part of management is needed to control the situation.

Wait and See Strategy

In the wait and see strategy, the organization decides that it will take no positive action until the marketplace "shakes out" and there is proof, one way or the other, on the feasibility of the open architecture concept. If an organization has some CASE tools available, it continues to use these and enhance their capabilities where possible, but that is the limit of its investment. If an organization has thus far made no investment in CASE technology, it continues to monitor the marketplace. In both situations, the organization can take positive steps to improve the systems design and development environment and prepare it for CASE products. This may include emphasizing CASE educational activities, introducing a specific life cycle or methodology such as information engineering, and training individuals in new techniques such as joint application development and concepts such as change management.

With this strategy in place, the organization can then proceed to select the best CASE product(s) to fit that strategy, examining all of the functions and features discussed earlier. That examination will be significantly enhanced if prior to beginning its research the organization defines its requirements for CASE. This definition should reflect:

- The life cycle and methodology principles supported by the organization.
- The amount of rigor and discipline management wishes to impose on work practices.
- The type of design and development work that represent a high priority for the organization (e.g., centralization of data resources, database conversion, new development, redevelopment, fixes to fairly new systems, or major enhancements to old systems).
- The hardware and software platforms available for application and database development work.
- The hardware and software platforms available for production applications and databases.

CASE IMPLEMENTATION ISSUES

The first organizations to implement CASE tools from 1985 to 1988 learned a great deal from the experience. The experience of that five percent of potential users identified a predictive set of issues that must be addressed when implementing CASE tools. These issues are grouped into seven categories as defined in Fig. 4.6. These issues were identified in a study of nineteen organizations conducted by the authors in 1988. It has been supplemented with their experience subsequent to the study.

Issue 1: Learning Curve

The start up period for a CASE tool is always longer than anticipated (Fig. 4.7.) Even when tool users receive formal training, learning the tool is a slow process. Casual use of a tool can lengthen the learning curve further. A tool must be used often if a user is to exercise its more sophisticated capabilities productively. Tutorials do help, but a user may need several weeks of tool use to fully comprehend and benefit from a single six hour session.

In addition, the first time a tool is used on an actual project, there is often a painful and time consuming relearning experience to be endured. This situation can be exacerbated if tool users insist on asking how they can make the tool support a present set of work practices and assumptions rather than allowing the

Learning curve	The ability to perform a task at a given skill level over time. A learning curve can show an increase, plateau, or decrease in skill performance over time.
Resistance	The reluctance of an individual to accept new work practices and a changed work environment. This resistance can be seen in active behavior (sabotage), passive behavior (neglect and nonfollow through) and passive aggressive behavior (special studies to show that something cannot work).
Methodology	A systematic and disciplined process used to accomplish a task based on certain theoretical principles. (A method is a way of doing something.) The more formal, structured, and disciplined a methodology, the greater the chance for achieving consistency and high-quality performance across a group of individuals.
Analyst behavioral skills	Skills in verbal and nonverbal communication and interaction with other individuals. These skills include the ability to manage groups, resolve conflicts, create consensus and motivate others.
Knowledge/skill building	Knowledge is an understanding of concepts and practices that can be demonstrated through performance of a task or through verbal and written testing. Knowledge is built through education. A skill represents the ability to perform a task to a certain degree of accuracy and completeness. It is built through training and demonstrated through action. The effective utilization of a skill is often dependent on the acquisition of a specific area of knowledge.
Data collection techniques	The gathering of information from individuals and groups. Techniques should provide an organized and systematic way to identify information patterns and trends.
Coordination of support efforts	The assignment and scheduling of resources to ensure that events occur in the most effective manner.

Figure 4.6   CASE implementation issues.

tool to dictate certain procedures. Attempting to force a tool to mimic a non-CASE environment will slow down implementation considerably and inevitably lead to disappointment for first time use. Everyone involved must accept that initial implementation of a CASE tool will slow down design and development work. Extensive support is required to get through that initial period.

Issue 2: Resistance

The most experienced analysts and programmers often fight the introduction and implementation of CASE tools more vigorously than other systems personnel. Veterans with fifteen to twenty years of experience may be the most difficult to convert. In some organizations where code generators are installed,

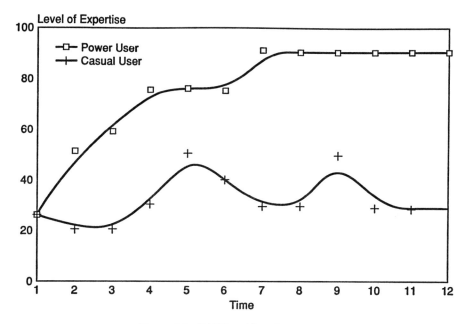

Figure 4.7 CASE tool learning curve.

veteran programmers, rather than refuse to use these tools, find performance problems with the generated code and insist that these problems can only be solved through manual coding. One reason for this problem is that CASE tools challenge the philosophical basis of design for those who consider themselves craftsmen. Another is the fear on the part of these veterans that their skills and expertise have become obsolete. One manager confronted with this problem compared it to the difficulties involved in the introduction of structured programming.

Another cause of resistance may be found in the lack of specific rewards for the use of new tools. In one organization, a systems manager described a project manager's view of programmers as ". . . so busy doing what they have to do, they haven't had the time to think about it (CASE)." Generally, these systems managers and project managers are veteran analysts and programmers themselves, having worked their way up through the ranks. They know the old way of doing business, as well as how to work the political system to obtain resources, and they are often under tremendous pressure to deliver applications on unrealistic deadlines. Without a specific incentive for these managers to overcome their natural resistance to a new tool, they will be unwilling to take people off projects, have them trained on an unproven tool, and then use that tool on a high visibility, critical project. The risk is too great and, some believe, unnecessary. Upper management, if committed to CASE, must realize this and develop an incentive and reward program for these individuals.

Issue 3: Methodology

In order for CASE to be successful, a formal methodology, like information engineering, must be put in place, must be accepted by the analysts and programmers as an organization standard, and must be enforced by systems management. The larger the project, the greater the need to have a methodology structure in place prior to tool use. Although this situation is changing, it is still true today that many programmers, analysts, project managers, and systems managers have only limited knowledge of the front end of the life cycle, particularly the logical design phase. Their training and interest begins with physical design, and logical design is often seen as no more than a quick stopover on the way to coding.

CASE tools raise this issue to a crisis point in some organizations. Programmers and analysts may not have a full life cycle view of an application. They relate principally to the life cycle activities in which they participate. Analysts see little need to maintain design documentation after initial creation because they are not impacted by the code generation process, and programmers see little need for program documentation because they know the code. When CASE is installed, this problem will be intensified if code is generated from nonmaintained design diagrams. Automation, in and of itself, does not guarantee up-to-date specifications. Without enforcement and rewards from management, results will not be consistent. This dramatically reduces the benefits of CASE. Even the CASE vendors recognize the problem, and many advise their customers of the importance of implementing a formal methodology along with their products. If analysts and programmers are not ready for a structured and disciplined methodology, they are probably not ready for CASE.

Some organizations hesitate to move from a vague or absent set of methodology principles to a sophisticated information engineering driven design and development life cycle because they believe the leap is simply too great. They should not be concerned about this. Information engineering principles should not be beyond the reach of any competent programmer or analyst. If, however, the organization wants to begin by instructing staff in the principles of structured analysis, this can also be a good way to introduce a common set of standards and practices. The choice of one methodology over another is probably less important than a strong commitment to a specific set of principles.

Issue 4: Analyst Behavioral Skills

An important job performed by today's analyst is that of communicating with business users and assisting them in reaching decisions. Good interpersonal skills are required to make this interaction with users effective and meaningful. While CASE tools can provide diagrams and prototypes that assist in the communication process, analysts cannot expect the tool to handle all of their communication problems for them. In fact, if not properly used, CASE tools can impede communication. Some of the diagrams produced by these tools end up looking like computer chip wiring diagrams, thus inhibiting rather than enhancing communication. In addition, if users do not understand the basic methodological assumptions behind the diagrams created by the tool, they may have trouble in interpreting those diagrams. Prototypes too can cause problems if they are improperly used. When unreasonable expectations for prototypes have been created, or when prototypes are not developed with a strong user interface in mind, they can cause users to question the value of the design process and the quality of the system that it will produce.

In other words, CASE can help, but only if the analyst understands how to use it to achieve specific communication objectives. The communication skills required by the analyst include:

- Identifying and clarifying issues and problems.
- Managing conflicts and constructing negotiated solutions.
- Building consensus among diverse individuals and groups.
- Translating user decisions and requests into design information to feed the code generation process.

Although it is not generally recognized, these skills are vital to the success of the implementation of CASE. Without these skills, the analyst will not achieve the highest possible quality in his CASE input. And without high-quality CASE input, the analyst runs the risk of producing an inferior system product.

Issue 5: Knowledge and Skill Building

Tool knowledge is built both through a formal process of education and through an informal process of building awareness, setting expectations and developing commitment. It is relatively easy to address the need for formal education. This is readily supplied by tool vendors and CASE education specialists. The informal process of building awareness must be conducted within the organization and it requires customization to be truly successful. It is worth the time required, though, for it can make the difference between CASE implementation success and failure. There are several different audiences for CASE training. These audiences include systems managers, programmers, analysts, project managers, and selected business users at various levels within the organization. The type of training each group receives may depend on a variety of internal cultural and environmental factors. All of these individuals need an awareness of the objectives and capabilities of CASE and an understanding of how CASE fits into life cycle activities and impacts project planning and management. More specifically, they need to understand:

CASE concepts and tool capabilities. They need to be able to answer the questions: "What is CASE?" "Why do we need it?" "What can it do for me?" and, "How will it change what I do?"

Methodology principles and CASE concepts. They need to be able to answer the questions: "What is information engineering?" "Why do we need it?" "How is it going to change our work?" "How can we use it?" and, "How does it relate to CASE?"

Life cycle principles. They need to be able to answer the questions: "What concepts and procedures govern our development of systems?" "What should a rapid application development life cycle contain?" "How does this impact the way we manage projects?" "What benefits are there to this approach?" and, "What is my role in this new life cycle?"

The informal education required to answer these questions can be conducted within the organization by a small group of committed CASE users who understand and support the new approach adopted by the organization. These individuals should be able to answer the questions identified and to present this information in a positive and convincing manner. Their job is really commitment building, and this requires both strong education and sales skills.

Issue 6: Data Collection Techniques

Both business users and analysts need to understand the specific input requirements of the CASE tool they are using. These can vary from tool to tool, with some tools requiring that information be collected and entered in a certain manner and others providing a more open set of possibilities. Data collection needs may also vary depending on project documentation requirements. A high-level planning project will not have the same requirements as a transaction system design project. No matter what the tool or project type, however, it is imperative that the information collected be of the highest quality and reliability. One vendor's brochure illustrates the CASE experience with a picture of several business experts standing around an analyst seated in front of a PC. The experts are gesturing at the screen, while the analyst is presumably hard at work entering information into the CASE tool. Needless to say, this does not represent a realistic or even desirable view of the data collection process. It is not likely to provide the quality or reliability that is required.

In order to meet the high standards of data collection, a process like joint application development is required. That is why we call the relationship between CASE and JAD a partnership. Joint application development provides high-quality CASE input, and CASE provides high-quality information validation and aids in system construction. If they are to be successful, those charged with implementing CASE within the organization must acknowledge the importance of the issue of quality input and take steps to address it. We think they will find that joint application development is the answer.

Issue 7: Coordination of Support Efforts

There are a number of activities that fall under the heading of coordination of support efforts. These activities must be addressed if user frustration and poor performance is to be avoided. Systems managers must commit adequate resources to ensure that appropriate support is maintained.

One type of support is the formal training that was mentioned earlier. Full-tool utilization cannot be obtained if tool users are not provided with high-quality training. It is also important that this training be provided at an appropriate time. The individual who has just been trained needs immediate access to the tool in order to practice his new skills and an opportunity to exercise these skills on a real project fairly quickly after training has been completed. The best type of training will focus on "how to" skills and on two important conceptual areas: the relationship between tool capabilities and methodology principles, and the relationship between tool capabilities and specific project needs.

Another type of support relates to the establishment of common practices regarding the application of tool capabilities to projects across the different project teams that may be operating within the organization. Three factors appear to guide how tools are accepted and utilized within the organization:

- Dictated policy: "Thou shalt use . . ."
- Project team sophistication and experience
- Tool capabilities

Certain policies regarding CASE tool use must be dictated. Some organizations, for example, require that specific CASE tools be used for projects over a certain size (e.g., 400 hours) and that for smaller projects, a team may choose its tools from several options. Others define tool utilization policy based on data requirements, project type (e.g., new development) or the need for prototyping. Dictated policy has the advantage of giving CASE a certain legitimacy and authority, as well as ensuring some degree of consistency, and hence higher quality, in its implementation.

It is not possible, however, to predefine every aspect of CASE tool usage. For this reason, the organization must consider the level of sophistication and extent of experience present in the project team and the particular capabilities available in the tool. In initial projects, the project team will want to exercise only the most basic capabilities of the tool, but over time, they will be able to add the use of more sophisticated capabilities. The team, for example, may begin by using all of the default specifications for graphics development or report generation. Over time the team will start to introduce customized versions of graphics and reports. This can yield benefits for both the project team and the organization. If project teams are permitted a certain degree of flexibility in using the tool, their commitment to its use will increase, as will their level of satisfaction.

This leads to another type of support that the organization can provide. It should create mechanisms to continue the CASE education and commitment building process. Mechanisms such as CASE user groups, CASE newsletters, and financial support for individuals who want to attend relevant national conferences can all enhance the level of sophistication and commitment exhibited by tool users.

PREREQUISITES FOR EFFECTIVE CASE USE

Those who have been through the experience of selecting and implementing CASE tools have recommended that those responsible for tool implementation lay the groundwork in the following way:

Understanding the Methodology.

Each tool embraces certain assumptions about the systems planning and development life cycle and the user must understand these assumptions. CASE implementors must identify the methodological principles that are supported by the target tool(s) and determine whether or not sufficient knowledge of these principles is in place in the organization for effective tool use. If sufficient knowledge is not in place (either among the systems professionals or the business users), then a plan for delivering this education must be developed.

Matching the Methodology to the Life Cycle.

A tool will have a greater chance for success if its definition of life cycle phases and deliverables matches those of the accepted life cycle. Changes may be required to the life cycle to ensure that this happens. CASE tools are less easily changed, but if one has been selected carefully and if options for customization are utilized, this may also help in ensuring that the tool and the life cycle are supportive of each other.

Defining Project Scope.

No tool will be used exactly the same way in all situations. Project type, complexity, span, and size all play a part in defining tool use. Standard project scoping techniques should be implemented in order to ensure that these project characteristics are clearly identified at project inception. Improper scope definition has been shown to be a major cause of project failure, with or without CASE tools. It is wise to use the introduction of CASE to bring a new set of standards to bear here, especially if this has been a problem in the past.

Developing Skills within the Organization.

CASE tools can add discipline to a sound set of skills, but they cannot make up for poor analytical thinking. These thinking skills need to be developed for an analyst to do his best work. One way to build these skills is through methodology training that emphasizes the application of principles to real business problems. To be successful, this training should encourage a structured approach to problem solving and be presented as a discipline, not as a collection of arbitrary rules.

Supporting CASE Users.

Information must be available for all systems managers and potential CASE tool users. They must know what tools are available, what benefits these tools can provide, when each should be used, and how each should be used. CASE implementation should be a project itself, complete with budget, an accountable project manager, and team members from across the organization and from all levels within it. The project team should report directly to a senior systems executive, and be removed as far as possible from organization politics.

Meeting Hardware Needs.

Many CASE tools require dedicated hardware as an addition to the standard PC configurations already present in the organization. The organization must be prepared to make a sufficient financial commitment to providing adequate hardware resources to ensure that users have easy access to CASE software. In addition, while some tools will function at a basic level on a minimal hardware configuration, it is important to provide more than the minimum in most cases. If tool users find that they have to wait for an unreasonable amount of time for the tool to process data or produce reports, their acceptance of the tool will be jeopardized.

IMPACT ON THE SYSTEMS ENVIRONMENT

CASE tools are often the catalyst for behavioral and procedural changes to the systems design and development life cycle. The larger the organization, however, the more time it takes for CASE to have an impact, either positive or negative. Depending on the emphasis placed on CASE, it can take from several months to several years before the real impacts can be measured.

These impacts will not be evenly distributed across an organization. Different groups are affected in different ways. Clearly, the roles of analyst and programmer will change most dramatically. Data administration activities, too, may be strongly effected. Other groups such as operations and technical support, on the other hand, may remain fairly unaffected. The specific impact areas to watch should include:

- Financial
- Productivity
- Job restructuring
- Change management
- Maintenance
- Performance measurement
- Internal communication

Financial Impact

For many organizations, the most significant impact area that will have to be addressed in the initial implementation of CASE is financial. If implemented across the systems organization and supported by a full education and training program, CASE can indeed be expensive. It is a capital investment, but one that should provide a return in the future through decreased project costs. CASE cannot be justified as a short-term expense because the productivity savings that lead to decreased project costs cannot be realized immediately. It should be remembered too that hardware and software account for only thirty-five percent of the total cost of CASE implementation. Labor costs are affected by CASE also, as are the costs of training and management. In one organization, a study showed that it actually cost about $30,000 for five days of CASE training for one individual when the cost of lost productivity was taken into account. On the other hand, the organization can also predict the savings brought by CASE by projecting time saved in construction and maintenance. All of these financial impacts must be evaluated when a commitment to CASE is discussed.

Productivity Impact

The initial decrease in productivity experienced by first time CASE tool users increases the stress felt by everyone involved in a project. For this reason it is particularly important that unreasonable delivery dates not be set for such projects. Initial data entry into the tool always takes longer than expected and the learning curve is a steep one. Expectations must be carefully managed, especially for initial pilot projects. Quality should be stressed instead of speed. This is an immediately obtainable goal that can be demonstrated even in a single life cycle phase. Productivity gains, on the other hand, will best be measured in the life cycle as a whole.

Job Restructuring Impact

Initially, programmers may resist the arrival of CASE for fear that their jobs may be eliminated. This happens when the code generation capabilities of the tool are overemphasized. This is really a misconception of the impact of CASE, however. It is unlikely that human programmers will be eliminated until code can be generated far more easily and completely than it can today. What does occur is a change in the way analysis and programming are performed. Analysts become internal consultants to business groups, facilitating the definition of process and information needs. Programmers give up much of their manual code writing for code module construction. This change is similar to changes in the home construction business. Carpenters, moving from custom home to modular home construction, still build houses, but the type of work they do has changed. Where specialty work must be done, their expertise is still highly respected.

Change Management Impact

CASE requires adaptation to a new work environment. As systems professionals, we have few skills for managing organization change. We assume new technology will be absorbed without notice. This will not happen. Change brings pain to all individuals at all levels in the organization. CASE begins the process of retooling the systems life cycle. It changes the way project teams work. As a result, the impact on people can be dramatic. The older and more mature the organization, the more difficult adaptation becomes. Younger, smaller organizations tend to adapt more easily. They are more experienced with change and less committed to an old way of doing business.

Maintenance Impact

One area where CASE will have an important and beneficial impact is in the maintenance of systems. When changes are required, they will be easier to identify and easier to execute. The regeneration of code may be performed automatically, thus saving time, and the maintenance of the design will be easier, thus ensuring continued quality. One organization found that maintenance was reduced over forty percent with their initial generated applications. This freed programmer time for new development, thus reducing their backlog problem dramatically.

Performance Measurement Impact

CASE tools provide a strong motivating force for the measurement of the systems organization's productivity and performance. The introduction of CASE tools forces the delivery of standard work products such as models, logical and physical designs, and generated code and databases. This facilitates the implementation of measurement standards. These standards must be carefully chosen, however. Measurement performed with reference to the standard unit of lines of code is not effective. The organization must move to a more meaningful standard of measurement. A number of organizations use function points as a standard unit of complexity. Future releases of CASE tools may incorporate measurement capabilities.

Internal Communication Impact

CASE also can benefit internal communication within the systems organization. CASE is a vehicle for enhanced communication and information sharing among such groups as data administration and application development project teams. The encyclopedia becomes a common focus for these different groups. It gives them a common language with which to communicate. If differences exist among these groups, CASE tool installation provides a focal point for their resolution.

Today's CASE tool marketplace is very fragmented. New players appear to be entering daily and established vendors disappear, perhaps to re-emerge at a later time. Vendors promise new releases of tools with advanced capabilities, but miss projected delivery dates by months or even years. It is difficult, if not impossible, to keep up with everything that is happening. One recent survey found that although over eighty percent of potential customers have bought tools, only twenty-five percent of that number had used the tool more than once, and only five percent of those who had purchased CASE tools were actually using them in a production environment.

Faced with over fifty tools that can be classified into the four CASE types—front end, back end, seamless, and special function—no organization will find the process of selecting and implementing tools to be an easy one. Even an organization with CASE experience that wants to upgrade its CASE profile may feel quite rightly that the marketplace presents too many options for an easy decision. While these technical issues surrounding the selection of CASE tools, like the organizational issues with their impacts on organization philosophy, policies, methods, procedures, and job descriptions, cannot be easily resolved, the organization must address them nevertheless. Only the organization that recognizes the profound impact of CASE and that plans for this challenge will be able to fully realize the benefits of these potentially valuable tools.

5

The Methodology Dimension:
Information Engineering

THE IMPACT OF IE

     The world of information systems design and development is a dynamic one, and no one philosophy or set of methodological principles could be expected to satisfy all of those involved in it. Nevertheless, if we put aside fads and prejudices, it is possible to identify a number of common concepts that are contained in one form or another in the development process endorsed by most organizations. These concepts are expressed, although with different emphasis and focus, in the three most prominent methodological schools competing for leadership today. Advocates of these three development approaches, structured analysis, information engineering (IE), and object oriented systems analysis, probably have more in common than they would readily admit. For this reason, we believe that any of the three may be effectively combined with JAD techniques and CASE tools to create a strong FUSION environment. Nevertheless, because of certain aspects of its approach, we find the information engineering school of philosophy to be the one that best supports the FUSION concept. In order to demonstrate this, it is necessary to look at information engineering as a distinctive philosophy, discipline, and rule set for computer systems design and development.

     Like other methodologies, IE is a type of language that may be used for analyzing and discussing the problems involved in systems design and development. Its unique character (as well as its commonalities with other disciplines) may best be seen by examining the following characteristics:

- **Structure:** the components of the language; usually defined as a series of phases.
- **Symbology:** the vocabulary of the methodology; the symbols and icons that carry information.
- **Diagrams:** the grammar of the methodology; the patterns used to structure the information presented.
- **Procedural instructions:** the rules for constructing and using the diagrams and symbols within the context of the language.

By looking at these four characteristics, it is possible to understand the contribution that IE makes to FUSION and to see where and how it interacts with JAD and CASE. Of course, no methodology is stagnant. Each methodology in use today is evolving as new types of user requirements and technological challenges make this necessary. For a methodology user to become an expert, then, he has to educate himself continually about the current status of principles and techniques. In addition, because methodologies are dynamic rather than static, they tend to merge into each other. Useful ideas from one are integrated into the others. There may, in fact, be no one accepted version of a methodology. It may exist only in multiple versions, varying with the needs and prejudices of the user. Many proponents of the structured analysis methodology, for example, have adopted E.F. Codd's information analysis techniques, thus embracing a process formerly said to be owned by the advocates of information engineering. Consider, too, the debate over whether object orientation is a subset of information engineering or whether it is a separate and distinctive methodology that grew out of object oriented programming languages.

The FUSION approach supports the information engineering methodology because we believe it is the most useful one for solving today's information management problems. The characteristics that make IE such a useful tool for problem solving are:

- A strategic, future based orientation to systems planning.
- A balanced approach to examining business process and information needs.
- Simplicity of diagrams.
- Continuity and auditability from logical design to physical design and development.

Strategic, Future-Based Orientation

As a methodology, information engineering has a clear bias toward the future. It focuses on planning for tomorrow's needs, rather than today's and defines these needs in terms of the strategic direction of the business. The business is always primary; systems are secondary. Users of an IE methodology must be prepared to ask themselves such questions as: "What will this business look like ten years from now?" "Who will our customers be?" "What products and services will we be selling?" "What will our priorities be: sales volume? cost benefit ratios? profitability figures?" IE uses a top down structure to overcome the operational focus of most systems designers and users and turns information planning and management into a strategic business activity, forging a stronger role for the systems organization in basic business decision making. By drawing a strong connection between strategic business plans and the systems that result from them, it ensures auditability and linkage from strategic (not just tactical and operational) business needs to application detail. Those who have previously used other methodologies that focused on an analysis of the existing business environment and omitted a planning component may find this approach challenging. We think that after trying it out they will agree that its benefits are substantial.

A Balanced Approach

A business has both processing and information needs, and each must be supported by any information systems plan and the applications that result from it. The processing needs of the business define the actions that it takes. The information needs of the business define the data that it stores and manipulates. Both types of needs must be met if the managers of the business are to solve problems and make sound decisions. A methodology that focuses principally on the analysis of business processes may be practical for building transaction processing applications or for re-engineering processes that have become outmoded, but it will be less than adequate for supporting complex decision making. A methodology that focuses principally on information analysis may be useful for providing decision making support, but it may not provide for efficient definition of processing requirements. Most businesses require a balance of analytical techniques to address both processing and information needs.

Information engineering provides the ability to support projects with either a process or a data bias by providing techniques that support both types of analysis and that clarify the relationship of one type of analysis to the other. IE supports the use of decomposition and dependency diagrams for independent process analysis and the use of entity relationship diagrams and entity tables for independent information analysis. The interaction of process and data can be examined through the use of such diagrams of data flow, action, data navigation, or state transition. These two types of analysis can be conducted jointly or in sequence. The selection of an approach is based on the orientation of the project and the perspectives of the users to be involved in the analysis. Experience shows that:

- Users who have procedural or rule based jobs (e.g., accountants, operations personnel and engineers) may find it difficult to think about their information needs apart from the processes of their work.

- Users who have jobs that emphasize abstract concepts rather than procedures (e.g., salespeople, marketing personnel, planners, and high-level executives) may find independent information analysis easy and procedural analysis difficult.
- Business re-engineering projects and transaction processing application development projects often require that process analysis be performed prior to information analysis.
- Strategic planning projects and complex decision support application development projects often require that information analysis be performed prior to process analysis or that the two types of analysis be performed independently of each other.

Simplicity of Diagrams

Some methodologies focus on the use of complex diagramming techniques as the basis for analysis. In some instances, the source of this complexity is the attempt to represent both data and process in the same picture. One example of this is the data flow diagram (DFD). At high levels of analysis, the DFD can greatly simplify the analysis of process and data, but at lower levels of analysis where complexity increases, the DFD can prove difficult to create and maintain. Its advantage is that it enables analysts to work out process and data requirements at the same time, but this is also its disadvantage. When analysts are required to think about business processes and data at the same time, important relationships can be revealed. This can be very useful, but it may also in some circumstances unnecessarily complicate the analysis of a business need, turning the DFD into something resembling an electrical wiring diagram.

An information engineering approach, on the other hand, simplifies the analysis process by providing tools for analyzing process separately from data. One way to do this is through the development of a decomposition diagram, which may be used to define a hierarchy of business processes independently of their relationships within an information flow. The dependency diagram, also promoted by information engineering adherents, may be used to examine the relationship of one business process to others without considering the data manipulated within each process. When it is useful to examine data separately from process, IE supports the use of a diagram to meet this need. The entity relationship diagram (ERD) is used to define information needs independently of the processes that create, read, update, or delete the information. Once this independent analysis of process and data is completed, the process-entity matrix and other diagrams (including the DFD) may be used to examine the total picture, revealing the relationships between process and data that must be defined to fully support a complex information management activity.

STRUCTURED ANALYSIS

1. Process-data integration	Data flow diagram
2. Data analysis	Entity relationship diagram Entity table
3. Process analysis	Decision table

INFORMATION ENGINEERING

1. Data analysis	Entity relationship diagram Entity table
2. Process analysis	Decomposition diagram Dependency diagram
3. Process-data integration	Data navigation diagram Action diagram Matrix

OBJECT-ORIENTED ANALYSIS

1. Data analysis	Entity relationship diagram Entity table
2. Process analysis	None
3. Process-data integration	State transition diagram

Figure 5.1 Methodology diagram summary and comparison.

It is true, of course, that the separation of process and data is somewhat artificial. Nevertheless, the analysis results produced when these two aspects of the information processing model are examined separately often justify the approach. It is particularly useful today when so many of our system development efforts are directed at solving complex information management problems. Neither does IE suggest that a single series of diagrams produced in a predefined sequence will solve every information management problem. Rather it puts the burden on the analyst to select and sequence the appropriate diagrams to meet a specific need. Figure 5.1 provides a summary and comparison of the diagrams available to the analyst.

Continuity and Auditability

Information engineering addresses a shortcoming found in some other approaches by providing a mechanism for the seamless transition from the viewpoint of the user of an information management solution as expressed in a logical design to the viewpoint of the developer of that solution as expressed in a physical design. Too often in the past, programmers had a tendency to set aside the logical design developed by the user community and, in effect, redesign the application in the physical design phase of the life cycle. This made it impossible to trace back physical design requirements to logical requirements.

Information engineering addresses this need for a link between the user and programmer views of an application by recommending the use of the action diagram, the ERD, and entity tables. These analysis tools, when combined with high-level fourth generation languages and automated CASE tool code generation capabilities, create a smooth, almost seamless, transition from logical design to physical design and development. When these diagramming techniques are used, the differences between the user view and the programmer view are limited to the vocabulary used in the diagram statements. For example, when a set of action diagrams prepared by the users are handed off to the development team, the programmers replace the English words with language geared toward technical construction requirements. The physical implementation of the design then is directly linked to the logical.

This clear link between logical and physical design results in better quality systems. Because the transition is smooth, user requirements are not likely to be lost or distorted. Neither is time wasted in the preparation of complex logical design diagrams that are seldom consulted after their time consuming creation.

The principles previously defined are common to all information engineering approaches, but it would be incorrect to suggest that IE is itself a single set of principles propounded by a unified school of philosophers. There are, in fact, several IE methodologies, with each evolving over time. Looking at the two most prominent IE methodologies, those advocated by James Martin and Clive Finkelstein, can reveal much about the distinctive IE approach to the solution of information management problems. Both men have had a profound impact on the way people think about systems today. Their approaches are distinctive and offer enough differences to give the analyst a substantive choice in IE approaches. Both, for example, make a clear distinction between process analysis and data analysis, but Martin gives priority to each at different points in his methodology structure. Finkelstein, on the other hand, while he clearly distinguishes between the two types of analysis, consistently sets a higher priority on data analysis and presents process analysis as a secondary, or derivative, type of analysis at the application logical design level. These preferences lead to other distinctions between the two approaches, but it is not our purpose here to examine these distinctions in detail. Rather, we believe that the common characteristics of the two approaches, when examined from a pragmatic point of view, can serve as an excellent guideline for the implementation of an advanced systems development life cycle.

Components	Objectives	Deliverables
Planning (Business unit)	Business needs Standards Business areas Project priorities	Business visions and plans Technical architectures Development plans
Analysis (Business area)	Information needs Processing needs Redesign business operations	Data model Process model Process-data relationship model Revised development plans

Design (Application)	Automation needs:
	  for information
	  for processing
		Logical design
		Physical design

Construction (Application)	Build the:
	  applications
	  databases
		Programs
		Physical databases

Add-on life cycle components

Install into production	Implement:
	  applications
	  databases
		Documentation
		Operational systems

Customer support	Fix and enhance:
	  applications
	  databases
		Change priorities
		New release plans
		System evaluations

Figure 5.2   IE components, objectives, and deliverables.

THE IMPORTANCE OF IE METHODOLOGY FOR JAD AND CASE

If we were able to follow information engineering theory precisely, all systems work for any business unit would begin with an IE planning project from which business area analysis projects and then application projects would be identified, scoped, and prioritized (Fig. 5.2). Some organizations have been able to do this. In these organizations, there is a commitment to make business plans and architectures drive application and database project definition. As a result, business units are able to examine their strategic, operational and tactical information, and processing needs in light of business plans. In this truly top down approach to systems development, the first project is always an IE planning project for the business unit.

However, most of us live in a less than perfect world. The larger and more complex the organization in which we live, the more difficult it becomes to follow the theory. We cannot take a vacation from current project work to go back into the business unit to rethink our information management approach from the ground up. What we really need, more than a theory, is a practical approach to decreasing our backlog of projects and ensuring that new projects reflect strategic, future oriented requirements. For this practical approach to work, we must decide not only how to apply a set of IE principles, but how, when, and where JAD and CASE should be used as well. The FUSION concept, which uses information engineering principles to drive JAD and CASE tool use, can provide this practical approach, enabling the organization to select and prioritize projects and carry them forward in the most productive way possible.

IE supports many different types of projects. A project may encompass work within just one methodology component (e.g., an analysis of a business unit's information needs), or it may span several components (e.g., a common manufacturing application which requires business re-engineering within a business area in addition to application design and construction). The flexibility of the IE methodology allows the analyst to define an appropriate territory for a project, just as it allows him to define a set of diagramming tools to support the analysis of that territory. In fact, the size and complexity of this territory plays a large part in the identification and sequencing of the specific diagrams to be used in the analysis. Because many IE diagrams can be used at different levels of analysis and in varying combinations with other diagrams (Figs. 5.3 and 5.4), it is up to the analyst to create a plan for matching these analysis tools to the information problem at hand.

It is also up to the analyst to identify the specific ways in which CASE tools and JAD techniques will be used to support a given project. To do this effectively, the analyst must understand the methodological principles accepted by the organization and acceptable alternatives for implementing those principles for a given project. In order for the analyst to plan a FUSION project (i.e., one that combines the use of IE, CASE, and JAD), he must do the following:

1. Locate the project within the IE life cycle.
2. Clarify project objectives and deliverables.
3. Identify opportunities for JAD intervention.
4. Define use of CASE tool capabilities.

This process will provide answers to the questions: "What am I doing?" "Why am I doing it?" "What do I hope to produce as a result of my efforts?" and, "How am I going to do it?" Anyone unable to answer these questions has no business beginning a project.

The first step performed by the analyst is to map the project against the IE life cycle to identify the type of project being undertaken. The project may fit into the planning, analysis, design, and/or construction components. For example, if the stated purpose of the project is to find ways to use systems to improve the

Diagram	May be used in
Decomposition diagram	Business visions and plans Technical architectures Development plans Process model Logical design
Matrix	Business visions and plans Technical architectures Development plans Process-entity relationship model
Dependency diagram	Process model Logical design
Data flow diagram	Logical design Process-data relationship model
Entity relationship diagram	Business visions and plans Technical architectures Data model Logical design
Entity table	Data model Logical design Physical design
Data navigation diagram	Process-data relationship model Logical design
State transition diagram	Logical design
Decision table	Logical design Physical design
Action diagram	Logical design Physical design

Figure 5.3 IE diagram utilization summary.

competitive market position of the business, the analyst will conclude that the project lies within the IE planning component. If the purpose of the project is to identify and support more effective access to business information, the analyst will conclude that the project lies within the IE analysis component. If the purpose of the project is to build an integrated information management system, he will conclude that the project scope spans both the IE design and construction components.

Once a project type has been determined, the analyst and project manager will be able to identify other important characteristics of the project, including the

PLANNING COMPONENT	DIAGRAMS

Business visions and plans
  strategic
  tactical
  operational
	Decomposition diagram
	Matrix
	Entity relationship diagram

Technical architectures
  data architecture
  process (applications) architecture
  technology architecture
	Decomposition diagram
	Matrix
	Entity relationship diagram

Development plans
  new development priorities
  redevelopment priorities
  dependencies
  timeframes
	Dependency diagram
	Matrix

ANALYSIS COMPONENT	

Data model
  entities
  attributes
  business rules
	Entity relationship diagram
	Entity table

Process model
  business functions
  business processes
	Decomposition diagram
	Dependency diagram

Process-data relationship model	Matrix Data flow diagram Data navigation diagram
Revised development plans	Dependency diagram Matrix
DESIGN COMPONENT	

Logical design
  data model
  process model
  process-data relationship model
  access specifications
	Entity relationship diagram
	Entity table
	Decomposition diagram
	Dependency diagram
	Data navigation diagram
	Data flow diagram
	Decision table
	State transition diagram
	Action diagram
	Query statements
	Screen and report requirements
	Application navigation/dialogues

Physical design
  physical data base
  program specifications
  access specifications
	Data structure chart
	Action diagram
	Layouts
	Navigation dialogues

Figure 5.4   IE diagram summary by deliverable.

specific objectives of the project and the deliverables required. To do this, it is necessary to consider how the project has been framed by those who have proposed it. How do they see the project? How do they express its purpose, its dimensions, its focus? Further, what do they expect to see as a result of the project? No matter what methodology stands behind a project, it cannot be successful unless its required outcome is identified prior to project initiation.

Once the relevant IE component(s) have been identified and a preliminary set of objectives and deliverables have been defined, the project manager and/or lead analyst assigned to the project should consider the appropriate use of the JAD technique and CASE tools for the project. The use of JAD will vary from organization to organization, and even from project to project within a single organization. In addition, the value of the technique will vary from one IE component to another. In the construction component, for example, JAD is less valuable than in the other three components. Because JAD is such a flexible technique, however, there are many options for its use in IE planning, analysis, and design projects. The use of CASE, on the other hand, is more likely to be standardized within a specific project type, especially given an organization's strong commitment to a set of methodological principles. If the organization has defined a standard set of deliverables for each IE component, then CASE can be used to satisfy these with relatively little need for evaluating options every time a new project is begun.

The discussion of IE components that follows indicates how different projects may be approached.

IE Component One: Planning Projects

The most important function of the planning component is to provide a link from business strategy to automation planning. Its general purpose is to answer the questions: "What is our business today?" "What forces are affecting our business today?" "What changes will we need to make in the future?" and, "What strategies must we put in place to optimize our position in the future?" Projects that fall within this component will seek to achieve one or more of the following :

- To define the information required for strategic decision making.
- To define a global database architecture to support these information requirements.
- To identify applications required to gain and maintain a strategic, tactical or operational advantage.
- To redefine business area boundaries and develop and prioritize a project slate to support these strategic changes.

Ideally, planning work should begin at the highest possible level to ensure that a complete picture of the enterprise and its objectives are represented. It is not always possible to begin with a detailed analysis at the enterprise level, however. Often the enterprise, whether it is a corporation or government agency, is too large and complex for a detailed analysis to be conducted at that level. It is particularly difficult to accomplish this if the enterprise is a multinational corporation containing business units with fundamentally different markets, products, and management philosophies. In such a case, it is preferable to conduct a more generalized planning project at the highest level (to define corporate mission, objectives, and strategy), and to conduct a detailed planning project at the business unit level. In some cases, a well defined slice of the business (e.g., manufacturing plant management, customer ordering processing, customer service and product support, or sales management) might better serve as the subject for an IE planning project. Such a slice cuts across organizational units, but will be easier for both analysts and users to handle.

The benefits of conducting this type of project are great. The IE planning project provides a structure for participants to analyze business objectives and strategy and examine current assumptions about products, services, and customers. Most organizations review their basic assumptions far too seldom, and one of the principal benefits of the IE approach is to emphasize the importance of this activity. Further, it provides the organization with a strategy for optimizing its information and automation resources in support of its objectives. It sets the stage for the creation of an automation plan that is closely tied to the organization's strategic objectives.

The planning project can also have an unexpected benefit for those organizations with a troublesome maintenance backlog. By requiring project participants to redefine their objectives and priorities, it may make it possible to substantially reduce that backlog. Projects that once seemed vital may be revealed to be of limited strategic importance. Other projects may be consolidated with little loss to information quality or processing performance. In one organization, for example, a corporate division, after completing a two-day JAD workshop in support of an IE planning project, was able to cut its application maintenance backlog forty percent and to dismantle an application maintenance group of ten people and reassign these individuals to new development projects.

The result of the planning project is, not surprisingly, a plan. There are a number of different types of plans that may be created. The three most common focus on strategic business direction, architecture, and systems development. All three would collect some of the same information, but the conclusions reached would vary according to the specific objectives of the project. It is possible, in fact, for an organization to require several different planning projects to produce all of the information and to make all of the decisions that are needed.

Where most systems development methodologies assume that an organization has a strategic business plan already in place, information engineering acknowledges that such may not be the case. It, therefore, provides guidelines for collecting and analyzing the information necessary for the organization to set out its strategic goals and direction. Strategic business planning projects can vary greatly, however. They can be conducted at different organization levels (e.g., enterprise, division, department, etc.), and their focus can vary from project to project. A project with a strategic focus, for example, might look at services provided to customers, with an eye on options for adding to, dropping, or modifying those services. One with a tactical focus might look at the problems and opportunities associated with the relationships between customer service representatives and customers. One with an operational focus might look at the availability and quality of customer records. Whatever the level and focus of analysis, the plan is likely to contain the following types of information:

- A definition of business organization structure to identify key accountable executives.
- A listing of business functions to identify key operating requirements.
- An identification of business locations to identify the distribution of resources.
- A listing of primary data subject areas to identify key information categories.

These four elements—organization, functions, locations, data subject areas—may then be compared through a series of matrix diagrams to identify key dependencies and to provide a framework for another planning perspective—business goal and problem analysis. This analysis will often identify factors critical to business success and highlight key business decisions that must be made, information designed to assist the organization in making the transition from the current to the future environment.

Two other approaches to business planning conducted from an information engineering perspective are gap analysis and mission analysis. Gap analysis, recommended by Clive Finkelstein for organizations that have already adopted high-level strategic plans, begins with the identification of the organization's current business strategy followed by parallel external and internal appraisals. The external appraisal identifies threats and opportunities present in the business unit. The internal appraisal identifies the weaknesses and strengths of the business unit. From this information, a gap analysis is completed to identify required changes in strategy and to select among the alternatives presented. A new, revised strategy is then developed and documented using a series of strategic statements. The mission approach, which Finkelstein recommends for groups that have no prior strategic planning experience, begins by asking project participants to define the mission and purpose of the business unit. From there, concerns and issues are identified along with specific business goals and objectives. From these two analyses come business policy statements as well as strategic and tactical statements covering markets, products and services, and distribution channels.

Another type of planning involves the production of an architecture plan. This type of plan can assist the project manager in answering one or more of the following questions:

- What information is required by the organization for it to be successful?
- What automated support is required to satisfy these information needs?
- What technology and standards are required to develop and maintain the required applications and databases?

Three architectures are at the foundation of this vision:

Data or information architecture.   This architecture is represented by a data model identifying data required to support the business unit and standards for data expression.

Process architecture.   This architecture is represented by a process model identifying the business processes required to support the business unit and the applications needed (transaction, decision support, expert, etc.) to create, maintain and access required data.

Technology architecture.   This architecture document required hardware platforms, physical distribution, and structuring of software, databases, and protocols, and standards for communication and networking configurations. This architecture is based on a knowledge of the current and emerging technology and an analysis of business unit locations, functions, organizations and data subject areas.

One or more of these architectural models may be developed during an IE planning project. Further work on refining them can be conducted as part of a separate IE analysis project.

A third type of IE planning project results in the creation of a systems development plan. This type of plan will answer the following questions:

- What in the existing systems environment must be replaced or modified?
- What are the potential benefits, impacts, and probability for success for each proposed project given the existing cultural and technological environments?
- What are the dependencies and interrelationships which must be considered in setting project priorities?
- In what sequence and timeframe should projects be executed?

A development plan is sometimes called a migration plan or an implementation plan. In either case, its purpose is to provide a road map for moving from today's computing environment to tomorrow's. To develop this plan, it is wise to analyze the existing applications and databases as well as the existing political and organizational culture within the business unit in the light of business and systems objectives. This may be done by segmenting and prioritizing the business unit into business areas and project areas. Within these business or project areas, specific projects may be created to:

- Resolve open issues (business or technical) that may inhibit plan implementation success.
- Re-engineer business processes prior to application or database development.
- Upgrade or replace technology across a business unit.
- Further analyze process and/or data needs of the business areas to define specific application and database projects.
- Begin new development or redevelopment of databases and applications.

It is always helpful when a business plan and an architecture plan for the business unit have been completed first. This creates a foundation, or road map, that will assist participants in a systems development planning project in making the decisions that are necessary.

Once the objectives of the planning project have been clearly identified, the deliverables must be defined in detail. This should involve more than a brief statement that a planning document will be produced. The content of that document should be identified in two ways. First, a draft table of contents should be prepared, and second, a listing of the specific diagrams that will be used to support the analysis should be provided. Unless this is done, there is a real possibility that the final document will not reflect the needs or intentions of some of the participants in the project.

Information engineering offers a number of different diagrams that may be used to analyze planning information, and it is unlikely that any two planning projects will use the same diagrams in the same way. If diagramming techniques are carefully selected, however, they can create a strong foundation for further work in IE analysis and design projects. The diagrams most frequently used in IE planning projects include:

Decomposition. May be used to define the hierarchical relationships within organizations, functions, and/or locations (Fig. 5.5).

Entity relationship. May be used to list information groups (data subject areas) and to provide definitions and identify basic relationships (Fig. 5.6).

Matrix. May be used to perform a comparative analysis and/or cluster analysis of items (Fig. 5.7).

These diagrams may be used in the preparation of business plans, architecture plans, and system development plans. All are supported by the major CASE tools. Some of these tools will provide more flexibility than others in creating the

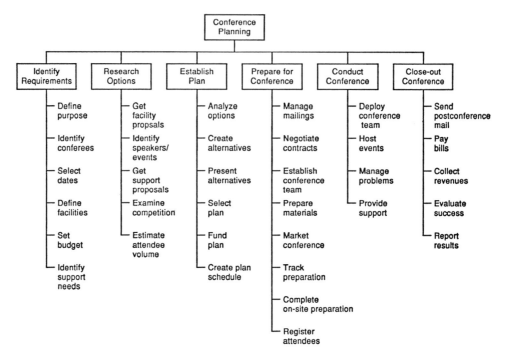

Figure 5.5   Example decomposition diagram.

diagrams; other tools will provide a more rigorous enforcement of methodology principles. The tools chosen should support the organization's standards and the objectives of the project.

IE planning projects provide great value to the organization, but because of their complexity, because they ask participants to question basic assumptions about the business, and because they generally touch such a wide cross-section of the organization, they are difficult to carry out. They are particularly susceptible to failure when organization commitment is not demonstrated at both the executive and middle management levels. These projects also challenge traditional approaches to gathering information such as the interview technique. Too much complex information must be gathered for the interview approach to be successful.

The chances for success are greatly increased, however, when the JAD technique is applied to IE planning projects. The use of JAD is generally initiated by the project manager who appoints a JAD facilitator to run one or more workshops where relevant information is captured and key decisions are made. A series of workshops is often required for planning projects. This series may be designed to gather information across a wide span of the organization, or it may be designed to steer a smaller slice of the organization through the definition of business, architecture, and systems development plans. If JAD is used, the time required for planning projects can be cut dramatically. In addition, an IE planning project

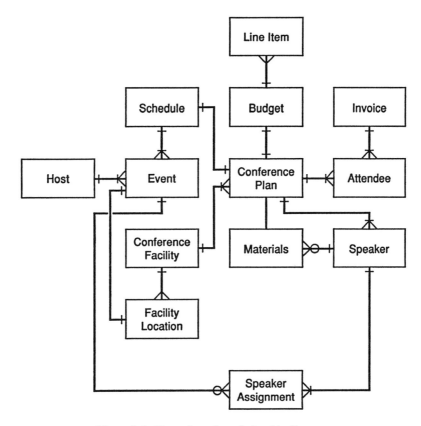

Figure 5.6 Example entity relationship diagram.

that uses JAD will also be much more likely to build a consensus in support of the changes proposed. When IE planning concepts and JAD are matched together, they provide a strong vehicle for analysis and an excellent catalyst for change.

An IE planning project is often a precursor to application design and construction projects which may be undertaken using rapid application development (RAD) techniques. The types of projects that may result from an IE planning project include:

- Backlog analysis projects to reassign maintenance priorities and resources.
- Specific application development or database design projects.
- Detailed business unit data and process analysis projects to refine ERDs and functional decomposition diagrams and to re-engineer business unit operations.

Business unit planning and business area analysis set priorities and boundaries for application and database design and construction projects that will use a

Entities Functions	Plan	Attendee	Speaker	Facility	Materials	Schedule	Events
Identify requirements	C						
Research options	R						
Establish plan	R, U		C	C		C	C
Prepare for conference	R, U	C	R, U	R, U	C	R, U	R, U
Conduct conference	R, U	C, R, U	R	R	R	R	R
Close-out conference	R	R	R	R	C, R, U	R	R

C = Create, R = Read, U = Update

Business functions to entities

Figure 5.7 Example matrix diagram.

RAD approach (Fig. 5.8). They provide the foundation on which RAD activities will proceed.

IE Component Two: Analysis Projects

If possible, an analysis project should be preceded by a planning project. This will help to ensure that the scope of the project and its objectives will be reasonable and appropriate. IE analysis projects can be more difficult than IE planning projects, however, because the analysis work is more precise, requires a more intensive effort, and relies on a more detailed knowledge of the business. The most important function of the analysis component is to define the information used by the business and the processes performed on it. Projects included within this component will seek to achieve one or more of the following objectives:

- To identify the essential processes of a business area.
- To identify the data required to operate a business area, generate work products, and make strategic, tactical, and operational decisions.
- To define the most effective way to manage the business area.
- To define data and process architectures for a business area.

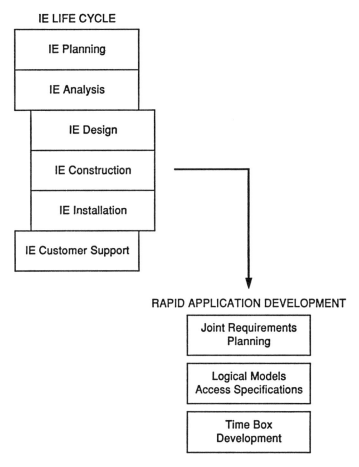

Figure 5.8 The IE relationship to RAD.

- To identify and prioritize application and database development projects for a business area.

A well conducted IE analysis project will enable management to examine the information and processing needs of a business unit in detail. This will ensure that future development activities will be structured to support these needs in the most efficient and productive way possible. In addition, IE analysis projects can be used to define requirements for re-engineering or redesigning a business unit (or part of a business unit) before specific application or database design and construction projects are begun. The results of an IE analysis project may impact current activities within a business area in several ways. It may cause modifications in current data and process architectures, redefine the scope or emphasis of current application and database design and construction projects, or reorder project priorities. Without this type of analysis above the application level, over-lapping, duplicative, or unnecessary applications and databases may be built or redeveloped.

The scope of a business area to be addressed by an analysis project may be defined as:

- An entire business unit, if the business unit is of a manageable size.
- A part of a business unit if clear subdivisions exist along functional (business process) lines.
- A part of a business unit if clear subdivisions exist along informational (data) lines.

The objectives of analysis projects vary, and therefore, so do their re-sults. Often, a project will be undertaken to produce a model of the information required by the business. This data model provides a view of the information groups and the specific items of data used in the business area under consider-ation. It also identifies the relationships among those data items and data groups. These projects provide a framework from which a series of applications and supporting databases may be constructed. As a next step, application design projects would be carried out to confirm and enhance the data and process models produced by the analysis project.

The techniques for data modeling as defined by E.F. Codd provide us with the ability to model the information needs of a business area. Codd's work in relational data modeling techniques and his rules for data normalization have had a major impact on our ability to effectively analyze information. The normalization process provides us with a straightforward way of organizing data logically (from the viewpoint of the data user) in a nonredundant and nonduplicative man-ner. When Codd's rules are followed, the resulting logical data model provides the basis for a smooth transition to the design of physical databases and processing.

There are different ways to frame or bound the scope of a modeling ef-fort. Martin, for example, suggests beginning data analysis by constructing a diagram representing the functional decomposition of the business. Finkelstein, on the other hand, starts with statements defining the strategic, tactical and/or operational business plan. Others suggest that existing databases be used as a framework for creating a logical data model. The FUSION approach endorses a combination of the Martin and Finkelstein approaches. First, a functional decom-position of the business should be created. A diagram that decomposes the basic functions of the business down to two or three levels is generally adequate. Then using that framework, a set of statements should be prepared that define strategic, tactical, and/or operational:

- Decisions (both predictable and extraordinary) that are made when perform-ing business functions.

EVENT

Number	Title	Date	Start Time	End Time	Host Code
322	Open/Intro	6/11	830	900	Jones, MJ
356	New Ideas	6/12	900	1030	Smith, KC
799	Problems	6/11	1000	1200	Larson, T
344	92 Plans	6/11	900	1000	Donnelly, K

Figure 5.9 Example entity table.

- Products (e.g., invoices, credit statements) that are produced in the course of conducting the business.
- Questions that must be answered regularly by those who work in and manage the business.

Each statement should be specifically associated with one or more of the business functions identified in the decomposition diagram. From these statements, the data required to perform the business can be easily identified, and generally at this point, a list of data items is prepared. This list may be carefully constructed to include only true data entities, or it may be constructed of data elements (attributes), or it may be used to collect an unrefined listing that mixes the two together, with the understanding that the list will be refined at a later time. This two dimensional framework also provides data auditability. Each data item that eventually ends up on a computer display can be traced back to a specific business need. Conversely, no data items should be captured, manipulated, or maintained that do not meet a specific need.

As a next step, two diagrams are developed to model the data that is identified as a result of the completion of the two dimensional framework. These are:

Entity relationship diagram.   The ERD is created as a result of an analysis of the data item list. It displays data groups and their relationships to each other.

Entity table.   Sometimes called the *entity list,* this graphic displays all the data items associated with a data group and, optionally, provides examples of each. Those data items that serve as a unique identifier for a particular occurrence of a data group are called *"keys."* Keys are generally underlined or specially annotated. Each table will represent one data group identified in the ERD (Fig. 5.9).

To understand the power of unique identification and definition which takes place in the building of a data model, examine the old view of data prior to Codd's work and a data model after Codd's work.

PRELOGICAL DATA MODEL VIEW

Application Defined Data
Accounts Receivable Application
Customer = Person Billed
Sales Management Application
Customer = Store Owner Name
Corporate Finance Application
Customer = Company Name and HQ Location

LOGICAL DATA MODEL VIEW

Business Area Data Model
Corporate Customer = Company Name and HQ Location
Sales Customer = Store Owner Name
Billing Customer = Person Billed

In the three applications in the old view of data, it is not possible to identify the real customer. Each application defines the customer differently, and each is correct. What happens when an executive asks for an analysis of revenues by customer? Which is the correct customer to reference? When data is defined prior to application design, each customer type is uniquely identified, so there is no overlap or redundancy of definition. When an executive asks for an analysis of customer revenues, he can then be prompted for a specific type of customer—corporate, sales, or billing.

Supporters of the information engineering approach have always had something of a bias toward the study of data over process. It is their contention that over time data is more stable than the processes that manipulate it. Therefore, they reason, if we capture a model of the data, we are more likely to build systems that will last longer and serve us better. Lately that view has modulated a bit to suggest that even if data is primary, process is important as well.

In some analysis projects, a process model will be created following the development of a data model. In other projects, it will be developed concurrently or even on its own. This process model generally offers a hierarchical view of the business processes performed within a defined area. Each level within the hierarchy may carry a specific name (function, activity, task, etc.) or be numbered (process 1.0, process 1.2, process 1.2.1, etc.). It may also identify the relationships of those processes to each other.

Some businesses and organizations require that we understand not only its information needs, but that we also understand its transaction processing needs. A process model should be included in the project deliverable if it is important to answer the following questions:

- How should work flow through the business?
- What is the most effective way to structure business processes?
- Which business processes require automation?

One valuable use of the process model is to eliminate redundancy, inefficiency, and complexity in the business. The process model documents business functions independently of their organizational implementation. In other words, it separates the organizational aspects of the business (who performs the processes) from the processes themselves (what is done). This allows for an analysis focused on cause and effect, action taken and result achieved. When a process produces either a negative result or no result at all, then it is clear that the process is a candidate for modification or elimination. When processes duplicate each other, they are also candidates for change.

The two diagrams that are generally considered essential to the process model are the decomposition diagram and the dependency diagram. They are usually constructed in this sequence:

Decomposition diagram.   This diagram defines a hierarchy of business functions and processes. The first one or two levels of this diagram may have been developed during a preceding IE planning project.

Dependency diagram.   This diagram identifies relationships among groups of processes at a particular level in the hierarchy of the decomposition diagram (Fig. 5.10).

The dependency diagram is a useful complement to the decomposition diagram. Without it, the analyst can have only an imperfect understanding of the relationships among the processes that support a given business function. Actually, it is useful to remember that any one diagram constructed to analyze an automation need will always represent a distortion of that need to some extent. Only by looking at an information management need from several angles can a complete, or nearly complete, picture of it be obtained.

Once both data and process models have been developed, it is possible to go further and produce a combined data/process model. This model provides a view of the relationship of information groups to business processes. That view may indicate whether those processes require that data be created, read, updated or deleted by each process. It may also indicate all the processes that each primary information group may transition through during its life cycle. It can be an extremely valuable tool in assessing the effectiveness and efficiency of current systems and in planning for the future. Most organizations that have used this analysis approach find that they are able to get a far greater return for their investment in systems development. It is a great aid in reducing redundancy and eliminating unnecessary data collection, manipulation, and processing.

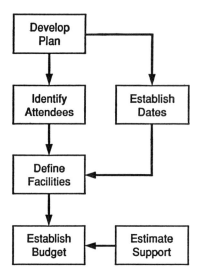

Process: Identify requirements

Figure 5.10 Example dependency diagram.

It is possible that the relationship of data (information groups) to process (business functions/activities) was delineated in a matrix diagram in a planning project. If such a diagram was not constructed before, it may be built in an analysis project. In either case, after its construction, it may be refined, and other diagrams may be added as well to further add substance to analysis activities. These diagrams are discussed next.

Process-Entity matrix.   This matrix identifies relationships between business processes and information groups. It may also define these relationships by indicating which processes create, read, update, or delete given information groups. If it builds on a previous matrix, it may refine the analysis by moving down a level of detail. Where business functions or activities formed one axis of the matrix in the previous diagram, here a function or activity may be broken down into component processes. Where data subject areas may have formed the other axis, here each data subject area may be broken down into information groups or even entities. When relationships seem to be missing (e.g., no processes link to a given information group), further investigation is required to determine if a process is missing or if an interface to another business area exists. If redundancy seems to exist (e.g., many processes appear to have the capability to create, update, or delete a given information group) further investigation is required to determine if one or more processes can be eliminated. This diagram, when used in conjunction with a revised process-organization matrix, may identify ways to redesign business operations.

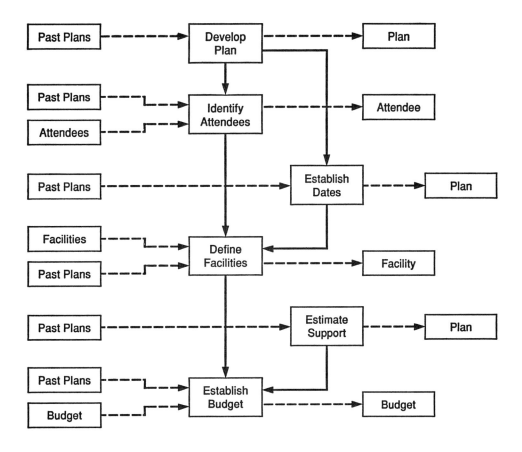

Process: Identify requirements

Figure 5.11   Example data flow diagram.

Existing systems-entities matrix.   This matrix documents data sources within an existing systems environment. This information can aid in defining project boundaries for new applications and/or databases. It may also point to application and database overlaps and duplications which can be eliminated through the redesign of existing applications or the redesign or development of new databases. This matrix can be compared to an existing system—process matrix diagram to find areas in need of automation support.

Data flow diagram.   This diagram may be built independently or may be built on the base of a dependency diagram. It documents the information groups transformed by each process (Fig. 5.11). The DFD can be used to validate the

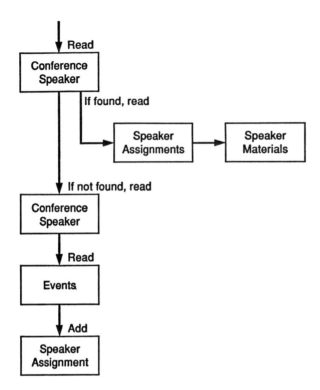

Process: Confirm speaker assignment

Figure 5.12 Example data navigation diagram.

various business process matrix diagrams to ensure that all information groups and processes have been addressed appropriately.

Data model navigation.   This diagram is actually a series of overlays on the entity relationship diagram. The overlays are created to ensure that the information required in the business area is supported with data in the model. Although most often used in application design for analyzing performance requirements, it can also be used to validate the data model (Fig. 5.12).

These diagrams are supported by most of the major CASE tools. As in planning projects, however, it is up to those managing an analysis project to define the way a given CASE tool will be used to produce these.

As in planning projects, the chances for a successful analysis project can be greatly enhanced if JAD is used to build consensus among business area executives and middle managers on key issues of scope and priority. It is a rare analysis project that fails to uncover controversial issues or raise key business concerns. The decisions that result from these projects can have far reaching consequences, affecting database design and application construction for years to come. Further, because an organization's ability to compete in the marketplace is tied to the quality of an organization's information resources, the decisions made in an analysis project can impact the success or failure of the organization's strategic plan. Without JAD and the commitment to new ideas it can build, there exists a danger that changes required to business systems and procedures will be ignored or resisted.

Many of these disagreements can be avoided if a planning project precedes the analysis project. If an IE planning project has not preceded the business area IE analysis project, business users may have to take extra time to identify their business directions and strategy. They may have to answer such questions as: "What products will we be producing in the next five years?" "Will our target markets change?" and "What strategies will our competitors adopt?" Answering these questions may be difficult if the individuals selected to participate in the analysis project do not have the information or authority to answer them. The JAD facilitator can identify these concerns before a JAD workshop session and create a strategy for resolving them before the analysis project is begun.

There are other challenges in this type of project that the JAD facilitator can address as well. Systems analysts and programmers may be too eager to rush from the logical view of an information management problem to its technical solution. The JAD facilitator can keep the participant team on track and focused on the logical view of the problem and its solution. This will prevent the technical team from making a precipitous jump to a physical solution, a solution that may not be the best answer to the problem.

Information users too may have difficulty in focusing on the logical view of the problem. Sometimes this occurs because a clear context or framework for the analysis project has not been identified. The JAD facilitator can assist here by ensuring that this context is defined in terms of information needs, business functionality, or business strategic, tactical or operational plans. JAD places a great deal of emphasis on this initial definition of the scope of a project to avoid a situation where the boundaries, emphasis, and objectives of the work are unclear. The JAD facilitator can also assist users in focusing their attention on what is needed rather than what presently exists. This applies equally to both information and process analysis. A great danger in analysis projects is that they will fail to examine assumptions about the business that may have outlived their usefulness. In today's dynamic business environment, it would be most unwise to assume that today's products, services, markets, or management strategies will be tomorrow's. In fact, the easiest prediction to make is that all businesses will undergo profound changes.

As noted earlier, there are many diagram options for IE analysis projects, and the JAD facilitator may assist the project manager in selecting some or all of these options for inclusion in project deliverables. A determination on the content of the deliverable should be based on the objectives of the project. Consideration should also be given to the capabilities of the project team. Certain diagram options may be more familiar or simply easier to use for a given group of participants. In addition, if the analysis project follows a planning project, the diagram options should take into account the input that may be provided by the deliverable produced in the previous project. The plan produced by the previous group of participants should be used as input to the analysis project, and it may also provide a guideline or model for the selection of analysis tools and techniques.

The analysis project itself may provide input to a subsequent application or database design project and is, therefore, generally considered to precede rapid application development (RAD) activities. The analysis project continues the definition of application and database project priorities and boundaries. The analysis project provides the data and process models from which specific RAD application and database projects may be derived.

IE Component Three: Design Projects

Ideally, before beginning an IE design project, the project team (or others) will have completed planning and analysis activities which will have defined the scope and objectives of this project. If this has not been done, the project manager and/or the project's JAD facilitator will need to address these issues in preparation activities. However, even if formal planning and analysis projects have been undertaken, some uncertainties about the detailed requirements of the business will remain when design work begins. These must be addressed if the project is to be a success.

In the traditional approach to a systems development project, the life cycle would begin with a feasibility study for the proposed system. Once feasibility was proven (or, rarely, not proven), then a design would be created. That design would encompass both required processing routines and databases. Often, though, no distinction was made between logical and physical design. The analyst/programmer routinely translated the user's requirements into a physical representation using a preselected technology. Work with the users centered around the design of printed reports and information display screens, not models of business process and data. Early prototyping efforts took this approach also, which led to endless iterations of the system. Information engineering approaches the design phase with a set of assumptions that differs markedly from this traditional view. It supports the following assumptions about the design phase of the life cycle:

- There is a vital distinction between the user view of business processes and information requirements (logical design) and the programmer view of processing routines and data (physical design).
- A logical design must be constructed first. A physical design may then be derived from the logical design through a series of refinement activities. Code is created based on the physical design. It may either be generated automatically, or it may be manually written.

- Databases may be constructed and implemented separately from the applications that will access those databases.
- Applications may obtain access to required data from multiple databases without interfacing with other applications.
- Application processing, at its most essential level, is the manipulation or transformation of data. Therefore, the logical design of an application process defines the interaction of that process with the database in terms of the requirement to create, read, update, or delete specific data.
- Requirements for application display screens and printed reports are specified by users after all process and data models have been defined for the application. These requirements are derived from the models, not the other way round.
- Application navigation or dialogue menus define the movement by users from screen to screen. Users should define these human interface requirements with the support of systems specialists in order to make the best use of available capabilities.

The primary objective of an IE design project is to define the logical and physical requirements for construction of an application and/or database. The product of this component should be all of the information required by the programming team or the automated code generator. As with the first two IE components, cooperation and consensus is required from the project participant group in order to ensure that the design is accurate and appropriate. Therefore, JAD is again critical to the success of the project work performed here. CASE can be important, too, for documenting design requirements and for generating code, if that option is selected by the project manager.

For IE design projects, the following deliverables may be included:

Logical design.   The user view of the application or database requirements and specifications for use.

Physical design.   The programmer view of the application or database required for automated or manual coding in a specific software language and hardware implementation.

The essential elements of the logical design are:

- Logical data model
- Logical process model
- Access specifications

If an application is classified as decision support, query, or management information, a process model may be omitted completely or may be limited to a very high-level view. For applications that support heavy transaction processing, a process model is required, and in fact, for most applications, a process model is a useful part of a complete logical design.

The logical data model may be the same as or a subset of the business area data model created during an IE analysis project. The purpose of this data model is to define a database from a logical, or user, view. When an entity relationship diagram is created here, it should contain information needed to calculate storage capacity and performance requirements. This information will provide guidance for building the physical structure of the database. Entity tables constructed here should document access requirements. This information may be generated through a data utilization analysis. The analysis would consist of:

- Navigating the logical data model by tracking business decisions, questions, and products that the application must support.
- Navigating the logical data model by tracking processes that must be automated by the application.
- Navigating the logical data model by tracking screen and report data requirements.

The logical process model may be the same as or a subset of a previously constructed business area process model. This model defines the scope of automated processing support, and may be documented using a decomposition diagram, a data-flow diagram, and/or a dependency diagram. The processes at the lowest level of detail may be used as the basis for the development of action diagrams. These diagrams will document the logic that must be supported by physical design and then code generation.

Logical designs for all types of applications require the definition of access specifications. These may consist of:

- Query statements
- Screen and report specifications
- Action diagrams
- Application navigation dialogues

The identification of queries to the database will be easy if business decisions and questions have been previously defined as a means of defining information requirements. If this has not been done, it should be done now. These queries may serve as the basis for the creation of SQL statements to be used to retrieve data from the database. The physical implementation of the database (e.g., DB2, ORACLE) will follow, including all necessary support such as error handling, recovery, and security provisions.

Display screens and printed reports are also included in the logical design for most applications. Display screens allow users to enter, view, manipulate, and delete data from databases accessed by the application. Although some consider screens to be part of physical design, the fact that they are (or should be) user designed more reasonably places them within the logical design. Reports too should be user designed and are, therefore, part of logical design.

Much of the extensive work once associated with screen and report design was required because there were no standards for this activity. Now, with SAA (Systems Application Architecture) and, in some cases, organization standards for screens and reports, the need for detailed layout specifications has been substantially reduced. In addition, the quality of screens and reports has increased dramatically. Today's technology makes it easy to include graphs, charts, and art work. If technology experts work with users to define report and screen requirements, the latest technology can be harnessed to create the most effective man machine interface. When user input to screen and report definition is obtained, prototypes are much more likely to be acceptable to users, and many tedious hours of revisions can be avoided.

Screen and report specifications should answer the following questions:

Functionality.   Will the screen/report be used to enter data, view data, inquire about data, change data, or some combination of these?

Volume and response times.   How often will this screen/report be generated or accessed by each user? How many total users are there? What performance volume may be expected at peak loads?

Purpose.   What questions will the screen/report answer? What business decisions can be supported by it? What business process(es) does it support?

Data.   What items of information should be displayed on the screen/report?

Processing.   Which data requires editing? What calculations must be performed? What other manipulation of data is required? In what sequence should the data be processed or displayed?

Action diagrams.   An action diagram defines the way in which items from the database are accessed or acted on. Action diagrams can be initiated by an event that triggers manipulation of data, a transaction, an error handling routine, calculations, edits, or construction of a screen or report. Any process taken from the lowest level of defined process model detail may be translated into one or more action diagrams (Fig. 5.13).

Those familiar with structured programming techniques will have no difficulty using action diagrams. Action diagrams are created by using the five familiar programming constructs of:

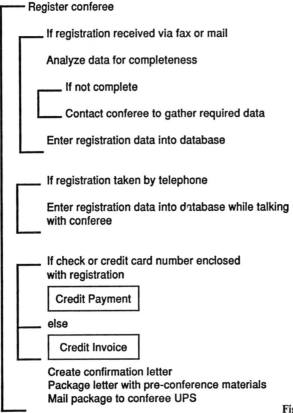

Figure 5.13 Example action diagram.

- Sequencing: to indicate the order of actions.
- Condition statements: to indicate that an action is to take place only if certain conditions are met.
- Case statements: to identify alternative actions to be taken given certain values.
- Repetition: to identify actions to be taken until certain values are exhausted.
- Nesting: action diagrams can be nested and refer to other action diagrams.

Finally, before physical design can get underway, the developers need to know how the users wish to move among the screens and reports they have defined. Because of advanced technology like SAA and Microsoft's Windows, much of what had to be uniquely defined in the past has been standardized. However, application generation requires some information about how the users wish to move from screen-to-screen. The diagrams that support menu definition are CASE tool dependent.

Once a logical design has been prepared, a physical design may be developed if the application or database is to be constructed by an in-house team. In a sense, the difference between logical and physical design is a matter of technology. Physical design begins when the analyst or developer no longer applies plain English to action diagrams or the data model and begins to use the code generator or the programming language. The amount of work this entails, as well as any diagramming techniques to be used, will vary based on the technology used for application and/or database construction.

Physical design requires developers to define exactly how to implement the database. In order to do this, they must ask a number of questions. These include:

- Should there be multiple copies of the same database at different locations? How is update consistency ensured?
- Should subsets of the central database be stored at different locations and secured for that location's access alone? How are updates to be timed and coordinated?
- Does the database need to be restructured to meet capacity and response time requirements?
- Are there different hardware and software at different locations? What impact will this have?
- Must the database be distributed among locations when no central database is in existence?
- Can the database be stored centrally for equal access by all?
- Is the database to be distributed among multiple locations but accessed through a network by everyone?
- Does the central database need to extract data from different transaction systems?

The information gathered and documented in the logical design will assist in answering these questions. In addition to that information, other information must be gathered and decisions must by made by the project team. Issues such as data availability, data transmission cost, response time requirements, security needs, and conversion options must all be addressed.

In the IE methodology, the physical design may be seen as a refinement of the logical design, but while the logical design may be simple and straightforward, it may have a physical implementation that is quite complex. For example, the logical design for a customer information application for a banking institution is fairly straightforward. Salespeople need access to a defined set of customer, product, account, and transaction history information. However, the physical implementation of the database required to support that application can require complex simultaneous on-line access to timely accurate data by users in hundreds of branch offices, nationwide, or internationally. In some cases, the logical design may be very complex, as with a manufacturing management application that supports multiple plant production functions such as shipping and receiving, shop floor scheduling, cost accounting, and parts distribution. The physical implementation of the application may require that the application be divided into modules which can be phased into operation.

Physical design, in the form of action diagrams, screen layouts, and other CASE technology dependent diagrams such as data structure charts, is important in today's code generation environment. Applications and databases developed in a CASE environment will be maintained at the physical design level, at least in the short term. In fact, many of the tools do not save generated source code. Programmers have no choice but to maintain applications through physical designs until such time as CASE tool technology allows a logical design to be translated automatically into a physical design or when the logical design can feed the code generator directly.

The results of IE design projects can be utilized in several different ways. One use for the design developed by the participants is as an aid to estimating the extent of the application development effort. This can provide valuable input for the manager who is considering whether or not to proceed with the construction of a proposed application. The design can also be used as the basis for the construction of a prototype. By viewing a working model of an application, the users can review and refine their design decisions quickly. This also provides them with a greater sense of involvement than if they were simply reviewing a paper document. A third use for the design is as the basis for purchase of a software package to meet the needs identified by the project participants. Although it is not customary to develop a detailed design prior to software package selection, this process would enable many organizations to avoid costly selection mistakes. Finally, the most common use for the design would be as the basis for proceeding into the construction phase of the life cycle.

An IE design project using JAD to capture design information and decisions and CASE to refine and validate the design can initiate rapid applications development activities. The most effective RAD approach combines the use of JAD, prototyping, timebox project management techniques, and CASE technology to deliver applications faster than with traditional approaches (Fig. 5.14). IE design and construction projects need not be developed using a RAD approach to be successful, but the organization that is moving into an IE environment should at least consider the use of RAD concepts. Where IE adds significantly to the quality of information management for the organization, RAD adds to the productivity of the systems organization in achieving that improvement. A time when the organization has proven its openness to new ideas by incorporating IE concepts into its life cycle is generally a good time to try out other enhancements as well.

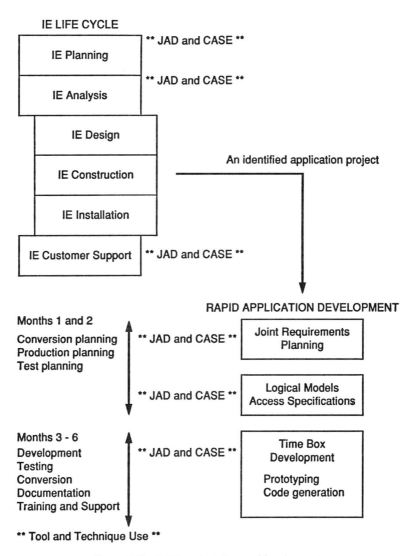

Figure 5.14   RAD project time and involvement.

IE Component Four: Construction Projects

The objective of an IE construction project is to build an application and/or database either manually or with the use of CASE code generation technology. This effort may be as simple as invoking the code generator, selecting the target language and operating platform, and pushing a button. It may be as difficult as manually coding and debugging all the program modules and databases. For large applications, it may mean integrating the tested modular programs into a working system.

For IE construction projects, the deliverables include any prototypes developed as well as the production systems developed, supported by all required program and operational documentation. Such projects may also produce implementation plans for testing, installation, training, and on-going support. JAD has not generally been viewed as a construction tool, but it can assist the project team in producing some of these deliverables. Although no one has yet perfected the concept of the JAD coding workshop (code generators seem by far the more productive approach), JAD workshops can be used to assist in prototype evaluation and to develop testing and implementation plans. In this way, user participation and commitment in the latter part of the life cycle can be maximized. Whenever joint decision making is required, JAD workshops can provide the process for achieving this.

In addition to coding, construction activities include:

Testing.   Different levels of application testing are necessary to find and remove errors. The IE methodology and the use of JAD techniques in earlier life cycle phases should reduce the number of errors dramatically, but there will always be small mistakes that will be uncovered through testing. JAD can assist in incorporating user input into the creation of a test plan. This will greatly enhance the chances for user acceptance on project completion.

Conversion.   Existing databases must be converted for utilization by the new application, or incorporated into new databases. JAD can be used to bring together representatives of the various databases to determine the best conversion solution.

Production planning.   Planning is required to ensure that the transition to a new production environment is smooth. Configuration control of old and new applications must be planned out, as well as storage capacity requirements and communications needs. Mini-JAD sessions can be used to bring together the people who have the information and authority to make production planning decisions.

Documentation.   Documentation for business users and production operations personnel must be created and maintained. Users will also require on-line or paper reference and training materials. Production personnel will need run books and recovery documentation.

Training and support.   Training and support for the user community will be needed initially and on an on-going basis.

MAPPING THE IE METHODOLOGY INTO AN EXISTING LIFE CYCLE

In selecting an information engineering methodology that fits the culture of your organization, you may want to adopt a specific interpretation of IE, or you may want to integrate ideas from several different IE perspectives. You may want to replace your current life cycle, or you may want to adapt the life cycle you presently use. There is a continuum of options available, from making a dramatic change to a highly prescriptive IE approach to modifying a current life cycle to include selected IE concepts, diagrams, and procedures. The option that you select should suit your organization's culture and information management requirements. No one option is right for every organization. Many organizations, for example, have moved toward an IE orientation by adding a "Planning for Systems" phase to the front end of their life cycles. Some systems organizations call this new phase "Discovery" or "Exploration," with the idea of including a number of different types of open-ended planning projects. They want the flexibility to address crisis projects, as well as more deliberate planning projects. Other organizations may choose to add IE-type diagrams to their current life cycle deliverables to take advantage of CASE capabilities and to enhance rapid application development ability. This too can be a useful introduction to IE concepts.

Actually, the whole concept of the life cycle is a bit different in an IE environment. Where more traditional life cycles favor a ladder of steps in which each step or phase is fairly discrete, in an IE life cycle, phases may overlap. This is particularly true when IE is combined with RAD. For example, in a RAD interpretation of the IE approach, application installation and production planning is conducted at the same time as application design activities. With the introduction of IE planning projects, some required capacity and production planning activities are conducted very early in the life cycle when architecture and development plans are created.

Nonetheless, if we were to overlay the information engineering life cycle on the traditional life cycle used by most organizations, there would be more matches than misses. However, the misses are important for an organization interested in implementing IE concepts without throwing out its current life cycle. One difference between IE and traditional life cycles is that less time is generally spent in each phase of the IE life cycle than in traditional approaches. This is achieved by eliminating some activities found in the different phases and by overlapping others. Some activities are eliminated because of the future focused orientation of the methodology. IE supports a forward looking philosophy that discourages detailed analyses of present processes, databases, and systems. IE focuses on what is needed for the future, rather than what exists in the current environment. This is different from the position taken by some of the older life cycle approaches in place.

Another difference is that IE has fewer more inclusive phases than traditional life cycles where phases are more numerous, and where each phase promotes a more limited objective. This detailed prescriptive approach provides less opportunity for flexibility and creativity than is possible with the IE approach. IE places more emphasis on the objectives of each phase than on the procedures required to achieve those objectives. This puts more responsibility on the shoulders of the systems professionals who must define the procedures required to achieve objectives, but it also provides more opportunity for flexibility to meet unique project needs.

A comparison of life cycle phases in traditional and IE approaches also illustrates how they differ in the way that time and effort is distributed. More traditional approaches emphasize the construction phase of the life cycle, with much of the resources of the project expended there. As a result, programmers seem to take on the principal responsibility for project completion and success. IE, on the other hand, emphasizes the front end of the life cycle, particularly the planning phase, with a proportionally larger expenditure of resources in this initial life cycle component. Here the user community assumes a much larger part of the responsibility for project success.

IE consequently encourages the creation of a different type of project team. User input is sought more often and in more phases of the IE life cycle than is generally true in more traditional approaches. Users and systems professionals are more or less required to form strong relationships because of the insistence of IE on building systems to meet strategic business needs. In an IE environment, systems do not merely solve information management problems, they meet strategic business needs. This means that the interdependency between users and systems professionals is extremely high. In addition, the project team is more likely to work closely together in the IE approach, handing off assignments on an ad hoc basis in order to progress quickly. Once again, this is the result of a methodology more concerned with meeting phase objectives than in policing phase procedures.

IE's emphasis on the front end of the life cycle should not be taken as an endorsement of feasibility analysis, however. This initial life cycle activity often found in traditional approaches is not generally found in IE approaches. Feasibility is addressed in an IE life cycle, but not in the way generally found in other approaches. Rather than focusing on whether a project is technically feasible, IE focuses on how the project fits into the larger architecture of the organization's information management plan. One reason for this is simple. At this point in the history of systems development, there is just about always a technically feasible option for developing and installing a desired system. Technical feasibility is not the open question it once was. Neither is financial feasibility. Most information management problems can be addressed within a reasonable budget. Today feasibility is not a go/no go decision. Rather, it is merely a question of which options to take, and this question should be answered, IE maintains, in the context of the larger information management plan of the organization, and not on a single project basis.

A significant difference can be seen at the end of the life cycle as well, where IE redefines the management of maintenance activities for applications and databases. With IE, maintenance decisions are made at the business level rather than the application level. Maintenance requirements are analyzed in order to separate enhancement requirements from other maintenance work such as error correction and conversion to new technology platforms. This goes hand in hand with IE's emphasis on planning. IE maintains that each project should reflect both the higher business needs of the organization and the architectural context in which it participates. This is as true for maintenance projects as it is for new development work.

By comparing the IE methodology structure and diagrams to those required in an existing systems life cycle, an organization can begin to define a new path for systems planning and development. This new path will then have to be tested against the needs of a variety of projects for it to be perfected. Each project will provide a new opportunity to determine how IE fits the needs of the organization.

QUESTIONS MOST FREQUENTLY ASKED

Some people look at information engineering as an arcane technique that is best implemented by highly specialized professionals. The major principles of the methodology, however, are neither obscure nor complex. There is no reason why the astute analyst or project manager cannot implement this approach within the organization. Still, there are a number of areas that seem to concern new practitioners of the approach. Here are some of the questions most frequently asked about the implementation of IE, and some pragmatic approaches to dealing with the issues they raise.

1. Why should initial data and process analysis be conducted separately?

While information engineering adherents are interested in the relationships between data and process, they maintain that initial data and process analysis activities should be conducted separately. One reason for doing so is that this approach simplifies the analysis process and enables the project team to work more quickly. If too much complication is introduced at an early stage in a project, it may falter from the weight of the participants' confusion. Another reason for conducting data and process analysis separately is that IE principles require the creation of separate data and process models. An important premise on which the information engineering philosophy is built is that data has more stability over time than process. Therefore, databases should be created as a primary activity, with the specific applications that will use that data being created as a secondary activity. These corporate databases serve as a stable resource. If created carefully, they should require relatively little change over time. The applications that access these databases, however, are dynamic resources. They will change over time to accommodate new circumstances and requirements.

2. Which comes first, data analysis or process analysis?

Assuming that we pursue data and process analysis separately initially, the next question is which of the two to focus on first. This question is interesting for the passion it can arouse. Some analysts maintain that data analysis must always come first; others argue just the opposite. As in most such debates, however, neither side is absolutely correct. The needs and objectives of any project should always dictate the answer to this question. As a general guideline, however, data analysis should precede process analysis for planning projects and for those analysis and design projects that will lead to the development of MIS and decision support applications. For design projects leading to the development of applications that will support heavy transaction processing, process analysis should probably come first. In this type of project, the user participants may have an easier time of it if they review their business processes first.

In either case, however, some analysis of business functionality must be performed in the early stages of the project to define its framework and to set its boundaries. It is very difficult for the project manager to plan a project or for project participants to discuss their needs without a strong sense of what is within the scope of the project and what is outside it. This is best done through a preliminary analysis of functionality. This is not a recommendation for the creation of a detailed process model up front; rather it is a proposal (based on extensive experience) to examine the basic business functions of the organization before the scope of a project is defined.

3. How are the relationships between process and data established?

For any given IE project, separate data and process models will be defined as a first step. Once these models have been defined, the relationships between data and process may be identified. This type of relationship analysis is critical for many projects. Data and process integration points include the following:

- In IE planning projects, a matrix diagram may be developed in order to define relationships between business processes and data subject areas or information groups.
- In IE analysis projects, a set of data flow diagrams may be developed to validate the data each process creates, accesses, updates, or deletes.
- In IE design projects, a state transition diagram may be developed to identify possible status conditions for primary information groups and the required processing for each status condition.
- In IE analysis projects or IE design projects, a data navigation diagram may be developed to define how the data model is accessed when a process is carried out, a screen is constructed, data is provided to support business decisions, questions must be answered or work products created.
- In IE design projects, a decision diagram may be constructed to define the relationship between a given status for a specific information group and

process actions required for that status or particular combination of status conditions.

- In IE design projects, a set of action diagrams may be constructed to define processing procedures required for code generation.

4. Why does IE emphasize an ideal or future-oriented view of business processes, rather than a present view?

In most cases, process analysis should be conducted from a future oriented, or "ideal," perspective. This means that the project team should put aside its knowledge of how the business processes are performed today and define its view of how the business processes should be carried out to optimize their performance. Where some methodologies require a detailed examination of the current process model, information engineering adherents consider this in most cases to be a nonproductive task. In some cases it may even be counterproductive in its emphasis on the familiar rather than the new and creative. IE starts from the assumption that the current process model is not the optimal model, and instead requires that an ideal model be constructed with special attention to the strategic goals and objectives of the organization. It asks project participants to derive the definition of business processes from those strategic goals and objectives and to avoid the introduction of redundancies. This will ensure that current processes will not be maintained just because things have always been done that way. It will also avoid a situation where project participants focus on current problems, directing their attention particularly at those problems caused by competing interests among the participants. This future orientation applies to the analysis of current automated systems as much as to current process structures.

Some individuals, particularly those engaged in operations and engineering work, may have difficulty exploring the future without examining current processes first. They are much more comfortable psychologically with the process structure they know than with speculation about an unknown structure. This can be complicated further if political considerations are involved, as they often are. In one manufacturing company, for example, an analysis conducted of the current process structure revealed that a particular engineering department was duplicating the work of other engineering departments. Project participants could not agree to address the problem directly and eliminate the unnecessary department, however, because of political considerations. Their solution to the problem was to make minor modifications in the process model and to assume that this would simplify their work processes. They could have made much more progress in addressing their real needs if they had focused on a new ideal process model derived from a set of predefined strategic business objectives. In this way, no one individual or department would be seen as gaining or losing. All project participants would be equally involved in the creation of a new structure clearly tied to business needs.

There are times, however, when an organization will decide that it is necessary to examine the current environment. This might happen when a current process model is considered to be very effective generally but not well suited to meeting a specific and limited need. A modification to the current process model might be required, for example, when a new product or service is added to those already offered by the marketing department. In this case, a complete new process model is not required; a modification of the current model will be sufficient. Here the organization needs to test the current model against the needs created by the new product or service. Exceptions to the current model can be noted and options for adapting the model to meet these needs can be identified and evaluated. Another case where an evaluation of the current process model may be appropriate is when the organization needs to evaluate its current strengths and weaknesses. The approach here is to look for "pockets of opportunity" by posing questions (e.g., "Can we decentralize our management of personnel resources?). It may also be appropriate to consider using a "gap analysis" approach. In this approach, the project participants first create an ideal process model and then compare this to a current model to identify where proposed changes will impact the existing environment. Sometimes a different group of people from those who defined the ideal model can define the required changes. This may help to remove politics from the re-engineering of business operations.

5. What is the difference between top down and bottom up data analysis? Is one better than the other?

In top down data analysis, the first step is to identify relevant information groups. The second step is to define the relationships among these groups, and the third step is to identify the attributes, or characteristics, of each group. This is an intuitive approach to creating a data model. It works well when project participants are well acquainted with the business area being addressed and are able to think quickly and creatively. Sometimes this approach works well. When project participants are not particularly creative, however, it may be difficult for them to use, and even with an excellent group of participants, the top down approach seldom results in a fully complete data model. The first step in the bottom up, or data normalization, approach as defined by E.F. Codd is the identification of data attributes, or "items." Once a comprehensive list of items has been created, the second step requires that natural groupings of items be identified. In the third step, each grouping is reviewed and items within each grouping are organized with the aim of identifying dependencies and reducing redundancy. This approach works well with project participants who need a lot of support in identifying individual data items and defining their relationships. It can be tedious, however, for people who have the ability to move quickly and are familiar with both the business area under consideration and the data modeling process.

Ultimately most analysts, either from necessity or by design, find that they use the two approaches together. They may begin by identifying obvious information groups and brainstorming a list of related attributes, but to complete the listing of attributes and to clarify dependencies and remove redundancies within the information groups, they then turn to the data normalization process. An initial ERD may be used to document the first step in this dual approach, with an entity table used to document the second step. The ERD will document the existing information groups and the relationships among those groups, and the entity table will document the individual information groups, or entities.

6. Should data analysis be application independent?

One of the great benefits of information engineering is the opportunity to address the information needs of a business area rather than just those of an application. Every effort should be made to build and maintain logical data models at the business area level. A business area data model can greatly enhance data consistency and integrity across the applications that provide and use the data contained in the model.

To build a successful business area data model, issues of business strategy and conflicting needs and priorities among model users must be addressed. It is critical that consensus be reached on the identification and definition of all information groups and data items. In addition, there are systems issues that must be resolved in order for the model to be successful. These concern the administration of the model, the hardware and software platform on which the model will be implemented, and the control of access to the model for use in development and maintenance of applications utilizing the model.

7. Once developed, are data and process models stable?

Experience shows that no data or process model is ever completely stable. Just as business needs evolve and change, models must evolve and change to support them. The models are organic because the business they support is organic. The number and frequency of modifications required depends entirely on the dynamic nature of the business. Some businesses will be able to develop fairly stable models. Others, perhaps experiencing corporate restructuring, mergers, or acquisitions, will be forced continually to refine their models to meet new needs. When the changes affecting the business are fairly dramatic ones, they may affect both data and process models. When the changes are somewhat less dramatic, it is likely that data models will be affected to a lesser degree.

8. How are the data and process models developed at the business area level integrated with application-level models?

If the broader business area models are developed first, then all application models should be a subset of the larger data and/or process model. The application models that are developed will provide additional detail not available initially at the business area level. Many organizations, however, will build data and process models at the application level out of the necessity to serve user needs before business area models are available. In such a case, the following applies:

- In order to prepare for the creation of a business area-level data model, the information groups defined in the application-level data models must be analyzed to identify inconsistencies and redundancies. To prepare for the creation of a business area process model, application-level business processes must be analyzed to identify duplications, overlaps and missing processes.
- Knowledgeable business users must resolve all inconsistencies and conflicts through the use of a consensus building approach.
- A disciplined data administration group supported by automated tools must integrate the application models into a business area model and then manage and maintain that model, inform the users of the model about its content, and provide support to the users as required.

KEY PROBLEMS ENCOUNTERED IN IMPLEMENTING THE IE METHODOLOGY

Implementing any new methodology can be difficult. Information engineering is no exception. The proper implementation of IE requires a great deal of effort on the part of all involved. This includes both the user community and the systems community, and high-level executives as well as those working at lower levels within the organization. The individuals responsible for making this change should consider the following suggestions for addressing the most common problems.

Difficulty in Focusing on the Future

Information engineering stresses a future-oriented perspective. It seeks to guide project participants in building information management solutions for tomorrow, not merely today. Some business users, particularly those at the operations level, may lack a broad perspective about their responsibilities. They may have had a long history of performing their jobs in a particular way and find it difficult to imagine doing things differently. Some may have worked for a single company, perhaps even a single organization for all of their working lives. They may never have been encouraged to offer new ideas before. So it is understandable that they may have difficulty in defining an alternative to their current business approach.

This problem can handicap a project, and it must be overcome if the project is to succeed. Project participants have to be shaken out of their comfortable assumptions, and this is generally the responsibility of a JAD facilitator. This individual must recognize the problem early in the project, and develop a strategy to deal with it. The most critical time for future oriented thinking is the workshop. There creative thinking can be encouraged through special exercises using brainstorming, displayed thinking, and decision round robins. Sometimes, bringing outside experts into workshops can provide new ideas that participants can use as a model for their own solutions.

Expanding Project Boundaries

IE emphasizes a modular approach to project management. This is why it may be applied so successfully to large and unwieldy projects. Unfortunately, this modular approach may be undermined by a common problem. "Scope creep" is a serious threat to the modular structure of projects favored by IE. This problem occurs when for reasons of political expediency, personal ambition, or just plain ignorance a project is allowed to keep growing until it is too large to be managed in a successful manner. If the problem is a technical one and project boundaries keep expanding because of an imperfect understanding of business functionality and organization structure, then decomposition diagrams representing business processes and organizations and matrices comparing the two can be helpful in keeping control of the scope of the analysis effort. If the problem is a political one, then top management intervention may be required. Scope expansion is a serious problem that can undermine the success of a project, and it must be addressed very early in the project life cycle if the project is to survive.

Lost Participant Focus

Because information engineering asks participants to look at the business from the very highest strategic level to the most detailed level of analysis, it can sometimes be difficult to get project participants to focus on the correct level of analysis for a particular activity. Some participants may want to focus on very detailed aspects of business functionality when they should be considering broader questions of strategy and objectives. In this way they may avoid dealing with larger issues that will require uncomfortable decisions. Others, when specific information is required about standard business processes, may want to focus on generalities, making grand statements about the future of the business or the true meaning of marketing. To overcome these problems when they arise in a workshop, the JAD facilitator must constantly keep participants on track, sometimes using examples to illustrate the appropriate level of analysis. Without such guidance, project participants can spend a great deal of time on nonproductive discussion.

Inappropriate Degree of Resolution in Data and Process Models

Because information engineering favors a flexible approach to the definition of data and process models, the degree of detail maintained in those models should be appropriate for the type of decision making for which the model was constructed. Many information management problems will require the construction of business area data models utilizing entity relationship diagrams, but a smaller number require application of the data normalization process and the construction of entity tables. Process models displaying a decomposition hierarchy of three to five levels may be adequate for business area and MIS and decision support application projects; transaction application design projects often require the addition of dependency diagrams.

Two types of problems can arise here. Inadequate resolution of data and process models can undermine the effectiveness and productivity of those members of the project team who must base their own work (defining the boundaries of applications to be developed, developing physical models, writing code, etc.) on them. On the other hand, too much detail in these models where it is not required can waste time, lower productivity, and cause confusion. To contain the level of detail and avoid this problem, some project managers and JAD facilitators set a time limit beyond which no more analysis will be done. In both cases, the best way to deal with the problem of incorrect resolution of detail is to ensure that an adequate understanding of the needs of the project and its participants is obtained at the outset. This means that the specific objectives of the project must be identified as soon as possible, and that the needs of those who will be receiving the models be clearly defined as well.

Inadequate User Involvement/Key Player Commitment

Because the information engineering approach draws a clear connection between business needs and system solutions, it requires strong participation from individuals at all levels within the business community and strong commitment from those at the top of the organization. If knowledgeable business users are not involved in the project at an early stage, the outcome of the project may be seriously jeopardized. A false view of information management requirements may be developed, or, even if an accurate view is developed, it may be rejected by those who have not been consulted in its development.

To encourage the participation of knowledgeable individuals, a clear presentation of the benefits of involvement must be offered to them. They must see their efforts rewarded. These rewards can come through professional recognition, improved working conditions, or an enhanced understanding of the application of automated tools in solving information management problems. To encourage the demonstration of commitment from top individuals within the organization, it may be useful to demonstrate the value of a successful project in promoting career development and enhancing the competitive position of the organization. In order to obtain strong project support from both business users and executives, the use of joint application development techniques should be encouraged. JAD can play a critical role in obtaining commitment and ensuring effective involvement of the right people in a project.

Competing Needs: Maintaining Today's Systems and Building for the Future

One of the biggest problems in introducing an information engineering approach (some would say the biggest problem) is how to continue to maintain our current information management capabilities and at the same time move to a future-oriented IE environment. To take one example, how do we continue to maintain our old payroll system to ensure that it produces checks on schedule and at the same time introduce a new human resources database? A great deal of the skepticism that greets the promoters of information engineering is based on the difficulties created by competing priorities. While this is not an easy problem to solve, it must be solved if an organization is to move ahead. Techniques for addressing this problem include the following:

- Application development projects currently underway can be expedited through the use of IE diagrams to speed the transition from logical design to coding. This can create positive expectations for future projects.
- A "cross-functional" application project (preferably one with easily defined data and process requirements) can be selected as an IE pilot project in order to demonstrate the value of IE concepts to a large number of business organizations at the same time and to demonstrate the value of IE concepts in dealing with difficult and complex projects.
- Working within a business area where individuals are already motivated to modernize their work operations, or where there is a great and immediate need for a new or redeveloped application can be a key to generating enthusiasm for IE.

Absence of Strong Project Management

IE is just like any other methodology in its requirement for strong project management. This requirement touches all aspects of project work, from personnel selection to scheduling to budgeting to maintaining firm control over project scope and direction. In an IE environment, it also means taking a firm hand to ensure that there is a future orientation to the work, that business objectives are always in clear view, and that diagramming techniques are utilized correctly within the project. In addition, strong change control standards and procedures are required to ensure that consistency is maintained throughout the project both internally and externally with respect to other ongoing related projects.

Premature Introduction of Technical Considerations

IE methodology emphasizes the need for a clear understanding of the strategic direction of the business. It insists that technical considerations should follow business needs and not the other way around. This is not to reject the idea that constraints must be respected within the project. There are often technical constraints that will influence the direction of a project without regard to project objectives or strategy. These must be considered up front in order to save time and avoid a situation where an information management solution is designed that cannot be implemented. However, where there are technology alternatives for solving a problem, an analysis of these alternatives should be delayed until after the business needs have been clearly and completely defined. Only then should a selection among alternatives be made. For information engineering, the business need always drives the technology solution.

Absence of Education/Understanding

Many methodologies assume that only methodology practitioners need to be experts in the principles and techniques embodied in the approach. Information engineering cannot be effectively implemented, however, unless all of those involved in a project—users and systems professionals alike—are well educated in the elements of the methodology. All project participants need at least a basic understanding of the IE life cycle, data and process modeling, and common IE diagramming techniques. The participants will benefit from a sound education in these areas, as will the project itself. While an uneducated user can make only a minimal contribution to a project, an educated user can be an enormously valuable asset.

6

FUSION: Integrating IE, CASE, and JAD

WEAVING THE DIMENSIONS TOGETHER

Each of the dimensions of FUSION is powerful on its own. Many organizations have gained greatly from simply adding CASE tools to their current life cycle methods and procedures. Other organizations have benefited from introducing JAD techniques or IE concepts. No organization that implements only one of these dimensions, however, has as powerful an approach to information systems planning and management as the organization that implements a total FUSION approach. This may seem a bit overwhelming at first, and it is true that the implementation of the FUSION approach can have a profound effect on an organization. However, the organization that accepts this challenge will quickly discover that the benefits of FUSION far surpass the effort required for implementation.

If we were able to follow information engineering theory to the letter, all systems work in a given business unit could be traced back to an IE planning project. That project would have made possible the definition of business area analysis projects, and these would have led to specific application projects. In our ideal world, there would be a commitment to create business plans and architectures and to use them to drive application and database project definition. Business would develop information management plans based on strategic business plans,

and all plans and requirements definitions would be developed through the cooperative efforts of participants knowledgeable about and committed to the goals of the
business.

However, most of us live in a less than perfect world. The larger and more
complex our business or organization, the more difficult it becomes to follow
theory. It is not possible to take a hiatus from existing project development work
to rethink systems in every business unit. We are saddled with large and small
application projects that must be installed and running "come hell or high water."
What we need, therefore, is a practical way to continue to work on already
identified projects and gain the benefits of IE, JAD, and CASE without having to
shut down and start from the beginning. Because FUSION was designed as a
pragmatic, rather than a theoretical approach, this is possible. While FUSION
does recommend stopping those projects that are totally inappropriate, it allows
those projects that cannot be delayed to proceed while the organization is working
on implementing the full IE-JAD-CASE approach.

Before the FUSION of IE, JAD, and CASE, a project team might jump into
a project without a clear definition of the scope of the project, an understanding
of its relationship to other projects being conducted by the organization, or an
understanding of the relationship of the project to the strategic objectives of the
business. This view of the project as an isolated unit, unique and self-contained,
and justified by virtue of its own existence, has caused more project failures than
any error in technical judgment ever has. With FUSION a project team can place
the project within its larger context and ensure that it will justify the effort expended
on it.

The steps required for achieving FUSION (Figure 6.1) are:

1. Define project scope.
2. Identify IE analysis approach.
3. Define project deliverable requirements.
4. Identify opportunities for JAD intervention.
5. Identify application of CASE tool capabilities.
6. Design JAD technical agenda.
7. Design JAD workshop agenda.

DEFINE PROJECT SCOPE

Let's begin with the assumption that a project has been identified and that its
principal objective is known. The first step in the FUSION approach, is to identify
the scope of that project by mapping it to, on the one hand, the IE life cycle, and
on the other hand, the organization. In this way we gain both a temporal and
spatial view of the project. The temporal view of the project places it against a
theoretical IE time line. It tells us where the project fits into the IE life cycle,

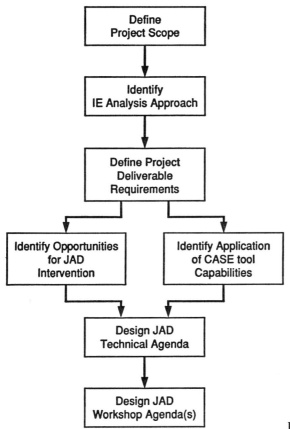

Figure 6.1 The steps of FUSION.

whether in strategic planning at the beginning of the life cycle, in application construction at the end of the life cycle, or somewhere in between. The spatial view of the project focuses on corporate geography. It examines how the project maps against the organization structure, whether it impacts one small business area or several major business units.

For example, if the principal objective of a project is to improve the competitive market position of a business through the enhancement of its information management resources, we can deduce that the project lies within the IE planning component. Further, if this objective embraces all product lines and support functions, then we know that the geography under examination is the entire business. If the principal objective of another project is to build an integrated accounting system, we can deduce that the project includes both IE design and construction components. If the accounting system will be utilized by all domestic business units of a large international corporation, then we know that the geography of the project is bounded by the Atlantic and Pacific oceans. Figure 6.2 summarizes the relationship of project objectives to IE components.

This step should provide answers to the following questions:

1. Where does this project fit within the IE life cycle?
2. How does this project map to the geography of the organization?
3. What major business functions will be impacted by the project?
4. Who should be a member of the project team?
5. What type of support and sponsorship is required from senior management?
6. What are the potential areas of cultural and political impact?
7. In broad outline, what deliverables will be required?

IDENTIFY IE ANALYSIS APPROACH

Once the scope of a project has been defined, it is necessary to decide which analytical techniques will be utilized to reach its principal objective. The principal objective of the project will be the determining factor in deciding which techniques will be selected (Fig. 6.3). For example, the principal objective of a project may be to define the information management needs of a business unit (say a chain of fast food restaurants). The appropriate analytical technique for defining a set of information management needs is the construction of a data model. On the other hand, if the principal objective of the project is to re-engineer certain business operations (e.g., to cut food delivery time), the appropriate analytical technique is the construction of both data and process models. If the principal objective of the project is to create an accounting system for the fast food unit, then the construction of a data-process relationship model may be required. If the principal objective of a project is to select and install an off-the-shelf software package, then the analytical technique to be selected would be the development of a logical design. This design would include access specifications as well as data and process models.

This step should provide answers to the following questions:

- Is there a requirement to model the information needs of the organization? If so, at what level should this information model be presented?
- Is there a requirement to model the business processes performed by the organization? If so, at what level should these processes be examined?
- Is there a requirement for an integrated view of data and process?
- Is there a requirement for a comparative analysis (i.e., models that contrast two views of data or process)? Or for an integrated analysis (i.e., one model that combines information from two sources)?

IE Component	Example Project Objectives
Planning	Define how systems can give the business a competitive advantage
	Define how systems must evolve to match the business vision
	Define the overall systems architecture to support the business vision
	Define business priorities that must drive systems support
Analysis	Understand the business current or future information needs
	Improve or re-engineer how the business conducts its works
	Define development and maintenance priorities for systems
	Develop concrete modernization and support plans for a business area
Development Construction Installation	Develop or change specific applications and data bases
	Define the requirements for selecting and purchasing off-the-shelf software packages and/or hardware
Customer support	Analyze change requests to understand the scope and impact of the next releases of application(s) on both the technical and business environments
	Define change request priorities for the next system release

Figure 6.2 IE components and project objectives.

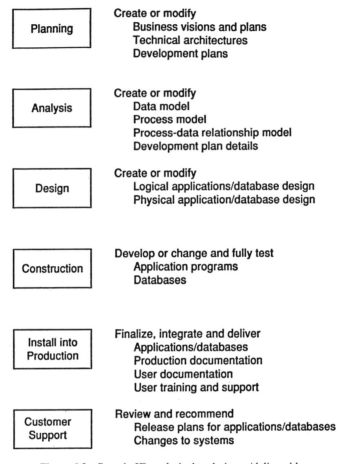

Figure 6.3 Sample IE analytical techniques/deliverables.

• Is there a requirement for other types of information (e.g., system access information, detailed information on corporate objectives and strategy, cost benefit ratios, marketing/implementation strategies, etc.)?

DEFINE PROJECT DELIVERABLE REQUIREMENTS

Once the analytical techniques required to reach a project's principal objective have been identified, the format in which the results of that analysis will be presented must be determined. Several options exist for the display of the analytical information gathered. The options chosen will reflect the needs of the project, the sophistication of the project team, and the projected next steps for the proj-

IE Deliverable	**IE Diagrams**
Business visions and plans	Decomposition Matrix Entity relationship
Technical architectures	Decomposition Matrix
Development plans	Matrix
Data model	Entity relationship Entity table
Process model	Decomposition Dependency
Process-data relationship model	Process-entity matrix Existing systems matrix Data flow Data navigation State transition

Logical design	Diagrams for the three models
	Access specifications:
	   query statements
	   screen and report layouts
	   action
	   application navigation/dialogues

Physical design	Data structure Entity table Action Screen and report layouts Applications navigation/dialogues

Figure 6.4 Sample IE deliverables and supporting diagrams.

ect. It is always necessary to keep in mind two questions: ''Who will be using the information documented in this project deliverable?'' and ''How will it be used?''

While the FUSION approach suggests that certain deliverables will probably fit the needs of most projects that fall within a specific life cycle phase, it does not dictate that specific graphic techniques be selected to represent data and process models. Deliverable content is suggested, but only as a set of options (Fig. 6.4). If, for example, the principal objective of a project is to select an off-the-shelf software package to support inventory operations, FUSION does not require that a detailed logical design be created. Only those elements of the design necessary for package selection are required. There might be no need, therefore, to include database navigation specifications or action diagrams. For example, we may have a project where our principal objective is the definition of the strategic information needs of a business area. We have already determined that the most appropriate analytical technique in this case is the creation of a data model, but we have a number of options for the display of that data model. In itself a data model is an abstraction. When we determine how best to document that model, we are defining specific project deliverable requirements. In this case, we may document the data model through the use of an entity relationship diagram and entity table diagrams, and we may choose to normalize the model to the fifth normal form if an expected outcome of the project is a series of on-line database inquiries. On the other hand, we may choose to document the data model with an ERD maintained in first normal form and without the use of entity table diagrams if an expected outcome of the project is the identification of overlapping applications.

By addressing deliverable requirements as a unique issue with every new project, FUSION attempts to strip out extraneous and time consuming content often contained in project deliverables. However, the FUSION approach can add to as well as limit deliverable content. Because FUSION insists on addressing the political and cultural context of the project as well as technical requirements, it may be necessary to go beyond traditional, or technical, content of the deliverable. For example, a determination of the cost benefit ratio of changing the process model for a business area may be a key to a successful project. In this case, the deliverable must contain information identifying resource savings achieved when a comparison is made between the old way of doing business and an alternative way of doing business. In another project, an organization may need to decide whether a complete redevelopment of existing systems is required to support the information needs created when a new product is added to an existing product line. Here the deliverable may have to include detailed cross referencing of information needs to existing systems in order for a decision to be made.

This step should provide answers to the following questions:

- What graphic techniques will best serve to display the information collected through the use of the analytical techniques defined in the previous step?
- What level of detail should be presented in these graphic representations?
- What textual (nongraphic) information is required? In what format should it be displayed?
- How do these graphic and textual components meet the needs identified in the principal objective of the project?

IDENTIFY OPPORTUNITIES FOR JAD INTERVENTION

Once the "what" of a project is defined through the definition of a project deliverable, the "how" of the project must be addressed. FUSION tells us to look at the options that JAD provides for detailing that "how." Depending on the project, all or a part of the deliverables required may be produced through the use of JAD workshops. In one project, for example, JAD workshops may supply all of the information required for the logical design deliverable, but the project team may construct the physical design and the application prototype by using a more traditional development approach. In another project, JAD workshops may produce all of the information that is required. This may happen in a project designed to produce a model of information needs for a business unit.

This step should provide answers to the following questions:

- Which of the deliverable items required can be produced faster and better through the use of a JAD workshop (or series of workshops)?
- How should the workshop(s) be structured?
- Who should be involved?
- What schedule should be adopted?
- Will the use of the JAD technique require any modifications or additions to the previously identified project deliverables?

IDENTIFY APPLICATION OF CASE TOOL CAPABILITIES

Just as opportunities for JAD intervention should be identified based on deliverable requirements, so too should opportunities for the application of CASE tool capabilities. Tool capabilities that will contribute to the development of the deliverable should be identified, and any special considerations caused by use of the tool should be examined. At this point, it is also useful to determine whether the tool will be used before, during, and/or after the JAD workshops. Once available CASE tool capabilities have been reviewed, the need for additional automated support should be determined. Word processing and graphic capabilities outside the scope of available CASE tools may be required. If so, options for supplying these capabilities should be considered.

This step should provide answers to the following questions:

- Which CASE tool capabilities are available to support the graphic and textual requirements identified in the definition of the project deliverable?
- Which project deliverable requirements cannot be supported by available CASE tools? How will these requirements be supported? Will integration of multiple software tools be easy or difficult?
- Will the CASE tool (or other automated tools) be used before JAD workshops? During workshops? After workshops?
- What hardware will be required to support the CASE tools used within the workshops? Will adequate printing facilities be available?
- Will it be possible to provide easy to read printouts of information maintained in the CASE tool to participants during the workshop(s)? Will special hardware or software be required to do this?

- How difficult will it be to input material produced in a workshop (perhaps on multiple easel pages) to the CASE tool? What accommodations will be required to achieve an easy flow from workshop to tool and back again to participants for review?

DESIGN JAD TECHNICAL AGENDA

At this point in the FUSION process, the scope of the project and its objectives have been defined. The IE analytical techniques required to support those objectives have also been identified. It is clear, for example, if a detailed process model will be required for the project. Based on this knowledge, the deliverable needs of the project have been determined. To continue with our example, we know how we will produce the detailed process model. Perhaps we have decided to use a hierarchical decomposition diagram followed by a set of dependency diagrams to gather, analyze, and document the process model. Further, we have determined how we will use JAD techniques and CASE technology to support the production of these diagrams. It is now time to pull these project elements together. We do this in a JAD technical agenda. Because we use this agenda to pull together all of the critical FUSION elements, the creation of a strong JAD technical agenda is a key to FUSION success.

The JAD technical agenda must combine all three FUSION elements: IE, JAD, and CASE. Its creation is guided by the principles of information engineering, it utilizes the JAD technique and takes advantage of CASE technology. The technical agenda specifies what information is to be gathered and analyzed during the workshop (or workshops), how JAD techniques will be used to gather and analyze it, in what diagrammatic format that information will be presented, and what CASE tools will be employed to store and maintain it. The technical agenda for any project represents a unique combination of elements. It includes the diagrams already selected to meet the analysis and documentation needs of the project, a JAD workshop structure created with both project objectives and constraints in mind, and a definition of specific CASE capabilities that will be utilized.

The JAD technical agenda brings all of these elements together to support one or more of five possible technical objectives, or "topic areas" (Fig. 6.5). These areas include:

- Project framework
- Data model
- Process model
- Data-process relationship model
- Access specifications

These five topic areas (or some subset of these areas) will form the basis of the JAD technical agenda. To construct the agenda, follow these steps.

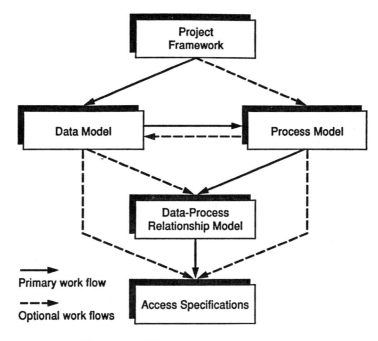

Figure 6.5 JAD technical agenda topic areas.

Step One

The first step is to identify those topic areas that will be addressed by the project. This should not be difficult. The decisions made in FUSION step two, which requires the identification of an IE analysis approach for the project, should lead you in the right direction. The need for a process model, for example, should already have been determined. The one topic area that may not have been considered previously would be the "project framework" topic area. Special consideration should be given to including this topic area in order to ensure that the scope of the project has been correctly defined and that all workshop participants share the same understanding of that scope. It is not necessary for each project to address all five topic areas, however. Some projects will address three or four, and others only one.

The number of deliverable items required for each topic area should also be identified. Each topic area will be supported by one or more deliverable items. The decisions made in FUSION step three, which requires the identification of project deliverable requirements, should guide you here. Just as we reviewed our previous decision to create a process model, we review here our decision from step three to support the creation of that model through the use of decomposition and dependency diagrams. It is also important to remember that while many of the items to be included in the technical agenda will be expressed as diagrams, nondiagrammatic items may be included as well. These items might be expressed as other types of graphic representations, descriptive statements, definitions of terms, prioritized lists, or other textual material.

Finally, it is possible that topic areas not included on this list will also be required for the technical agenda. A strategic planning project, for example, might require a detailed look at resource impacts of a proposed plan. When appropriate, special topic areas should be created to meet such needs.

Step Two

Each topic area that will be addressed will form a section of the technical agenda. The next step in the FUSION process is to identify and sequence the deliverable items that are required within each section. To continue with the example provided earlier, the items within the data model topic area would be sequenced with the ERD first and the entity table second. This is done because information from the first item would be needed to produce the second item. This takes into account the sequence in which these items would be addressed within a workshop.

The JAD facilitator and project manager must use their best judgment in deciding how and when to capture this information. They should ask themselves, "What must we know in order to capture the information required in a given agenda item?" For example, one of the information items required in a technical agenda may be an estimate of resource savings from redesigned business processes on a cost per person per transaction basis. This information, which relies on the identification of differences between existing and future business operations, may best be gathered after diagrams depicting present and future process decomposition and present and future process dependency information.

Step Three

The third step is to identify one or more exercises that can be used to obtain the information required within each section. Each exercise selected must satisfy a dual set of needs. It must further the analysis of technical information and it must advance the cause of building a project team. When selecting exercises, it is important to consider the capabilities of the workshop participants, the level of detail required, the time available, CASE tools that will be used, and workshop pacing and timing requirements. Just as no two technical agendas will be precisely the same, no two sets of exercises will be identical.

Step Four

Next, the JAD data collection forms and room displays that will be required during the exercises must be designed and prepared. As before, the capabilities of the workshop participants, the level of detail required, the time available, CASE tools that will be used, and workshop pacing and timing requirements should be considered in the design of the forms and displays. In addition, any special equipment required by the participants and the JAD facilitator should be identified. In a very sophisticated FUSION environment where all data collection and analysis is automated, for example, each participant or participant group might require a workstation to enter information to complete data collection forms. In a less automated environment, data collection forms may be prepared on paper and designed to serve as input documents for a CASE tool. Room displays may be prepared for presentation on simple paper easel sheets, on vinyl sheets for display on an overhead projector, or on a computer for display through the use of a special projection device.

Step Five

At this point, the specific use of the CASE tool(s) throughout the life cycle of the project should be defined. If information will be input in the preworkshop phase, the manner of input should be determined as well as the need for any reports. For information that will be input during the workshop, it will be important to identify the need for interim reports. It is necessary to identify what reports might be required during the workshop, how these reports will be produced, and any special accommodations that must be made to ensure that they are readily available and easy to use. Both paper printouts and overhead displays should be considered. If the information contained in these reports will be required as input to or guidance for other exercises, paper printouts will probably be needed. If the information will be validated by the total group at one time, then projection may be quite acceptable.

This step should provide answers to the following questions:

- What topic areas will be covered in the workshops?
- What diagrams and other outputs will be produced to support each topic area?
- What exercises will be used to capture the information required to produce the diagrams and other outputs?
- In what order will these exercises be conducted?
- What data collection forms and display materials will be required?
- How will CASE tools be used to support the collection of information?

DESIGN JAD WORKSHOP AGENDA

Once the technical agenda is completed, the project manager and JAD facilitator must determine how it will be implemented. Perhaps most important, they must determine how many workshops will be needed to complete all of the exercises in the agenda and what the content, participation, and length of each workshop should be. Behavioral exercises may be added at the opening and closing of each workshop and, if appropriate to the project and participants, woven into the technical agenda to support team building and ensure project success. The length of each workshop and the mix of behavioral and technical exercises will be based on the following factors:

- The nature of the topic areas covered in the JAD technical agenda.

  Certain sequences of topic areas provide natural breakpoints between workshops. This in between time can be used for consolidating and preparing documentation. For example, in a technical agenda created in support of a project to produce a logical application design, a natural breakpoint occurs after process and data analysis has been completed and before the definition of access specifications is begun.
- Participant willingness and commitment to the project.

  The less enthusiasm there exists for a project, the greater the need for action to build commitment and increase the chances for project success. If, for example, a project is promoted by top level executives but not supported by lower level staff, there will be an increased chance of project failure. In order to reduce this chance of failure, educational opportunities and commitment building exercises may be introduced into the project. This can mean that the life cycle of the project will be extended. In some cases, it may be advisable to break up a project into small units that can be better tolerated by participants who would object to an aggressive, time consuming schedule. Perhaps the desire to avoid trespassing on a staff holiday or getting in the way of another important assignment may also make prolonging the schedule advisable.
- Project concreteness and clearness of purpose.

  The more well defined the project and the less it overlaps with other projects, the easier it will be for participants to make decisions and reach consensus. The more ambiguous and ill defined the objectives of the project, the more time and exercises will be needed to assist participants in clarifying the objectives and defining a focus for the project. Simply put, if the objectives and focus of a project are not defined at the outset, the participants will be forced to take this task upon themselves as part of the project itself.
- Participant relationships.

  The more hostility among the participants or participant groups involved in the project, the more the need for exercises to bring participants to a common understanding and the more time the JAD facilitator will consume in managing discussions, issues, and conflicts. If participants are neutral in their relationships but are located in different organizational units, time will be needed to assist them in developing a common language. This will add time to the project, particularly in the workshop phase, because discussions will take increased time until a common language is developed.

* Participant resistance.

If the project has the potential to significantly change the business, participants may be anxious about this change and the impact on their jobs, responsibilities, and work environment. They may also be less willing to make decisions about the nature of the change. Participants may have trouble fully entering into workshop discussions if their attention is diverted (correctly or incorrectly) by visions of layoffs, relocations or the elimination of business functions. It may be valuable in such a case to add time to the agenda to review and define project benefits and to allow participants to vent concerns about potential changes.

This work should provide answers to the following questions:

* How many workshops will be required to complete the exercises comprising the technical agenda?
* Which exercises will be covered in each workshop?
* Which parts of the final deliverable will be produced in each workshop?
* How much time will be required for each workshop?
* Who will participate in each workshop?

TECHNICAL AGENDA SAMPLES

The following three sample technical agendas and workshop script excerpts are provided to show how a deliverable gets translated into a JAD technical agenda. Ideas for translating technical agendas into JAD workshops are also provided. One example is presented for each of the three IE components where JAD is most effectively utilized, planning, analysis, and design. Each can be considered to represent a single project. The deliverables, agendas and selected exercises presented, however, are only examples of the broad range of options and opportunities that are available to a JAD facilitator in the FUSION approach.

A Strategic Planning Project

A large corporation contains within it a strategic business unit (SBU) that markets window blinds to the residential marketplace. This strategic business unit was purchased by the corporation last year. Since then it has become apparent that all is not well with the operation. The SBU is faced with growing competition and needs to modernize its manufacturing operations to increase output and to reduce per unit costs.

Initially, the SBU planning manager approached the manager of the systems organization, and asked him to develop a new customer and product tracking system so that the SBU could better manage its marketplace activities. After a few initial questions about how this new application might overlap with the existing order processing system and how this system would fit into the overall plan for technology support for the business in the next five years, the systems manager determined that a FUSION approach would be appropriate for the project. The planning manager of the SBU agreed. A senior JAD facilitator was called in to conduct preworkshop activities. When the JAD facilitator, the systems manager and the individual appointed to be systems project manager gathered some background information, they discovered that the unit had never conducted a formal strategic planning project before.

The three key players agreed that the first requirement for the SBU was the development of a strategic business plan. However, instead of letting the staff of the business unit develop this plan on their own, the systems organization suggested that they remain involved. Based on this business plan, the SBU and the systems organization would then examine how the SBU could more effectively utilize automation and computer systems to give it a competitive advantage. From that beginning, a technology plan would be developed to support integrated information databases and a set of application projects. Because the key individuals involved wanted to accomplish this planning work within six to eight weeks, a FUSION approach utilizing one or more JAD workshops was clearly indicated. The JAD facilitator defined the project as an IE planning project and determined that it consisted of three IE deliverables—a five-year business plan, an architecture plan and a development plan. For phase one of the project, JAD would be used to define the five-year business plan. The phase one deliverable would also include a list of business and technical issues to be addressed in phases two and three of the project. Content of the phase one JAD deliverable is defined in Fig. 6.6. The JAD technical agenda required to support this deliverable focuses on the project framework topic area. The agenda is outlined in Fig. 6.7. This technical agenda can be executed in one JAD workshop of four days if the level of detail required in the last content section, "Opportunities for Change," is limited to idea generation. Script excerpts providing instructions for creating matrix diagrams for this technical agenda are found in Fig. 6.8. Opening and closing workshop exercises should be added to the agenda along with an exercise to change the tone of the workshop environment after the completion of the agenda section, "Definition of the Future View of the Business."

If more detailed information were required for the "Opportunities for Change" section, then two JAD workshops would be recommended—a three-day workshop to cover the sections through "Defining a Future View of the Business," and a two to three-day workshop to define "Opportunities for Change." Each JAD workshop would also have opening and closing workshop exercises.

I.   Current Business Structure and Relationships

        a. SBU business functions
        b. SBU organization structure
        c. SBU geographic layout
        d. SBU existing systems support

II.   External Impact Analysis

        a. Market trends — customers
        b. Market trends — products and services
        c. Market trends — economics
        d. Market trends — competition
        e. Industry opportunities/issues

III.   Internal Impact Analysis

        a. Strengths/weaknesses — human resources
        b. Strengths/weaknesses — products and services
        c. Strengths/weakness — business operations
        d. Strengths/weakness — customer relations
        e. SBU opportunities/issues (short and long term)

IV.   Future View of the Business

        a. Mission statement
        b. Business goals and objectives
        c. Measures of goal achievement
        d. Statements of business policy
        e. Statements of strategic direction
        f. Actions needed to control the future

V.   Opportunities for Change

        a. Business operations redesign for increased effectiveness
        b. Technology improvements for competitive advantage
        c. Business and technology open issues

Figure 6.6   Sample strategic plan deliverable created through JAD workshops.

An Information Analysis Project

The new vice president of sales at a fast growing professional services business is having difficulty in getting timely feedback on sales results and related information. He and his managers need data on a daily and weekly basis, but data is currently provided on a monthly basis. This data is used to support strategic, tactical and operational decision making. In order to remedy the situation, the vice president has approached the systems organization with the idea of extracting data from existing systems to obtain more integrated information support to his

Topic Area	Content Section	Content Item
Project Framework	Validate:	

	SBU business functions	Decomposition diagram
	SBU organization structure	Decomposition diagram
	SBU geographic layout	Decomposition diagram
	SBU existing systems support	Itemized list

The facilitator leads a total group discussion to validate the diagrams and lists which have been stored in the CASE tool. Each diagram is displayed using overhead projection directly from the CASE tool. Changes and additions to the diagrams and lists which result from discussions are posted on easel boards. The CASE tool diagrams are updated off line and printed out for later use in the workshop.

Define Relationships:

	SBU process — organization	Matrix diagram
	SBU process — geographic layout	Matrix diagram
	SBU process — existing systems	Matrix diagram

The facilitator divides the participants into three subteams. Each subteam develops one of the process relationship diagrams using easel board display. Then each team presents to the total participant group the subteam recommendations for their assigned process matrix. Changes, additions and deletions are collected by the facilitator during the total group discussions on room display easel boards. The matrices are created, stored and produced off line with the CASE tool by JAD/CASE specialist.

Define External Impacts:

	Market trends — customers	Handouts
	Market trends — products/service	Handouts
	Market trends — economics	Handouts
	Market trends — competition	Handouts

Figure 6.7   Sample JAD technical agenda to create a strategic plan.

organization. He has discovered, however, that this will not be so easy to achieve. The systems manager in charge of supporting the sales business area explained to the vice president that there was a considerable problem with overlapping, inconsistent, and redundant data in the existing systems. He suggested that before they begin further system development it would be a good idea to review their current information needs. He also recommended that they use a FUSION approach. This would ensure that they would be able to move quickly, to address high-priority information needs first and involve the right people. The vice president agreed and assigned his three direct reports to work as an executive sponsor team for the project.

Subject matter experts (either participants or outside experts who participate only as presenters in this content section) present their information to the total group. The facilitator moderates the question and answer sessions which follow the formal presentations. CASE tools are not used.

Industry opportunities/issues   Prioritized list

The facilitator leads the group in a nominal group technique exercise to generate issues and opportunities. The JAD/CASE specialist documents the definition of each opportunity/issue as it is defined by the nominal group technique. Each issue and opportunity is entered into the CASE tool off line. These may be utilized in later analysis inside or outside of the workshop.

Define Internal Impacts:

Strengths/weaknesses — human resources   List
Strengths/weaknesses — products/services   List
Strengths/weaknesses — business operations   List
Strengths/weaknesses — customer relations   List

The facilitator assigns each of four subteams one of the strength/weakness analyses. The subteams use displayed thinking to identify and define strengths and weaknesses of the internal business. The strengths and weaknesses are listed using room displays. Each strength and weakness definition is documented on a form. The CASE tool is not used.

SBU internal opportunities/issues   Prioritized list

The facilitator conducts a force-field analysis exercise. The exercise requires room displays and forms completed by the JAD/CASE specialist. The information is entered into the CASE tool after the ranking of opportunities and issues is complete.

Create a Future Business View:

Mission statement

Leading a total group discussion, the facilitator creates a new mission statement for the business. As each part of the statement is created, the facilitator boards the results using the room display. After completion of the exercise, the JAD/CASE specialist completes a form to record the mission statement.

Figure 6.7   *(Cont.)*

Business goals and objectives   Decomposition diagram
Measures of achievement   List

Using the exercise of displayed thinking, the facilitator has the total
group create business goals, objectives and measures. After the
decomposition diagram has been created using the room display, the
JAD/CASE specialist can enter it into the CASE tool off line. Printouts
can be made available to the group.

Statements of business policy
Statements of strategic direction

The facilitator divides the group into subteams. Each subteam
creates, boards and presents to the total group recommendations for
business policy and strategic direction for the business. The facilitator
moderates the discussion until consensus is reached.

Actions needed to control the future   Prioritized list

The facilitator leads the total group in a generation of possible
actions. To assist in determining which actions are seen as most
important by the group, a forced-pair comparisons exercise is used to
prioritize the actions quantitatively.

Recommendations for Change Opportunities:

Business operations changes   Decomposition diagram
                                       Matrices
Technology improvements   Prioritized lists

Using all the materials generated in the workshop, the subteams work
to create proposals for changes in the internal business operations to
make them more effective and proposals for leveraging technology to
achieve the new business directions, goals and objectives. Room
displays are used so that total group discussions that follow the
subteam work can be easily understood by the group. The facilitator
moderates the total group discussion. Diagrams in the CASE tool are
added or the existing ones are updated based upon the results of the
discussions.

Figure 6.7 (*Cont.*)

A senior JAD facilitator was called in. He immediately began preworkshop
activities with the three sales managers, the systems manager, and a newly
assigned project manager. The JAD facilitator identified a two-phase approach
for the project, with an IE analysis project as the first phase, and an optional
IE design and construction project as an optional second phase. For the analysis
project, the JAD facilitator recommended a full review of sales area information
needs. This would cover both strategic and tactical decision making and
operational level processing information needs. JAD workshops would deliver

the information and decisions required. Then the project team could take over in a second phase of the project to conduct a sourcing and technology analysis to identify the best way to deliver on-line information support to the sales organization. The deliverable for the analysis phase of the project is outlined in Fig. 6.9.

The technical agenda (Fig. 6.10) for this project should include the project framework and data model topic areas. It is likely that the agenda could be executed in one JAD workshop of four to five days. Opening and closing workshop exercises should be added, along with an exercise to change the tone of the workshop environment after the completion of the data normalization section. Script excerpts containing instructions for creating a data model are outlined in Fig. 6.11. If the project team wished to spare the participants some of the more detailed technical work, two JAD workshops would be recommended. The first workshop, a three-day effort, would complete all work through data normalization. Then the project team would construct a draft ERD, put all the data into the CASE tool, run exception reports, and bring the participants back for a one-day workshop to validate the draft ERD and modify it where necessary.

An Application Design Project

A systems manager, in a review of the maintenance backlog, discovered that forty percent of the maintenance requests made over the past six months could be associated with the current customer order support (COS) system. These changes ranged from requests for new reports for the sales organization to the addition of data and functionality from the product management organization. In addition, the warehousing units had requested new interfaces with the inventory management system. Rather than parcel out these changes to the maintenance group, the systems manager decided to take a FUSION approach. He suspected that there were sufficient business changes to think about redevelopment of the system. Because the technology of the existing COS system was almost eight years old, this seemed a sensible approach.

A senior JAD facilitator was called in to conduct preworkshop activities. After assembling representatives from all the requesting organizations at a target meeting for project definition and scoping, the JAD facilitator and systems manager conducted project research using focus groups in the sales, product management, and warehousing groups. The JAD facilitator and systems manager determined that they needed to redevelop the existing system using a new relational technology. The vice president of business operations agreed to act as executive sponsor and fund the creation of a logical design and construction of a prototype of a new COS system. Money was tight, and the project would not be able to move into full production without strong justification. The deliverable for the IE design work was to be a logical design for the Customer Order Support System as outlined in Fig. 6.12.

Topic Area/ Content Section	Facilitator Script

Project Framework

Define Relationships

The facilitator tells the group, "Now that we have validated the business functions, structure, geography, and existing systems support, let's look at the relationship of the business functions and processes to the other aspects of the business. This information will begin to show you such things as the: (a) redundancy and complexity of business operations and support, (b) distances hindering efficiency and communications, and (3) business activities not currently supported with automation."

(60 minutes for subteams)

The facilitator assigns a relationship analysis to each team, distributes the blank matrix forms to each team and instructs them, through an example, in how to construct and complete the process relationship matrices. The facilitator suggests that during initial construction, the subteams use an easel board room display and Post-It® notes so that the subteams can easily make changes. The matrix diagram instructions should include the following:

1. "On the vertical axis of the matrix diagram, list the business processes from the lowest level of the business function decomposition diagram we just validated."

2. "On the horizontal axis of the matrix diagram, list the items for which the relationship will be analyzed. For example, for organization structure, select the groups from the most appropriate level of the organization decomposition diagram."

Figure 6.8   Excerpt from strategic planning JAD workshop script.

The technical agenda (Fig. 6.13) for this project should include the following topic areas: project framework, data model, process model, integrated data/process model, and access specifications. The technical agenda would require two JAD workshops of four to five days each for execution because of the level of detail required. The first workshop would complete all work through the data model navigation section. The second workshop would complete the definition of access specifications. Prototyping could be included in this second workshop if prototype development could be accomplished after workshop hours or in the background during the workshop. Each JAD workshop would have opening and closing workshop exercises as well. Script excerpts outlined in Fig. 6.14 describe

3. "Identify the relationship or interaction
the cells should define. For example, in the
relationship of business process and
organization structure, you may want to
define whether the organization group starts,
ends, or contributes to a business process.
You may want to record how many people
participate in the process, or whether the
group is financially responsible or
accountable for the process. Create codes to
reflect the relationship or interaction, if
necessary."

4. "Look at each cell in the matrix, discuss the
relationship it represents and enter the codes
that reflect the relationship."

5. "If it would help your analysis of the
relationships, reorder the matrix cells to
pattern the cell contents from top-to-bottom
and left-to-right."

6. "Group or cluster the matrix using personal
judgment."

7. "Analyze the results and derive conclusions
about the current environment that you want
the total group to consider as it moves
forward with the strategic planning in the
workshop."

(30–60 minutes   Starting with one of the subteams, the facilitator
per subteam   has the subteam report the results of its analysis. The
in the total group)   facilitator then moderates changes, additions, and deletions
to the matrix relationship as well as handling other questions
regarding subteam conclusions. The total group work
continues until all subteams have reported and consensus
on the matrices has been reached.

Figure 6.8   *(Cont.)*

instructions for dependency diagramming. The time allowed for between workshops should be approximately one week.

A CENTER FOR FUSION POWER

In each of the projects described earlier, the project manager was able to turn to
a single resource for FUSION support. That support came in the form of a JAD
facilitator who was knowledgeable about FUSION, experienced in its application,

I.   Sales Area Scope

a. Functions and processes performed in the business area
b. Organization units supporting the business area
c. Business decisions, business questions, and business
   work products in need of information support

II.   Data Model

a. Entity relationships
b. Entity tables
c. Entity and attribute definitions

III.   Business and Technology Open Issues

Figure 6.9   Sample business information model deliverable created through JAD workshops.

and able to provide access to the technical tools required to support it. In order for FUSION to be fully implemented within the organization, there must be a way for project teams to access the following services:

- FUSION education
- Information engineering training
- CASE tool acquisition and installation
- CASE tool training
- JAD workshop facilities
- JAD facilitators
- JAD/CASE specialist training
- Life cycle training
- Team building
- Project planning and management
- Project leadership training

One way to supply these services is to create a FUSION Center. The FUSION Center is both a facility and a team of people. It is the focus for implementation of the IE methodology, JAD techniques, and CASE technology. In the FUSION Center, a trained group of professionals can assist project teams in implementing this approach to meet a wide variety of objectives. Organizations today are involved in creating such centers. Some of these centers have been created with minimal investment. They consist of a conference room, a set of PCs loaded with CASE software, and a group of JAD trained professionals. Other organizations with access to more extravagant budgets have created specially outfitted rooms with advanced hardware and software capabilities, and a permanent staff of professionals trained and experienced in joint application development, advanced facilitation techniques, and such other areas as project management, methodology development, and strategic planning.

It is exciting if a brand new facility full of high-tech equipment can be specially constructed for the center, but this is not necessary. Nor is it necessary, generally, to hire an entirely new organization to staff the center. A basic FUSION Center can generally be created within existing space and by using equipment currently owned by the organization. The staff, too, can often be obtained by reviewing the credentials of individuals currently employed by the organization, although special training for these individuals is required. If an organization wishes to begin by experimenting with FUSION concepts, it may want to take the modest approach outlined earlier. If so, it is important to appoint a committee made up of members from many areas within the organization in order to ensure that basic decisions about the physical facilities and equipment provided by the center and its staff will be made by and supported by the individuals who will utilize its services. In addition, the committee should address the important changes that will be introduced by the implementation of the FUSION approach. These include:

- New job functions, roles and accountabilities (e.g., JAD facilitator, JAD/CASE specialist, FUSION Center coordinator, etc.).
- Changed job functions, roles and accountabilities (e.g., project manager, systems manager, programmer, analyst, etc.).
- Realignment of staff resources through organizational change, hiring, firing and/or attrition.
- New and changed methods and procedures.
- Changes in project team structures, modes of management and operation, and role accountabilities.

It would be difficult to provide a complete checklist for creating a FUSION Center because each organization will have to face this issue mindful of its unique needs, but we attempt in subsequent chapters to provide strategies for managing change and implementing FUSION techniques.

FUSION: THE DRIVER TO RAPID APPLICATION DEVELOPMENT

Many organizations today are interested in utilizing the principles of rapid application development (RAD) to speed their systems development activities (Fig. 6.15). This raises the question of how the FUSION approach fits with a RAD approach. The answer is that the two approaches are quite complementary. FUSION easily embraces the major assumptions of RAD: speeding up of the development process, overlapping of tasks within the life cycle, application of new tools and techniques, use of well structured teams, and careful definition of the

Topic Area	Content Section	Content Item
Project Framework	Validate:	
	Business function scope	Decomposition diagram

The facilitator has the total group review the business functions that are within the scope of the project. Then subteams are assigned one or more of the functions. Their job is to confirm the four to seven business processes within the assigned functions. Each subteam works on different functions so work is not duplicated. Each subteam then reports out its conclusions to the total group under the direction of the facilitator who manages the changes, additions and deletions to each of the functions.

Once this level of decomposition is completed, the group may decide to decompose one more level of detail to fully understand the business. Room displays and subteam completed forms are used to document the decomposition. The JAD/CASE specialist enters and/or updates the decomposition diagrams into the CASE tool after completion of discussions.

| | Organization units | Decomposition diagram |
| | | Matrix diagram (process) |

Using easel board room displays, the facilitator leads a total group discussion to identify and then map the organization units into the business processes using the lowest level of business decomposition completed in the previous exercise. The JAD/CASE specialist enters the matrix and decomposition diagrams into the CASE tool after the discussions are concluded.

| | Generate: | |
| | Business questions and decisions | List |

Figure 6.10   Sample JAD technical agenda to create a business information model.

project to limit its size and scope. RAD just as clearly embraces the FUSION approach through its support of the information engineering methodology and its advocacy of new tools and techniques.

James Martin, who first popularized the term, has recommended and promoted RAD as a full life cycle approach. To be fully implemented, RAD requires the complete re-engineering of the system life cycle and the installation of a new infrastructure for the organization that has four essential aspects.

- A technical architecture that allows the integrated use of CASE technology, the reusability of models and designs, code generation for easy development and maintenance, and the portability of software across hardware platforms.

The facilitator assigns each subteam one or more of the business functions. Using nominal group technique, team members generate candidate lists of strategic, operational and tactical questions and decisions made in that part of the business. After the questions and decisions are collected and boarded by the facilitator, he leads a total group discussion to understand each question and decision that was generated. The JAD/CASE specialist records each question on a form and documents the reasons for its use in the business as they are revealed in the discussions. If the CASE tool allows this type of data storage, the JAD/CASE specialist enters the questions and decisions into the tool off line.

Data Model

Generate:

Information groups   Entity relationship diagram

The facilitator leads a total group discussion to generate primary entities for the business area. The facilitator may try to create a first cut entity relationship diagram. If the group becomes bogged down in attempting to define the entities, the facilitator may stop this exercise and switch to the next exercise. Room display is used to document each entity so all can reference it later.

Attributes   Attribute definitions

The facilitator distributes documented questions and decisions among pairs of workshop participants. Each pair identifies the data needed to answer the business questions and make the business decisions. Each data item is placed on a Post-It® and is added to the room display under the entity that seems most appropriate.

Data normalization   Entity tables

The facilitator leads the total group in the normalization of the data. As entities and attributes are defined, the JAD/CASE specialist enters the definitions directly into the CASE tool, if convenient, or records the definitions on forms for later data entry.

Refine:

Entity relationships   Entity relationship diagram

With data normalization complete, the facilitator may lead a total group discussion to construct an entity relationship diagram to refine and validate the data normalization exercise.

Figure 6.10 (*Cont.*)

Topic Area/ Content Section	Facilitator Script
Data Model	
Data Normalization	In preparation for this exercise, the room display consists of blank easel board paper taped to a wall. The entities and attributes identified in the previous exercises are written on Post-It®s (one per Post-It®) and affixed to the paper.
	The facilitator tells the total group, "Now that we have identified the major information groups and what we need to know about each group, it is time to organize that data so both business people and technical people can understand it better. The exercise you are about to experience will assist in simplifying the data and eliminating data redundancy. The result will be a model of business area information needs as the business users view it. This model can later be translated into a physical structure for a data base which the users can then access."
(15 attributes/hour)	The facilitator goes to an entity on the room display, selects it and asks the group, "Is there a data item (within this entity) that can uniquely identify an occurrence of this entity?"
	Once this key is selected, the facilitator asks the group to provide a full definition of the attribute. Once defined, the attribute is placed in the entity and is marked (e.g., underlined) to denote a primary key.
	The facilitator selects another attribute from the entity list and asks the group, "What is the definition of this item of data?" The facilitator has the group confirm that the data should be associated with this particular entity and then asks the question, "Can there be more than one of these attributes in a single occurence of this entity?"

Figure 6.11 Excerpt from business information modeling JAD workshop script.

- A formalized methodology, enforced and implemented through the use of CASE tools and technical architecture, that provides a common language, discipline and structure for a strategic approach to application and database planning, design and development.
- A small team approach that involves expert business users and highly skilled systems professionals.
- A committed management that invests in new tools, techniques, and training to enhance the capabilities of systems professionals and improve the quality of their work environment.

The contribution that FUSION makes to RAD can be seen by looking at its three dimensions. Information engineering, the methodology dimension of the FUSION approach, provides any project team with a number of benefits. It

If the answer is no, the facilitator leaves the attribute where it is, marks it complete, and goes onto the next attribute.

If the answer is yes, the facilitator may need to create a new entity if an appropriate existing entity is not found. The new entity name consists of the original entity name combined with a noun. The key for this new entity will consist of the original entity key "hooked to" another appropriate attribute which uniquely identifies a single occurence of the new entity. The facilitator then moves the attribute under discussion to the new entity and marks it complete. The facilitator explains, "We have just removed a repeating attribute from the first entity. This new entity presents a simpler and more straightforward view of that attribute and how it is used in the business."

The facilitator continues with this exercise until all entities and attributes have been discussed. This completes first normal form for the data modeling section. The JAD/CASE specialist should document each definition on a form or in a CASE tool. A second specialist may be required to keep up with the pace of the group. The group should be given a short break every 90 minutes.

The facilitator may have the group complete second, third, fourth, and/or fifth normal forms also. However, those forms may be completed outside the workshop by a smaller team of people. The majority of business rules are generated from this first normal form exercise.

Figure 6.11 *(Cont.)*

enables the team to set project priorities for the organization, to identify an appropriate project, to clearly define its scope, and to select the best available diagrammatic tools for analysis and documentation of project findings. It provides the focus and structure needed to keep a project on track and ensure that it produces sound results. These characteristics of the IE approach are as necessary to the successful implementation of a rapid application development approach as they are to FUSION. This can be seen even in the initial stages of a RAD project. Martin's RAD approach calls for Joint Requirements Planning (JRP) workshop as a precursor to a JAD logical design workshop. This planning workshop must define project scope, boundaries and priorities, or review and refine a draft definition of these project characteristics. Without this upfront activity, it would be very difficult to correctly divide large projects into smaller systems development modules. This project breakdown activity is critical to project success in the case of large complex projects. It enables us to take these difficult projects and cut them down to size. Where the whole of the project may be too complicated to address successfully, these units are manageable and easily understood, and perhaps most important of all in a large project, the deliverables of the separate modules will be easy to integrate. When modules are correctly defined, decisions regarding the sequence and content of logical design workshops can easily be made. The meth-

I.   Functional Scope

          a. Business processes to be supported
          b. Business organizations involved in processes
          c. Data subject areas to be supported

II.   Data Model

          a. Entity relationships
          b. Entity tables
          c. Entity and attribute definitions

III.   Process Model

          a. Process decomposition
          b. Process dependencies

IV.   Data–Process Relationship Model

          a. Data model navigation
          b. State transaction analysis

V.   Access Specifications

          a. Query specifications
          b. Screen and report specifications
          c. Action diagrams for order editing
          d. Application navigation requirements

Figure 6.12   Sample logical design deliverable created through JAD workshops.

odology dimension of FUSION, information engineering, provides the structure for making such decisions.

The second FUSION dimension, JAD, also has strong ties to the RAD concept. While it is possible to develop successful applications using more traditional user involvement techniques, it can be difficult to develop such applications quickly and with strong user support. JAD makes it possible to move quickly through the life cycle because it expedites decision making and ensures that there will be a minimum of second-guessing. By bringing the key players together at one time and in one place, it eliminates situations where project work comes to a halt because an important decision has not been made. By involving users early in the process, it ensures that when an application is implemented, it will be accepted, and substantial reworking will not be required. In this way it supports the speed advocated by RAD. RAD also calls for the use of project teams and the involvement of those teams at all stages in the life cycle. JAD is the best technique available for structuring and managing those teams. Poorly managed teams can bog down the life cycle and create an excuse for inaction. JAD ensures that this does not happen. To a significant extent, then, JAD makes RAD possible.

Finally, CASE, the third dimension of FUSION, can easily be seen to support the RAD concept. CASE assists in moving a project along quickly and ensuring its high quality. It does this by providing the tools needed for analyzing and documenting project information, for developing reusable data and process models at multiple levels of complexity, for developing and presenting application prototypes, and for generating code. All of these tools increase the speed and quality with which systems planning, design, and development projects can be completed. Clearly, then, CASE too contributes to the implementation of RAD.

By contributing through each of its three dimensions, FUSION provides the foundation for rapid application development.

READINESS FOR FUSION IMPLEMENTATION

Even if an organization has embraced the concept of FUSION, there is still much work to be done before it becomes a reality. Implementation of the FUSION approach can be quite a challenge. This is particularly true for large organizations, organizations with multiple management centers or work sites, and organizations where change is an infrequent and unwelcome visitor. Even in organizations that are not large or complex and that have enlightened management teams, issues of politics, limited resources, and mounting backlogs can get in the way of implementing this powerful new idea. This is particularly true when organizations recognize that the implementation of FUSION requires even more than the investment of their dollars in hardware and software. It requires individuals to modify their behavior and accept a new set of values. The difficulty of this undertaking should not be underestimated.

In thinking about how to approach the implementation of FUSION, it quickly becomes clear that strong leadership from top management is a requirement. This leadership can only come from managers who can:

- Overcome their own reluctance to change and transform the reluctance of others.
- Manage the chaos of change.
- Assist all members of their organizations to prepare for and accept change.
- Change the competitive and territorial values of many systems professionals to the values of cooperation, sharing, and team orientation.

THE BREAKTHROUGH PROJECT: SYSTEM LIFE
CYCLE REDEFINITION

Where do we begin? There are many approaches to implementing FUSION, but the most successful approach in the long term will be one that builds internal commitment at all levels within the organization and energizes individuals to take

Topic Area	Content Section	Content Item
Project Framework	(Same as Technical Agenda for Business Information Model)	
Data Model	(Same as Technical Agenda for Business Information Model)	
Process Model	Develop:	
	Process detail	Decomposition diagram

The facilitator assigns the subteams portions of the business decomposition. Working with the lowest level of detail, each team decomposes its assigned processes one more level and then details information about each process on a process documentation form.

The facilitator moderates the presentation of each subteam to the group using room displays of the decomposition. Changes, additions and deletions are annotated on the forms after the discussions and consensus is reached with the total group. The JAD/CASE specialist updates the decomposition diagram and process descriptions in the CASE tool off line.

	Process dependencies	Dependency diagram

The facilitator has one of the systems participants present the standards for the dependency diagramming exercise. Continuing to work with their assigned functions and processes, the subteams create a dependency diagram using room displays. The exercise begins with the lowest level of process detail. Once diagrams are shared with the total group and consensus is reached, the teams can return to create higher level dependency diagrams if required for the project.

Figure 6.13   Sample JAD technical agenda to create an application logical design.

action in support of the changes introduced. A valuable technique for implementing FUSION in an organization is to identify an important need within the organization and to convince top management to apply the FUSION approach to meet this need. Properly handled, this initial FUSION project can become a breakthrough project for the organization. In a short period of time (depending upon project requirements, as short as four weeks), it can both demonstrate the value of the approach and create a committed group of people, a kind of "clan of the curious," who will become the energizing force behind FUSION. Different types of projects can provide the opportunity for this initial implementation. The selection of a breakthrough project will depend upon the needs, priorities, and values of the organization. The best type of project will be one that the organization widely recognizes as significant and challenging. It can be placed at any point in the life cycle, from systems planning to design, to development. Because so many organizations are in the process of re-examining their life cycles, however, the

**Process-Data
Relationship
Model**

Define:

| State transitions of the primary entities | State transition diagram |

To integrate process and data, the facilitator asks the total group to select the primary entities which represent major information or work flows through the business. The facilitator leads a total group discussion to create a state transition diagram for one primary entity. The facilitator then assigns entities to the subteams for further analysis and documentation on forms. Subteam recommendations are discussed with the total group moderated by the facilitator. When all changes, additions and deletions are collected, the JAD/CASE specialist enters the diagrams and supporting information into the CASE tool.

| Data model navigation for usage views | Entity relationship diagram |

Working with the total group, the facilitator teaches the participants how to trace through the data model the information needed to answer a question, make a decision, or complete a process. Questions, decisions, and processes are assigned to the subteams for their analysis and recommendations to the total group. Through total group discussion after the subteam work, changes and additions are made to the information model and the business processes as needed.

Figure 6.13 (*Cont.*)

example offered here is a breakthrough project that has as its principal objective the definition of a new systems development life cycle. This example serves a dual purpose. It presents the technique for utilizing a breakthrough project and at the same time provides recommendations for integrating the FUSION approach into the system life cycle.

Two deliverables are generally produced by this type of project. The first is a life cycle document that describes how to utilize IE, JAD, and CASE in the organization. Depending upon the needs of the organization, this document may be used to update an existing life cycle methodology, to serve as the first release of a completely new life cycle, or to define requirements for the purchase of an off-the-shelf life cycle product. The second deliverable is a FUSION implementation strategy and plan.

In addition to these deliverables, the organization can expect to derive other benefits from the project. Where the previously defined deliverables provide tangible benefits to the organization, these other benefits are less concrete but no less important. They lay the foundation for future behavior within the organization by providing a new set of values that define:

Access
Specifications

Specify:

Screens, reports and queries   Lists

The facilitator presents a review of all that has been accomplished. Room displays of the business processes, questions and decisions, data model and organization groups (users) are posted or distributed throughout the group. The facilitator uses the nominal group technique to generate a list of potential screens, reports and queries. Through a total group discussion, the facilitator assists the group in creating a single list of appropriate screens, reports, and queries that will be supported by the application. Each screen, report or query must be traceable back into the models.

Specify:

Standards and capabilities   Handouts

The facilitator asks a systems subject matter expert to present to the total group the standards for screen and report design and to demonstrate the capabilities of the hardware and software which may enhance or shape screen, report and query specifications.

Screens, reports and queries   Specifications

The facilitator assigns screens, reports, and queries to triads for detailed specification using forms which can be handed off to CASE tool prototyping specialists as they are completed. Once the prototypes are constructed, they can be reviewed by the total group for refinement purposes. Changes are made based on the consensus of the group and recommendations of the subject matter screen and report design experts.

Special routines   Action diagram

The transaction processing which the application must support may require the definition of programming routines that can be documented using the action diagram. The facilitator will present an example of how to construct an action diagram along with the standards (e.g., verbs) to be used. Based on expertise and interest, participants are paired or grouped into triads and assigned one or more routines to diagram. Questions and issues encountered should be brought to the total group for discussion and consensus. The JAD/CASE specialist enters the diagrams into the CASE tool after consensus is reached.

Application navigation   Decomposition diagram

The facilitator leads a total group discussion to identify menus (dialogues) and their use by users of the application. These can be prototyped directly from the room display created by the facilitator or from documentation forms created by the JAD/CASE specialist as the discussions take place. Once prototyped, they can be reviewed for refinement by the total group.

Figure 6.13 *(Cont.)*

- The role of the systems organization within the context of the total organization.
- How the systems organization will work with its customers, the users, and others outside of the systems organization.
- The importance of individuals to the new environment and how their expertise and contributions will be developed and supported.
- How people will work together in teams, how those teams will function, the responsibilities they will accept, and the tasks for which they will be held accountable in the new FUSION environment.

Benefits

The breakthrough project facilitates FUSION implementation in a number of ways. One of the major benefits is controlled experimentation. Without committing to a large scale change, the organization can experiment with FUSION concepts and determine how they fit the needs of the organization. This is particularly effective when a broad base of participants is involved in the experiment. This provides the added benefit of involvement for those individuals. Through their involvement in the breakthrough project, they will gain experience in and build commitment to the FUSION approach.

A second major benefit of the breakthrough project is the result of the project itself. When a good product is produced by the project, that in itself is a convincing argument in favor of the FUSION approach. In the case of the breakthrough project recommended here, the life cycle product will have a substantial impact on the organization. For most organizations it will provide a badly needed look at the accepted way of doing business. If, as it should, the project results in a life cycle that is well suited to the needs and culture of the organization, then the FUSION process will be perceived in a positive light, and the chances that implementation will succeed will be enhanced.

While it would be possible to select a system development effort as a breakthrough project, a particular benefit of the type of breakthrough project recommended here is that it forces a detailed analysis of the systems organization. In order to effectively examine the organization's life cycle needs, the culture and values of the organization must be examined as well as its operational processes. This examination will reveal areas of strength and weakness, all of which can affect the success of the FUSION approach when it is implemented. The areas which the participants should examine during the project include:

- Project authorization and approval processes
- Project manager authority and accountability
- Systems organization structure and reporting relationships
- Managerial reward systems
- Employee training and development—both technical and behavioral

Topic Area/ Content Section	Facilitator Script
Data-Process Relationship Model	
Define State Transitions of the Primary Entities	The facilitator tells the participant group, "One way in which we can validate the processing requirements for the business to be supported by the application is to examine the key information groups (entities) in our data model to see how they get acted upon in our business. The following exercise and diagram construction will do this for us."
(60 minutes for subteams)	The facilitator reviews the instructions for state transition analysis using an example like the one that follows. The instructions should be displayed so that the subteams can reference them in their work.

1. "Select a primary entity for transition analysis." For example, ORDER.

2. "Name and define the statuses through which the entity will pass during its existence." For example, an ORDER may have the statuses of RECEIVED, IN PROCESS, BACK ORDERED, DELIVERED, CLOSED, and ON HOLD.

3. "For each status, starting with the first,

   a. Identify the decisions or actions that can take place at the end of the status which allow the entity to move to a different status." For example, an ORDER remains in the RECEIVED status until the salesperson has received a ten percent payment from the customer and verified the delivery date with the plant expediter.

Figure 6.14   Excerpt from Logical Design JAD workshop script.

- Conflicts between upper and middle management
- Level of trust and commitment within and between upper and middle management

Another benefit of the breakthrough project is that it can provide the organization with an understanding of the constraints and limitations within which FUSION must operate. Some organizations are initially skeptical of the many benefits that

b. "Identify the events or conditions that cause the entity to enter the status." For example, an ORDER enters the received status when the order entry screen is completed.

c. "Identify the processes or actions that must be completed while the entity is in that status." For example, while in a RECEIVED status, the customer credit must be checked, the product manufacturing schedule must be checked, the delivery date must be negotiated with the customer and the delivery location and total price including delivery charge must be agreed upon. Note: The previously defined business processes can be referenced and integrated into the state transition diagram at this point.

(20 minutes per subteam for total group consensus)

The facilitator has the total group confirm or select the entities to be submitted to state transition analysis and has the subteams take on assignments for the analysis based upon their expertise and interest. After completing this first level of status analysis, the subteams report out their results using room displays. The facilitator moderates the consensus building and the integration of changes into the diagrams. The JAD/CASE specialist enters the diagrams into the CASE tool off line after consensus is reached.

If an additional level of state transition analysis is required for complete understanding, the subteams can go down one more level of detail, creating a state transition diagram for each process (or just selected processes) within each status.

Figure 6.14   *(Cont.)*

FUSION can bring, but others are so enthusiastic that they overestimate the potential benefits. A well managed breakthrough project can help people to develop reasonable expectations for the process. In addition, if it is to be successful, the FUSION implementation strategy selected must respect the financial and resource constraints of the organization. These constraints and limitations should be identified early and integrated into the working assumptions of the project. Such constraints and limitations normally encompass three areas—limits on annual capital investments or expense budgets, human resource limitations on expanding or replacing staff, and limits presented by the existing application environment and critical work in progress. If these constraints and limitations are not addressed, they may prevent FUSION success.

If the breakthrough project is to perform its function effectively, it should demonstrate the benefits of all three of the FUSION dimensions. Clearly, however, most projects will rely to a greater extent on one or two of the dimen-

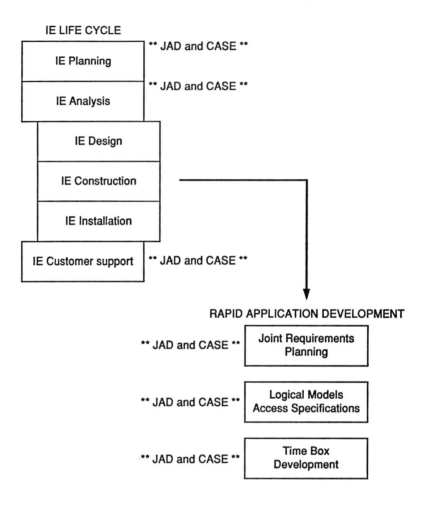

Figure 6.15 A FUSION approach to RAD.

sions. This is not a problem, although if the organization is already experiencing difficulties with use of its CASE tools, for example, it might be wise to select as a breakthrough project one that will show off the benefits of FUSION in this area. It is also helpful to consider whether any of the dimensions will provoke resistance within the organization in order to be able to neutralize this problem early in the project. Of the three FUSION dimensions, JAD often encounters more resistance (at least from the systems organization) than the others. Perhaps because it is people focused and not technology focused, the technique is viewed with skepticism by systems professionals. If this is true, it will be useful to emphasize JAD education and awareness building in the project.

Goals and Objectives

The breakthrough project has three major goals and supporting objectives.

Goal One.   To raise the awareness of individuals regarding the potential of the FUSION approach to enhance the information management capabilities and strategic position of the organization.

- Objective: To identify the reasons why the organization needs to change.
- Objective: To show the relationship of the FUSION approach to current needs and problems.
- Objective: To demonstrate a working environment in which current problems are reduced or eliminated.

Goal Two.   To identify a workable strategy to support FUSION implementation.

- Objective: To identify organization and individual values and behavior that will enhance FUSION success.
- Objective: To reveal limitations and constraints that must be addressed.
- Objective: To prepare an integrated solution that meets the organization's needs and addresses organization issues.
- Objective: To create a six to twelve-month action plan with clear accountabilities, deliverables, and tasks.

Goal Three.   To energize the systems organization for change.

- Objective: To create momentum for change using planning, leadership, education, marketing, and public relations skills.
- Objective: To create a commitment to follow through at all levels within the organization by rewarding action and risk taking.
- Objective: To identify techniques for involving people at all levels of the organization in implementation activities.
- Objective: To initiate changes in behavior and values and to support the development of technical skills required for FUSION success at all levels of the organization.

Critical Success Factors

The life cycle breakthrough project utilizes each of the dimensions of FUSION to a different degree. The application of information engineering principles is fairly straightforward. The IE life cycle is used as a guideline for evaluating and modifying or replacing the organization's current life cycle. The application of CASE technology to the project, though not so obvious, can be defined as well. CASE tools can be used, for example, to analyze and document the attribution of tasks to organizations performing them (through matrices) and the relationship of tasks within life cycle phases to each other (through dependency charts).

In the case of a life cycle project, however, JAD is clearly the unifying dimension. It provides the structure for the project and the principal technique for moving it forward. JAD facilitates the consensus building and decision making that is vital to the development of a life cycle. Because JAD requires a certain amount of customization in order to support a business operations re-engineering project, it can provide a test of the organization's ability to adapt the FUSION approach for its own purposes. With the benefit of flexibility, however, comes the need for integrity. Adaptation of the JAD technique is only successful when critical success factors are respected. In addition, the very sensitive nature of the project (where people are asked to examine their values, take unaccustomed risks, and change familiar methods and procedures), requires special attention to the roles of the executive sponsor, the project manager, and the JAD facilitator. The people who fill these roles with their individual commitment, talent, and experience have the power to make or break the project. They include:

Executive sponsor.   The person most critical to the breakthrough project is the head of the systems organization in which FUSION is to be implemented. This is the person who must provide the leadership, focus, and commitment for FUSION, and who must energize the organization for action. No one else can fill this role because anyone lower in the reporting hierarchy will be tempted to place the special interests of his own group first. He may or may not have been the one who first recognized the need for FUSION, but he must be responsible for the implementation of the approach and must express to everyone within the organization the values and behavior that are required for FUSION success. His leadership and commitment should be expressed in the following ways:

- Visibility: He must first accept the role of executive sponsor for the breakthrough project. He must ensure that all required personnel are made available for JAD workshops and other project activities. He must talk to others about his commitment, FUSION values, and the importance of the breakthrough project both in informal settings and at preparatory meetings. Finally, he must commit to accept the results of the breakthrough project and act on them.

- Accountability: The executive sponsor must also secure the funding required to complete the breakthrough project and begin implementation of FUSION. He must be responsible for the actions of the manager of the breakthrough project who should report directly to him. This will assist the project manager is overcoming in-house political positioning as well as demonstrate executive commitment to change. This person must be willing to be held accountable for resolving issues assigned to him as a result of project work and be ready to begin formal FUSION implementation.

- Role Model: More than any other person, the executive sponsor must model the values and behavior he wants to see in his direct reports and the rest of the organization. He must cut through political and territorial issues that may arise from the breakthrough project. He must demonstrate through his own behavior how to be a communicator, negotiator, and obstacle remover. He must empower the people in his own organization to create a FUSION implementation plan and be willing to act on it if he wants his managers to empower their own people, and he cannot second-guess those he has empowered. He must set boundaries, constraints, and guidelines before, not after, the work begins. He must remove the discrepancy between what is said and what is done if he is to overcome the cynicism of those of the employees who have seen too many unsuccessful attempts at change in the past.

Project manager.   The project manager for the breakthrough project must bring strong experience and expertise to his work. He is the champion for FUSION at the working level. He must have the respect of his bosses, his peers, and those at lower levels. Through his behavior, he must show people that he is not afraid to take risks, that he is willing to cut through red tape, and that he has the flexibility to work in a new way. He must be a direct and open person. A timid person in this position would be overwhelmed by the other players, their politics, and the potential impact of the project on the organization. A rigid person in this position would resist experimenting with new behavior and values. The breakthrough project manager should model the new role of project manager in the FUSION environment. He should demonstrate to people through his own behavior how to be a communicator, negotiator, and obstacle remover. He must empower the participants in the project to make decisions and be willing to sell these decisions to the executive sponsor if necessary. He must use the authority given him to seek out boundaries, constraints, and guidelines before, not after, he finds himself in trouble. Finally, he must bring people into the process, not exclude them from it.

JAD facilitator.   Experience and creativity are critical requirements for the JAD facilitator for this project. Any first project requires a highly experienced JAD facilitator, and this is doubly true for this project because of the need for customization of the JAD technique, the involvement of multiple levels within the organization, and the need to examine basic organization values and behavior. The JAD facilitator must be able to work through every aspect of the project with the project manager. Deliverable design and agenda construction are critical. In addition, team building during the workshops is critical, and the JAD facilitator must energize project participants and mold them into a cohesive and committed unit. In some cases, the JAD facilitator will need to break through the cynicism

√ Programmer/Analyst

√ Systems/Business Analyst

√ Project Manager/Leader

√ Data Administrator

√ Systems Manager

√ Director

√ Business Customer/User Liaison

√ Operations Manager

√ Capacity Planner

√ Systems Planner

Figure 6.16 Sample breakthrough project participants.

that has built up over the years. JAD facilitators can come from within the organization, but many organizations turn to an outside source for a facilitator for the breakthrough project to obtain the expertise and objectivity required.

Participants. Breakthrough project participants should be drawn from all groups and levels within the organization and should represent both the systems organization and user organizations. If expertise in IE, JAD, and CASE are lacking internally, outside experts may be invited to serve as participants as well. One very large company, for example, included within its participant group one individual from each of its ten divisions, three people from corporate management and three outside experts. A smaller organization selected an individual from each hierarchial level across each of its six directorates along with two customers and two outside experts. Figure 6.16 presents a typical workshop participant list by title.

Breakthrough Project Deliverables

The breakthrough project will result in two deliverables. The first is a life cycle document that will create a structure for managing systems projects and will define the utilization of methodology, tools, and techniques within a project environment. The second is a FUSION implementation strategy and plan. Both documents should reflect the following FUSION principles and values:

Evolutionary change. The life cycle methodology developed should be seen as a living document, one that allows for change and enhancement. As with applications that are enhanced through the release of new versions, the new life cycle document should be updated and reissued every one to two years. The implementation plan should allow for updates as required.

Practical guidance. Both documents should emphasize the application of the FUSION approach to different types of projects. The life cycle document should provide guidance on the use of IE, JAD, and CASE based upon real world experience and should not be overly prescriptive. For example, it should not require the preparation of a business area analysis before every development project because that is neither practical nor necessary. On the other hand, it should not encourage the cutting of corners if those cuts will jeopardize project success. The implementation plan should be equally pragmatic and emphasize change management issues, not theory.

Easy to use approach. Both documents should provide checklists and reminders (where appropriate) for those who coach and work with project managers and their teams. For example, the life cycle document should spell out the decisions supported by each life cycle deliverable, the information that should be contained in that deliverable, and what to look for in a quality deliverable.

Emphasis on accountability and decisions required. The life cycle document should define the individuals involved in each phase of the life cycle and their responsibilities. It should allow for the use of different techniques to carry out these responsibilities and refrain from overly prescriptive statements about the behavior of individuals carrying out the various roles. Similarly, the implementation plan should make clear what decisions have to be made and by whom. It should also allow for team based input into decision making.

Emphasis on business needs, not technology solutions. The life cycle document should support the information engineering principle of beginning with the needs of the business. It should ensure that questions of technology appropriate to the solution of a problem are not addressed until a business need is clearly defined. It should provide alternatives for using different tools and techniques for solving these problems and identify resources for support in these areas. The implementation plan too should focus on matching high level business strategy to FUSION benefits.

Promotion of a proactive culture. The life cycle document should provide assistance in identifying questions that should be asked and problems that may be anticipated for different project types. It should refrain from specifying each and every task required to complete a project. Rather, it should provide opportunities for the organization to customize the activities of a phase to meet unusual needs or circumstances. It should focus on the creation of a problem solving environment. The implementation plan too should allow organization members to contribute to the strategy and encourage them to take responsibility for identifying implementation problems and solving them.

The life cycle document is a description of a new systems culture within the FUSION environment. It defines the language, behavior, roles, and deliverables for that environment. It is simple and direct, offering support for political as well as technical problem solving and allows flexibility for different environments and applications. The life cycle document should not be a multivolume book attempting to provide a rule for every occasion. Rather, it should present a basic value set and behavioral framework in which people have the freedom to decide what is best depending on the unique situation of their own project. It should promote the continuous improvement of quality as work is performed, not controls for making changes after work is completed.

Several vendors offer automated life cycles with complex integrated capabilities for project documentation and management. Is automating the life cycle itself a necessity? With large projects, automated project planning and estimating support can be very helpful. However, too often automated methodologies place too much emphasis on the generation of reports. Users of the automated life cycle tool sometimes begin to believe that they are servants of the tool, entering information because the tool requires it, rather that using the tool for the sake of the project. Most critical documentation and measurement needs for a project can actually be met by standard CASE tools. And in the event that a true rapid application development approach is applied to a large project, the modularized format recommended by RAD will eliminate the need for complex project management and tracking schemes.

The second breakthrough project deliverable is the FUSION implementation plan. The plan should be divided into three phases—Phase I for start up activities, Phase II for proliferation activities, and Phase III for the definition of continuing support and improvement. The typical organization needs six months to complete Phase I, followed by six to twelve months to complete Phase II. Phase III is monitored on an annual or semiannual basis. The accompanying action plan defines a strategic framework, activities, deliverables, schedules, financial budgets, human resource allocations, and role accountability assignments for each of the following areas critical to FUSION implementation success:

- Fully Committed Executive Sponsorship and Management Buy-In: Creating and maintaining support at executive levels during each of the implementation phases.
- Organization Environmental Modifications: Preparing the organization for FUSION by organization restructuring to support a FUSION Center, redefinition of project authorization and budget approval procedures, facilities changes, job function and authority changes, and project team membership and working relationship changes.
- FUSION Compatibility with the System Development Life Cycle: Redefining the work practices of systems design and development to incorporate

FUSION concepts, values and practices and then proliferate them through-out the organization.

- Education and Training: Purchasing or developing formal and informal educa-tion and training mechanisms for people at all levels within the organiza-tion. Subjects covered should include: life cycle phases, IE principles, CASE and JAD technical skills, and value analysis and behavioral skills devel-opment.

- Marketing and Commitment Building: Creating a welcoming environment for FUSION by producing newsletters to promote FUSION success, holding open houses for customers and staff, and disseminating promotional materials such as mugs and shirts with special logos designed to bring attention to FUSION and build personal commitment to the change process.

- Acquisition and Installation of IE, CASE, and JAD: Conducting research into, piloting and customizing FUSION vendor products and services, devel-oping FUSION products and services in-house, and/or expanding existing FUSION products and services within the organization.

- FUSION Coordination and Support: Creating a FUSION Center and taking other actions required to provide and coordinate quality support for project teams in their use of the three FUSION dimensions.

- Change Management Support: Purchasing or developing special training to enhance the change management and support skills of managers at all levels of the organization. Encouraging managers and executives to act to relieve political pressures, to assist individuals threatened by FUSION change, and to provide appropriate incentives for staff for supporting the transition to a FUSION environment.

The FUSION implementation plan is the project management roadmap for the FUSION implementation team. The team coordinates, communicates, negoti-ates, and supports the organization through implementation activities and removes obstacles in the way of the line project teams who are implementing FUSION in their work and those who have been assigned accountabilities for issue resolution within the FUSION implementation plan.

Breakthrough Project Schedule

The breakthrough project follows the basic JAD format of preworkshop, workshop and postworkshop activities. Figure 6.17 outlines a typical six-week schedule for a breakthrough project. This schedule will vary depending on the amount of time needed for preworkshop activities and the amount of time needed to review and finalize the project deliverables. This schedule starts with the identi-fication and commitment of the executive sponsor, the head of the systems organi-

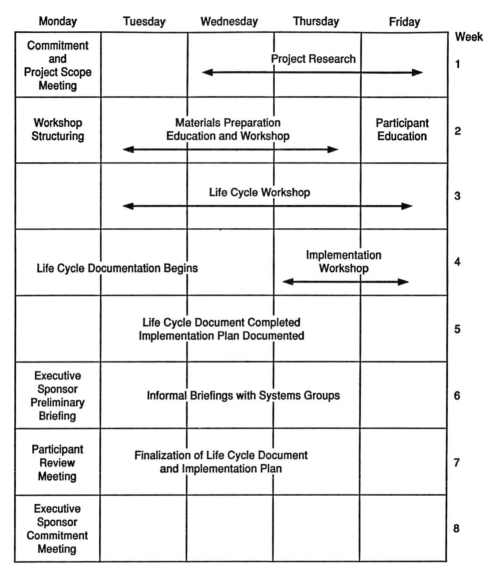

Figure 6.17 Breakthrough project activity schedule.

zation, to proceed with the project. Weeks, perhaps months, may be needed to obtain that approval. In some cases it will be easy to obtain this support. In others, it may require the identification of a particular project that can benefit from FUSION, a failure or crisis within the organization, or some good salesmanship by those within the organization who have been charged with implementation of one or more of the FUSION dimensions.

PREWORKSHOP ACTIVITIES

The JAD facilitator should customize preworkshop activities according to the following guidelines:

Project Definition and Scoping

To ensure commitment to a strong change process for the implementation of FUSION and prevent a false start, the executive sponsor for the breakthrough project, his direct reports and the breakthrough project manager and his team should spend four to eight hours in a project definition and scoping target meeting. The JAD facilitator should use the target meeting to reinforce executive sponsor commitment, define desired FUSION values, set project boundaries, clarify strategic organization direction and define the constraints of the breakthrough project and subsequent FUSION implementation. Special attention should be paid to the roles and responsibilities of the executive sponsor, project manager and JAD facilitator for this breakthrough project.

Project Research

The focus of project research in the breakthrough project should be on life cycle needs and current organization standards and values. Life cycle needs must be defined in order to identify the type of projects being performed by the organization and the type of support they require. Current standards and values should be investigated as well in order to match these standards and values to those required for FUSION success. The best technique for gathering this information is the focus group interview. A series of such interviews should be set up to gather this information. In addition to obtaining the required information, these interviews will also be useful for establishing the organization's readiness for change and identifying likely impacts (positive and negative) of FUSION implementation. (For additional guidance on managing focus groups, see the chapters on the JAD dimension.)

Focus groups should include participants from the following groups:

- Middle managers: those who supervise project managers
- Project managers: from systems and user communities
- Business users/customers
- Programmers and analysts
- Individuals who can contribute special expertise such as technology specialists, measurements experts, data administration managers, capacity planners, user liaisons, organization/strategic planners, and development center staff

- Individuals from administrative and employee support groups such as systems training and human resources

Deliverable Definition and Workshop Structure

The JAD facilitator should work with the breakthrough project manager and his team to finalize requirements for both the life cycle and FUSION implementation plan deliverables. The facilitator should encourage the team to be creative in their design effort. They should focus on usability, portability and access. In order to achieve these objectives, some organizations have created downsized documents, color coding, multiple cross reference systems, and quick reference formats to obtain a new look in their materials as well as to emphasize the human factors values of these documents.

Two workshops will be required for the project, as indicated in the sample project schedule. The first workshop should focus on defining the new systems culture and operating environment and on translating that culture into a FUSION life cycle. Four to five days are generally required for this workshop. The second workshop should focus on developing a FUSION implementation plan and consolidating the energy, enthusiasm and commitment initiated in the first workshop. Two to three days are generally sufficient for this work.

Workshop participants should be chosen carefully to ensure that representation is cross organizational and multilevel. Participation should be limited, however, to no more than twenty individuals to ensure that the group is not too large. Organization leaders and influencers should be included, both from the systems organization and from user organizations. Subject matter experts may be included as well if FUSION expertise is limited within the organization. The JAD facilitator must, of course, possess this knowledge, but expertise on FUSION within the participant group is required as well or the group will run the danger of turning repeatedly to the facilitator for decisions. Decision making must come from the group, not the JAD facilitator.

Materials Preparation

A preworkshop deliverable for the breakthrough project should be provided to participants prior to the workshops. It should include the following information:

Project background. A summary of the problems, issues and history behind the initiation of the breakthrough project, and FUSION implementation.

Project objectives. A statement of the objectives for the new life cycle methodology, the specific measurable benefits projected for FUSION implementation, and current and future issues and problems that will be addressed by a new life cycle, and the implementation of the FUSION approach.

SAMPLE 1:

Enterprise Wide Planning
Technology Research
Business Area Analysis
Product Design
Product Development
Product Installation
Customer Support

SAMPLE 2:

Exploration
Project Definition
Project Design
Project Development
Project Implementation
Customer Service

SAMPLE 3:

Architecture Planning
Application Design
Application Development
Application Implementation
Customer Support

Figure 6.18   Sample FUSION life cycle components.

Project scope.   A definition of the boundaries for the life cycle including a preliminary look at components (Fig. 6.18) and decisions to be supported by each component, and a statement on the strategic direction and values that should be reflected in the new life cycle.

Project complexity.   A description and analysis of organization structure, business functions, staff skill mix, and opportunities for growth and change.

Project impacts.   A summary of the potential change impacts of the FUSION approach and a new life cycle on the existing organization including such areas as: structure, policies, job functions, cultural values, operating procedures, technology utilization, communication patterns, and user relationships.

Assumptions, issues, and constraints.   An identification of assumptions related to the project and expectations for it, as well as a statement of existing constraints in such areas as budgets, resource allocations, time frames, and so forth. All political, technical, and other issues raised during preworkshop activities should be documented and identified for workshop or implementation resolution.

Risks and rewards.   The clear delineation of what is at stake if the organization is not successful in moving to a FUSION environment. The executive sponsor should also identify techniques for recognizing individual and team contributions to the restructuring of the organization and for rewarding the display of new values and behavior.

The workshop agenda and supporting workshop exercises and data collection forms should be constructed with the objectives of the project and the projected content of the deliverables in mind. Special attention should be given as well to use of the workshop for team building and the reinforcement of FUSION values.

Participant Education and Preparation

It is not only important to educate and prepare the workshop participants in a breakthrough project, but it is also critically important to begin to educate the systems organization itself. Therefore, a target meeting should be held to achieve two objectives: to brief the participants on their workshop responsibilities; and to inform the participants and other interested members of the organization about the scope and goals of the project. This meeting will provide an opportunity for the executive sponsor to demonstrate his commitment to the FUSION approach and to set a "breakthrough" tone for the project.

If the project manager and JAD facilitator believe it is needed, a special education and awareness building session on FUSION and its dimensions may also be held prior to the workshop. This type of half-day or day long session can help to bring participants to an equal level of awareness. FUSION concepts can be discussed, and previous organizational experiences with IE, CASE, and JAD (if any) can be shared.

Workshop I: Defining the New Life Cycle

The JAD technical agenda for the life cycle definition workshop must allow for extended discussion and analysis and be well integrated with team building exercises. All technical decisions regarding the new life cycle should be docu-

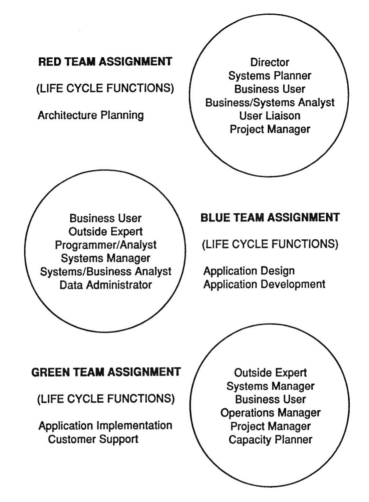

Figure 6.19 Sample life cycle component subteams.

mented using workshop data collection forms. A variety of exercises to generate ideas without judgment, analyze and evaluate ideas, and support decision making should be designed into the workshop agenda. The workshop should emphasize the identification of key project decisions rather than the procedures or tasks required to get the project work done. In other words, the life cycle document should define what needs to be done and not be overly prescriptive about how to do it.

The participant group should be divided into life cycle component subteams (Fig. 6.19). Teams should be heterogeneous, composed of members from varying locations within the organization, and at varying levels. This will encourage team building and help to expedite discussions.

A typical agenda for the workshop would look like this:

- DAY 1
  Open the workshop:
    Establish group norms
    Bring participants to a common level of understanding
    Establish vision for working with customers and each other
  Validate life cycle components:
    Component purpose
    Actions that trigger component activities
    Key component activities
    Component activity sponsorship and funding
    Project team composition, roles and accountabilities
    Component final deliverable
    Related work outside of the component
  Define component details:
    Interim deliverables (if required) and purposes
    Start and end component measurements
    Indicators of component failure or lack of quality
  Define critical success factors for each component:
    Values
    Working relationships
    Sponsorship
    Involvement (users and others)
    Required support
- DAY 2
  Define component deliverables:
    Decisions to be supported by the deliverable
    Accountable roles
    Critical content sections and value adding information
    Dependencies for constructing deliverables
- DAY 3
  Define technique and tool utilization for each component activity:
    Tool/technique purpose and deliverable supported
    Conditions for tool/technique use
    Advantages of tool/technique use
    Critical skills/knowledge required
    Resources required to effectively utilize tool/technique
- DAY 4
  Component relationship analysis:
    Sequencing and overlap (components may not be completed in a linear
    fashion, parallel activities are possible in a RAD environment)
    Decision points for project authorization and continuation

Information and/or workflow documentation
Quality and speed assurance analysis for each component:
   Actions to ensure speed of work completion
   Identification of quality measures and checkpoints
   Remedial actions for substandard work
Close the workshop:
   Identify issue assignment and resolution responsibilities
   Identify next steps
   Conduct workshop evaluations

Some organizations may want to customize the life cycle to accommodate different types of projects conducted by the systems organization. These project types might include new development, technology conversions, and enhancement projects. This should present no problem if the project team is able to agree on project types without too much dissension. Other organizations may want to include projects that are not strictly systems oriented such as strategic planning projects or market analysis projects. This can be done as well, but it may add to the time required for the workshop and might better be left to a later workshop where other life cycle uses are discussed. If project types are addressed (whether systems oriented or not), analysis of component and deliverable impact for each project type should be integrated into the agenda to identify customization requirements.

Workshop II: FUSION Implementation Planning

Following a short break, the project team should reassemble in a second workshop to develop the FUSION implementation plan. The workshop should open up with a team reinforcement exercise prior. As before, a mix of exercises should be integrated into the design of the technical agenda. A typical agenda for the workshop would look like this:

* DAY 1
  Exploring implementation inhibitors and enhancers within the current environment:
     Organization operating problems and opportunities—policies, procedures, practices
     Education and training and related employee development support
     Current cultural values and attitudes toward change
     Current IE, JAD, and CASE utilization within the organization
     Management and supervisory politics, attitudes, and pressures
  Defining strategies for FUSION Phase I implementation:
     Organization environmental modifications
     FUSION education and training
     Marketing and commitment building

Acquisition and installation of IE, JAD, and CASE
IE, JAD, and CASE administration and management
Management and supervisory change support
* DAY 2
Develop Phase I FUSION action implementation plan:
Activities and deliverables
Accountabilities for activities
Integrated implementation area schedules with dates beginning with the end of this second workshop
Evaluation and decision points
Resource requirements—people, dollars, equipment, etc.
Reinforce commitment for FUSION implementation:
Recommendations for resolving open issues
Implementation project team membership and support
Participant responsibilities for Phase I

POSTWORKSHOP ACTIVITIES

Once the workshops are completed, the breakthrough project manager is responsible for completing the two deliverables and presenting their results to the executive sponsor. He may want to do this jointly with project team members in order to demonstrate the commitment of all of those involved. The executive sponsor will then have to decide whether or not to authorize the breakthrough project manager to move forward with FUSION implementation as outlined in the plan. If the groundwork is carefully laid before the workshops, however, this will not be a problem.

Open Issue Resolution

The assigned open issues and the FUSION implementation plan become the working agenda for the FUSION implementation project team. To provide a technique for ongoing problem solving during the implementation process, a forum should be established. The purpose of the forum would be to review implementation issues and resolve any problems as they come up. Participants in the forum should include the executive sponsor for the project as well as representatives from throughout the organization. The forum itself should be a structured meeting, and it should be held on a regular basis.

Transitioning Needs

In some cases, the FUSION implementation project manager will not be the same person as the breakthrough project manager. If an implementation project manager has not been appointed prior to the conclusion of the breakthrough project, time must be built into the schedule for the appointment of this individual. Time will also be required for a transition from one manager to the next. FUSION implementation team members may be appointed as full or part time team members depending on the amount of overall coordination required for implementation activities. Some of these individuals may have been participants on the breakthrough project team, but it is not necessary that the breakthrough project team and the implementation project team be identical. It is probably better, in fact, if new faces are brought into the process, and some members of the first team are excused to go on to other work. This will increase the number of people who play a part in the transition and should help to increase organization commitment.

Some time will be required for completion and review of release 1.0 of the life cycle document, although a delay here is not advisable. People will be eager to see the results of the project, and the sooner they have the document in their hands the better. Identification of initial pilot projects, as well as many of the marketing and commitment building activities which implementation requires, depend upon access to the new life cycle document. Delays during the writing, publication, and distribution process can cause interrupt implementation momentum and may be perceived by organization members as a reluctance to move forward.

The breakthrough project is an excellent vehicle for the establishment of implementation momentum, but in order to exploit it fully, it is necessary to see that the project and implementation plan that follows do not get caught up in second-guessing and politics.

7

FUSION Implementation: A Strategy for Restructuring Systems Development

FUSION TRANSLATED INTO REALITY

While experimentation with IE methodology, CASE tools and JAD techniques can help an organization test the waters and gain an appreciation for the potential difficulties involved in more widespread FUSION implementation, there is no substitute for a clearly defined and carefully executed FUSION implementation strategy and plan. A building contractor would not build a house without a set of blueprints, nor would a venture capitalist invest in a company unless there were detailed business plans outlining all the risks as well as the benefits. FUSION requires the same kind of planning. A successful transition from the current environment to a FUSION environment requires the willingness to invest in the future, the ability to redirect the resources of the organization, and a detailed action plan. The introduction of FUSION constitutes the restructuring of all systems development policies and practices. FUSION brings changes to the organizational structure, job functions, responsibilities and authorities, employee skill and knowledge requirements, and management and project team working relationships. But just as important, FUSION brings new values, attitudes and behavior to the organization. Such changes cannot be treated lightly. It takes time and support to implement them successfully.

Each organization must implement FUSION somewhat differently because of its unique culture, and all organizations will face the problems that accompany the introduction of any change. In some organizations, established attitudes and work habits are as hard to change as the ruts in an old dirt road after years of use. In these organizations, FUSION implementation will introduce discipline for the first time into an environment where users and systems people exist in two armed camps and where new ideas are seen as threatening and are vigorously resisted. In other cases, FUSION implementation will require only a minor shift to a new set of structured work methods and the formalization of existing communication strategies that characterize systems/user relationships. In most cases, however, FUSION implementors face a mixture of these two extremes. The first step, then, is for the organization to review its strengths, its weaknesses, its structure, its rules, its quirks—what makes it tick. Once an organization has examined what it is, then it can plan for what it can be.

Overcoming Planning Problems

The problem with planning is that the planning process itself is an ambiguous effort, accompanied by many risks. Some planning efforts take too long and result in plans that are irrelevant by the time they are finally approved. Others are conducted in haste and offer unsupported conclusions. For FUSION planning to be effective, it must avoid these potential problems. The team responsible for creating a successful FUSION implementation plan should:

Model the projected FUSION environment.   Planning activities should be conducted using the techniques that will be implemented in the FUSION environment.

Be time sensitive.   Planning activities should be completed as quickly as possible (without omitting required tasks) by using a phased approach.

Include an intervention strategy.   The use of a breakthrough project demonstrates the benefits of the projected change. Perhaps more important, though, it provides the momentum the organization needs to initiate the change process. As with a chemically dependent person who begins the road to recovery through a family supported, professionally orchestrated "intervention," an organization that is "addicted" to old inefficient work habits can begin the process of changing to a FUSION lifestyle through the intervention of a breakthrough project.

Target specific planning areas.   The critical success factors required for FUSION success will dictate the specific planning areas that must be addressed within the plan. These areas are discussed next.

Planning Phases

The FUSION implementation plan should be divided into three phases:

- Phase I: Start Up
- Phase II: Proliferation
- Phase III: Continuous Improvement and Support

Phase I of the implementation plan typically requires six months. This phase has two major objectives: the acquisition or development of the FUSION products and services required to support each of the three dimensions; and the preparation of the organization for the changes that will follow. Once the organization obtains IE, JAD, and CASE products and services, it must pilot and install them. During this time, key individuals will develop the knowledge and skills needed to expand this initial implementation beyond the controlled start up environment. In addition, FUSION effectiveness will be demonstrated on real projects, success stories will be developed, and commitment to the principles and practices of the FUSION concept will be created.

The FUSION proliferation phase takes FUSION out into the organization at large and weaves FUSION into the fabric of all systems activities. Phase II generally requires approximately twelve months. During FUSION proliferation, new values and work practices are disseminated throughout the organization, as are lessons learned from the start up phase. The development of general education and training programs is a critical success factor in this phase, as is the development of effective resource distribution and change management strategies.

Phase III of the implementation plan requires the development of an on-going strategy for quality improvement. Feedback mechanisms must be developed to ensure that people understand which actions have been successful, which require refinement and what changes must be addressed. In addition, productivity and quality measurements must be developed. Phase III requires the support of a significant cross section of the organization as new people become involved, as customer needs change and as technology advances.

CRITICAL SUCCESS FACTORS FOR
FUSION IMPLEMENTATION

FUSION implementation can be considered a success when the existing organization has transitioned to a new way of working that:

- Increases the speed of project completion.
- Improves the quality of the product produced.

- Reduces the maintenance effort required.
- Increases the effectiveness of resource utilization.

In order for these objectives to be achieved, certain fundamental critical success factors must be adhered to in the FUSION implementation project. These include:

- Fully committed executive sponsorship and management buy-in
- FUSION coordination and support
- Organization marketing and commitment building
- Organization environmental modifications
- Education and training
- Change management support
- Acquisition and installation of FUSION products and services
- FUSION integration with the systems development life cycle

Fully Committed Executive Sponsorship and Management Buy-In

Although a commitment to FUSION is required throughout the organization for successful implementation, commitment must begin at the highest executive level within the systems organization. The demonstration of support for FUSION implementation by the executive sponsor must be highly visible. At a minimum, it must include:

- Demonstrating the values and behavior he wants to see in his direct reports and others. He must be willing to cut through political and territorial issues that will arise during phase I—start up and phase II—proliferation activities. He must be a communicator, negotiator, and obstacle remover. He must empower the people in the organization to act. He must set boundaries and define guidelines for FUSION before the effects of implementation are felt. Finally, he must be willing to embrace the FUSION plan developed by the project team and proceed with implementation.
- Providing the funds and personnel required to support FUSION planning and implementation. This includes chartering the FUSION implementation project team, staffing it, and providing funding for FUSION implementation.
- Taking responsibility for the actions of the implementation project manager and project team, particularly during phase I activities. He must assist the team in problem solving and overcoming obstacles encountered as implementation proceeds. This support includes making himself available for meetings and other public activities required to develop a constituency for change as recommended by the project team.

- Providing strong support for those projects selected as pilots for phase I. This support must include extending time limits for projects when this is made necessary by the learning curve. It must also include support for the project managers and project teams who participate in these pilot projects. He should personally encourage those participating in the implementation plan, particularly during start-up activities.

Before JAD, IE, and CASE are applied to projects in the start up phase, there must be a core of middle and lower managers who want FUSION to succeed and who are willing to work hard to make this happen. When they are presented with the benefits of the FUSION approach, these champions of change will line up to be the first to participate and lend their support. They will be willing to take risks because they know that more learning takes place in a dynamic environment than in a static one. These champions will be followed by the more cautious individuals in the organization who will accept FUSION only when the approach has been proven.

When resources are limited for FUSION implementation (as they almost always are), some technique must be found to determine how best to apply those resources that are available. The concept of triage can be helpful here. Used during military actions and civil emergencies by medical teams with limited resources, the triage approach assumes that a body of people under stress can be divided into three groups. These three groups include: individuals so severely damaged that they will be lost no matter what actions are taken, individuals who are hurt but who will survive without immediate attention, and individuals who will survive only if immediate attention is provided. If we follow the triage approach, we will attend to the third group of people first.

Within the typical organization, there will be project managers who not only require help, but who recognize that they can succeed only with special assistance. These are the individuals who should be sought out by the implementation project team. These managers will probably recognize the benefits of FUSION, and it is likely that they will be willing to assume the risks of a new approach. Because their projects are at risk, they will know failure is a possibility, but they will not want to fail. Once they understand that FUSION can make a significant difference in the outcome of their projects, they will be willing to work with the FUSION implementation team and utilize their expertise. After these initial successes, other project managers and project teams will start lining up to apply FUSION principles to their projects.

FUSION Coordination and Support

A boat, no matter how well designed, will not sail unless the skipper knows how to hoist and trim the sails to effectively utilize the wind. But the principles of sail trim become second nature only after much training and practice. The same applies to project teams and FUSION. The use of IE methodology, JAD technique, and CASE tools will become part of the culture and an accepted way of working only after much learning, guidance, practice, and encouragement.

The roles and responsibilities involved in FUSION implementation must be specific, clear, and measurable. This requires that FUSION support responsibilities become a part of the performance objectives and performance plans of individual managers and project teams. Specific responsibilities and performance objectives must also be defined for the FUSION implementation team and the staff of the FUSION Center. Participation on FUSION implementation teams, task forces or standing committees must be formally recognized within the organization's performance appraisal system. Achievement or nonachievement of specific objectives must be rewarded accordingly. This will encourage a serious attitude toward FUSION implementation responsibilities and assist all of those involved in monitoring and enhancing their performance of implementation tasks.

During phase I, the key group involved in implementation is the ad hoc FUSION implementation team. During the second implementation phase, the proliferation phase, implementation support must come from the staff of a new FUSION Center or (if no center has been established) from a core group created for this purpose. These coordination points for FUSION provide support to project teams and managers, manage quality assurance and initiate continuous improvement mechanisms for FUSION and the systems organization as a whole.

In small centralized systems organizations, FUSION coordination and support can be managed by a team of two or three people. In large decentralized organizations, multiple core support groups may be required. If appropriate, one group may be created to manage each dimension, with all three groups reporting to a single FUSION coordination manager. In such a case, each group would be responsible for ensuring that a strategy is implemented to ensure that the products and services associated with its dimension are fully implemented throughout the organization through the development of training, marketing and pilot project programs. These core groups would then be supported in each division or region by FUSION implementation teams and, possibly, a FUSION Center staff that would report by dotted line to the FUSION coordination manager (Fig. 7.1). These division or regional groups would provide direct project team support.

The FUSION implementation team and FUSION Centers are not directly responsible for utilizing IE, CASE, and JAD on projects. Instead, they are responsible for supporting line project teams and project managers by providing technical assistance, sharing information, identifying problems, and offering solutions, and in general, acting as knowledgeable consultants. The project teams themselves will be the actual implementers of FUSION tools and techniques. The FUSION implementation teams and FUSION Centers are responsible for such actions as:

- Building commitment and managing expectations of executives and managers.
- Motivating individuals at lower levels to use IE, JAD, and CASE tools and techniques.

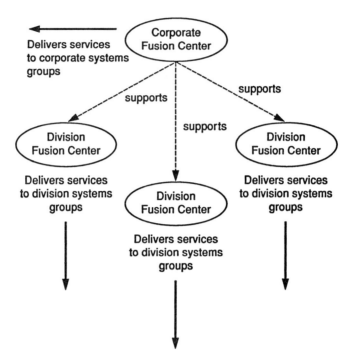

Figure 7.1 Sample FUSION support structure.

- Developing and proliferating guidelines for IE, JAD, and CASE utilization on projects.
- Assisting project teams in FUSION implementation by providing JAD facilitators, JAD/CASE specialists, information engineering expertise and life cycle planning expertise through in-house staff or outside vendors.
- Educating and training project teams and managers in FUSION change management skills directly or through outside vendors.
- Providing a mechanism for continuous productivity and quality improvement through FUSION utilization.
- Researching, selecting, and customizing an IE methodology, JAD technique, and CASE tools.
- Coordinating information sharing and skill transfer among project teams.

FUSION coordination and support practices developed and tested during the start up phase will be implemented during the proliferation phase and carried into the continuous improvement phase. Responsibility for coordination and support will transfer from the temporary implementation team(s) to the permanent FUSION Center(s) at the beginning of phase II—proliferation.

Without the coordination and support services provided to project teams by the FUSION implementation teams and FUSION Centers, there is a risk that people will misuse FUSION methodology, tools and techniques. In extreme cases, there may even be individuals who will attempt to sabotage the FUSION effort. "We tried it, but it didn't work," is a frequent retort of reluctant and frustrated project teams that were not provided with strong coordination and support services.

Once FUSION has been successfully implemented, the job of the implementors is not done. It is the responsibility of the FUSION Center staff to create and maintain a program for the continuing enhancement of FUSION tools and techniques. Depending upon organization needs, this may include the adoption of measurement techniques such as function point analysis for identifying and tracking productivity gains, or the development of specialized feedback mechanisms to enable project teams to translate their experience into updates to FUSION principles, tools, and techniques. Continuing improvement is an important on-going objective that will prevent stagnation and subsequent productivity loss. The needs of the organization will change over time, and the FUSION approach must change as well.

The key to productive and effective FUSION is to make this evaluation and enhancement process a part of the FUSION approach, rather than an activity that intrudes and disrupts the organization. It is important to avoid a situation where FUSION users say, "They're changing it again. Can't they ever get it right?" To avoid this, a release approach should be utilized, and FUSION users should be made aware of this. The organization should look forward to changes and enhancements. Generally, an organization will need to update its FUSION approach every one to two years. The rule is "learn by doing, and then share the knowledge."

Organization Marketing and Commitment Building

People can be trained in FUSION skills, but until they value the principles of FUSION, they will not be successful in applying them to their work activities. To begin to effect this change in the values of individuals, the organization must adopt a marketing plan. Marketing begins the value change process. If raises the awareness of FUSION concepts and educates people about FUSION benefits. It convinces people that this new idea is worth an investment of time and energy and stimulates their curiosity. FUSION should be marketed based on the needs and biases of the organization and its project teams. For example, one implementation team may market FUSION as "a new approach that will save maintenance costs." Another team may position FUSION as "the continuing evolution of structured analysis." If marketing is not part of the FUSION implementation effort, people will not see any reason for changing their valucs and work practices.

The FUSION implementation team must develop a strategy for marketing FUSION. They must decide what they want people to visualize, think about, and sense when they hear the words FUSION, IE, JAD, and CASE. They must also decide what qualities they want the FUSION implementation team to represent. Do they want the team to convey an image of service and expertise? Do they want their audience to focus on a picture of old practices evolving into new ones, or do they want to suggest a revolutionary change? Do they want people to focus on a picture of integration, where the best of the new and the old are combined? Once they decide what message they want to send, the FUSION implementation team must then determine what words, pictures, and actions will best convey that message. With strategy and images defined, the mechanics of creating presentations and materials to tell the FUSION story can begin.

Once their interest in FUSION has been stimulated, people will need a conceptual understanding of FUSION, training in the dimensions of IE, CASE, and JAD, and specific information about how FUSION benefits can be delivered. This knowledge will help them begin to relate the FUSION approach to their own responsibilities and work activities. There is a strategic marketing process at work here. First, interest must be stimulated, then knowledge must be transferred, and then commitment can be developed. The evidence of commitment is the ability of individuals to envision themselves as involved in the FUSION process. They can see themselves taking part in JAD sessions, building IE diagrams, and using CASE tools. They see how the benefits of FUSION apply both to their individual roles and to their participation in work groups. They will also be able to identify project situations where FUSION is appropriate and situations where it is not appropriate.

The FUSION team must not reject the idea of selling the process for fear that selling an idea is somehow demeaning or inappropriate in a business setting. Some people view commitment building activities negatively because they believe that sales tactics are only used to get people to buy something they don't really need. That is coercion, not selling. If the implementation team believes in FUSION and values its benefits, then the team is only fulfilling its responsibility by helping others in the organization to come to the same conclusion.

In addition to the FUSION implementation team, managers have an important role to play in selling the FUSION approach. They need to work against both active resistance ("I won't do it that way.") and passive resistance ("We'll let them think we agree and then, when they're gone, we'll do what we please.") in the organization. Managers must prepare the work environment and the people within that environment to accept FUSION and the changes it brings to the organization (Fig. 7.2).

Organization Environmental Modifications

All aspects of the systems organization, its culture, values, and operations may be affected by the introduction of FUSION. Some aspects of the organization will require adaptation and change in order to properly support FUSION. Those aspects that are already supportive of the FUSION approach may only require

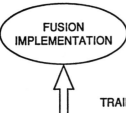

TRAINING to develop the skills for change.

SELLING to build commitment for change.

EDUCATION programs to overcome
the roadblock of ignorance.

MARKETING to raise awareness
for the potential of change.

Figure 7.2 Marketing and sales in
FUSION implementation.

strengthening. Those aspects that tend to work against FUSION success may have to undergo substantial modification. In either case, the organizational environment cannot be ignored, or the success of the approach may be seriously undermined. It will be necessary, therefore, to conduct an assessment of the current environment in order to identify potential impact areas and to address the issues that will affect FUSION success. Phase I of the implementation plan should contain activities to address and resolve these issues before an attempt is made to disseminate FUSION concepts throughout the organization. Issue areas that are most likely to be identified and to require clarification or remedial action include, but are certainly not limited to:

- Project authorization and approval processes
- Project manager authority and accountability
- Systems organization structure and reporting relationships
- Managerial reward systems
- Employee training and development—technical and behavioral
- Political conflicts between upper and middle management
- Commitment of upper and middle management
- Fiscal and other resource constraints and limitations

Some organizations will adopt the FUSION approach in part to shake up the organization. The more emphasis there is on the implementation of FUSION as a revolutionary act, the more swiftly and directly these issues must be addressed. If, on the other hand, the introduction of FUSION is seen as an evolutionary act, then changes in these areas will be less dramatic and can spread out over a longer period of time. In either case, the integration strategy adopted by the implementation team should focus on overcoming the strongest inhibitors and reinforcing the best enhancers to FUSION within the systems environment.

Education and Training

Education and training are both required in the FUSION implementation process, and while these two concepts are mutually reinforcing, it is important to understand how they differ. The purpose of education is to build knowledge and to overcome ignorance. The purpose of training is to develop skills that can be tested through the demonstration of specific behavior. While education transfers knowledge about "what" is involved in FUSION and cultural change, training transfers required skills, the "how to" of implementing FUSION concepts in the work environment.

An integrated education and training strategy is critical to FUSION success. The education part of the strategy must stress an understanding of the principles of information engineering, the way those principles are embodied in CASE tools, and the theoretical basis of group facilitation and team building that underlies JAD. The training part of the strategy must stress the technical skills needed for utilizing CASE tools, constructing IE diagrams, designing workshop agendas, and facilitating workshop sessions. A strong FUSION curriculum must also touch on related concepts. It should include programs to transfer both theoretical knowledge and practical skills in such areas as communication, change management, and personal development.

It is critical to consider the population addressed by this program. Too often the educational or theoretical part of this curriculum is directed at members of the business user community, while the skills training part is addressed to members of the systems organization. FUSION success is best guaranteed if the full curriculum is available to the entire organization, and users are encouraged to take skills training courses, while systems professionals are encouraged to take theoretical or knowledge building courses. One of the purposes of FUSION is to eliminate the artificial division between the two groups, and a strong education and training program can further this objective. An on-going education and training curriculum must be in place to serve both systems professionals and users at all levels of the organization. It should be developed and tested during phase I and should be ready for full implementation during phase II. Some organizations will want to bring in outside experts to assist in the development of this curriculum. Others will find the expertise they need within the organization. Outside consultants can be helpful in expediting the curriculum development and piloting process, but in the long run for FUSION to become part of the organization's culture, the more members of the organization that are involved in the delivery and management of the new curriculum, the greater the chance for FUSION success.

Educational programs may be structured in a variety of formal and informal formats including informational presentations for staff and special project teams, video tapes, brochures, pamphlets, conferences, seminars, and other short formats designed to stimulate the audience's interest in FUSION and provide a forum to discuss their concerns. Skills training programs are usually more formal in their presentation style, although a key to their success is the degree to which they are customized. The value of a skills training program increases in proportion to the extent that the application of skills to real world problems is stressed. Both classroom and on-the-job reinforcement training is needed. In order for this part of the program to be successful, good trainers are a necessity. These individuals should be expert both in FUSION skills (IE diagramming techniques, JAD, and CASE) and in the project requirements of the organization. In addition, they must know how to teach, a skill sometimes in short supply. Without competent professionals to execute IE, CASE, and JAD, FUSION implementation success is not possible.

Change Management Support

Just as the organization's work environment will have to change to make the most of the FUSION approach, the personnel of the organization, both management and staff will also need to change. This is particularly true for the systems organization, where the changes will be felt most profoundly. Many systems professionals will find the change to FUSION threatening. Managers must be prepared to deal with their own insecurities in the face of this change, as well as the fears of their employees. Classroom training alone will not be sufficient to dispel all of these fears. In the past, systems organizations have elevated technical skills and downplayed so called "people skills." Promotion practices have followed this tendency. Managers have too seldom been rewarded for exercising excellent skills in communication, team building, motivation, and values development. This will have to change if FUSION is to be successful.

The positive changes introduced by FUSION will not get past the start up phase if managers throughout the organization are not prepared to build alliances and focus on the good of the organization as a whole. Political maneuvering in particular can destroy a FUSION implementation effort in the early stages. FUSION requires commitment as well as skills. Rapid application development demands highly skilled systems professionals working long hours in intense, close relationships with users. Once FUSION moves beyond the controlled environment of the pilot projects of phase I into full implementation, special training, coaching and other types of support may be necessary to enable managers to rebuild and renew their project teams.

Acquisition and Installation of FUSION Products and Services

Although the acquisition and installation of FUSION products and services should not be allowed to take center stage in FUSION implementation, it is an important factor in FUSION success. This is probably the most well defined of all implementation activities, and for that reason it can take on a life of its own if not properly managed. It should not be allowed to force other implementation issues to the sidelines. Acquisition and installation activities may take place throughout the start up and proliferation phases. If customization of products or services is required, this should be done in phase I. Pilot testing and modification, if required, should be completed before FUSION proliferation is begun.

FUSION Integration with the Systems Development Life Cycle

The systems development life cycle codifies the work practices and cultural values of the systems organization. All three FUSION dimensions must be fully integrated into the life cycle for FUSION success. In cases where there is no life cycle, FUSION provides the basis for building a comprehensive life cycle and standards for the deliverables within that life cycle. If required, a breakthrough pilot project can be used to address the need for life cycle creation or modification. FUSION provides a particularly effective means for doing so because it involves the users of the life cycle in its creation and modification. Some organizations will face more change than others. At a minimum, IE deliverables must be mapped to established life cycle deliverables, and JAD techniques and CASE tool utilization must be mapped to the activity set of the existing life cycle. This mapping bridges old and new work practices.

Some organizations will want to consider modifying an existing life cycle, especially if the approach currently used is widely supported by the organization. That life cycle can be changed to reflect the terminology, deliverables and processes found in the FUSION approach. Some organizations will want to consider modifying the three FUSION dimensions in some way in order to make them more compatible with an established life cycle noted for its widespread support and effectiveness. This customization may include such changes as:

Terminology.   Using established life cycle terminology in place of terms more commonly used by IE, JAD, or CASE experts. Generally, these changes affect terms used for life cycle components, activities/tasks, and deliverables.

Deliverables.   Enhancing standard IE deliverables to meet existing system life cycle deliverable requirements. Generally, these changes require that additional content be included in deliverables.

Process.   Enhancing JAD techniques to match the common practices of the established systems development life cycle. Generally, these changes require that JAD accommodate factors in the cultural environment.

Once documented, phase one, start up activities should include pilot projects to test different life cycle components on real projects. Based on the results of those pilots, the life cycle should be revised and reissued at the beginning of phase two, proliferation activities.

FIVE KEY MISTAKES TO AVOID

Change is a difficult process, especially when its subject is a large complex organization. It takes time, patience, and commitment. Systems organizations have been attempting to implement significant change within their organizations for years. From their experience, we can identify some mistakes to avoid.

1. Ignoring the unique character of the organization.

    The most frequent mistake made by systems groups in implementing new methodologies, tools and techniques is to focus attention first on finding the most perfect, most complete and most clearly state-of-the-art solution. This external focus is bound to fail because it emphasizes tools and techniques and fails to address the unique needs of the organization and organizational politics. These factors must be taken into account if the solution selected is to gain widespread acceptance. If a solution is selected before the needs, goals and directions of the organization are known, then the implementation exercise becomes one of force fitting the organization to the solution. Implementation should provide a fusing of IE, CASE, and JAD dimensions with the organization in a way that encourages individuals to welcome the opportunity to be a part of the effort and to accept a new way of working.

    Another related mistake is not providing post installation support. Too often it is assumed that the benefits of a proposed solution will be recognized instantly and that the products and services selected will be utilized immediately. The result is a short burst of change followed by a quick relapse to the old way of doing business. Again, this fails to take into account the organization's need for a period of testing of new ideas and accommodation to them.

2. Failing to develop political support.

    Another mistake often made in an organization wide change effort is to assume that such an effort can be accomplished by one or two individuals who have no budget and no authority over the most powerful and influential individuals or groups within in the organization. The designated implementors, often provided with such titles as "Productivity Improvement Manager," cannot meet their objectives if they are not positioned for success within the organization. No matter how enthusiastic and dedicated to the implementation task they are, their efforts will be doomed to failure. Without clear accountability, executive sponsorship, budget authority, and the active participation of powerful and influential line managers and professionals, they cannot succeed.

3. Expecting too much too soon.

A typical mistake is to expect too much too soon. Changes that impact both the culture and technology environment of an organization inevitably take time. Sometimes the process involves taking one step back in order to take two steps forward. People need time to accept change and to adjust to a new environment, and along the way, adjustments must be made as the change is experienced and more is learned. Patience is required as well as a good understanding of the nature of organizations and individual needs. Many of today's systems organizations have an organizational history that dates back for twenty or more years. They will not be dramatically altered in a mere six months. Most successful change plans are multiyear efforts, with two to five-year horizons. The amount of time required for a given organization will be a result of several factors: the age of the organization, its size and complexity, the experience of the organization with previous changes, and the commitment to change of top management.

4. Failing to develop a FUSION marketing plan.

A typical mistake of change implementors is to fail to respond to the continuing need for awareness and commitment building activities at all levels of the organization. People will not take risks for what they do not value. Implementors must be able to assist people in becoming involved in change and in recognizing the benefits that they themselves will obtain. Most implementors need to learn the marketing and sales skills that will help them to present FUSION effectively. Few already have them. Nevertheless, they must become part of the implementation team's repertoire. Effective marketing of the FUSION concept is not a nice-to-have. It is a necessity.

5. Expecting FUSION to solve all problems.

Some organizations expect FUSION to address problems outside its scope. If there are major problems within the organization, it is unfair to expect the implementation of the FUSION approach to solve these. Many organizations are under tremendous stress today. This stress may be the result of changes in consumer priorities, increasing competitive pressures from abroad, disturbances caused by mergers and acquisitions, internal political conflicts, or other factors. No one set of tools and techniques, no matter how well structured and integrated can address all of these issues. Those responsible for implementation of FUSION within the organization should take these factors into account when they look at the internal environment into which FUSION will be placed. With strong planning and continuing support, FUSION can succeed in a stressed environment, but it cannot completely transform that environment.

FUSION IMPLEMENTATION IN THE COMPLEX ORGANIZATION

In a smaller systems organization (one with fewer than two hundred people), orchestrating the move to FUSION is a task of reasonable size. Although politics will still have an impact, the smaller size of the organization provides distinct advantages. Generally, it is easy to identify the key executive. This individual will have the authority to direct and support the changes FUSION requires. He is probably fairly accessible to people within the organization. In addition, in the smaller organization the number of people affected by the implementation of FUSION is not too great. For this reason it is easier to coordinate FUSION implementation activities and build commitment. It takes less time to accomplish tasks. People know each other and are often co-located. Finally, it is easier to see the impact of FUSION in a smaller organization. Every success has high visibility. The formal and informal communication paths that transmit the news about FUSION are generally more direct and straightforward than in larger organizations.

A more difficult challenge for FUSION implementation is found in larger, more complex systems organizations, particularly those that are decentralized. Often the corporate systems vice president has no direct control over the budgets, priorities, and practices of divisional or regional systems organizations (Fig. 7.3). It may be difficult for this executive, who may have as few as five to twenty staff, to get the division directors, who each have hundreds of staff, to participate in FUSION implementation. How does he get these divisions to move toward an integrated, corporately compatible architecture for systems work? How does he get divisional systems executives to see the larger systems picture?

To examine these and other questions raised by the challenge of the complex organization, it is useful to look at the experience of a large midwest based international manufacturing company. In 1985, the corporate systems executive director was told to standardize the work practices and integrate the systems of twelve independent operating divisions with a total of over three thousand employees. Although each division was satisfied with its own business strategy, the corporation was taking a beating in the marketplace. The corporation suffered from a lack of timely, high quality information, insufficient product quality and a too long product development cycle. As a result, the executive director of the organization was told by the corporate vice president to meet the following objectives:

- Reduce total division expenditures for systems activities by constructing common systems and databases.

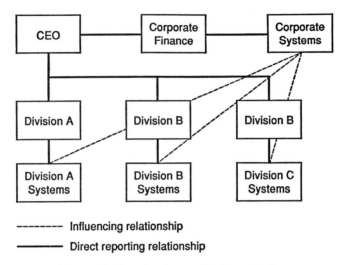

- - - - - - - - Influencing relationship

───────── Direct reporting relationship

Figure 7.3   Complex decentralized organization.

- Integrate division and corporate information and make this resource accessible worldwide.
- Bring common work standards and technologies to the division systems organizations so that resources can be shared.

After five years of work, substantial progress has been made toward the achievement of all objectives. The company is utilizing FUSION in all of its divisions and has had major successes in the use of rapid application development, the construction of integrated databases and the implementation of new technologies. It has moved beyond the start up phase and is nearing completion of the proliferation phase. The critical success factors here include a well thought out plan, a strong commitment to FUSION success by top management, and a combination of realistic expectations and patience.

Creating the Infrastructure for Change

One of the first activities undertaken by the corporate systems executive director was to market FUSION at the executive level within the divisions to raise the awareness of the business issues behind the need for change. These issues were easily recognized as critical by the executives. They all were aware that applications were consistently delivered late, that divisions had trouble getting skilled people, and that buying new technologies was a challenge given budget constraints. This initial marketing effort accomplished the following:

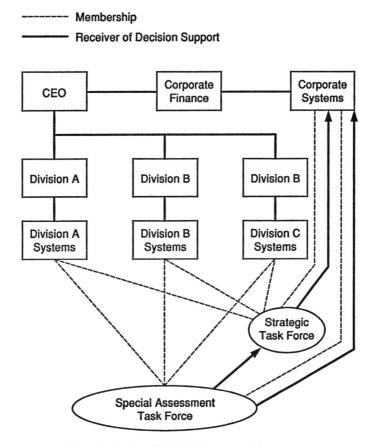

-------- Membership
———— Receiver of Decision Support

Figure 7.4 Sample FUSION support infrastructure.

- Identification of support for the first common systems initiatives.
- Creation of a multidivision commitment to participate on two task forces—a strategic decision support systems task force and a special assessment task force.
- Identification of specific pockets of resistance and available support for change.

The assignment of the two task forces was critical to the overall strategy for involving a broad spectrum of the organization. These groups were empowered to provide direction on meeting the corporate challenges that had been identified. Together they provided an infrastructure for change planning and implementation throughout the company (Fig. 7.4). The strategic task force reviewed and approved plans offered by members of the organization and the special assessment task force. No step was taken without their concurrence. The special assessment task force was chartered to explore new tools, techniques, methodologies, training, and anything else that might help solve systems problems. They developed plans, sponsored experiments, and built division commitment for change. They were, in effect, the FUSION implementation team. The corporate systems executive director and the strategic task force of systems managers together filled the role of executive sponsor for the project. Both task forces were accountable for finding and supporting solutions. They were decision makers, the focus of action.

These two task forces sponsored and planned a breakthrough project that had the objective of defining a new life cycle for the systems organizations. This was made easier because they had a budget to help defray the costs of experimentation. As a team, they reviewed vendor products and services and made recommendations for utilization and corporate wide adoption when appropriate. They were responsible for FUSION implementation strategy and planning, as well as coordination and execution. They recommended and authorized the expansion of the corporate systems staff and gave it responsibility for a new FUSION Center. These people became internal consultants to the divisions. The important lesson here is that the corporate systems executive director accomplished his task by giving others the power to help him, by demonstrating his commitment through his behavior (he was known for doing the unusual and dramatic), and understanding that success would require time as well as effort.

Identifying Opportunities for Implementing FUSION

Another reason for the success of this implementation effort is that the executive director of systems chose his opportunities with care. He did not start integrating databases and building common systems in divisional areas where he had no direct control. Instead, he began FUSION utilization on corporate projects. Two project areas that provided good opportunities for FUSION implementation were corporate financial systems and human resources systems where staff reported directly to him. Each division had its own accounts payable, receiving and personnel systems, but these systems suffered from the problems of duplication of data, inconsistency of data and overlapping processing. Since the different divisions had overlapping information requirements, it was clear that commonization of systems was a high priority. When systems are "common," they are designed as a single set of applications accessing a single database. Once this design is developed, certain processing and data requirements can be customized for a given user group if its unique requirements justify this.

FUSION clearly demonstrates its value in this type of project. The data and process modeling techniques provided by information engineering, the consensus building process provided by JAD, and the analysis and documentation capabilities of CASE are well adapted to handle this type of systems need. In this case, experienced user representatives from all divisions were brought together with the stated purpose of creating a consensus on common practices and information needs. IE data and process modeling techniques were used to analyze require-

ments, and CASE tools were used to document the results. Perhaps most important of all, the executive sponsor did not dictate what the requirements for the new
system would be. Instead, he gave this responsibility to those most affected by
the proposed change.

This was not an overnight effort. Many individuals and work groups were
involved. This gave the organization time to experiment with the new approach
and widespread experience with the tools and techniques involved. As success
stories proliferated, the divisions themselves became interested in applying
FUSION principles to their own internal projects. Because a FUSION infrastructure was in place, this was easy to do. The people on the task force were well
equipped to assist their own organizations in supporting and guiding early FUSION
efforts.

This FUSION implementation plan was created with the idea of minimizing
the need for additional personnel resources. Instead it relied on the development
of new skills and knowledge in existing personnel and the reallocation of current
staff to new job functions. FUSION staff were drawn from the existing division
and corporate staff of project analysts and managers.

The FUSION Center

The executive director of systems drew the staff of the FUSION Center from
his own corporate staff. In addition, he encouraged the divisions to create their
own centers to deliver what the central group could not. The corporate FUSION
Center took responsibility for:

- The coordination of information about and access to approved vendors and
  products and services available to support FUSION projects.
- The creation of an internal consulting team to provide planning, assessment,
  and training support to systems groups.
- Continuing enhancement of the life cycle and the selection of standard tools
  and techniques for systems design and development.

The FUSION Centers located within the divisions provided direct expertise
to their project teams in the form of JAD facilitation, CASE/JAD skills, and IE
concepts and diagramming expertise.

THE FUSION IMPLEMENTATION PLAN:
STRUCTURE AND ELEMENTS

There is no perfect FUSION implementation plan. Each organization must
develop an approach that is right for itself. It is also important to try to complete
the planning effort as quickly as possible given the organization's strengths and

limitations. The goal after all is not the creation of a plan. The goal is FUSION implementation. It is important, however, to document the plan carefully. The quality of the written plan is generally a key factor in obtaining plan approval and in justifying requests for funding approval for implementation activities. The documented plan also becomes the project management road map for the FUSION implementation team. Therefore, it must contain certain information to support decision making and implementation management. This information should include:

FUSION implementation strategy.   A description of the overall strategy for FUSION implementation for each of the three phases—start up, proliferation, and continuing improvement and support.

Critical success factor (CSF) action plans.   There are eight critical success factors for FUSION implementation. Each should be supported by an action plan that includes all three implementation phases. These CSF plans should have the following:

Measurable objectives for achievement
Directional thrusts guiding implementation activity selection
Activities required to achieve objectives
Deliverables produced as a result of one or more activities
Individual and group roles and accountabilities for each activity
Activity schedules and time line
Total resource requirements and costs associated with the accomplishment of the objectives and each individual activity

Phase action plans.   Each implementation phase should be supported by a phase action plan that integrates all individual critical success factor plans in support of FUSION implementation. The action plan for phase one will generally require from six to twelve months for completion, the phase two plan will require from twelve to eighteen months, and the phase three plan will require a series of quarterly reports to top management.

Accountability plans.   Each phase will also require a definition of roles, responsibilities, and action due dates. This should be provided to each participating individual and group, along with a checklist of work to be accomplished.

THE STEPS TO FUSION IMPLEMENTATION

The FUSION implementation plan begins with the appointment of a FUSION implementation project manager and the execution of the breakthrough project to provide a catalyst for the planning effort. The following examples illustrate typical planning steps.

- Steps to create FUSION implementation strategies and plan.
  Step 1:   Get the Support of the "King." Identify a powerful source of high-level executive support, or if one is not apparent, create one.
  Step 2:   Assess Internal Environmental Readiness for FUSION. Identify those aspects of the organization that require change, those aspects that favor the introduction of change, and those that will constrain change.
  Step 3:   Research the Marketplace. Identify the most appropriate FUSION products and services for the organization given its requirements and constraints.
  Step 4:   Create the "Clan of the Curious." Build a core of management and staff support through the introduction of a breakthrough project.
  Step 5:   Create a FUSION Vision. Redesign the systems development life cycle and the systems culture through the completion of a breakthrough project.
  Step 6:   Create a FUSION Implementation Plan. Create a three phase FUSION implementation plan taking advantage of the insight gained through the breakthrough project.
- Steps to confirm and reinforce commitment to FUSION.
  Step 7:   Package the Plan. Finalize the plan for decision making and distribution.
  Step 8:   Get "the King" to Bless and Fund the Plan. Obtain final funding and resource approvals to begin phase I—start-up activities.
- Steps to execute FUSION Implementation.
  Step 9:   Implement Phase I—Start-Up Action Plan. Begin the transition to the FUSION environment through acquisition, development, testing, marketing, commitment building, education, training, and piloting activities.
  Step 10:   Implement Phase II—Proliferation Action Plan. When start-up objectives have been achieved, begin to transition from a temporary to permanent support environment and install FUSION throughout the systems organization on all projects. Sell success and make midcourse corrections as needed.
  Step 11:   Implement Phase III—Continuous Improvement and Support Action Plan. Once the organization has transitioned to the FUSION environment, begin on-going measurement and support activities.

Each organization will proceed with this type of implementation effort differently. However, there are some aspects of the implementation effort that will present a special challenge to all organizations. These areas include:

- Getting started
- Techniques for internal assessment
- Techniques for marketplace research
- Planning ideas
- Packaging ideas

To make the planning effort a success, individual leadership is a necessity. Assume that you have just been appointed by your director to be the project manager for CASE tool implementation. Some experimental applications of CASE technology have been conducted with mixed results. Your director says to you, "We really need to get into rapid application development. We know enough about CASE technology, and with a little research we can get a tool set in here fairly quickly. The vice president thinks it's time, and I agree with him."

You realize that CASE tools and rapid application development cannot be successful in your organization without the other FUSION dimensions of IE and JAD, but what is your first step? How do you go about designing a FUSION plan, getting consensus on its objectives and strategy, building commitment to it, and then managing FUSION implementation?

Getting Started: Confirming Executive Support

You have to start by getting support from the head of the systems organization. Your director represents only one section of the total systems group. Without executive sponsorship from the key systems executive, your planning effort may fail. You and your director must sit down with the vice president to discuss how FUSION implementation can help the systems organization to achieve its goals and objectives and to resolve difficult issues and problems. This initial commitment and objective setting activity is critical. It provides the charter to start the FUSION implementation project and to integrate it into the total business plan for the organization. Make sure to have the following:

- Agreement on the part of the vice president and your boss that the need for CASE tools cannot be addressed without also addressing the other two dimensions of FUSION.
- A commitment to the development of a FUSION implementation plan using a breakthrough project.
- A direct reporting relationship for you in your role as FUSION implementation project manager to the vice president for implementation plan development and initiation.
- A meeting date to review the completed plan to gain the vice president's final approval.

- A commitment from the vice president to assign the right people (at your request) to participate on the team to conduct research and perform an internal assessment; to make others available to participate in the breakthrough project; and to provide sufficient budget to get to the final approval planning step.
- A letter with the vice president's signature chartering the FUSION implementation project and requesting that all managers and staff cooperate with the planning effort.

Without the formal face-to-face support of the key systems executive, your work may be easily derailed by some short or long term crisis. Budget can get reallocated, activities can be postponed, and personnel resources can evaporate. You are asking the vice president to empower you and others in the organization to retool the manufacturing operation of systems design and development. That is a big investment. It will, in the long term, profoundly affect the total operation. You know it, and the vice president and your boss should know it too.

Getting the Right People Involved

Once the FUSION implementation charter is established, you must create a strong implementation team. Those who should participate are those who will be most affected by FUSION, both systems professionals and members of the various user communities. Team members and breakthrough project participants should have a stake in the outcome. The people who participate in the planning and support of the implementation effort must represent all of the powerful and influential segments of the systems organization. All hierarchial levels should be represented as well. The individuals included should be respected and influential members of their own groups and should know the larger organization well, including its established system life cycle, development standards, actual work practices, and culture. These individuals should have experience in different life cycle components, including customer support. They should also be familiar with any productivity experiments with IE, CASE, or JAD that might have been conducted by their own work groups.

Participants should be willing to put in the time required to develop the FUSION implementation plan. You do not want people who are resistant to the idea of FUSION. Skeptics are welcome, but not those individuals who feel threatened by change. In addition, you should look for individuals with good communication and listening skills, as well as a good sense of the basic organization structure and strategic direction of the business.

Team members may participate on a part time or full time basis. People may participate in research and assessment activities intensely for limited periods of time, perhaps for two to six weeks. After the plan is delivered, these people may return to their regular jobs or to new ones depending on the implementation strategy recommended. As a result, you may need the support of as few as two (but probably closer to eight) team members. The breakthrough workshop project will expand participation to at least twenty.

You may wish to have an outside consultant coordinate and facilitate the team's activities. An outsider can be the catalyst an organization needs, and generally the cachet attached to hiring a consultant can add importance to the perception of the team's work. "They're paying real money to get the plan developed," the theory goes. "They must be serious." In addition, an outside consultant can provide an objective view of the organization and provide feedback to the team to keep members on track.

You, your director and the vice president may decide to create an infrastructure to support the FUSION implementation process. If an infrastructure is established (such as the one created for the complex, decentralized organization previously discussed), those people who sit on the task force(s) can be a great resource. They may nominate themselves or others to participate in the breakthrough project or to participate on the implementation team.

Preparing the FUSION Implementation Team

Once the team members are selected, you should begin to meet together to develop the team as a functioning group. The activities conducted in this readiness building stage should include:

- Defining and reaching consensus on FUSION values.
- Developing team communication and operations rules.
- Defining planning objectives.
- Educating and training participants in FUSION dimensions.
- Developing a schedule, roles, and accountabilities for plan development.

Defining and reaching consensus on FUSION values.   Team members must look at what they value and what the implementation of FUSION will mean to their own values and those of the organization. The greater the consistency between the value sets, the easier FUSION implementation work will be. The greater the discrepancy between those value sets, the more work FUSION implementation will involve since behavior is driven by what we believe, our values. If the organization has not traditionally valued user involvement, for example, FUSION implementation must address that value discrepancy. Team members must understand and embrace FUSION values before they are able to give their full support to the implementation effort.

Developing team communication and operations rules.   Successful teams should spend some time when they first get together to learn how to:

- Work together.
- Utilize each other's strengths.
- Set up ways to communicate effectively, raise issues and resolve conflicts.

Ideally, team members should be co-located. This enhances the quality of their work as well as their ability to move quickly and reach consensus. If they cannot be co-located, then a special attempt must be made to ensure that sufficient contact takes place and that team members see themselves as an interdependent unit.

Defining planning objectives. It is obvious that the primary objective of the planning effort is to create a FUSION implementation plan that will be supported and funded by the executive sponsor. However, there are other important objectives that should not be overlooked. These include:

- Building a partnership relationship between the systems and user communities.
- Building commitment and acceptance to the changes that will be introduced by the transition to FUSION.
- Increasing the organization's knowledge and increasing individual interest in IE, JAD, and CASE at all levels within the organization.
- Developing a positive image for FUSION and its dimensions of IE, JAD, and CASE throughout the organization.

Educating and training participants in FUSION dimensions. To ensure that all team members have a sufficient level of knowledge about FUSION, the team should get their basic education as a group and then divide into small groups of two or three to pursue more in-depth knowledge. For example, the team as a whole might begin by reading this book and attending one or two seminars in information engineering, JAD, and CASE concepts. Then the team could divide responsibilities for in-depth education, with one small group studying IE, another JAD, and a third CASE.

Developing a schedule, roles and accountabilities for plan development. Finally, the team will need to develop a fully detailed action schedule and define each member's roles and accountabilities for conducting the research and assessment work and managing the breakthrough project.

Conducting an Internal Environmental Assessment

With the team educated, you are now ready to identify the problems, issues and opportunities that must be anticipated and addressed in the FUSION implementation plan. The discoveries made in the internal assessment will result in modifications to the organization environment and the development of a strategy to support change management throughout the organization. Some of this work may be accomplished through the breakthrough project research step, but the team may wish to expand upon that work. The formal steps for internal assessment include:

- Creating an assessment methodology.
- Identifying interviewees and preparing data collection materials.
- Conducting the assessment.
- Analyzing findings to identify implementation needs.

Creating an assessment methodology.   The way in which the implementation team conducts the assessment will determine the quality of the information gathered. The nature of the assessment process will also have an impact on the way the FUSION implementation team is viewed by the rest of the organization. People will equate FUSION with the perceptions they have of the FUSION team, and because one of the FUSION planning objectives is to build enthusiasm and interest in FUSION, it is important that the team utilize a marketing orientation in its assessment work.

The construction of the assessment methodology consists of setting the scope of the assessment, selecting assessment interviewees, and selecting appropriate information gathering vehicles. In creating this methodology, the team will determine what should be assessed, who should be involved in the assessment, and how the assessment will be conducted.

Identifying interviewees and preparing data collection materials.   Questionnaires alone are not sufficient for the data gathering that must take place during phase one of the implementation plan, nor is this technique personal enough to support the marketing orientation that FUSION implementation requires. Instead, a combination of one-on-one interviews and focus group sessions is recommended as the primary source for organizational information. Selecting the right interviewees for the assessment process is critical to obtaining valid and comprehensive results. It is not necessary to interview everyone. Interviewees should represent the diversity of opinion within the organization, the political influences at work, and different interest groups among the population as a whole. Clearly, the individuals selected should also be knowledgeable. It is important to remember that the process works two ways. Individuals who feel that the interview or focus group experience was worthwhile will probably share this feeling with their colleagues and add credibility to the assessment process.

To identify interviewees, the team should generate an initial list of candidates using the selection guide in Figure 7.5. The team may wish to ask the executive sponsor and his direct reports for nominations and then add names to that list as required to ensure that the organization population is fully represented.

1. Identify at least five major user groups. Select interviewees from each group at all levels who interact with the systems organization.

2. Identify five to ten major systems project teams and select interviewees from all levels.

3. Identify interviewees from the following systems groups: data administration, database administration, systems training, development center, systems planning, capacity planning, and production operations.

4. Identify key systems executives to serve as interviewees.

5. Identify interviewees from projects that have utilized FUSION dimensions on an experimental or on-going basis.

6. Identify other individuals with a particular contribution to make such as a marketing expert or individuals who have had successful experience implementing other significant changes within the organization.

Figure 7.5   Informant selection guidelines.

It is best to ask interviewees to participate in a formal invitation letter from the executive sponsor. They should also be contacted personally by an implementation team member. Follow up letters to confirm attendance at the interview and thank you letters after completion of the assessment are also recommended.

The scope of the internal assessment is the examination of relevant organization issues. Data collection questionnaires should be structured to collect information about these important areas:

• Organization structure and accountabilities
• Resource levels and responsibilities
• Life cycle standards and deliverables
• Formal and informal policies, procedures and work practices
• User/systems relationships and project team structures
• Attitudes toward change
• Management values, philosophies and work pressures
• IE, JAD, and CASE knowledge, skills and experience

Conducting the assessment.   With effective scheduling and utilization of implementation team members, data collection should be completed within one to two weeks. Unless the organization is extremely large, the entire assessment should not take more than four or five weeks. When assessments extend beyond this time, people can become frustrated and lose interest. It is counterproductive

1.   Find a quiet, comfortable room in which to conduct the interview. Make certain that there are no working telephones available. It is best to select a room in the territory of the interviewees. Do not use individual offices, however, unless no other space is available and telephone calls can be screened out.

2.   Limit the time of the interviews to no more than one hour for one-on-one interviews and no more than two hours for focus group interviews.

3.   Use a prepared set of ten to twelve open ended questions in order to direct the interview, ensure consistency of data collection across interviews, and avoid getting off the topic.

4.   Questions should be carefully focused and neither too broad nor too specific. They should not be designed to evaluate or intimidate the informant. They should be neutral and not designed to elicit a predetermined response. Questions should be tested ahead of time.

5.   Introduce yourself and describe the purpose of the interview before beginning questioning.

6.   Listen to interviewee responses and ask for clarification wherever necessary. Ask for examples to back up general statements.

7.   Employ communication skills such as active listening and rephrasing to test your comprehension of what is said.

8.   Balance your listening and note taking activities to enhance personal interaction. If possible, two team members should conduct an interview, one to ask questions and one to take notes.

9.   At the completion of the interview, thank interviewees for their time. Get permission to check back for issue clarification and make sure that you have their phone numbers.

Figure 7.6   Guidelines for one-on-one and focus group interviews.

to get bogged down in data collection. In addition, it is important to identify any relevant documentation that should be reviewed. This can be done before, during or after the scheduled interviews and focus groups. Guidelines for interviews are provided in Fig. 7.6.

In some situations the team may not be able to conduct in person interviews due to geographical location and the expense of traveling. Telephone conference call interviews can be substituted for face-to-face interviews. These interviews can be supplemented with (but not substituted by) written questionnaires and a review of existing formal documentation.

One-on-One Interviews.   The one-on-one interview is the simplest and most basic information gathering technique, involving the interviewee responding to questions posed by the interviewer. It is used most frequently with key executives and in situations where an interviewee has unique or especially private information.

Focus Group Interviews. The focus group interview was originally a market research vehicle. It is used with small groups of people to elicit in-depth information and opinions. The focus group generally consists of a small group of participants and a facilitator. It meets for at most three hours. A provocative question is used to start a lively conversation among the participants. The facilitator's role is to control the conversation and ensures that it stays on track. He should not encourage the expression of conflict, but neither should he use the focus group as an occasion for consensus building. It is primarily an opportunity for generating and exploring ideas without judging them.

Questionnaires. Questionnaires can be used as a supplementary data collection technique, but they cannot be used alone because they do not provide sufficiently detailed information. In addition, when one of the objectives of the implementation project team is to model the behavior of FUSION, it is important to demonstrate direct involvement in research activities. A question on a piece of paper cannot do this. Direct personal contact is a necessity. Questionnaires lend themselves better to statistical analysis than the more subjective data produced by one-on-one interviews and focus groups, but they are unlikely to reveal much about organization culture and values. Questionnaires are best used to supplement personal interviews in order to validate interview results and to gather factual information. The questionnaire should be easy to complete and not too lengthy. It should provide a section for detailed responses as well as multiple choice selections. You may want to ask respondents to provide their names, or, if you think the questions are somewhat controversial, you may want to make this optional. If you use this information gathering format, you should probably expect a return rate of forty to sixty percent.

Documentation Review. The purpose of the documentation review is to obtain background information on the organization and its work practices and to determine what standards have been promulgated and which of these have been adhered to. The review consists of gathering and reading any existing life cycle definition or specification documents, procedure and practice manuals, sample deliverables from actual projects, policy statements, organizational plans, organizational charts, CASE tool documentation, and other related materials. After the review, the team can analyze the differences between formal and actual work practices and FUSION practices. The quantity of documentation reviewed is less important than the quality and relevance of the documentation. Examples of requirements definition projects, design projects, and other project types should be examined for variations and commonalities.

Analyzing findings to identify implementation needs. In analyzing interview and questionnaire data, the team should search for response patterns and distinctive issues. All of the responses to each question should be gathered together and reviewed in order to understand the full range of organization opinion on each issue. The results of the assessment may be organized into the following categories:

- Organizational structure and accountabilities
- Resource levels and responsibilities
- Life cycle standards and deliverables
- Formal and informal policies, procedures, and work practices
- Relationships between user and systems groups and possible changes to project team structures
- Attitudes toward change
- Management philosophy and values
- IE, JAD, and CASE knowledge and skills

This information defines the extent of the changes the organization will need to make in order for FUSION to be successfully implemented.

Techniques for Marketplace Research

Researching the marketplace in order to select the most appropriate IE methodology, JAD technique, and CASE tools is an important team activity. This activity will provide your team with the required data to select, create and integrate IE, JAD, and CASE products and services into the systems development life cycle. Some of this work may be conducted in parallel with the internal environmental assessment. However, the internal assessment provides direction for marketplace research, and no final decisions on selection of products and services can be made before the environmental assessment is completed. The assessment may reveal that there are products and services already in use within the organization that may serve as a model for FUSION implementation. It may also reveal certain organization values, policies and practices, or constraints and limitations that may steer the team toward or away from certain IE, JAD, and CASE products and services.

The steps for conducting marketplace research include:

- Defining a marketplace research methodology.
- Conducting the research.
- Analyzing research results.

The process of surveying the marketplace for the best products and services must be closely managed. With well over one hundred different CASE products available and many reputable IE and JAD vendors to choose from, it is possible to prolong the survey far beyond what is needed. Encourage team members to focus on those products and services that have the best reputation, the longest history of use, and the best vendor support systems. If your company has experience with FUSION products and services, be sure to include these in your candidate list. Consider products and services for each FUSION dimension independently and then look at how much difficulty might be involved in integrating potential selections. Some vendors offer products and services in more than one dimension. Some have alliances with other vendors. These factors may enhance product compatibility and make integration easier. In addition, talk with other companies that have needs similar to your own, and review books and computer industry trade magazines. After a general review, select two to three vendors for each FUSION dimension for a detailed evaluation.

Research Basics

A marketplace research methodology is developed by defining a set of research criteria, creating a candidate list of products and services, and selecting appropriate data gathering techniques. The methodology should define what will be researched, who will be involved in the research, and how the research will be conducted.

Marketplace research criteria define the baseline for all product and service evaluation and selections. The criteria define those needs of the organization that must be met in each FUSION dimension. The criteria should be limited in number and prioritized by importance. Items that may appear on your criteria list include:

- The ability to customize a product or service to meet the needs of the existing culture and the current life cycle.
- The presence of diagramming techniques, task definitions, language, and deliverables that match those in current use in the organization.
- The likelihood that the product or service will continue to evolve in sophistication over time.
- The ability of the vendor to work with your organization to install and customize the product or service.
- The ability of the vendor to work with your organization to integrate the produce or service with those products and services already in place.
- The internal logic and coherence of the product or service.
- The degree of discipline and self-enforcing rigor provided by the product or service.
- The quality of the training and education provided by the vendor.
- The estimated longevity of the product or service.
- Cost of installation and annual maintenance support.
- Delivery dates available.

There are four principal marketplace research data collection and evaluation techniques. They include:

- Vendor marketing and demonstration meetings
- Visits to working sites
- Baseline project testing
- In-house product or service pilot

In most situations, the first three techniques will be used to narrow the selection to a first choice for each category. The last technique, an in-house pilot, will finalize the decision making. If time, resources and money are available, the first and second product and service choices may be tested as well to obtain a more complete view. Piloting generally is part of phase one activities.

Vendor marketing and demonstration meetings.   This data gathering technique involves a formal presentation by the vendor, a question and answer period, a product demonstration using vendor examples, and a review of appropriate product or service documentation. Your team may be required to sign nondisclosure agreements with the vendor to obtain the information you want. To be most effective, the meeting should be a structured experience. Each vendor should be allotted time to spend with the team. The team should want to get as much information as possible from the meeting.

Therefore, to ensure the success of this meeting:

- Talk with the vendor prior to the meeting. Cover the purpose of the meeting, who will attend, and what the likely outcome will be. Agree to an agenda and provide him with the questions for which your team is seeking answers.
- Make sure you have all the facilities available that the vendor will require.
- Team members should be good listeners. They should be open to new ideas and attempt to create a positive atmosphere. Vendor presentations can provide a powerful learning experience, even when the product or service presented is not appropriate to the particular organization. Team members should take advantage of this educational opportunity.

Visits to working sites.   This technique is generally a second step in the research methodology. The opportunity to talk with those who have used products and services you are considering can be invaluable. Preferably, the team should divide into small groups, and these groups should make two to three hour visits to target sites without the vendor present. Questions for these visits should be developed after vendor presentations. Ten to twelve open ended questions should stimulate the discussion. They should not elicit company confidential or competitive information. Neither should they be designed to intimidate or test your hosts.

Because the visitation site will have a different culture, standards, and organization environment from your own, your hosts' appraisal of a product or service must be seen as somewhat subjective. Focus instead on product capabilities and characteristics of vendor services that are culturally independent. If certain characteristics of the host organization closely resemble your own, however, this can provide you with additional clues as to which products or services may fit that culture best.

Baseline project testing. An important market research technique is the "baseline evaluation project." This project provides a scenario against which each product and service under consideration can be demonstrated and evaluated. If such a project is attempted, the team may want to design a test case project to represent the future project needs of the organization, or the team may utilize an actual project experience (perhaps one noted for its level of difficulty). This will provide a common reference point for evaluation.

A baseline project is best used after a thorough review of available products and services makes it possible to narrow the search to a few finalists, those that best meet the selection criteria for your organization. The vendor is asked to demonstrate the utilization of his product or service on the baseline project. This demonstration should be attended by all team members and should take, depending on the vendor's needs, no more than one day.

To ensure the success of the test, the baseline project should be given to the vendor at least one week prior to the demonstration. He should be able to call a team member for clarification to questions during his preparation time. The vendor should be able to bring additional expertise to the meeting. The meeting should be neutral, but focused on getting information for criteria evaluation.

In-house product or service pilot. The objective of a pilot may be to test a product or service alone or to test the compatibility of two or more products and/or services. Most organizations find it too expensive and time consuming to pilot more than one or two products or services for each FUSION dimension, and this should not be necessary if the products or services to be piloted are carefully selected. Depending on the organization's needs, a thorough evaluation activity for a product or service may require as little as four weeks or as much as six months.

Successful execution of a pilot requires the following:

- Staff that have been well trained in use of the product or service (or strong outside support) to avoid problems associated with the learning curve.
- Project managers and participants who are willing to take part in the pilot.
- Installed and tested products.
- Clear objectives and structured evaluation procedures for the evaluation of the pilot.
- Careful monitoring of resources utilized.

Pilots also have a side benefit. They open the decision making process to a wide variety of people, and by doing so they can build enthusiasm for FUSION and position the organization for change. The implementation team should work closely with vendors throughout this piloting period.

Piloting is particularly beneficial if:

- The organization has no experience with the products or services within a FUSION dimension.
- Support for FUSION products and services needs to be encouraged within the organization.
- Previous negative experiences must be overcome.
- Experimentation can be conducted cost effectively without causing delays that might alienate potential FUSION supporters.
- There are one or more projects where a pilot can have a significant impact on the outcome. It is important, however, that these projects not be so critical that problems in a pilot will spell failure for the entire FUSION effort.

Research Results

In analyzing the data collected from vendor meetings, visits with customers of the products and services, baseline project evaluation and pilot projects, the team should focus on those products and services that rate high on the most heavily weighted selection criteria. The team may use different evaluation techniques ranging from highly scientific mathematical formulas to the development of a general consensus after a discussion of results. In any case, the research data must be consolidated and documented before the analysis can be completed.

The ultimate use of the marketplace research data is to provide information to answer these questions:

- Which products and services should be obtained to support FUSION implementation across the organization?
- Which aspects of the selected products or services must be modified in order to be
  compatible with other selected products and services?
  effectively installed within our organization environment?
- Which aspects of the selected products and services may limit or enhance chances for success when they are implemented in the organization?
- Which aspects of the organization environment should be changed in order to successfully implement the selected products and services?

Planning Ideas

With the environmental readiness assessment and market research completed, the FUSION implementation team has sufficient information to conduct a breakthrough project workshop and to begin to formulate a FUSION implementation plan. To assist the team in preparing for the planning activity, review this list of some of the questions that should be answered as you create the framework for each critical success factor.

Executive Sponsorship and Management Buy-in

- Is there a need for a task force infrastructure during FUSION implementation? Who should participate on the task force? What should the charter of the task force be?
- Are the direct reports to the executive sponsor sufficiently committed to make FUSION implementation possible? What must be done to reinforce their commitment? Where else in the management structure does this commitment issue show itself? Will the executive sponsor take action to remedy any problems? Does the executive sponsor's commitment require reinforcement as well?

FUSION Coordination and Support

- Should the FUSION implementation team continue on as the coordination and support team for implementation? Should a FUSION Center be permanently established before the proliferation phase? Should an existing organization (e.g., a development center) take on FUSION Center roles and responsibilities?
- Should the style of the FUSION Center be directive? Consultative? What services should be provided? Should a FUSION facility with specialized JAD rooms be created?
- What outside consulting support should be provided? For how long? Where should consulting efforts be directed?
- Should FUSION be implemented on a project basis or on an organization basis in the start up phase? In the proliferation phase? Are certain types of projects or systems groups better FUSION utilization candidates than others?

Acquisition and Installation of FUSION Products and Services

- Should FUSION products and services be piloted during the start up phase or should purchase decisions be made now? Should more than one product or service be available in each dimension? Should there be a final selection for standard products or services in one or more of the dimensions?
- Should any products or services be developed completely in-house? Are time, talent, and money available to do this adequately? What justifies such an approach?

- Should the products and services be customized before they are installed or after a period of piloting? How should buy-in by line development groups be created during the customization process?
- Should we focus on the in-house development of education and training for the products and services? Should we rely on vendors for this support?

Organization Environmental Modifications

- Should FUSION implementation begin prior to, at the start of, or after organizational structural changes are made? Are such changes really necessary?
- Is the environmental modification process a political as well as a technical exercise? How should line managers and professionals be involved to improve their acceptance of change?
- Should the emphasis be on making the easiest changes first, with more difficult changes instituted over time? Should we "bite the bullet" and make the most difficult changes first?

Marketing and Commitment Building

- Should we focus on individuals or groups? Should there be a formal program approach for commitment building?
- Are distinctive commitment building approaches needed for different management levels, special groups, and/or individuals?
- Should marketing and commitment building activities emphasize the innovative nature of FUSION or its easy fit with the organization's culture and historically accepted methods and procedures?

Education and Training

- How should education and training be administered in each implementation phase? Should we use regular training channels or create a special structure for this effort?
- Where can we obtain training in behavioral skills? How should this training be integrated into the technical curriculum?
- How should education and training be timed with FUSION utilization? What is recommended for the education and training mix? Who should get what training and education?
- Should the training and education programs be provided in-house or by external sources?

Change Management Support

- What support must be given to relieve work pressures?
- What support is needed to improve the change management skills of managers and supervisors?
- Must staffing be assumed to be static or can support for change be enhanced by putting the most flexible people in sensitive positions?
- How should change management skills be developed and maintained in managers and supervisors?

FUSION Compatibility with the System Development Life Cycle

- What must be done to package and prepare the new life cycle for distribution? How can this be tied to FUSION marketing and commitment building activities?
- What must be done to pilot the new life cycle? How do we get people involved in using it, and how will we obtain feedback?
- What types of revisions may be necessary before phase II—proliferation of the FUSION life cycle, can begin?

Sometimes a particular planning activity can support more than one critical success factor. As each activity is agreed to, deliverables for the activity, measures of completion, accountabilities for activity completion, and start and end dates should be identified. Some of the activities will be on-going, while others may be performed only once. Some may require extensive preparation and approval, while others may not. Some may require outside expertise, while others may draw on the expertise present within the organization. Your team will want to consider all of these possibilities. Consider the constraints identified in the assessment. Constraints on personnel resources and funding must be addressed in the plan. The plan should also include a monitoring process to ensure task completion, regular review of activities and identification of modifications as required.

It may be politically advantageous for the plan to include options or alternatives from which the infrastructure task forces and/or executive sponsor may choose. By giving these key individuals options (those options that your team agrees can be successful), you enhance the likelihood that the executive sponsor and task force will support the plan.

The creation of a realistic FUSION implementation plan may require extensive discussion with the executive sponsor and his task force, as well as with other key managers within the systems organization who have not participated in the breakthrough project. The FUSION implementation project manager and team members should check with key managers to ensure that the plan will support the business objectives of the organization. Without the agreement of these important individuals, your team may create an exciting FUSION plan that cannot be implemented. It must also be remembered that time will not stand still during the development of the plan. Two to three months may have passed since the FUSION implementation team was chartered. Events or decisions outside the scope of the team's work may impact the final plan. The impact of such changes should be accounted for within the plan.

Packaging Ideas

The completed FUSION implementation plan should be well documented. It should utilize graphics such as Gantt charts, PERT charts, and other visual representations to aid in clarity of presentation. In addition to the FUSION implementation plan itself, the document may contain assessment and research results and an executive summary defining the decisions required for moving forward with implementation, including those related to funding, personnel and time required to make FUSION a success. Because documentation is used to assist in gaining executive sponsor approval for FUSION implementation, it is important that the report contain a valid representation of the organization's needs and a strong presentation of the team's ideas and plans for FUSION implementation.

In defining report content and format, consider your audience. In deciding who will see the report, consider the need for information of the different segments of the audience. Some people will require only an executive summary, while others will require the full report. If appropriate, the report can be presented in a number of different versions.

The level of detail presented is a factor in plan acceptance. Too much detail can make the report unreadable. Too little detail leaves too many questions unanswered. As with any report, this one should be presented in clear language, should be organized in a logical pattern, and should demonstrate a clear focus. Consider too the politics of what is reported. There may be certain language that is appropriate or inappropriate for the organization. This report has an important sales objective. It is to convince its readers of the soundness and practicality of the plan and to gain their commitment to it. Any rhetorical devices that you can use to accomplish this should be included. You may choose to distribute a draft copy of the plan to a short list of key individuals and breakthrough project participants for their review. You will certainly need to show a draft copy to the executive sponsor if you wish to include a cover letter from him in the final distributed edition of the plan.

Although people may nod their heads in agreement with the recommendations of the FUSION implementation plan, the plan is only paper until the key executive, the executive sponsor for FUSION implementation, allocates budget, people, and time for its execution. Then his direct reports and other managers must commit projects, time, and people to support the activities required by the plan. Although seemingly simple, this step can be a political juggernaut for the uninitiated. It will require patience, fortitude, and resilience.

8

Concepts in Managing Change

CHOOSING THE FUTURE

When the FUSION approach is implemented in an organization, it brings with it numerous changes including new technologies, new methods and procedures, and new working relationships. It requires people at all levels of the organization, from top executives to clerks, to make individual and fundamental changes to their technical activities, their communication techniques, their working relationships with people, and their work roles and responsibilities. This personal level of change must be addressed for FUSION to be successful, because only if the people of the organization are willing to adopt FUSION values, will they ensure its ultimate success.

If people do not believe in and highly value the FUSION approach to systems design and development, it will fail. It is their willingness to invest their energy in FUSION implementation, to embrace the changes it brings, and to accept ownership of this new way of doing business that will enable them to reap the rewards promised by FUSION. This level of commitment cannot be created through education and training programs alone, no matter how good those programs might be. "You cannot train anybody to do anything that he does not fundamentally believe in," said Robert Haas, the chairman and CEO of Levi Strauss & Co. when interviewed about his company's efforts to change. If the individual feels lost within the organization, if he sees no unique role for himself, he will lose his commitment to the organization's goals and he will take his skills to another organization.

Much has been said in this volume about the importance of the three elements of FUSION: IE, JAD, and CASE. We cannot afford to forget the human element, however. Without careful attention to this element, the FUSION solution will be rejected. Our attempts to use the traditional approach to systems design and development have revealed some important implementation critical success factors. These attempts have taught us that you cannot dictate to people what they should do and expect them to do it. People cannot be treated like replaceable parts of a machine, with no attention paid to their ideas and values, with no opportunity to make decisions about their work environment. For FUSION to succeed, the people who will be most affected by it, both systems professionals and users, must define what FUSION is and how it should be implemented in a positive, collaborative effort.

We have also learned from our past experience that bureaucratic approval procedures can be so burdensome that they can delay or kill projects no matter what methodology, techniques, and tools are adopted. In a FUSION environment, people must be empowered to make the decisions needed to act quickly. The organization that adopts FUSION will find that it leads to a dissemination of power throughout the systems organization and its project teams. It requires that systems and project managers stop seeing themselves as controllers and enforcers and start seeing themselves as negotiators, communicators, and obstacle removers. They need to give the people who report to them the freedom to act based on their own skills, experience and willingness to be held accountable. The manager, in short, needs to stop seeing himself as an autocrat and start seeing himself as a leader.

FUSION requires that managers model the values and behavior that they want their employees to exhibit. Managers must communicate openly, directly, effectively, and frequently. They must give people permission to disagree, to engage in honest and open discussion. They must encourage risk taking by admitting their own mistakes and accepting the mistakes of others as the price of innovation. They must encourage team work by participating rather than dictating when decisions are required. And they must be willing to commit the time and money required for training people in communication skills, problem solving and decision making techniques, leadership, and team work, as well as the technical knowledge and skills needed for IE, JAD, and CASE.

The traditional systems organization has too often failed to reward managers for their ability to develop their people and create a team work environment. It has rewarded people for getting the job done, no matter what the quality of the product delivered. Too often, reward systems have reinforced the resistance to change, the creation of large, slow moving staff structures, and independent rather than collaborative action. If FUSION is to succeed, managers must be rewarded for taking actions which are supportive of team-based values and cooperative behavior. Measurable objectives that support the new value system must be set by each manager and staff member. Managers should be rewarded for empowering their people, developing their skills and reducing turnover, and for delivering high quality products to satisfied user customers. It is clear that such fundamental value and behavioral changes cannot take place overnight, just as the new ideas, tools, and techniques represented by IE, JAD, and CASE cannot become a way of life overnight. The more top management does to promote, encourage and model these new values and behavior, however, the more quickly the people within the organization will respond.

The values of the FUSION environment are best exhibited in an organization where:

- All levels of the systems organization and the user groups they serve are involved in defining and implementing FUSION.
- People performing basic business functions are empowered to make decisions regarding how those functions will be performed based upon their experience, skills, and willingness to be held accountable.
- There is no discrepancy between what the organization says it values and what it actually values and rewards. Managers coach and counsel their people and encourage risk taking, collaboration and team work. People take on objectives that support the new value system, are held accountable for achieving those objectives, and are rewarded when they do so.
- The organization invests in developing its people both technically and behaviorally. It recognizes that their commitment is the most important element in the success of FUSION. Without highly skilled, dedicated people at all levels of the organization, FUSION will not become an accepted way of designing and developing systems, users will continue to be disappointed, and the systems organization will have missed an opportunity to make a strategic difference within the corporation.

THE CHAOS OF CHANGE

As executives providing the leadership for FUSION and as managers and supervisors charged with making FUSION work within the organization, we must prepare ourselves to work with individuals and groups of people. No matter how well we plan for a major change like FUSION, there will be an increased level of uncertainty and stress during the transition period. The confusion and disorder that can result from this change may affect productivity as the old way of doing business is replaced by new work methods and procedures. Change may be easy for some, those who are flexible and open to new ideas. Others may have great difficulty with change or even be traumatized by it. They may be unable to work in a new environment and find it impossible to adapt to new job requirements.

We cannot treat everyone in the organization as if they were the same. This would be like a doctor prescribing the same drug for all his patients no matter what their symptoms. As managers of change, we need to know how to diagnose and respond to different reactions to change. We must understand three concepts—how people think, how people respond to threats, and the stages of accepting change. With an understanding of this framework, managers can begin to build the skills needed to assist individuals in dealing with change and to work with others in the organization to construct and implement successful change plans.

HOW PEOPLE THINK: THE THEORETICAL PERSPECTIVE

There has long been a debate among theorists as to whether it is possible to influence the behavior of individuals by modifying the attitudes and values that drive that behavior. One school of thought maintains that attitudes and values are not directly tied to behavior and that we cannot influence how people act by addressing their thoughts and beliefs. Our experience does not bear this theory out. We believe that attitudes and values, the way we think and how we judge, are clearly linked to human behavior. If we intend to influence human behavior, then, we must take individual attitudes and values into account. The more closely personal values are aligned with organizational values, the easier it is for the individual to commit his energies to his work and to accept personal responsibility for his actions.

The work of Robert S. Hartman and other philosophers and psychologists in the discipline of axiology, the philosophy of values, has provided us with systematic and predictable way of measuring how people make the judgments that underlay their behavior. Over the past twenty-five years, Hartman's work has offered important insight into the patterns of thought that lead to an understanding of the individual's motivation, his ability to perform and his commitment to performance. Hartman believes that individuals and work groups must be aware of and understand:

- How they think.
- Which values and attitudes are positive and helpful and which may be negative or blocking.
- How those values and attitudes contribute to the potential for success in their jobs.

Then they are better able to make self-determining decisions regarding what is needed to be more effective. With this information, work groups and project teams can employ their strengths and develop their potential to move faster, more effectively and with greater commitment to success.

Some individuals find it easy to change; for others the change process can be difficult, even traumatic. Often, people who find the change process difficult are those who believe that they have no choices, that their values and ideas are permanently fixed. This is a misconception. Consider the way an individual's values and thought patterns change as he grows from adolescence to old age. Ideas

OUTER WORLD	INNER WORLD
Empathy Accept others as unique	**Self-esteem** Accept self as unique
Practical Thinking Make comparative judgments	**Role Awareness** Appreciate one's role
System Judgment Accept structure, ideas and order	**Self-direction** Have inner principles that drive behavior

Figure 8.1 Hartman value and thinking structure.

about the importance of sex, security, money and companionship change through the acquisition of life experience. At the cultural level, (the societal or organizational level), values can change over time too. This can be seen in the shifts in American social values over the last twenty-five years. Attitudes about such issues as the role of women in society, the nature of the family, and the concept of racial and ethnic identity all demonstrate the volatility of our values over time.

It is possible to explain the dynamic nature of our thinking by looking at the two perspectives through which the individual defines the world (Fig. 8.1). One is the outer world—the factors that define how we view that which is outside ourselves. The elements of this outer world include empathy, practical judgment, and system judgment. By this we mean the ability to:

- See and accept others as they are. Assigning value to others without respect to what they do or how well they do it.
- Make comparisons from a practical perspective. Judge one thing or person against another. We value others in terms of their roles, functions and relationships.
- Understand the structure, authority, and concepts of the world around us. Decide "what ought to be" in relation to an ideal or the world around us.

The second world is the inner world of the self, focusing on how we perceive ourselves. The elements of this inner world include self-esteem, role awareness, and self-direction. By this we mean the ability to:

- See and accept ourselves as unique human beings without comparison against others or an ideal. Seeing ourselves as infinitely valuable while acknowledging our strengths and weaknesses.

- Appreciate our role in society and our social contribution. View ourselves in relation to our functions in life or our work, its meaning and usefulness. In this way, we present a certain image to the rest of the world.
- See where we ought to go and make a commitment to do so. Here we measure ourselves against an internal measure of perfection. Our inner principles, concepts and ideas of who we ought to be drive us into the future.

These six elements tell us about the structure of our thinking, about how we make decisions. The degree to which each individual understands the particular structure of his own thought is directly related to the effectiveness of his ability to act. Knowledge of how we think and what we value helps us to clarify our biases and identify specific areas that need further development. Is our thinking clear or fuzzy? Is our thinking balanced across the dimensions or is the structure skewed toward one or more elements? The answers to these questions can help us to identify the values and attitudes which have potential for promoting positive behavior and those which have the potential for promoting blocking or negative behavior. When we compare these potentials against a model thinking structure of high performers for our job, we can identify areas in need of development. These areas represent important opportunities for growth. When we compare these potentials against the potentials of others in our group or team, we can take advantage of each individual's strengths and improve working relationships among the whole group. This will help us to eliminate the frustration that results from unnecessary conflicts, mismatches in tasks and abilities, and futile attempts to work in areas in which we are not well suited.

FUSION Applications

Studies that focus on systems professionals seem to indicate that the values and thought patterns common in this group are not consistent with an open or welcoming attitude toward change. The work of J. D. Couger and R. A. Zowacki describes the typical personality type in this group as strong on analytical ability but not particularly flexible or adaptable. They suggest that the thought patterns that make an individual a talented computer systems developer are the same thought patterns that make it difficult for him to accept change. These thought patterns include:

- A need to see the world as systematic and well structured.
- A perspective that favors practical judgment and rational, logical thinking.
- An emphasis on facts; a tendency to view people and things in terms of black and white.

People who value structure, order, and rules in their environment also generally want what is expected of them clearly defined. Without these externally imposed expectations, many systems professionals and others like them have difficulty setting their own goals and direction. In addition to high-level goals, they also prefer that an external authority define such aspects of their work as the schedule of daily activities, office assignments, and procedural routines. But these same people who like structure do not want to be dictated to. They want work objectives to be explained to them, and they want knowledgeable direction. They are likely to view changes in routine procedures with suspicion unless they are fully explained. Ambiguous, ill defined, or generalized directions may confuse and frustrate them. If a request or command fails to fit within the well structured framework of their expectations, systems professionals are likely to react in a negative way. They become "stuck," unable to take action. If such an individual is asked to do something different for a customer, he may react by saying, "But, I've never worked that way before. I don't think that's part of my job." These people need a well-defined structure in order to be comfortable in a world that they see as ambiguous, even threatening. Changes that affect any aspect of that world can be difficult for them to incorporate into their tightly structured perspective.

In addition to their tightly structured world view, systems professionals are characterized by a preference for deductive thinking over inductive thinking. These individuals prefer the step-by-step reasoning process embodied in decision trees and data flow diagrams to more open or intuitive approaches such as idea generation and free association, and their education in math and computer science reinforces this bias. Much of organizational life, however, including the politics and sociology of organization communication and decision making, cannot be explained through an appeal to deductive reasoning. This confuses and frustrates systems professionals who are reluctant to accept and integrate the irrational aspects of the organization into their world view.

As a result systems professionals are inhibited in their ability to manage project teams, work groups, and larger organizational units. Neither is it easy for them to work with users whose thought patterns are more likely to favor inductive reasoning than deductive reasoning. When users are unable to convey their needs in specific terms, systems people get frustrated. This in turn may generate hostility on the part of users who see the systems professionals as unwilling to listen and uninterested in helping them meet their needs. Because systems professionals often do not have the skills required to help users articulate their needs or translate them into a tightly structured design, they can misjudge users and assume that they do not know what they want.

From the viewpoint of many systems professionals, the world is made up of unambiguous facts. It is a black and white world, with little or no room for ambiguity. Anything that suggests the presence of a gray element, a "maybe" or a "sometimes," is a source of frustration. This is understandable. From a programming point of view, things either are or they are not. Grays cannot exist. Grays cannot be programmed.

This black and white perspective has caused systems professionals to underestimate the difficulty involved in creating expert systems and artificial intelligence systems. They expect these systems to serve as simple decision machines that operate on clearly defined, even mathematically precise, logic. However, when they attempt to capture the judgments of experts in the design of these systems, they discover that much of the decision making that is performed by these experts is intuitive. This is not to suggest that computer professionals in general are not intelligent. On the contrary, it is just to suggest that their particular intelligence is bounded by a world view that makes it difficult for many of them to appreciate the value of intuition and to be patient when confronted with ambiguity.

In the terminology of today's popular psychology studies, individuals who choose a computer systems career are "left brained," while their colleagues in the marketing and personnel departments are "right brained." This implies that systems people are generally analytical, deductive, and linear in their thinking while their colleagues are creative, intuitive, and holistic. Their ability to adapt, to "go with the flow" and to maintain their equilibrium despite the ambiguity present in their environment is somewhat limited. As a result, their ability to adapt to the changes that accompany the transition to a FUSION environment will also be limited. To assist them in making this transition, top executives and managers must offer leadership and training to provide the opportunity for positive personal change.

HOW PEOPLE RESPOND TO THREATS: THE THEORETICAL PERSPECTIVE

Depending on the individual, change can be threatening or stimulating. Each person interprets change differently based upon his own values and needs. It is possible to influence this interpretation by using external incentives, but this is not always easy to do. A monetary incentive or an opportunity for peer recognition may mean little to someone who is threatened with the loss of his work group affiliation or the loss of his job. External disincentives can be even less effective. The threat of the loss of status or financial compensation intensifies the negative atmosphere and can cause an already volatile situation to erupt. People cannot be coerced into change. It may be possible in the short term to coerce them into falling in line, but in the long term they will retaliate through acts of sabotage ranging from passive resistance to outright aggressive destruction. We need to give individuals the right to choose whether to accept a changed environment or to remove themselves from it. Along the way, they need support and counseling to assist them in seeing opportunities as well as threats.

In order to help people better accept change and to reduce their perception of change as invariably threatening, we have to understand the different ways that individuals react to threats. The work of Abraham Maslow, a leading industrial psychologist, is helpful here. Maslow developed a behavioral model that describes the multidimensional character of human needs. After years of study and analysis,

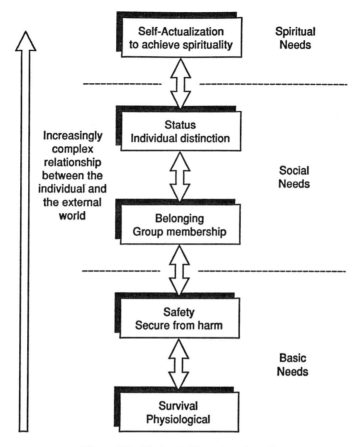

Figure 8.2 Maslow's hierarchy of needs.

he concluded that the individual has a hierarchy of needs, and that the individual will always work to attain or maintain a certain level of need gratification. Further, he states that if a person has a need level that cannot be met, or if his need level is threatened once it is satisfied, the individual will be forced to retreat to a lower need level (Fig. 8.2). Maslow concludes that if an individual cannot meet his most basic needs, then he cannot move upwards to achieve higher, more social need levels.

One of our most basic needs as human beings is the need for survival. This includes the basic physiological needs for food, air, sex, elimination, and sensing. Deprived of these needs, a person cannot care about such higher needs as the need for friendship, social status, or personal fulfillment. Some people live much of their lives without consciously addressing the need for survival. These fortunate individuals find that their basic needs are met with little exertion on their part. Others work very hard to meet these needs, and, indeed all of us eventually come face to face with them when we are forced to confront the consequences of a terminal illness, a natural catastrophe, an accident, or financial reversals.

To understand how the need to survive can overtake even the most fortunate individual, consider what happens to your thinking processes and abilities when you have to go to the bathroom but are prevented from doing so because you are in the car caught in traffic or in a meeting where you cannot leave. Your survival need for elimination becomes an obsession. You cannot pay attention to what is going on around you. You don't care what others are saying or doing. You just want to find relief. At this point, your physiology takes over and any higher needs you might be involved in satisfying are ignored until this survival need is met.

If the need for survival can be met, the individual can then attempt to meet a new need, the need for safety and protection from bodily harm. This concept of safety includes the need for a job that will supply an income that can be used to obtain a safe shelter, food to eat, and other necessities above the survival level. If a person's job is threatened, his basic need for security is threatened, and the threat of job loss need not be real for someone to feel threatened. Many people who hold very secure jobs feel threatened with little provocation, while others whose jobs are much less secure may not feel threatened until directly confronted by the prospect.

People who feel their jobs are threatened are not likely to be concerned about their work group, its achievements, or the morale of the organization. They are likely to be fixated on keeping their jobs. But their reaction to the threat may not be what is expected. Some people may react by working harder to prove their worth. Other people react by shutting down and becoming nonproductive because they feel the decision is out of their control. Some may become angry and act out their anger, thus increasing their chances of being dismissed, or they may devote their time to mobilizing an employee action to save jobs.

With the needs for survival and safety met, the individual is capable of attending to social needs. The need to belong, to be part of a group, is one of these needs. Everyone, at some level, needs to be part of a group. Primary group membership in our society is defined by the family, but work and professional groups, political and religious groups, and play or recreational groups are also important. In the absence of a family group, people may turn to one of the other groups as their primary group to meet their need to belong. Even the most private individual belongs to at least one group in which he claims membership.

Belonging defines a person's need for love, affection, attention and for being part of something greater than himself. Membership in the group can be formal or informal. Membership can be pleasant or may include conflict and worry. It is the membership that is important. People vary greatly in their need for membership and belonging. Those people who are most "other people" oriented may belong to ten or more groups. Those people who are least "people oriented" may rely on only one group, their family or their religious group, for meeting this need.

The belonging need is threatened when a person's membership in a group is threatened. A divorce that ends a family membership group, a move to a new city that threatens membership in an informal circle of neighbors or friends, or the loss of a job within a particular work group are all examples of threats to belonging. The reaction to a threat to one's sense of group membership may be minor. The individual may turn to another group for support. However, some individuals will suffer more severe feelings of rejection. They may suffer a loss of self-esteem because they perceive themselves as being rejected by others. Feeling themselves isolated, some will become passive, while others will become angry. Some may be mobilized to action.

For some people, just belonging to a group is sufficient to meet their social needs. For others, an additional need may surface once the need for group identification has been satisfied. This is the need to see one's self as unique and different from others within the group and, in association with that need, to obtain the approval of the perceived power structure. The need to be seen as special can be very important to some individuals, as is the need to gain the respect and recognition of others. Many of our motivational systems in business build upon this need to gain recognition. Promotions and sales awards are designed to give such recognition, to demonstrate that the individual has earned the approval of the organization. Nonmonetary status rewards like big offices, limousines, or a name on the letterhead all confer individual recognition.

When people do not have high status needs, such reward systems fail to produce the expected results. Despite the promotion, the money and the corner office, some people will decide to leave the job, act with disloyalty, or oppose the power structure. Business executives frequently make the mistake of assuming that everyone has the same need for status and recognition that they have. Some people just do not care what others think. They find their satisfaction in internal values, not those defined by society.

When an individual's need for status is threatened, he may suffer rejection and depression, or he may protest and fight the action that threatens him. A reorganization that flattens the organization hierarchy, changes in reporting relationships, or shifts in authority levels can all threaten status. A facility reorganization that does away with private offices and replaces them with cubicles can threaten visual evidence of special status. If a reward system that measures job performance based on the number of subordinates managed by an individual is changed to judge instead quantity and quality of work delivered, this can seriously threaten the status of the individuals involved.

When a person moves beyond the external environment, the social structure, and approval and reward systems, he starts to look within his own self for definition instead of looking to others. Such a person is expressing the need for self-actualization. Self-actualization occurs when a person has achieved a "oneness" with his environment. In this state, his external environment no longer plays a role in his need to demonstrate achievement. When a person is self-actualized, he takes an action because that action is in perfect harmony with his inner beliefs and thoughts. He does not act to gain anyone's approval or to prove anything to himself. People often speak of moments or occasions of self-actualization. Whether it occurs when camping in the wilderness or when speaking in front of a crowd of several hundred people, this moment can provide an individual with a feeling of completeness and contentment, a total satisfaction with who he is and what he is doing. Many eastern religions such as Buddhism focus on the attainment of self-actualized states, directing followers on a path that leads away from external distractions and toward inner peace.

Some people may not recognize the need for self-actualization within themselves. Others who do recognize this need may yet not be able to achieve a constant state of self-actualization. Generally, this is a state that is only attained for limited moments in time. Those people in whom the need is particularly pronounced are often also those who are curious about life in general. They are interested in discovering new types of personal expression to serve as vehicles for self-actualization. Threats to this need arise when such opportunities are taken away. For example, if a sailor who loves the water can no longer go to sea, his inner self is threatened. The same may be true of a programmer who loves his work but who is told that he is to use a code generator to write code. He may view this innovation as a threat to his need for self-actualization.

The needs for personal safety and survival are basic needs. When faced with threats to the satisfaction of these needs, people can react dramatically and irrationally. However, the next level of needs, the social needs of belonging and status, are in part determined by the culture in which an individual lives. Some cultures, such as the Japanese culture, stress group membership and place a higher value on the community than on the individual. Other cultures, such as the American culture, put more emphasis on the individual, his personal achievement and his ability to exist independently of others. Neither emphasis is good or bad. A culture can change and evolve over time because the society's values change. By looking at the values of our society and at our own individual values, we can better understand our social and self-actualization needs.

FUSION Applications

Maslow's work teaches us that while different need levels surface at different times, lower, more fundamental needs tend to overpower higher needs. People are all different, however, and they experience different needs with different intensities. It is important, therefore, that we recognize that individuals have different needs and that we understand when and why these needs are threatened. Once we do so, we can be more effective in managing change within the systems organization. We will consequently be in a better position to protect our investment in people, the most important element in FUSION implementation.

The changes that FUSION brings to the organization in the form of new skill requirements, new job descriptions, and new working relationships will be seen as threatening by many people. Some will view the changes brought by FUSION as a threat to their job security. They may believe that their skills will not be needed any longer. Others may worry about their status within the organizational hierarchy. They may see themselves as being stripped of power and authority. Some may see their need to belong to a community threatened. They may feel a strong sense of belonging in the community as it is presently constituted, but be uncertain if they can find a place in a new type of group environment.

These individuals may reveal their concerns through the exhibition of certain types of behavior or through what they say, but these indications are only a warning signal. In order to understand the nature of the threat as perceived by a given individual, it is necessary to look further. Let's consider an example. In the days following a meeting at which a commitment to implement a FUSION approach was announced, the systems manager noticed that several of his programmers were displaying unusual hostility. One of his most experienced programmers was unavailable whenever a meeting was called. When approached, she seemed to be uncharacteristically sharp with other members of the staff. She seemed angry. Wanting to understand what was bothering her, the manager stopped by her office. He described what he had observed in the past few days, saying, "You seem to be out of sorts this week. You've snapped at several people on the staff and you haven't returned calls from our most important customer. It just isn't like you. What's wrong? How can I help?" The programmer was clearly hesitant. But finally she replied, "I just don't know what's going to happen to me with all these changes. I've worked hard to establish myself as the lead programmer. Now with all the changes, I just feel like I'm going to have to start all over again."

It was clear that the programmer in this example felt threatened by the changes that FUSION would bring. The typical systems manager in such a situation might offer some sort of noncommittal reassurance such as, "Don't worry. There will always be a place for you." But this is not enough. If this type of valued individual is to be won over to the side of FUSION, more must be done. First, the systems manager must discover as much as possible about the nature of the programmer's perception of the threat. One way to do this is by further questioning. He might ask, for example, "Do you feel that your role as group leader might disappear? That you might be left with no job?" What he may discover if he asks such questions is that his programmer is not afraid that her job will be lost, but that the status of her job will be diminished. "I don't know where I'll fit in," may well be what is on her mind. Once he understands that she has a high need for status and recognition, he can address those needs directly. Pat reassuring phrases will not help, but a specific discussion about her new role in the organization may make all the difference in obtaining her enthusiastic support for the change.

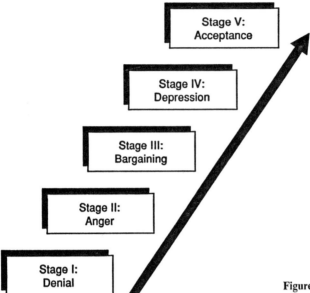

Figure 8.3 Kubler-Ross's stages to the acceptance of change.

THE STAGES TO ACCEPTING CHANGE:
THE THEORETICAL PERSPECTIVE

Although the changes brought by the implementation of FUSION may threaten individual needs for safety, belonging, status and self-actualization, they should in no way threaten the individual's physiological need to survive. Nevertheless, if we look at that most ultimate and traumatic change that threatens our need for survival, our own death, we can learn something about how we come to accept change and how we progress from the initial knowledge of this threat to the full acceptance of it. Dr. Elizabeth Kubler-Ross, a psychiatrist who formulated her theory in working with people who faced death prematurely due to terminal illness, identified five distinct stages through which people must pass before they can accept death (Fig. 8.3). Kubler-Ross found that an individual's ability to pass through these stages and reach a level of acceptance often depends on how other people react to the ill person's behavior. In other words, Kubler-Ross found that friends, family, doctors, and nurses could inhibit or enhance a person's ability to accept death. This important analysis of the individual's response to life's most difficult challenge can help to illuminate the difficulties people face when confronted with less traumatic, but still significant, challenges in their work environment. Kubler-Ross's theory can help us to identify actions that managers and peers can take in dealing with people suffering from the difficult changes that may accompany the implementation of FUSION. What managers say and how they act can make a great difference in helping people to adapt to the new culture FUSION brings to the systems organization. Reviewing Kubler-Ross's description of the stages of response to the ultimate threat of death can help us to understand the individual's response to the changes brought by FUSION, and this understanding, in turn, can guide us in the development of a plan for managing that response.

Stage 1: Denial.   The first step in the acceptance of change occurs when the individual learns of the change that he must expect. According to Kubler-Ross, the individual's first reaction is denial. In this stage, the individual simply refuses to believe that the change is happening. Denial can be total or partial, but the more traumatic the change, the greater the threat and the stronger the initial reaction of denial is likely to be. Kubler-Ross also found that the more traumatic the change, the more significant is the manner in which the change is communicated. If the communicator is uncomfortable talking about the change, he will project those feelings onto the person to whom he is delivering the message. Consequently, if news of a difficult change is being communicated, it is important for the communicator to consider how the message is presented. If he assures the affected individual that everything possible will be done to make the change easier, this is likely to have a positive effect.

Denial plays an important role in the acceptance of change. Denial acts as a buffer that diminishes the effect of news that is unexpected and shocking. It allows a person to collect himself, and with time mobilize less radical defenses. In assisting the individual to deal with change, Kubler-Ross believes that it is important for the communicator to be prepared to listen to the response of the individual and not brush aside his denial. The communicator must also be prepared to emphasize the steps that must be taken if the individual is to deal with the threat. The goal is to show the person affected by the change that the communicator is someone who cares, who is available, and who will remain involved. This helps the person to develop the confidence needed to share his feelings and to address the threat directly. When he is able to do so, the denial stage is over.

Stage 2: Anger.   After the individual has confronted the change, he is likely to ask the question, "Why me?" Denial is replaced with anger. The more traumatic the change to the individual, the deeper the feelings of anger, rage, resentment, and envy of those not affected. This anger can be directed at anyone and anything at any time. It can be rational or irrational. A natural reaction in those close to the affected individual is avoidance, the desire to stay away. This is not helpful, however. It increases the anger of the individual and adds to his isolation. Those people who wish to help him must listen to his anger without taking it personally. At times, the listener may even have to accept some of the anger. The anger the individual feels comes from his realization that he has lost control over his situation. His anger becomes associated with a feeling of helplessness, a feeling that his life is being manipulated by forces beyond his control. For individuals in whom the need to be in control is strong, the anger that follows their perception of losing control can be extreme. This provides us with another clue for assisting the individual. Kubler-Ross found that an individual can manage his anger better if he is provided with opportunities to make small decisions over those aspects of his life that he does still control.

Stage 3: Bargaining.   If a person is able to work through his anger when faced with a traumatic and threatening change, he will enter a third stage called "bargaining." Bargaining is the individual's attempt to postpone the inevitable. Kubler-Ross discovered that, like a child, a person faced with a traumatic change hopes he will be rewarded for good behavior and not have to go through with the punishment (the change). He promises good behavior and sets a self-imposed deadline. In bargaining, the individual makes the implicit promise that if his behavior is rewarded, he will not ask for more.

People who interact with a person in the bargaining stage must be careful not to promise what they cannot deliver. A patient who pleads, "If I take all my medication, I'll get better won't I?" is setting the doctor up for a false promise. The doctor must carefully respond, "If you take all your medication, your chances may improve, but I can't promise you that you will be cured." It is important for the doctor to reassure the individual that he will do everything he can to make the change as comfortable as possible.

Stage 4: Depression.   Kubler-Ross's fourth stage in the acceptance of change is characterized by the depression that comes from the sense of loss experienced by the person affected. There is a realization that things will not be the way they used to be, that the change is unavoidable. This stage is a grieving period where two types of depression are observed.

The first type of depression, reactive depression, results from a loss of self-esteem because the individual's previous sense of purpose and role in life is gone. He understands that life will go on without him. Those who interact with a person suffering from reactive depression need to reassure him that he is still a valuable person and that his unfinished work can yet be completed. This provides relief and eases the depression.

In the second type of depression, the individual prepares himself for the loss of his love objects. It is a time of sorrow that should not be met with attempts to cheer up the person with false encouragement or reassurance. It is often difficult for the depressed person to express his feelings about his loss of hope. He is accepting that the change cannot be stopped or delayed any longer. People who interact with a person at this stage of adjustment contribute most through their presence. Their ability to listen is far more important than anything they can say.

Stage 5: Acceptance.   In this final stage, the individual develops a sense of acceptance of the change that confronts him. In cases of traumatic change, this acceptance may seem to be characterized by the absence of feeling. Kubler-Ross found that at this stage the pain is gone, the struggle is seen to be over, and the individual begins a process of detachment. He feels at peace within himself and has regained his sense of personal dignity. The harder the individual struggles to avoid the inevitable change and the more he denies it, the more difficult it is for him to reach this final stage of acceptance.

FUSION Applications

A comparison between the way in which the terminally ill face the challenge of confronting their own death and the way in which employees face the challenge of a significant change to their work place can be revealing. Clearly, the degree of change is not the same. Even the loss of a job, while it can be perceived as traumatic by the individual involved, is in no way comparable to the loss of a life. However, the stages that lead to the acceptance of change can be seen to operate in both examples. If we understand how people meet the challenge of terminal illness, if we look at the strategies they use to cope with the change and the strategies that can be used to assist them through the coping process, we can use this knowledge to assist individuals in the work place to cope with change that is, if not traumatic, still difficult and unsettling. Systems executives and managers can make a significant difference in helping individuals in their organizations cope with the changes that FUSION brings if they see the introduction of this change as a powerful force with the potential for serious disruption of the work place. Consider the guidelines provided next for assisting people to move through the stages of adjustment to change and to come out on the other end as major supporters.

Stage 1: Denial.   In assisting people through the first stage of adjustment to the changes introduced by FUSION, a manager needs to be aware of his own discomfort in giving the individual news that he knows may cause pain. Whether the message is a traumatic one ("Your job may be eliminated.") or one that is less severe ("You're going to need to learn some new skills to stay in your current position."), the manager must work through his own discomfort before he talks with the employee. He needs to display empathy, assuring the individual that he understands that the message he is bringing may be a difficult one to accept. He must also be supportive, indicating that he will do everything he can to make the change as comfortable as possible.

Too often people are not directly and personally informed about pending changes that will affect them. They learn about important changes through the grapevine, in general announcements made in group meetings, or in memos issued by high level executives they have never met. Such communication vehicles do not provide people with an opportunity to express their concerns to the individual responsible for the change. Personal responsibility is important here. Any manager directly involved in implementing the change to a FUSION environment should conduct a private and personal conversation with each employee as soon as possible. Together the employee and the manager can assess the effect of the change and create an appropriate response. If people are not provided with individual attention, they may feel abandoned, isolated, even hopeless. Instead of working out their concerns with their manager, they may end up expressing their anxiety to their peers in a way that proves disruptive to the entire organization.

Some examples may clarify how denial impacts an organization affected by change. In hard economic times, a company had to cut back its staff by ten percent. This cut applied to the systems department, just as it did to the other parts of the organization. While the systems employees heard about the projected cutbacks, however, most did not believe that they would take place. Others who did believe that some cuts would be made still believed that the systems department would be spared. They were overheard making statements, such as: "It can't happen. Who's going to do my work? I've been here twenty-five years. It's just not true." Their reaction to a threatening change—denial.

In another revealing example, when a bank installed a code generation tool, a group of senior programmers resisted its use rather dramatically. Rather than spend their time learning the new tool, they conducted an extensive study to "prove" that the code generator could not provide efficient enough program code for their application. They recommended that manual coding was the only way to achieve the needed operational efficiencies of the application.

In one case, a group of independent insurance agents, when told of a new "smart" personal computer system that would make their offices "paperless," reduce clerical needs, and link them electronically to corporate headquarters, refused to participate in a requirements analysis and review of a prototype. They denied the need for the system. The project was dropped due to lack of support from the user community. It was four years before such a change was attempted again.

More recently, when a systems manager told his project manager that he would have to use a new information engineering methodology to define the logical design for his project's application and use a CASE tool to capture the design, the project manager's response was simple. "That won't work," he said. "You guys can do what you want. I know what I'm going to do to get the job done and it doesn't include any fancy new stuff."

When confronted with the denial response to the changes brought by the implementation of FUSION, managers must listen to the reactions of their staff and directly address their concerns. They need to ask questions like, "What is it about the change that concerns you?" This will help the manager to understand the threat at the heart of the denial. Then he can directly address these concerns in a way that will reassure the staff and reduce the trauma of the change. It is important that the manager not try to prove to the affected individuals how positive the change will be. That tells them that the manager is not listening. Through listening and questioning, the manager should be able to alleviate the concerns that forced the denial in the first place. Here is an example of what can be done.

Consider the case of Jamie, a systems manager, and Tom, a project manager. When Jamie called Tom into his office to tell him that his project had been selected to demonstrate the value of the FUSION approach, Tom's immediate reaction was, "This approach won't work. I'm going to do it my own way, a way I know I can succeed at. Are you trying to set me up for failure?" Jamie's response was, "Look Tom, I know you are upset about this, but it's important to the organization that we try a new way of working. This project looks like it might benefit greatly. What is it that concerns you?" "It's just too much for everyone to learn so quickly and we're really under the gun to deliver by January," Tom said. "Didn't you hear the sales executive in the user group talk about how he's tired of getting applications installed six months too late?" Jamie accepted the feedback, saying, "Tom, you're right. It is a lot to learn. I know it's not going to be easy. I'm going to get you and your team special training, and I'll work with you myself. If we need to get the delivery dates renegotiated, I'll do everything in my power to help you get what you need." Tom was still skeptical. "Oh, that sounds good," he said. "But I don't believe you can pull it off. The sales people won't stand for it." Jamie closed by saying, "I'll start on that issue immediately. I know this has not been good news for you, but I'll be here to listen to your problems and get you whatever help I can. You're a valuable person, and I'll do everything I can to work together with you and the rest of the team to make the project a success in these unique circumstances." About a week later after Tom's team had been through a brief training session on FUSION basics, Tom returned to Jamie's office to set dates for further training and get approval for two consultants to join the team, a JAD facilitator and an IE/CASE tool expert. Both were provided.

What is important in this example is that the systems manager did NOT:

- Dictate that the project manager had to use the new approach, although he assumed it in the conversation.
- Belittle or brush off the project manager's concerns with rosy pictures of how easy it would be or suggest that he was overreacting to the situation.
- Offer false promises—like automatically slipping the delivery date.

The systems manager DID:

- Actively listen to the project manager and reflect back to him his stated concerns.
- Offer support and reassurance based on what the project manager said.
- Maintain a concerned but positive attitude that left the door open for the project manager to return when he was ready.

Stage 2: Anger.   When faced with an angry employee, many managers will avoid the individual and encourage others to avoid him also. This isolating action only worsens the individual's sense of a loss of control, his feeling of helplessness and his perception that he is being manipulated. Systems managers must work with the employee to help that person regain his sense of control. In one situation, a project team member, Sharon, was having difficulty coping with the new work procedures of the JAD technique, particularly those related to the increased involvement of users and the use of CASE tool experts on the project. Her anger was expressed in several ways:

- She consistently forgot to turn in her weekly time report, thus forcing her manager to come to her to get it.
- She made all her own appointments with the users without informing her project team about what she was doing.
- She missed project team meetings where plans and strategies for the project were developed.
- She refused requests by the users to change a key meeting date, saying, "That's not the way I'm accustomed to working. Once the date is set, we keep to that schedule."
- She complained to the users about the intrusion of "outsiders" on the project team.

The natural reaction of a project manager to this situation would be to get this person off his project team through a transfer or reassignment. However, this person, when not threatened or angry, is a very talented, resourceful, dedicated and hard working individual. The project manager, Ray, wanted to help her overcome her anger rather than remove her from the team. Ray called a meeting with Sharon without the other team members present. He opened the conversation with, "Tell me about how the project is going from your perspective, Sharon." "Fine, I guess," she replied. "Why don't you ask the other team members? They should know." Her tone of voice was sarcastic, and she looked everywhere but at Ray. "Well, I have," he responded, "and they told me that you appear to have some problems with the project." "And there are situations which have occurred recently, Sharon, that have concerned me," Ray said looking directly into Sharon's eyes. He objectively described the behavior he had observed. He made no judgments, but was clear in his description.

"Boy, you sure do seem to get around," Sharon defended herself. "I know this project hasn't been easy, Sharon," Ray said. At this point, Sharon exploded. "I'll tell you it hasn't been easy. Everyone is telling me what to do, calling meetings. Even the users are telling me what to do. How did we get roped into this project in the first place?" Ray was firm. "It's actually a good project for us. It will lead to an opportunity to work on major databases that will serve the entire business area. I know it's not what you expected. What would you like to see happen?" Sharon launched into a thirty minute discourse on how she would have run the project if she had been the project manager in charge. Finally, she wound down.

Ray concluded that Sharon was having tremendous difficulty in working in a position subordinate to him. She was suffering from not having control of the project. "It's very important that we all work as a team on this project. Would you like me to call a meeting of the whole team to work out a better schedule so you won't have to miss the planning and strategy meetings?" Somewhat relieved, Sharon responded, "Well, maybe you could just check with me before you set a date for a meeting and get me an agenda. That way we can prepare better. And, I'm just concerned that these new CASE tool "experts" as you call them are going to mess things up. What are they supposed to do anyway?" "Would you like to schedule some time with the CASE tool folks to get a briefing on what they will do? Maybe some of the other team members have the same need as you."

Sharon had regained a sense of control. "Let me check my calendar and set up a meeting," she said. Ray closed the session by saying, "Sharon you are an important person in this project. The team needs your full participation. Thanks for talking with me. I want to know your concerns."

At the next project team meeting, Ray facilitated a discussion about what team members could do to keep each other informed and to work more closely so everyone would have an opportunity to contribute and to have their individual needs met. After the list was constructed, Ray had Sharon tell the group about the session she was going to schedule to learn about what the CASE experts were doing. Over the next three weeks, Ray made an effort to solicit ideas and feedback from the team and from individual team members in private sessions with them.

The surprise came when Sharon walked into Ray's office and said, "Listen, I want to apologize for complaining to the users about the CASE tool experts. I did not even realize that I was doing it. If I have a problem again, I'll come directly to you. I know I wouldn't want to hear something like that through the grapevine." Sharon had adjusted to being a team member and not a project manager.

It is important for managers who will be helping people adapt to the FUSION environment to develop their patience and listening skills. They must be able to confront employee anger and frustration in a positive, objective manner, and assist people in developing their own action plans. These managers should not see their role as "advice giver." Advice implies a sense of parental authority and confirms the individual's fear that he has lost control. The manager should work to discover the individual's concerns and then address them in a jointly created plan. He should not casually dismiss those concerns and then "solve" the problem by telling him what to do.

Stage 3: Bargaining.   Paul, a project manager, had been told that he must use an information engineering approach for his project. Paul did not know anything about IE and was afraid that his project would fail if he used IE. Paul could accept that the organization would have to use IE eventually, but hoped that he could delay the use of IE on this particular project. He approached his manager, Harry, with a bargain, "If I take the IE training, will you let me make the decision on whether or not to use IE on the project?" Harry smiled. One of Paul's peers,

Jake, had just tried to strike a similar bargain over using their new CASE tool by asking, "If I use the CASE tool for the diagrams, can I provide a back up narrative using a word processor?"

What should Harry do? Should he agree to the bargains proposed by Paul and Jake? If the bargain will actually postpone a change that must be implemented, a manager should not agree to the bargain, although, if he can, he may want to strike a bargain that will help the individual maintain control without affecting the change. Paul's bargain would delay IE implementation, so Harry said to Paul, "It's important that we start using the methodology. Maybe you won't need to use all the features for your project. If you take the training, I'll be glad to work with you to select the most appropriate aspects of the methodology to use on your project." In this way, Paul retained some decision making authority but not the ability to sabotage the change. Harry saw that in Jake's case the problem was not acceptance of the tool, but insecurity about its use. Harry said, "It may be a good idea to support the diagrams with narrative since we've never used them this extensively before. If you use the CASE tool to produce, analyze, and validate the diagrams, then back up word processing should be no problem at all." In this way, the manager successfully transformed two potential detractors of FUSION into supporters.

Stage 4: Depression.   Caring and concern are expressed when an individual makes himself available to another and demonstrates that he is involved in the other person's life. This demonstration of involvement can assist an individual in dealing with the depression that comes when a traumatic change is finally accepted as inevitable. A manager should not try to make everyone involved in the change to FUSION put on a falsely happy face. That type of behavior would display an insensitivity to the difficult emotions that some people experience during the change. Rather, the manager should demonstrate his concern in a way that indicates that he can see the situation from the affected individual's point of view.

In one situation, the implementation of FUSION took place during a downsizing effort by a company. As a consequence, when Jim created the FUSION Center, he had to reassign staff resources from existing project groups to support the center and eliminate some jobs. One of these was Keith's position as system manager. It had been a shock to everyone that a person who had been with the company for almost his entire career, had worked his way up the ladder to systems manager, would be asked to leave. Jim was able to help Keith find a new position with a different division of the company, a position with strong promotion potential, but it was clear that Jim was deeply hurt by the situation. When the final work day arrived, Keith sat in his office, silent and sad. Jim came in, sat down and said nothing as Keith loaded up the last of his boxes. After a few minutes, Keith stood, shook Jim's hand, put on his coat and said, "Thank you for caring." The pain in leaving could not be eliminated, no matter how bright the future or how satisfying the opportunities it would provide for Keith.

Stage 5: Acceptance. As supervisors and managers, we know that if an individual accepts a change, he can once again become enthusiastic, dedicated and productive. In one organization, the decision had been made to "quick start" FUSION by making every new development or redevelopment project use IE, JAD, and CASE. One project manager, Danny, perceived the whole effort as just another hair brained idea and took a passive aggressive strategy toward implementing FUSION. As the JAD facilitator conducted the preworkshop activities for the project, Danny became more angry and more quiet. He was required to participate by his boss, but Danny had decided that he would refuse to make decisions and take part in discussions. He would leave it all up to the outsider, the JAD facilitator. "You can take Danny to the well, but you cannot make him drink," a team member observed. The JAD facilitator, Miriam, took Danny to lunch two days before the first workshop to discuss Danny's concerns. After hearing him out, Miriam said, "Listen Danny, I know all this FUSION stuff sounds like a strange approach to take, but I also know it will produce results. Lots of companies, even our competitors, are doing this. So we really have no choice. You have an important role as the project manager. If you will just agree to participate in this first workshop, it will help everyone. After the workshop, if you really can't live with the FUSION approach, I'll go with you to your management to discuss the possible alternatives available to us for the rest of the project work." Reluctantly, Danny agreed to proceed with the workshop.

In the first day of the workshop, Danny was quiet and did not contribute much. On the second day, he started to participate in small team discussions on issues he felt were important. On the morning of the third day, he not only participated actively in the large group, but he took Miriam aside during a break to suggest a way to address an issue that the group was skirting around. Miriam prepared a special exercise for the afternoon session to clarify and resolve that issue. The question of the FUSION approach never came up between Danny and Miriam again. Miriam had been able to assist Danny to accept FUSION by:

- Giving him a sense of control, of choice.
- Providing consistent support of his feelings and concerns.
- Allowing him a bargain he could live with.
- Giving him time to work through his feelings without interfering.
- Not providing false hopes or promises.

BEGINNING THE CHANGE MANAGEMENT PROCESS

Not all individuals faced with a traumatic change will be able to work through all of the stages that have been described here. Some people remain angry or in denial, fighting everything and everyone. Others find accepting change easy. They are not threatened. What is important, though, is that the stages of acceptance behav-

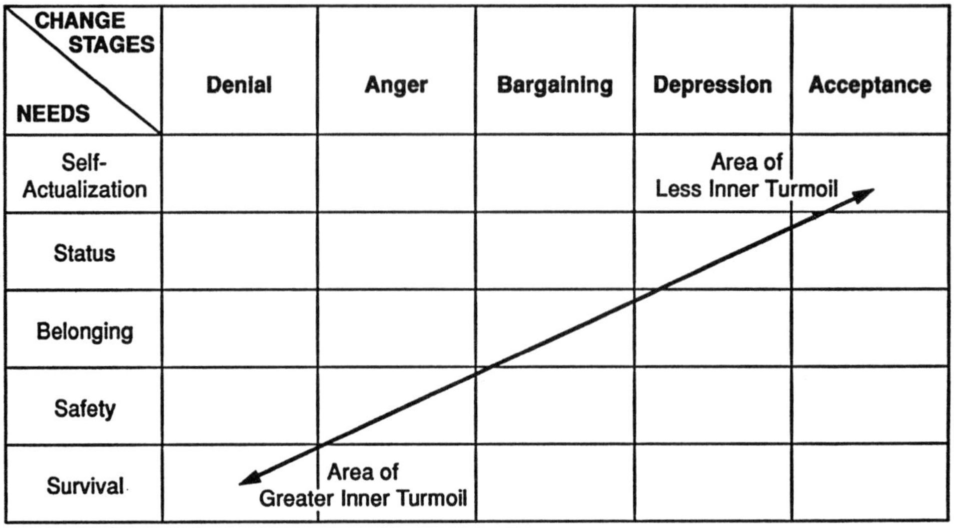

CHANGE STAGES / NEEDS	Denial	Anger	Bargaining	Depression	Acceptance
Self-Actualization				Area of Less Inner Turmoil	
Status					
Belonging					
Safety					
Survival	Area of Greater Inner Turmoil				

The more severely the threat is seen to impact the individual's social and basic needs, the greater the level of his internal turmoil or trauma and the stronger his behavioral reaction.

Figure 8.4 A model for change reaction assessment.

ior provide guidance for managers and supervisors. The stages show us how to work with individuals within the context of the larger change that is taking place. The approach benefits the organization as a whole, because FUSION can only be successful when it is supported by those involved.

Change is possible when the values of the organization are aligned with the values of the individuals within the organization, and belief in these values increases as people see the values acted out by executives and managers. The work of Maslow and Kubler-Ross provide important insights to help identify how people respond to the changes brought by FUSION implementation and to plan a strategy for dealing with these responses. By combining their models (Fig. 8.4), we can see how threats to our own needs impact the severity of the stages to change acceptance.

The more severe a threat is perceived to be by an individual, the greater the level of his internal turmoil or trauma and the stronger his reaction will be. The word "perceived" is important here. What one person perceives as temporary loss of status, another may perceive as a permanent loss of safety. The temporary loss of status may trigger a mild anger reaction, while the threat of permanent loss of safety may produce severe denial. For example, when faced with the introduction of a CASE tool, John felt his status threatened and reacted as follows:

- Denial: "I can't do this. I don't have the skills to do this."
- Anger: "Why haven't we been trained in this before?"
- Bargaining: "I'll only use it on my project if I get training."

- Depression: "This is just too much trouble. It was easier to do it the old way."
- Acceptance: "With some practice, we'll get better. All this additional data and analysis will really improve the quality of what we deliver."

However, Neville, when faced with the same situation was more seriously threatened. He reacted this way:

- Denial: "This can't happen. You can't replace what I do with a machine."
- Anger: "I won't be forced into something I can't do. I'll sue them if they fire me."
- Bargaining: "All right. I'll to go to the training and learn this tool. If I still can't do it, will you let me do my work the way I know how?"
- Depression: "The old way of doing things is really gone. There's no hope for old guys like me. We're not going to be able to compete in this new world."
- Acceptance: "I guess I can give it a try since they did train me, but it's not going to be easy.

The more threatened the individual, the more effort a manager must expend in listening to him, supporting him and accepting his reactions.

Managers and executives have the same types of needs and threat responses. Managers must remember not to project their own feelings and reactions onto others or to assume all people think the way they do. Managers cannot allow their own discomfort to interfere with their responsibility to assist the people on their teams to be the most effective and positive contributors possible.

Everyone, no matter how high in the organizational structure, how sophisticated, or how experienced, must pass through the five stages to change acceptance. The ease with which this occurs and the speed at which it occurs depends on the individual's own self knowledge, his internal values, how well those internal values are aligned with the external values of the organization, and the degree of disparity between the organization's actual values and its stated values.

As executives and managers we need to be trained in the concepts of values, needs and change stages. We need to learn how to work in an environment that emphasizes people instead of things. Such training needs to be instituted before the implementation of a major organization change such as FUSION and should be a prerequisite for key managers.

Selected Readings and References

ATKINSON, P.E. *Creating Culture Change: The Key to Successful Total Quality Management,* IFS Publications, United Kingdom, 1990.

ATRE, S. *Database: Structured Techniques for Design, Performance and Management,* John Wiley and Sons, New York, 1988.

BEER, M. ET AL. "Why Change Programs Don't Produce Change," *Harvard Business Review,* November-December, 1990, pages 158–66.

BRIDGES, W. PhD *Surviving Corporate Transitions,* Doubleday, New York, 1988.

BROOKS, F.B. JR. *The Mythical Man-Month: Essays on Software Engineering,* Addison-Wesley Publishing Co., Inc., Reading, MA, 1974.

CASE, A. JR. *Information Systems Development: Principles of Computer-Aided Software Engineering,* Prentice Hall, Englewood Cliffs, NJ, 1986.

CHEN, P.P. *Entity Relationship Approach to Systems Analysis and Design,* North-Holland, Amsterdam, 1980.

COAD, P. AND YOURDON, E. *Object Oriented Analysis,* Yourdon Press, Englewood Cliffs, NJ, 1991.

CODD, E.F. "Further Normalization of the Database Relational Model," IBM Research, San Jose, CA, August 31, 1991.

CONNELL, J.L. AND SHAFER, L.B. *Structured Rapid Prototyping,* Yourdon Press, Englewood Cliffs, NJ, 1989.

COUGER, J.D. AND ZOWACKI, R.A. *Motivating and Managing Computer Personnel,* John Wiley & Sons, New York, 1980.

DATE, C.J. *Database: A Primer,* Addison-Wesley Publishing Co., Inc., Reading, MA, 1985.

DAVENPORT, T. AND SHORT, J. "The New Industrial Engineering: Information Technology and Business," *Sloan Management Review,* Summer, 1990, pages 133–44.

DAVIS, G.B. *Management Information Systems: Conceptual Foundations, Structure and Development,* McGraw-Hill, New York, 1985.

DREGER, J. B. *Function Point Analysis,* Prentice Hall, Englewood Cliffs, NJ, 1989.

FINKELSTEIN, C. *An Introduction to Information Engineering: From Strategic Planning to Information Systems,* Addison-Wesley, New York, 1989.

FRANCIS, D. AND YOUNG, D. *Improving Work Groups: A Practical Manual for Team Building,* University Associates, San Diego, CA, 1979.

GANE, C. *Rapid Systems Development,* Rapid Systems Development, Inc., New York, 1987.

GANE, C. AND SARSON, T. *Structured System Analysis: Tools and Techniques,* Prentice Hall, Englewood Cliffs, NJ, 1979.

HAMMER, M. "Reengineering Work: Don't Automate, Obliterate," *Harvard Business Review,* July-August, 1990, pages 104–11.

HARTMAN, R.S. *The Structure of Value: Foundations of Scientific Axiology,* Southern Illinois University Press, Carbondale, IL, 1967.

HIGGINS, D.A. *Data Structured Software Maintenance: The Warnier-Orr Approach,* Dorset House Publishing Co., New York, 1986.

HOPKINS, T. *How to Master the Art of Selling* (2nd edition), Champion Press, 1982.

HOWARD, R. "Values Make the Company: An Interview with Robert Haas," *Harvard Business Review,* September-October, 1990, pages 133–44.

INMON, W.H. *Information Systems Architecture,* Prentice Hall, Englewood Cliffs, NJ, 1986.

JONES, C. *Programmer Productivity,* McGraw-Hill, New York, 1986.

JONES, C. *Applied Software Measurement,* McGraw-Hill, New York, 1991.

KERR, J.M. "The 10 Commandments of RAD," *Database Programming and Design,* May, 1991, pages 38–39.

KIEFFER, G.D. *The Strategy of Meetings,* Simon and Schuster, New York, 1988.

KUBLER-ROSS, E. M.D. *On Death and Dying,* Macmillan, New York, 1969.

———— *Questions and Answers on Death and Dying,* Macmillan, New York, 1974.

MARTIN, J. *Information Engineering: Book I Introduction,* Prentice Hall, Englewood Cliffs, NJ, 1989.

———— *Information Engineering: Book II Planning and Analysis,* Prentice Hall, Englewood Cliffs, NJ, 1990.

———— *Information Engineering: Book III Design and Construction,* Prentice Hall, Englewood Cliffs, NJ, 1990.

———— *Rapid Application Development,* Macmillan, New York, 1991.

MARTIN, J. AND MCCLURE, C. *Structured Techniques for Computing,* Prentice Hall, Englewood Cliffs, NJ, 1985.

MASLOW, A.H. *The Farther Reaches of Human Nature,* Viking Press, New York, 1971.

ORSBURN, et al. *Self Directed Work Teams: The New American Challenge,* Business One Irwin, Homewood, IL, 1990.

PFEIFFER, W., et al. *The Annual: Developing Human Resources,* University Associates, San Diego, CA, 1985–1990.

REES, F. *How to Lead Work Teams: Facilitation Skills,* Pfeiffer & Company, San Diego, 1991.

SANDHUSEN, R.L. *Marketing,* Barron's Educational Series, 1987.

SENGE, P.M. *The Fifth Discipline: The Art and Practice of the Learning Organization,* Doubleday, New York, 1990.

—— "The Leader's New Work: Building Learning Organizations," *Sloan Management Review,* Fall, 1990, pages 7–23.

SHLAER, S. AND MELLOR, S. *Object Oriented Systems Analysis—Modeling the World in Data,* Yourdon Press, Englewood Cliffs, NJ, 1988.

STRASSMANN, P. *Information Payoff,* The Free Press, New York, 1985.

STRAYER, R. "How I Learned to Let My Workers Lead," *Harvard Business Review,* November–December, 1990, pages 66–83.

TEMPLETON, J.F. *Focus Groups,* Probus, 1987.

WAITE, T.J. (ed.) "Business Reengineering," *Insights,* Index Group, Inc., Fall, 1989, Vol. **1,** Number 2, pages 2–8.

—— "Picking Apart Warehouse Processes at Ford Motor Company," *Insights,* Index Group, Inc., Fall, 1989, vol. **1,** Number 2, pages 2–8.

WOOD, J. AND SILVER, D. *Joint Application Design,* John Wiley & Sons, New York, 1989.

YAO, S.B. (editor) *Principles of Database Design, Volume 1, Logical Designs,* Prentice-Hall, NJ, 1985.

YOURDON, E. *Managing the Structured Techniques: Strategies for Software Development in the 1990's* (3rd edition), Yourdon Press, Englewood Cliffs, NJ, 1986.

—— *Modern Structured Analysis,* Prentice Hall, Englewood Cliffs, NJ, 1989.

ZUBOFF, S. *In the Age of the Smart Machine: The Future of Work and Power,* Basic Books, New York, 1988.

ZENGER, J.H., ET AL. "Leadership in a Team Environment," *Training and Development,* October, 1991, pages 47–52.

Index

J

K

L

M